W9-BCG-784

The Development of American Citizenship, 1608–1870

The Institute of Early American History and Culture
is sponsored jointly by
The College of William and Mary
and The Colonial Williamsburg Foundation.

This book was the winner of the Jamestown Prize for 1975.

The Development
of American Citizenship,
1608–1870

by
James H. Kettner

Published for the
Institute of Early American History and Culture
Williamsburg, Virginia
by The University of North Carolina Press
Chapel Hill, North Carolina

© 1978 by The University of North Carolina Press
All rights reserved
Manufactured in the United States of America
ISBN 0-8078-1326-5
Library of Congress Catalog Card Number 78-954

Library of Congress Cataloging in Publication Data

Kettner, James H.
  The development of American citizenship, 1608–1870.

  Includes index.
    1. Naturalization—United States—History.
2. Citizenship—United States—History.   I. Institute
of Early American History and Culture, Williamsburg,
Va.   II. Title.
JK1814.K47   323.6'0973   78-954
ISBN 0-8078-1326-5

Jan 25'79

To
My Mother and Father

Contents

Preface

I arrived at the subject of this work by a somewhat circuitous route. Fascinated by the complexity of the constitutional and institutional changes of the Revolutionary era, I first thought to trace the development of the American political community from about 1760 to 1820. I began investigating qualifications for suffrage, but my interest gradually came to focus on the sources of American citizenship, and I found it necessary both to broaden the chronological dimensions and to move into what for me were rather unfamiliar legal materials.

Perhaps it is not necessary to justify the temporal scope of this study—the reasons for my choice of period should be clear from the substance of the work—but a few comments on my extended use of legal sources may be in order.

Descended from all the nations of the world, richly (though too often divisively) pluralistic in ethnicity and culture, Americans almost by default came to rely on abstract legal criteria for defining the basis of their common nationality. They drew heavily upon the accumulated traditions of English law in articulating new ideas of citizenship, but the process involved more than the autonomous evolution of legal doctrine. At every stage of development, practical experience, political expediency, and personal hopes and fears helped shape their thinking.

The judges, lawyers, and legislators who slowly forged the legal concept of citizenship shared the pervasive social values and cultural prejudices that impeded the universalistic thrust of new ideas of membership and that dictated the subordination of certain groups or their exclusion from full privileges. Yet the jurists who figure centrally in this study were limited by special constraints peculiar to their profession—particularly by their reliance on precedent, by the impulse to make every argument or judgment "logical" in terms of what had gone before—that make their efforts to accommodate broader cultural values within the rationale of the law especially revealing of some of the fundamental problems and aspirations of Americans. Moreover, these judicial efforts were not merely academic exercises, interesting as theory but irrelevant in practice: plaintiffs and defendants were real people whose fates could be determined by subtle shifts in the interpretation of technical points of law. It made a difference—both to him and to the wider community—whether Dred Scott was legally a citizen. It makes a difference still.

I have tried throughout this study to keep the social and cultural context in mind while tracing changes of legal doctrine. Still, my main aim has not been to give a comprehensive account of the forces that at certain critical junctures may have impinged upon the development of the law. Changing attitudes and practices concerning the rights and roles of women, for example, deserve more focused attention than they have received here; the complex position of the Indians in American society, too, is worthy of far more extensive inquiry. I have dealt with such groups, but only to the extent that questions of their status intersected with the development of the law of citizenship before 1870.

It is my hope that this study will be of use to scholars whether trained in the law or not, and for this reason I have tried to avoid excessive reliance on technical legal language. I have used legal forms in citing certain kinds of sources, and those unfamiliar with these forms may wish to consult the "Note on Citation" following the text. As for any technical lapses that may remain evident to those whose training, unlike mine, has been in law rather than history, may I remind them of that useful maxim, *"De minimis non curat lex"*—the law does not concern itself with trifles—and plead for their indulgence.

The bulk of an earlier version of Chapter 7 appeared in article form in the July 1974 issue of the *American Journal of Legal History*, and scattered paragraphs of the text were included as part of an essay published in the June 1976 issue of the *Virginia Law Review*. I am grateful to the editors of both journals for permission to republish here.

I also wish to thank the Jamestown–Yorktown Foundation and the other sponsors of the Jamestown Prize for awarding the prize to my manuscript.

Many others have contributed to this work as well, often in ways they may not have realized. Had it not been for Dennis K. Rothhaar's willingness to risk coffee stains on his copy of *Black's Law Dictionary*, I would never have begun to understand the arcane language of legal reports, and had my good friends David T. Konig and Jon H. Roberts been less tolerant in their criticisms of early versions of the work, I might never have found the courage to submit it in dissertation form.

I have been equally fortunate in receiving advice from scholars who took time from their own busy schedules to aid me in shaping the final study. Morton J. Horwitz made many helpful suggestions, and Stanley N. Katz went far beyond the call of duty and friendship in critically reading several drafts. A great many of my Berkeley students and colleagues, too, have given me the benefit of their moral support and intellectual insight: Thomas G. Barnes, Gunther Barth, Paula S. Fass, Robert L. Middlekauff, and Kenneth M. Stampp only begin the roster of those whose assistance has been considerable.

David Ammerman, Joy Dickinson Barnes, and Clare Novak of the Institute of Early American History and Culture have been superb editors, responsible for innumerable improvements in substance and form, and hereby absolved from all blame for remaining infelicities and idiosyncracies of style.

My chief intellectual creditor, however, is Bernard Bailyn, and it is to him that I owe the largest debt of gratitude. His assistance in guiding the dissertation project from which this study has grown and his generous help since have been invaluable.

The Development of American Citizenship,
1608–1870

Prologue:
Subjects, Aliens, and Citizens

The concept of American citizenship that achieved full legal form and force in the mid-nineteenth century grew from English roots. It was the product of a development that stretched over three hundred years, a development in which the circumstances of life in the New World shaped and transformed the quasi-medieval ideas of seventeenth-century English jurists about membership, community, and allegiance. The process of change was gradual, and those who participated in it did not fully perceive its patterns or direction. Nevertheless, as Americans first experienced, then sought to articulate the meaning of, their transformation from subjects to citizens, they made piecemeal changes and partial modifications of English ideas that developed, step-by-step, into a new concept of citizenship.

Americans inherited a complex set of ideas about the sources and character of "subjectship." These ideas were rooted deep in the English past, but not until the early seventeenth century were they integrated into a coherent doctrine. The basic theory of subjectship was coeval with the beginnings of American colonization and was the product of the period that formed the bridge between the eras historians have categorized as "medieval" and "modern." Conflicting concepts of community characterized those two eras. The medieval notion of "allegiance" reflected the feudal sense that personal bonds between man and lord were the primary ligaments of the body politic; the modern notion of "nationality" assumed a legal tie

3

binding individuals to a territorial state and rendering them subject to its jurisdiction. The "community of allegiance" was in essence personal, the "national state" primarily territorial.[1]

Historians have discovered elements of the modern doctrine of nationality as far back as the fourteenth century, particularly in connection with practices of naturalization, but such notions clearly were planted and nourished in an intellectual context dominated by medieval ideas of personal subjection and by a wide variety of statuses. Indeed, despite the early emergence of some elements of "nationality," English law long continued to stress the personal nature of the subject-king relationship and the gradation of ranks characteristic of an older social and political order.[2]

Early English law had no fixed concept of subjectship or of nationality as a status; no consistent and fundamental distinction divided subject and alien.[3] Rather there were levels and ranks of persons with varying rights and privileges—or conversely with different disabilities—that defined a broad spectrum and hierarchy of possible individual statuses. The notion of a primary distinction between member and non-member emerged slowly, in response to specific issues of landholding, taxation, and access to the king's courts. Before the Tudor period there appears to have been no firm sense of a fixed "national" status identified with a more or less specific complex of rights from which "non-nationals" were excluded. Naturalization—in the modern sense of a grant of status with an accompanying package of rights—was preceded by, and

1. J. Mervyn Jones, *British Nationality: Law and Practice* (Oxford, 1947), 1–4. For a brief comparison of classical and medieval ideas of nationality that stresses modern elements in the latter, see W. A. Shaw, ed., *Letters of Denization and Acts of Naturalization for Aliens in England and Ireland, 1603–1700* (Huguenot Society of London, *Publications*, XVIII [Lymington, 1911]), i–ii, hereafter cited as Shaw, ed., *Denization and Naturalization, 1603–1700*. See also John W. Salmond, "Citizenship and Allegiance," *Law Quarterly Review*, XVII (1901), 270–282, XVIII (1902), 49–63.

2. Clive Parry, *British Nationality Law and the History of Naturalisation* (Milan, 1954), 8. Parry agrees with Sir Frederick Pollock, Frederic William Maitland, William S. Holdsworth, and others that a coherent law of nationality can be traced after the crown's loss of Normandy. Sir Alexander Cockburn, *Nationality: or the Laws Relating to Subjects and Aliens Considered with a View to Future Legislation* (London, 1869), 7, even argued that the *jus soli*—the rule that place of birth determines nationality—was a fixed principle of law in Anglo-Saxon times.

3. Parry, *British Nationality Law*, 7. Although the loss of lands in Normandy led to a crystallization of rules separating subjects and aliens generally, distinctions between the two were made in certain specific contexts earlier. The consolidation of aliens' customs duties in 1303 and 1305, for example, was the culmination of a long regulatory process based on such a distinction. *Ibid.*, 8, 15.

for a time coexisted with, the practice of removing disabilities and bestowing privileges piecemeal.[4] Medieval English law posited a continuum of ranks and rights, but did not create distinctly separate categories of subject and alien.

By the seventeenth century the line dividing subject and alien was well marked; yet traces of the older ideas remained. English subjectship still comprised a variety of ranks and relationships. Jurists distinguished between natural-born subjects, naturalized subjects, and "denizens," all of whom were members of the community in some sense, although there were important differences in the nature of the ties that bound them as subjects and in the rights that they could claim. The general category of aliens, too, embodied separate classes of persons—perpetual aliens, alien friends, and alien enemies—whose respective legal positions varied in detail. Procedures for adopting outsiders into the community had become standardized, even though the rationale behind the processes of admission would not receive an articulate theoretical justification until the mid-seventeenth century.

English jurists never attempted fully and explicitly to catalog the rights attached to subjectship. Rather they were content to define those rights implicitly by specifying the disabilities suffered by those who did not enjoy subject status. Most crucial was the restriction on real property rights that began to emerge in the fourteenth century. In 1324 the king claimed the escheat of lands descending to "any born beyond the seas whose ancestors were from the time of John under the allegiance of the king of France."[5] At the time, this confiscation was not considered permanent, but was directed against those who adhered to a hostile prince. The rights of persons affected were to be reconsidered if a lasting peace ever came. "Frenchmen" could not hold English lands because they were at war, not because they were aliens.[6]

4. Elias Daubeny was deemed *Anglicum purum* (a pure Englishman) by a "grant of the King's grace" in 1295. Although such unspecific grants of status do not appear frequently until the 15th century, piecemeal grants of privileges or exemptions were common and may be seen as the precursors to naturalization. *Ibid.*, 9; Shaw, ed., *Denization and Naturalization, 1603–1700*, iii–iv.

5. *Praerogativa regis*, 17 Edw. II, stat. 1 (1324). Owen Ruffhead *et al.*, eds., *The Statutes at Large . . .* (London, 1763–1800), I, 180, gives this date. The act is quoted in Shaw, ed., *Denization and Naturalization, 1603–1700*, ii. Hereafter, see the Table of Statutes, p. 367, for the source of British, U.S., and Confederate statutes cited in text or notes.

6. William S. Holdsworth, *A History of English Law*, IX (London, 1926), 92, notes that if such a person "claimed land he was not met, as in later common law, by the peremptory

Despite its ad hoc beginnings, this restriction upon landholding and inheritance had become axiomatic, generalized, and inclusive of all aliens long before the seventeenth century. Well into the nineteenth century aliens were barred from personally owning real property in England. Non-subjects could acquire and use land, but they did so only at the sufferance of the crown and for the use of the king.[7] The alien could at best gain only a temporary, "defeasible" title; his possession could be challenged by the king and his property confiscated through an "inquest of office" or similar legal procedure. He could convey this title to another, but it remained liable to royal challenge, for an alien could not convey a better title than the one by which he held. An alien could not inherit real property or transmit it to his children, even though they might be English subjects by virtue of birth within the realm.[8]

Because aliens were denied the right of property in land, it followed that they could not bring real actions at law.[9] It also followed that they could not exercise any franchises or hold offices to which real property qualifications were attached. Although an alien could "acquire property in goods, money, and other personal estate, or . . . hire a house for his habitation," and although he was protected in his person while residing within the dominions by permission, these "rights" were clearly concessions—indulgences "necessary for the advancement of trade"—that could be withdrawn when war turned friend to enemy.[10]

The course of time brought some elaboration and clarification of

plea that, being an alien, he could not hold land; but by the dilatory plea that he was a Frenchman and could not be answered here till Englishmen were answered in France."

7. Samuel MacClintock, *Aliens under the Federal Laws of the United States* (Chicago, 1909), 13. An alien could acquire land by "act of the parties" (i.e., by purchase or devise), but not by "operation of law" (descent, curtesy, or dower). His title could not be challenged by anyone but the crown, and until this was done, he had a claim to protection in his possession.

8. This rule was altered in 1699, when by the act of 11 & 12 Will. III, c. 6, natural-born subjects were enabled to inherit ancestors' estates even though their parents (through whom title was derived) were aliens. Previously the parents' alienage blocked the descent. The 1699 act was further explained by 25 Geo. II, c. 39 (1752).

9. Holdsworth, *History of English Law*, IX, 94. Sir Thomas Littleton was probably incorrect in suggesting that aliens could bring neither real nor personal actions. *Ibid.*, 93–94; Parry, *British Nationality Law*, 8.

10. St. George Tucker, ed., *Blackstone's Commentaries: with Notes of Reference, to the Constitution and Laws, of the Federal Government of the United States; and of the Commonwealth of Virginia* (Philadelphia, 1803), I:2, 372. Pagination is standardized, but Tucker divided the first volume of the *Commentaries* into two parts. I have checked all references with Edward Christian's 12th London edition, 4 vols., 1793–1795.

the privileges of subjectship and the disabilities of alienage. Commercial expansion mitigated some of the early strictness of the law, especially with respect to "alien enemies"—those who were subjects of sovereigns at war with the English king. The late seventeenth century saw the beginning of the concept of domicil, which in effect allowed place of residence rather than allegiance to determine status for some purposes.[11] An alien enemy thereafter might be allowed the more advantageous position of alien friend, while an English subject residing and carrying on business in a warring country would assume an alien character for the purpose of commercial retaliations.

The disadvantages suffered by aliens remained nonetheless significant, and in at least one area they increased. The navigation acts of the seventeenth century excluded merchant aliens from participation in the lucrative colonial trade, even though these aliens had specifically enjoyed a limited freedom to engage in commerce from the beginning of the fourteenth century.[12] The persistence of these legal impediments to full economic and political participation thus continued to distinguish subject and alien and to accentuate the advantages of English subjectship.

If the categories of subject and alien were clear by the time James I ascended the throne, the assumptions behind them were not. Although the law reflected a clear sense that members of the community ought to enjoy a status different from that accorded to outsiders, it had developed no explicit theory to explain the source, character, or effects of national status. It was not until Sir Edward Coke's influential opinion in *Calvin's Case* (1608) that a theory of allegiance and subjectship was fully articulated.

Coke's explication of the nature of membership and community may be seen as the first of four distinct phases in the development of the concept of citizenship. Written in response to the controversies surrounding the accession of James I, Coke's decision in *Calvin's Case* dominated English law for several centuries.[13] The central

11. Holdsworth, *History of English Law*, IX, 72, 93–99.
12. For the exclusion of aliens from the colonial trade, see Thomas C. Barrow, *Trade and Empire: The British Customs Service in Colonial America* (Cambridge, Mass., 1967), 5, and Charles M. Andrews, *The Colonial Period of American History* (New Haven, Conn., 1934–1938), IV, 65–66. Aliens paid higher duties than subjects until 1784. Henry Atton and Henry Hurst Holland, *The King's Customs . . .* , I (London, 1908), 321.
13. Statutory regulation largely superseded Calvin's Case after 1844, but in certain contexts Coke's opinion was still considered authoritative. See Isaacson v. Durant, 17

conclusion of this decision was that subjectship involved a personal relationship with the king, a relationship rooted in the laws of nature and hence perpetual and immutable. The conceptual analogue of the subject-king relationship was the natural bond between parent and child. Although England's law envisioned various types of subjectship, ranging from the natural status of the native-born to the legally acquired status of the naturalized alien, all varieties of membership mirrored permanent hierarchical principles of the natural order. Once a man became a subject—by birth or otherwise —he remained a subject forever, owing a lasting obedience to his natural superior the king.

Coke's quasi-medieval assumption that social and governmental organization grew out of natural principles of hierarchy and subordination preceded, and eventually conflicted with, newly emerging concepts of society and government as the product of individual consent and contract. Significantly, English jurists did not totally recast the law of allegiance to conform with the new ideas of government by consent. Rather Coke's authoritative interpretation of subjectship remained embedded in the law, where it continued to exert a profound influence. By the mid-eighteenth century English concepts of subjectship and community consequently encompassed a central ambiguity: on the one hand, society and government had come to be seen as resting on individual consent and compact; on the other, the legal status and obligations of the individual remained natural, perpetual, and immutable. In dealing with questions of status—for example, in analyzing the long-familiar practice of naturalization or in deciding cases involving treason, the betrayal of allegiance—English jurists tended to ignore the ideas of social compact articulated during the constitutional crises of the seventeenth century and continued to apply the increasingly anachronistic maxims and dicta of Coke.[14]

The second stage in the development of American theories about citizenship occurred across the Atlantic, where colonial attitudes

Q.B.D. 54 (1886), and Attorney General v. Prince Ernest Augustus of Hanover, A.C. 436 (1957). The latter case is discussed in T. B. Smith, *British Justice: The Scottish Contribution* (London, 1961), 24–27, and T. B. Smith, *Studies Critical and Comparative* (Edinburgh, 1962), 20–27. I thank Mr. Thomas Broun Smith for his kind response to my questions on this and other points of Scottish, English, and British law.

14. For an excellent survey of 17th-century English constitutional history, see Margaret Atwood Judson, *The Crisis of the Constitution: An Essay in Constitutional and Political Thought in England* (New Brunswick, N.J., 1949).

slowly diverged from those of Coke and his English successors. Circumstances in the New World led men to attenuate and modify these concepts of natural allegiance. Change was most apparent in the naturalization policies that quickly became a common feature of colonial governments. The concerns involved in the incorporation of aliens into colonial societies were preeminently practical, and little attention was paid to doctrinal consistency. There was at this time no attempt to rethink the traditional theory of membership from initial premise to ultimate conclusion. Americans continued to value their status as subjects and to affirm their allegiance to the king, but they also moved toward a new understanding of the ties that bind individuals to the community.

In the mid-seventeenth century when English judges turned their attention to the process of naturalization, they took as their starting point Coke's analysis of natural subjectship. Working from this theoretical base, the judges concluded that the essential purpose of naturalization was to make the alien legally the "same" as a native Englishman. Although in fact the adopted member's rights might remain somewhat less extensive than those of born subjects, in law his allegiance, though acquired by a legal process, must be considered to share the attributes that Coke had described; that is, it must be deemed natural, personal, and perpetual.

In the colonies this pattern of thinking was reversed. Americans first came to see the allegiance of adopted members as reflecting the character of the naturalization process. This legal procedure involved a form of contract between an alien who chose a new allegiance and a community that consented to adopt him as a subject, and the colonists began to view the allegiance that resulted as volitional and contractual. Should this consensual allegiance be limited to adopted subjects only? The need to attract settlers produced generous naturalization policies that promised aliens virtually the same rights as Englishmen. Despite some resistance from imperial authorities, the distinctions between the various categories of subjects—still quite real in the mother country—began to soften and blur. Naturalized subjects seemed in fact to share the same status as natives; thus their allegiance ought to be the same. Significantly, the colonists took the model of the naturalized subject as their starting point, and they ultimately concluded that all allegiance ought to be considered the result of a contract resting on consent.

A third phase in the development of an American concept of

citizenship occurred when the Revolution impelled the colonists to articulate in theoretical form this new concept of allegiance. Amidst the conflict and confusion that marked the imperial controversy of the 1760s, the War of Independence, and the long search for new forms of republican government, Americans sought to define principles of membership that adequately encompassed their ideals of individual liberty and community security. In large part they built upon the notion inherent in the process of naturalization that the tie between the individual and the community was contractual and volitional, not natural and perpetual. This idea shaped their response to the claims of Parliament and the king, legitimized their withdrawal from the British empire, controlled their reaction to the loyalists, and underwrote their creation of independent governments.

The Revolution created the status of "American citizen" and produced an expression of the general principles that ought to govern membership in a free society: republican citizenship ought to rest on consent; it ought to be uniform and without invidious gradations; and it ought to confer equal rights. But if general principles were clear, particular questions about the source, character, and effects of citizenship remained open well into the nineteenth century.

In the fourth and final phase of conceptual development, Americans sought to work out the implications of their ideas in the context of a federal republic based on the principle of popular sovereignty. Logic often led to conclusions that were unanticipated and, to many, unacceptable. The newly emergent principles of citizenship clashed with deep-seated prejudices, including the traditional exclusion of Indians and Negroes, to produce confusion and contention. Ultimately, the attempt to arrive at a consistent doctrine of citizenship would be settled neither in the Congress nor in the courts, but on the battlefields of the Civil War.

PART I

The English Background

CHAPTER 1

Natural-Born Subjects and the Theory of Natural Allegiance

English law held in practice, long before it explained in theory, that persons born within the royal dominions were the king's subjects. This general presumption was made explicit in 1368, and the basic principle was never successfully challenged.[1] Yet it did not follow that those born outside the dominions were necessarily aliens, for English jurists had no conscious attachment to the *jus soli*—the legal principle that place of birth alone determined one's status as subject or alien.[2] Ancestry could also determine who was a "natural-born subject" with an inherent claim to the rights of an Englishman.

A number of judicial pronouncements and legislative enactments clarified the status of foreign-born children whose parents were English subjects. There was little question about the position of the royal family. A declaration of 1343 affirmed that birth abroad could not affect the succession to the throne and that the king's children,

---

1. 42 Edw. III, c. 10 (1368), affirmed that infants born in Calais and "elsewhere within the lands and seignories pertaining to the king beyond the sea" could inherit "as other infants born within the realm," thus recognizing their subject status. See Shaw, ed., *Denization and Naturalization, 1603–1700*, iii. A bill introduced in 1580 (23 Eliz. I), but which failed of enactment, would have established that children born in England whose parents were aliens should not be deemed natural-born subjects. *Ibid.*, ix.

2. For discussions of the common law and early legislative enactments regarding English nationality in terms of competing principles of the *jus soli* (place of birth) and *jus sanguinis* (descent), see Cockburn, *Nationality*, 12, and Sir Francis Piggott, *Nationality, Including Naturalization and English Law on the High Seas and beyond the Realm*, I (London, 1907), 41.

13

wherever born, could inherit in England.[3] For common subjects, however, the issue was more ambiguous. An equivocal judicial decision of 1290 had allowed the foreign-born son of a native English mother to claim his inheritance in England, but accompanying dicta limited its use as a precedent in favor of "other aliens."[4] The status of such children born abroad remained uncertain until the statute *De natis ultra mare* (1350) dealt directly and authoritatively with the problem. Reaffirming that the English law "is and always hath been" that the king's children could inherit in England, the statute proceeded to declare that "all children inheritors, which from henceforth shall be born without the ligeance of the king, whose fathers and mothers, at the time of their birth, be, and shall be, at the faith and ligeance of the King of England, shall have, and shall enjoy, the same benefits and advantages . . . as other inheritors aforesaid in time to come; so always that the mothers of such children do pass the sea by the license and wills of their husbands."[5]

The interpretation of *De natis* in the English courts was not altogether consistent. A ruling of 1582 narrowed the statute, holding that children born abroad were to be considered aliens if the parents left the dominions without license or stayed outside the realm longer than their licenses permitted.[6] But other rulings worked to liberalize the act. In a case of 1627 involving the right of the children of an English merchant and his Polish wife to take a devise of copyhold, several judges not only affirmed the property right but also added that *De natis* required only that either the father or the mother be a natural-born subject.[7] To compound the confusion, three judges ruled in 1640 that the daughter of an English merchant, born in Poland after the father's death, was a subject and could

3. 17 Edw. III, Parliament Roll (1343).

4. See the case of Elyas de Rabayn (1290), discussed in Parry, *British Nationality Law*, 10. Parry infers that birth abroad made the son an alien; one could equally well argue that the son's status turned on the (presumed) alienage of his father. I suspect that neither the *jus soli* nor the *jus sanguinis* ruled here, rather that the case depended upon the father's foreign allegiance and upon the presumption that both mother and son assumed the father's condition. The case is worth mentioning as an example of the ambiguous nature of the evidence and of the danger of positing the controlling influence of abstract legal principles not explicitly alluded to by contemporaries.

5. *De natis ultra mare*, 25 Edw. III, stat. 2 (1350), quoted in Jones, *British Nationality*, 66.

6. Hyde v. Hill, Cro. Eliz. 3 (1582). See also Charles Viner, *A General Abridgment of Law and Equity* . . . , II (Aldershot, 1747), 261–262, under "Alien."

7. Rex v. Eaton, Lit. Rep. 23 (1627). Parry, *British Nationality Law*, 44, notes that five years later Sir Edward Littleton himself doubted his recollection of the decision, advising a client in a similar situation to avoid the question by obtaining letters of denization.

inherit by the common law. They grounded their decision on the maxim *partus sequitur patrem* (the offspring follows the condition of the father). They deemed the mother's status immaterial, as she was under the power of the husband: "*sub potestate viri*, and *quasi* under the allegiance of our King."[8]

Legislation in the seventeenth and eighteenth centuries partially clarified issues raised by the statute *De natis*. The status of foreign-born children of subjects in exile with Charles II was statutorily explained in 1676, and a similar act passed in 1698 defined the position of children born of parents engaged abroad in the service of the king against the French.[9] More important, a statute of 1709 explained that the "children inheritors" referred to in *De natis* were to be deemed natural-born subjects, not merely aliens with special property rights. Later acts not only confirmed this construction but also affirmed that the father alone had to be natural-born, excluded the children of persons attainted of treason and other serious crimes, and, finally, extended the right of subjectship to the second generation born abroad.[10]

Although over time there was some controversy over the details of the law, English jurists consistently maintained that either birth or descent could identify the natural-born subject. In modern analytical terms, the system combined the principles of the *jus soli* (birthplace) and the *jus sanguinis* (descent) in determining subjectship. But contemporaries did not use these categories to interpret the law. Building instead upon a fundamentally medieval conception of the political and social order, early English lawyers and legislators defined status in terms of simple and coherent principles of allegiance. This, at least, was Sir Edward Coke's perception when, "by one of those fortuitous events which make the growth of the law so haphazard, yet so full of happy surprises," he and the other judges of England's highest courts gathered together the

8. Bacon v. Bacon, Cro. Car. 601, 602 (1641).
9. The act 29 Car. II, c. 6 (1676), dealt with children born between June 14, 1641, and Mar. 24, 1660/1661, and a few other named persons. Those who wished to benefit from the act were required to take the Sacrament within seven years and the oaths of allegiance and supremacy within one month thereafter. The act 9 & 10 Will. III, c. 20 (1698), followed the same model. Shaw, ed., *Denization and Naturalization, 1603–1700*, ix–x; Parry, *British Nationality Law*, 50–52.
10. 7 Anne, c. 5, sec. 3 (1709). This section survived, though other sections of the act were repealed in 1712 (10 Anne, c. 5). 4 Geo. II, c. 21 (1731), extended the principle to the second generation. DeGeer v. Stone, 22 Ch. D. 243 (1882), affirmed that the third generation was alien. See Jones, *British Nationality*, 69–72.

"various scraps of precedent" to determine the issues in *Calvin's Case*.[11]

Calvin's Case, or the *Case of the Postnati* (1608), was a test case instituted primarily to determine the nature of the union wrought between Scotland and England by the accession of James I, who was already James VI of Scotland. The political issues involving the status and rights of subjects in the two dominions following the union had been fully debated in and out of Parliament since James's arrival in England.[12] A joint session of Scottish and English high commissioners had proposed that "the common law of both nations should be declared to be, that all born in either nation sithence His Majesty was king of both, were mutually naturalized in both," but the English Commons refused to agree.[13] In view of Parliament's inability to resolve the controversy, *Calvin's Case* was contrived to bring the matter into the English courts.

Formally, the litigation involved a dispute over land titles.[14] Two suits were introduced in the name of Robert Calvin, an infant born in Scotland in 1606 after the accession (a *postnatus*).[15] Calvin's counsel complained that their client had been prevented from taking possession of lands to which he was lawfully entitled. Opposing lawyers contended that as an alien, Calvin could neither inherit nor sue for lands in England. Since the determination of the infant's status as subject or alien raised fundamental questions about the

11. Joseph Henry Smith, *Appeals to the Privy Council from the American Plantations*, Columbia University School of Law, Publications of the Foundation for Research in Legal History (New York, 1950), 467.

12. Harvey Wheeler, "Calvin's Case (1608) and the McIlwain-Schuyler Debate," *American Historical Review*, LXI (1955–1956), 589.

13. Jones, *British Nationality*, 29. See also [W. Cobbett and John Wright, eds.], *Cobbett's Parliamentary History of England. From the Norman Conquest in 1066. To the Year, 1803* (London, 1806–1820), I, 1018. Note that the word "naturalized" here refers to the state of being a natural-born subject and not to the process by which aliens were incorporated into the community.

14. Calvin's Case, 7 Co. Rep. 1a (1608). T[homas] B[ayly] Howell, ed., *Cobbett's Complete Collection of State Trials . . .* (London, 1809–1826), II, 559–696, has Coke's report as well as Serjeant Francis Moore's account of the parliamentary debates on the union, Sir Francis Bacon's argument for Calvin, and Lord Chancellor Ellesmere's speech in the Court of Exchequer-Chamber.

15. One suit was brought in King's Bench for the freehold of lands in the English parish of Shoreditch; the other in Chancery for detaining the evidences of title and taking the profits of land in the parish of St. Botolph. Holdsworth, *History of English Law*, IX, 79.

English law and the constitution, the suits were adjourned to the Court of Exchequer-Chamber.[16]

Although four lawyers, fourteen judges, and the lord chancellor participated in *Calvin's Case*, the opinion of Lord Coke, chief justice of Common Pleas, emerged as the definitive statement of the law.[17] Coke's attention focused on the status of the natural-born subject —the individual who was born into the community of Englishmen. In the process of analyzing natural allegiance, however, Coke commented extensively on the nature of the community and the structure of political obligation. His wide-ranging conclusions— buttressed by his personal authority as one of England's most eminent jurists and made accessible in his *Reports*—constituted the first comprehensive theory of English subjectship.

Coke's argument in *Calvin's Case* was convoluted and complex, but it is worth examining in close detail. Because Anglo-American jurists and theorists subsequently focused on particular conclusions or maxims rather than on the underlying logic of the opinion, they often transformed Coke's meaning by quoting him out of context. Ultimately, different elements of *Calvin's Case* would sustain radically opposing visions of the meaning of allegiance, political authority, and constitutional legitimacy.

Coke began his analysis by noting that English law encompassed a number of different kinds of "ligeance" describing various kinds of relationships. Although there were four basic categories of allegiance—natural, acquired, local, and legal—his primary concern was with the "*ligeantia naturalis*" that characterized the natural-born subject.[18] Broadly defined, this allegiance was the "true and faithful

16. Howell, ed., *State Trials*, II, 559–562, 607–609. Solicitor General Bacon and Attorney General Henry Hobart argued for the plaintiff (Calvin), Laurance Hyde and Serjeant Richard Hutton for the defendants. Opinions were given by Edward Heron, James Altham, George Snigge, and Lawrence Tanfield of the Exchequer; Thomas Foster, William Daniel, Peter Warburton, Thomas Walmesley, and Edward Coke of Common Pleas; John Crook, David Williams, Christopher Yelverton, Edward Fenner, and Thomas Fleming of King's Bench; and by Thomas Eggerton, Lord Ellesmere, the lord chancellor. *Ibid.*, 609.

17. Jones, *British Nationality*, 28, calls this the "pure milk of the common law doctrine of allegiance to the crown." The "definitive" label is justified, too, by the invariable citation of this *Report* in the major legal digests and commentaries of the 17th and 18th centuries whenever issues touching allegiance, alienage, treason, and so forth are dealt with. Cases on both sides of the Atlantic are replete with references to Coke's arguments here.

18. *Ligeantia naturalis* defined the natural-born subject, and this was Coke's major concern. *Ligeantia acquisita* pertained to those who were subjects not by birth but by conquest, denization, or naturalization. *Ligeantia localis* encompassed the temporary obli-

obedience of the subject due to his sovereign. This ligeance and obedience is an incident inseparable to every subject: for as soon as he is born, he oweth by birth-right ligeance and obedience to his sovereign."[19] This obligation was natural and immutable, corresponding to the obligations a child owed his parents.

The object of natural allegiance was the sovereign who protected a person at the time of his birth. Protection, like allegiance, was a natural obligation, owed by the superior to the inferior, by the sovereign to the subject. Aristotle's authority confirmed that "to command and to obey is of nature," for "whatsoever is necessary and profitable for the society of man is due by the law of nature," and "magistracy and government are necessary and profitable for the society of man; therefore, magistracy and government are of nature." The bond between the subject and the sovereign thus involved reciprocal obligations, "for as the subject oweth to the king his true and faithful ligeance and obedience, so the sovereign is to govern and protect his subjects."[20]

Coke described allegiance and protection as a double, reciprocal bond (*"duplex et reciprocum ligamen"*), and he claimed that "power and protection draweth ligeance."[21] By this he did not mean that

---

gations owed by resident alien friends. Finally, "ligeance which is called legal" involved the obligations resulting from formal oaths of allegiance. See Calvin's Case, 7 Co. Rep. 1a, 5b–7a, and Sir Edward Coke, *The First Part of the Institutes of the Laws of England; or, A Commentary upon Littleton* . . . , ed. Francis Hargrave and Charles Butler, 1st Am. ed. from the 19th London ed., corrected (Philadelphia, 1853), I, 129a. Under feudal law, every male aged 12 and upwards was obliged to swear allegiance to the king. The oath merely affirmed a preexisting status; it did not create a new one. All men (but not women) —including resident aliens—took this oath confirming the allegiance (of whatever character) they already owed. See Jones, *British Nationality*, 58, and Sir Matthew Hale, *Historia Placitorum Coronae. The History of the Pleas of the Crown*, ed. Sollom Emlyn (London, 1736), I, 64–67. Coke observed that though some "persons be exempted from their personall coming to the tourne and leet [courts in which the oath was sworn], and many other persons never took the said oath of allegiance, yet all are subjects of what quality, profession, or sex soever, as firmly bounden to their allegiance, as if they had taken the oath, because it is written by the finger of the law in every one of their hearts, and the taking of the corporall oath, is but an outward declaration of the same." Sir Edward Coke, *The Second Part of the Institutes of the Laws of England* . . . (London, 1797), I, Statute of Marlebridge, chap. 10, 121.

19. Calvin's Case, 4b. In Owen alias Collin's Case, Godbolt 263, 264 (1615), Coke noted "that in point of allegiance none must serve the King with *ifs* and *ands*."

20. Calvin's Case, 12b–13a, 4b.

21. *Ibid.*, 5a, 9b. Wheeler, "Calvin's Case," *AHR*, LXI (1955–1956), 590, argues that Coke subtly shifted his definition of allegiance so that what began as a unilateral obligation became a reciprocal, contractual one. Here Wheeler fails to note the distinction between obligation and performance in Coke's understanding of "protection." Americans during the Revolutionary period would make the same misreading, arguing that allegiance was the

the subject-king relationship was a contractual one dependent on the continuous and effective exercise of protection. Rather a person born within the actual protection of the king would remain a subject even though that protection later might be lost. A natural-born subject inhabiting a territory conquered by a foreign sovereign, for example, would assume new obligations toward the conquering power, but this would not destroy his primal natural allegiance. Instead, the individual would now be *"ad fidem utriusque regis"* (in allegiance to both kings).[22] This double allegiance would characterize only the *antenati*, namely, those born before the loss of the territory. Children born within the protection of the new sovereign would owe allegiance to him alone.[23] Similarly, the sovereign who lost the territory would retain the natural obligation to protect the *antenati*, even though in fact he might not be able to exercise that protection; however, he would owe nothing to children born after the conquest. Because the primal obligations of allegiance and protection remained perpetual and inviolate, no subject could ever lose his natural allegiance. He might abjure the kingdom and leave the country, but he could not break the tie that bound him to his king, the father of his country.[24]

This analysis of birthright subjectship grew from a philosophical world view that saw government and society as reflections of natural principles of order and hierarchy. The bond between the subject and his sovereign mirrored the divinely ordained obligations of right and duty subsisting between the inferior and superior. Yet if the essence of the relationship was natural, its expression was political and legal, and Coke quickly turned his attention to an analysis of how the natural substance of subjectship shaped and controlled the constitutional forms of the English community.

The avowed aim of *Calvin's Case* was to determine the status in English law of an infant born in Scotland after the accession. Ac-

---

contractual reciprocal of continuous actual protection and using Coke to justify their withdrawal of allegiance after George III had withdrawn his protection.

22. Calvin's Case, 27b.

23. A clarifying analogy might be drawn here with the parent–child relationship. The natural relation between father and child cannot be altered, though the parents divorce and remarry. The child of the first marriage, accompanying the mother, might gain a "new" father, but nothing could destroy his natural relationship with his real father. Children of the second marriage, of course, would have no relationship to the first father.

24. As Coke put it, *"qui abjurat regnum amittit regnum, sed non regem, amittit patrem, sed non patrem patriae."* Calvin's Case, 9b.

cording to Coke's principles, the law of nature clearly made that infant James's subject. But James wore two crowns, and for Calvin's opponents the distinction between the crowns of England and Scotland was more important than their union in his person. Citing the civil law maxim, *"Quando duo jura concurrunt in una persona, aequum est ac si essent in diversis"* (when two rights meet in one person, it is the same as if they were in different persons), these lawyers insisted that Calvin was a subject of James VI of Scotland and an alien to James I of England.[25] In essence, they argued that natural allegiance, hence one's status as subject or alien, was defined by one's relationship to the crown (to the king as a legal construct) and not to the person who wore the crown.

Coke opened his attack on this contention by demonstrating that kingship existed in the natural order even before men created legal systems. It was "historically true," he argued, that "before judicial or municipal laws were made, kings did decide causes according to natural equity," and it was also evident that "government and subjection were long before municipal laws." Indeed, the formulation of laws would have been senseless unless allegiance already existed, for "it had been in vain to have prescribed laws to any, but to such as owed obedience, faith, and ligeance before, in respect whereof they were bound to obey and observe them."[26] Allegiance and protection, subjects and kings, were facts of nature; they preceded the emergence of governments and laws. Their essential character could not be defined in terms of man's legal constructs.

Although the superior natural man was king in the state of nature, Coke insisted that kingship in seventeenth-century England encompassed more than pure natural superiority. The real monarch was both a natural person and a legal construct; he consisted of two capacities: "One a natural body, being descended of the blood royal of the realm; and this body is the creation of Almighty God, and is subject to death, infirmity and such like: the other is a politick body or capacity, so called, because it is framed by the policy of man . . . and in this capacity the king is esteemed to be immortal, invisible, and not subject to death, infirmity, infancy, nonage, etc."[27] Alle-

25. *Ibid.*, 2b. This maxim was used for a different purpose in the debates preceding the American Revolution. See below, chap. 6, at n. 83.
26. *Ibid.*, 13a.
27. *Ibid.*, 10a. For an analysis of the origins and theological antecedents of this mode of thought, see Ernst H. Kantorowicz, *The King's Two Bodies: A Study in Mediaeval Political Theology* (Princeton, N.J., 1957), 3–23, and *passim*.

giance, declared Coke, was owed "to the natural person of the king, which is ever accompanied with the politick capacity, and the politick capacity, as it were appropriated to the natural capacity, and is not due to the politick capacity only, that is, to his crown or kingdom distinct from his natural capacity."[28] As in the state of nature, allegiance in England was owed to the person (natural capacity) of King James. But since James derived his superiority and his ability to protect subjects from his kingship, allegiance accrued to him only after he inherited the crown. In the state of organized society, the monarch was an inseparable combination of a natural person and of a legal construct or "body politic."[29]

Neither law nor logic would sustain the claim that allegiance in England could be defined by either capacity alone. To isolate the natural capacity as the focal point and determinant of allegiance was to conclude that the death of a king "denaturalized" all persons born under his protection. On the other hand, the king as a political entity could not actually exercise that protection which "draweth ligeance." The king's "crown," according to Coke, was

an hieroglyphic of the laws, where justice, etc. is administered. . . . Therefore, if you take that which is signified by the crown, that is, to do justice and judgment, to maintain the peace of the land, etc. to separate right from wrong, and the good from the ill; that is to be understood of that capacity of the king that "*in rei veritate*" hath capacity, and is adorned and endued with endowments as well of the soul, as of the body, and thereby able to do justice and judgment according to right and equity, and to maintain the peace, etc. and to find out and discern the truth, and not of the invisible and immortal capacity that hath no such endowments; for of itself it hath neither soul nor body.[30]

"Disembodied law" could not afford protection "in real matters," and thus it could not in itself elicit allegiance. A natural person was needed to make the system work; however, a natural person without the crown lacked the means of protection. Only after his accession, therefore, could he serve to define the community of subjects.

28. Calvin's Case, 10a. For the use of this dictum in the imperial debates of the early 1770s, see below, chap. 6, at nn. 82–85.

29. Coke declared that the law of England did not admit the notion of an interregnum. Coronation was "but a royal ornament and solemnization of the royal descent" and not an act essential to the transfer of the crown. *Ibid.*, 10b–11a; see also Kantorowicz, *The King's Two Bodies*, 317–333.

30. Calvin's Case, 11b.

Coke derived several important conclusions from his analysis of kingship as a necessary combination of natural and political capacities. First—and most immediately relevant for the outcome of *Calvin's Case*—all *postnati* Scotsmen were to be considered natural-born subjects in England. They had been born within the personal protection of the king of England, and it did not matter that the protection they enjoyed had been exercised through a separate political capacity—namely, through the independent system of Scottish courts and laws that James embodied as king of Scotland. On the other hand, the *antenati* Scots, those born before James became England's king, had been born under distinct persons and different crowns, and by English law they remained aliens.[31]

The union of capacities also explained why the *antenati/postnati* distinction did not apply when the crown changed heads within a particular kingdom. The political capacity was a legal construct "framed by the policy of man" and could acquire qualities not shared by ordinary persons.[32] According to legal principles already familiar and authoritative by 1608, "when the body politic is conjoined with [the natural body of the king], and one body is made of them both, the whole body shall have all the properties, qualities, and degrees of the body politic which is the greater and more worthy."[33] The political capacity was deemed immortal; the demise of

31. Wheeler, "Calvin's Case," *AHR*, LXI (1955–1956), 588n, dismisses the *antenati/postnati* distinction as a "compromise intended to provide for the gradual unification of the two realms during the span of a maturing generation." Holdsworth, *History of English Law*, IX, 80, sees the exclusion of the *antenati* as "a conclusion which followed from the territorial principle" of nationality rather than from the "personal principle." Charles Howard McIlwain, *The American Revolution: A Constitutional Interpretation* (New York, 1923), 92–93, also obscures the theoretical basis for the distinction by arguing that Coke stressed the natural capacity alone. The logical reasons for separating the two groups stem in fact from the theory that the two capacities were necessarily united, regardless of political motives and circumstances.

32. Calvin's Case, 10a, 12a–12b. Coke, *First Institutes*, ed. Hargrave and Butler, I, 15b, 115b, explicitly states that "by the common law, the king is a corporation," noting as well that the "common law hath no controller in any part of it, but the high court of parliament." Through the political capacity, then, Parliament could theoretically "control" the power that James exercised as king of England. Note, however, that this did not logically permit parliamentary interference with powers the king might have by virtue of non-English political capacities, a point that would be of particular importance for Americans in the 1760s.

33. Case of the Duchy of Lancaster, 1 Pl. Com. 212, 217 (1561). Coke cited this several times in Calvin's Case, and he referred his readers to it for an explanation of the "royal politique" in his *First Institutes*, ed. Hargrave and Butler, I, 43b. Kantorowicz, *The King's Two Bodies*, 16, 19, points to the resemblance between this concept and the religious ideas of the Trinity and the two natures of Christ, and he notes that "the crypto-theological idiom

the monarch merely meant that the incorporeal body politic was transferred from one natural body to another. Thus the natural-born subject of Elizabeth remained in allegiance to James I; allegiance focused on the new natural person, but it was owed to the "same king."[34]

This view of allegiance profoundly affected the whole structure of political power and authority. Coke's argument inevitably led to the conclusion that the community of allegiance was not coterminous with the political community of the English state. The natural community of allegiance was the aggregation of all those reciprocal relationships of allegiance and protection between individual subjects and the king. It resembled the natural family, where a common paternity made sons and daughters into brothers and sisters; it transcended the boundaries separating Scotland and England and brought *postnati* Scotsmen and native Englishmen together as fellow subjects; and it supplied authority and natural obligation to those legal and political systems created by man.

Coke carefully distinguished between this natural community of allegiance and the actual constitutional relationships existing among the various dominions under the king. England and Scotland remained constitutionally distinct and independent, although Ireland, for example, was subordinate to the ultimate supervisory jurisdiction of England's parliament because that kingdom had been brought under the king's protection by conquest in the time of

---

was not the personal spleen of any single one among the Tudor lawyers, nor was it restricted to a small coterie of judges."

34. Kantorowicz, *The King's Two Bodies*, 13n. This concept allowed jurists to posit a continuity of allegiance even though the crown was obtained in an irregular way. Although Mary and Elizabeth were "of the half-blood," they inherited the lands—and the subjects—of their predecessors as if they were the natural, direct, "full-blood" descendants of past monarchs. Analogously, Henry VII's attainder for treason, according to Coke, was absolved immediately and "without any other reversall" when the crown descended upon him. Coke, *First Institutes*, ed. Hargrave and Butler, I, 15b, 16a. Because "allegiance and protection are reciprocal terms," and because de facto kings controlled the means of protection, even a usurper became the "same" person in law as his de jure predecessors. The usurper, not the person "who has a right or title to the crown, without possession," was the object of the subject's allegiance. Sir John Kelyng, "A Treatise upon Treason," 17, in *Sir John Kelyng's Report of Crown Cases in the time of King Charles II, . . . Together with a Treatise upon the Law and Proceedings in cases of High Treason*, ed. Richard L. Loveland, 3d ed. (London, 1873). (The *Report* and the *Treatise* are paginated separately, with the title page of the latter bearing the imprint "London, 1793.") Kelyng observed that though Hale, *Historia Placitorum*, I, 60–61, had thought an act of hostility in favor of the rightful heir not to be treason, Coke argued that a de jure king, on gaining the crown, could punish treason committed against an earlier de facto king. For Coke's argument on this point, see Sir Edward Coke, *The Third Part of the Institutes of the Laws of England . . .* (London, 1797), 7.

Henry II. Parliament could not intervene in Scotland because the Scottish and English crowns settled upon the same person only by the accidental confluence of two independent laws of succession.

James's title to the kingdom of Scotland was established by the Scottish laws of royal succession. Since "by the laws of the kingdom he doth inherit the kingdom, he cannot change those laws of himself, without consent of [Scotland's] parliament."[35] James became king by law and was therefore limited by law. Yet because the legal systems of England and Scotland remained independent, the king's authority in the two dominions could only be limited by the parliament of the kingdom concerned. The community of allegiance that resulted when the crowns of the two dominions merged in a single person did not extend the authority of the political institutions of either kingdom.

The situation was different when the title to a kingdom derived from conquest, as was the case with Ireland. The conqueror's authority over a conquered population was absolute—it was the power of life and death (*"vitae necis et potestatem"*). By virtue of the victory, he could "alter and change" the laws of the defeated kingdom "at his pleasure." If the territory conquered had been a Christian kingdom, the "ancient laws" remained in force until the new ruler chose to alter them, which he could do unilaterally at any time. If, on the other hand, the vanquished kingdom had been an infidel one, its old laws were abrogated immediately, for they were "not only against Christianity, but against the laws of God and of nature."[36] In either situation, the conqueror's position rested upon a superiority of force and power, not upon law.

As a conqueror, the king held unlimited power over Ireland, including the authority to change or abolish Ireland's laws. Once he established new laws, however, he and his successors were constrained by those laws, which could no longer be altered unilaterally. As Coke put the point, "If a king hath a Christian kingdom, as Henry 2, had Ireland, after John had given unto them, being under his obedience and subjection, the laws of England for the government of that country, no succeeding king could alter the same without parliament."[37]

---

35. Calvin's Case, 17b.
36. *Ibid.*
37. *Ibid.* Compare Wheeler, "Calvin's Case," *AHR*, LXI (1955–1956), 593, for a different and highly questionable interpretation of this passage.

Coke's syntax here was convoluted, but his point was fundamental. In his view, the first three rulers of Ireland reigned there by right of conquest. Richard I followed Henry II not by operation of law (from the Irish perspective), but by military control. John followed Richard I and initially ruled as "king of Ireland" for the same reason, that is, because his dominance remained rooted in force and power.[38] But then John exercised the conqueror's right to alter the laws; he "had given unto them . . . the laws of England for the government of that country," and thereafter he and his successors became limited monarchs in Irish eyes, deriving their crown (their Irish political capacity) from Ireland's new law and changing that law only with the consent of Ireland's parliament.[39]

John gave Ireland the "laws of England," but this act fixed Ireland's internal constitutional relationships only and did not determine the relationship between the two dominions. Indeed, whatever laws John chose to give Ireland, that kingdom remained under the ultimate supervisory jurisdiction of England's parliament, for England had conquered Ireland. The power that enabled Henry II to undertake the conquest was the power that accompanied the crown of England. From England's point of view, Henry II, Richard I, and John followed each other by the ordinary operation of England's laws of royal succession, whatever the basis of their authority from Ireland's perspective. Although the king of Ireland had finally limited himself and his successors by establishing laws in the conquered kingdom—in much the same way that Duke William had limited himself by confirming England's laws after the Conquest—England had never legalized its position vis-à-vis Ireland. England's authority over its conquest still ultimately rested on naked power.

Ireland had never been merged with England; it remained a distinct kingdom. Yet Coke, citing a Year Book of Richard III,

38. Coke noted that King John added *"dominus Hiberniae"* to his title, "which title . . . he assumed as annexed to the crowne, albeit his father, in the 23 years of his raigne had created him king of Ireland in his lifetime." *First Institutes*, ed. Hargrave and Butler, I, 7b. For amplification of Coke's view of Ireland's relationship with England, see *The Fourth Part of the Institutes of the Laws of England* . . . (London, 1797), chap. 76, 349–361.

39. Many scholars have misread Coke on this point, assuming that "giving the laws" of England, rather than the actual conquest, formed the basis for extending parliamentary authority. See, e.g., Smith, *Appeals to the Privy Council*, 468, and Wheeler, "Calvin's Case," *AHR*, LXI (1955–1956), 593. When he used the word "parliament," Coke did not always mean the English parliament.

noted that "Ireland has a parliament, and makes laws, and our statutes do not bind them, who do not send knights to [our] parliament (which is to be understood, unless they be especially named) but their persons are subjects of the king, just as the inhabitants of Calais, Gascony, and Guienne."[40] Coke's parenthetical qualification—his claim that England's parliament retained jurisdiction over Ireland—was possible only because the relationship between the two kingdoms was still that of the conqueror and conquered. Ireland was not a part of the realm of England, but "the title thereof being by conquest, the same by judgment of law might by express words be bound by an act of the parliament of England."[41]

Coke thus postulated a distinction between the king's personal relationship with his subjects in various kingdoms and the constitutional relationship of those kingdoms. On the one hand, subjectship and allegiance depended upon the fact of protection; whoever was born under the protection of the person who was king was a natural subject, regardless of whether that protection consisted of a system of laws (as in England and Scotland) or of military force and power (as in the first stages of Irish dependency after the conquest). On the other hand, the political and constitutional relations among the several kingdoms depended upon historical, not natural, factors. The English parliament had no authority over Scotland because English law had nothing to do with the king's title there; however, Ireland remained a subordinate dominion because the title came by way of conquest.[42]

The jurisdiction of the several parliaments was or could be lim-

40. Calvin's Case, 22b, citing Y.B. 2 Rich. III, 12a. The citation, except for Coke's qualification (which was in English), reads: "*Hibernia habet parliamentum, et faciunt leges, et nostra statuta non ligant eos, quia non mittunt milites ad parliamentum . . . sed personae eorum sunt subjecti regis, sicut inhabitantes in Calesia, Gasconia, et Guyan.*"

41. *Ibid.*, 17b. A pamphlet of 1644, probably written by Patrick Darcy, contended that John might have given the "laws of Scotland, not England," to Ireland, and thus Parliament's authority was illegitimate if it rested on John's law-giving. Robert Livingston Schuyler, *Parliament and the British Empire: Some Constitutional Controversies concerning Imperial Legislative Jurisdiction* (New York, 1929), 64–68. Since Coke did not place Parliament's authority on this foundation but rather on England's conquest of Ireland, Darcy did not fully come to terms with Coke's analysis.

42. Scotland's independence remained unchanged until the formal union of 1707. The transfer of the Scottish crown from James II to William and Mary in 1689 was the result of the independent decision of the Scottish Convention. Ireland, on the other hand, automatically went to the new sovereigns. *Ibid.*, 74; David Ogg, *England in the Reigns of James II and William III* (Oxford, 1955), 266–267. The impact of the Act of Union is discussed below, chap. 3.

ited, but the rights and obligations of both the king and his subjects were as extensive as the community of allegiance. Robert Calvin and all other natural subjects could demand the rights of subjectship and protection in all the king's dominions. The monarch was morally and naturally obliged to extend protection to all these subjects by every means at his command. This natural obligation might be obstructed or regulated by the laws of a particular dominion, as exemplified by the situation of the Scottish *antenati*. The *antenatus* Scotsman had the same abstract claim as Calvin to James's protection, for all Scotsmen were subjects of James VI. But English law, having nothing to do with James's title as king of Scotland, was not obliged to recognize relationships previously created under that crown; it took cognizance of James only after he gained the English crown.[43] The *antenati* were aliens to James as king of England, and they were aliens to his English subjects.

The law of England thus viewed the *antenatus* Scotsman as an alien, even though James saw him as a subject. Since the law recognized a sphere of royal action beyond its immediate control (defined generally as the king's prerogative), it could not prevent James from treating the *antenati* with special consideration. But the law could and did bar the monarch from unilaterally granting aliens the same rights as natural-born subjects.[44] If James chose to fulfill his personal obligations toward the *antenatus* Scotsman by granting him those privileges at the disposal of the prerogative power, the law was bound to recognize that act; nevertheless, it recognized the

43. Titles to property purchased by the king—or descending to him from collateral ancestors—before his accession vested in his natural person. Lands he acquired as king vested in his political capacity and were annexed to the crown. Coke, *First Institutes*, ed. Hargrave and Butler, I, 15b, n. 4; see also the Duchy of Lancaster Case, 1 Pl. Com. 212, 214 (1561). The allegiance owed by the *antenati* Scots to James VI was like property acquired before the succession—it could descend separately. The allegiance of the *postnati*, on the other hand, was annexed to the crown of England and went to the royal heir of James I.

44. Coke observed that though the king could "by his letters patent . . . make a denizen," he could not "naturalize . . . to all purposes, as an act of parliament may do; neither can letters patent make any inheritable in this case, that by the common law cannot inherit." Calvin's Case, 7a, and below, chap. 2. Coke elsewhere noted that "the common law hath so admeasured the prerogatives of the king, that they should not take away, nor prejudice the inheritance of any: and the best inheritance that the subject hath, is the law of the realme." Coke, *Second Institutes*, I, Magna Charta, chap. 30, 63. The quotation both shows that the law set the boundaries of the prerogative and expresses the notion that subjectship gave a right to legal rights. James did show concern for the Scottish *antenati* in England. Parry, *British Nationality Law*, 54, notes that though clerks of the signet office usually received 30s. for preparing letters patent for aliens, they received "nothing for those of a pauper, and again nothing for those of a Scot."

king's act only and was not itself bound to meet the king's obligation.

Coke's analysis of allegiance would become a precedent of great significance both for explaining the character of the subject-king relationship and for determining the connection between subjectship and subordination to Parliament. Place and time of birth or descent from parents in allegiance might prove subjectship, but neither explained its origins.[45] God and nature, not men and laws, made natural-born subjects. The object of their allegiance and the character of their protection depended upon the law, but the obligation of allegiance and the right of protection did not. Nature made Calvin a subject; thus the law was bound to deal with him as such.

Natural allegiance defined a community of subjects whose status, obligations, and rights were reflected in, but not created by, the territorial state. The community of allegiance transcended political boundaries and legal jurisdictions. Subjectship created political authority, not vice versa, for allegiance obliged men to obey laws and governments. The legitimacy of every kingdom and state rested upon the hierarchical principles of the natural order.

Coke's conclusion that allegiance was natural and perpetual would help shape the theories articulated after 1608 respecting the status of other kinds of subjects. Moreover, his dicta about allegiance and political authority would exert a strong influence over the development of attitudes and doctrines concerning the constitutional character of the new imperial community in the eighteenth century. Americans in particular would seize upon elements of *Calvin's Case* to explain and legitimize their special relationship with the mother country. Although the ideas and assumptions that made the case a logical and convincing whole in 1608 would fade, its maxims and definitions would survive as guiding imperatives, serving as the source and inspiration for the ideas of future generations.

45. Holdsworth, *History of English Law*, IX, 80, misconstrues Calvin's Case by arguing that it rested on the "territorial principle." Birth within the dominions was presumptive evidence for but not the cause of allegiance.

CHAPTER 2

Acquired Subjects and the Theory of Naturalization

Native Scotsmen, Irishmen, and Englishmen were all natural subjects of the king, but they were not the only members of the community of allegiance. Men and laws completed what nature had begun. Aliens, born out of the protection of the English king and owing their natural obedience to another sovereign, could become adopted subjects and share the rights that others enjoyed as their natural inheritance.

By the seventeenth century English law provided two distinct procedures for incorporating aliens into the community. Parliamentary acts of naturalization, fairly standardized in form, adopted foreigners on terms that generally conferred the full rights of subjectship. Royal patents of denization, on the other hand, bestowed only limited rights, making the denizen a sort of halfway member who ranked above the alien yet somewhat below the native-born or naturalized subject. The modes of admission were thus distinguished by the locus of authority and by the nature and extent of the rights granted.

Until about the fifteenth century no such distinction between naturalization and denization had existed. Rather the king and Parliament worked together in bringing outsiders into the community of subjects. A foreigner who wished to acquire the status and privileges of an Englishman would petition Parliament, which would then authorize him to obtain a grant of royal letters patent under the great seal.[1] Just why the two elements of this operation became separated is not altogether clear, although the reasons seem to have been primarily procedural and practical. Parliament's orders for the admission of aliens tended toward fixed forms and standardized grants, while the monarch, whose prerogative authority was more flexible, could vary the terms of admission from case to case. And it frequently appeared to be in the royal interest to modify Parliament's orders that foreigners be granted full rights. When Parliament authorized such a grant to Henry Hansforth in 1431, the king responded with letters patent requiring that Hansforth continue to pay the aliens' duties, which were double those paid by native subjects. The Tudor monarchs, committed to the prerogative, preferred to adopt aliens by letters patent, and most of their grants contained similarly advantageous provisos respecting customs. The few parliamentary acts in the same period continued to confer full privileges.[2]

Although the distinction between admission procedures probably stemmed from practical concerns, it eventually acquired a kind of theoretical rationale. Denization came to be seen as "a high and incommunicable branch of the royal prerogative," a grant of the king's grace by which some, but not all, privileges of natural-born subjects were conferred.[3] The power to "naturalize a meere alien, and make him a subject borne," was confined to Parliament, whose jurisdiction was "so transcendent and absolute, as it cannot be confined either for causes or persons within any bounds."[4] Denization put a man "in a kind of middle state, between an alien and natural-born subject," while naturalization put him in "exactly the same state as if he had been born in the king's ligeance."[5]

The most important benefits conferred by the acquisition of one of these forms of subject status involved property rights. Aliens could purchase but not personally own real property, holding only for the use of the king.[6] Since "every Man" was "presumed to bear

1. Shaw, ed., *Denization and Naturalization, 1603–1700*, iii–iv.

2. *Ibid.*, vi–viii. Shaw observes that though there were numerous denizations in this period, there were only four parliamentary acts of naturalization under Henry VIII, two under Edward VI, one under Mary, and twelve under Elizabeth. An act of 23 Eliz. I (1581) was the first to use the word "naturalizing."

3. Tucker, ed., *Blackstone's Commentaries*, I:2, 373–374.

4. Coke, *Fourth Institutes*, chap. 1, 36.

5. Tucker, ed., *Blackstone's Commentaries*, I:2, 373–374.

6. See above, Prologue, n. 7.

Faith and Love to that Prince and Country where first he received Protection during his Infancy," the loyalty of an alien was not to be trusted. Property and other restrictions were imposed in part "that one Prince might not settle Spies in another's Country; but chiefly that the Rents and Revenues of one Country might not be drawn to the Subjects of another."[7]

Long residence, continued good behavior, and even swearing "legal allegiance" could not fully remove the taint of suspicion. Although resident alien friends owed temporary allegiance, could be adjudged guilty of a kind of treason,[8] and in common speech might be "capable of the title of his [Majesty's] loving and obedient subjects," they were not qualified for "the distinct title of natural subjects, which is usually in statute set in opposition against denizens and strangers."[9] Even if an alien friend "comes into England when he is an Infant, and for a long Time continues here, and is sworn to the king, yet he continues an alien."[10]

The formal grant of letters patent of denization removed some of the disabilities of alienage restricting property rights. The denizen could purchase and own lands, although he could not inherit them.[11] Moreover, the denizen's lands might descend to his children only in limited cases. If the children had been born abroad, they were aliens and of course were incapable of inheriting in England. If specifically included in the denization, they, like their father, could not inherit but only purchase. If born in England, they were subjects by birth, personally qualified to take by descent; but they could inherit their father's property only if born after his denization. Subject children born before their father's denization could not inherit from him because of his incapacity: at the time of their births, he was still an

---

7. Matthew Bacon, *A new abridgment of the law* . . . , 3d ed. corr., I (London, 1768), 76.

8. Sherley's Case, 2 Dyer 144a (1557). John Sherley, a Frenchman, was convicted of treason for participating in Stafford's rebellion. It was held that at the time of the offense France and England were at peace, and Sherley thus owed temporary allegiance as a resident alien friend.

9. Courteen's Case, Hobart 270 (n.d., ca. 1618?). The comment quoted referred to "the Dutch living here within the King's protection, being of a friend country."

10. Knightley D'Anvers, *A General Abridgment of the Common Law* . . . , 2d ed., I ([London], 1725), 322.

11. Andrews v. Baily, Style 139 (1648). The rule here stated that "denization by letters patent do enable the party to purchase lands, but not to inherit the lands of his ancestors as heirs at law; but as purchasor he may enjoy the lands of his ancestors." Parry, *British Nationality Law*, 58, presumes that an alien could take by descent after his denization. This error leads to some confusion in his discussion of retrospectivity and other distinctions between the two modes of admission.

alien.[12] Denization, in short, was not retrospective. It could not wipe away the stain of an alien birth, but could only grant rights prospectively.

The limitations of denization were determined by the authority by which it was conferred. *East India Company* v. *Sandys* (1683–1685), a case involving the king's power to grant a trading monopoly that abridged the rights of his subjects, explained the point clearly. Sir William Williams, one of the counsel, observed in the course of argument that

the law doth intrust the king by his letters patent, to make denizens of aliens, but not to naturalize them. . . . I humbly take the reason to proceed from the interest of the subject, that the right of the subject is immediately concerned in letting in aliens to have the same right, liberty and freedom with English subjects in England, and that this ought not to be granted to aliens, not by the king under his great seal, without the consent of the Lords and Commons, the representatives of the subjects in parliament.[13]

Coke had declared it a fixed principle of the common law that the king's prerogatives could not abridge the inheritance of his subjects.[14] This maxim would be violated if denization were allowed a retrospective operation, for it would then infringe the existing rights of others without their consent.

The case was otherwise with naturalization "because in an Act of Parliament every Man's consent is included."[15] This mode of ad-

12. Coke, *First Institutes*, ed. Hargrave and Butler, I, 129a. Coke noted that if a denizen "had issue in England before his denization, that issue is not inheritable to his father; but if his father be naturalized by parliament, such issue shall inherit." The defect in the first instance lay in the father, not the son. The father could transmit land only after his denization, and he could only have heirs in consequence of that grant.
13. East India Co. v. Sandys, 10 Howell *State Trials* 371, 499 (1683–1685).
14. See above, chap. 1, n. 44.
15. Bacon, *New abridgment of the law*, I, 79. If a subject married an alien woman, sold his lands, obtained a patent of denization for his wife, then died, his widow had no claim to a dower of those lands, for her capacity to take and the possibility of endowment dated from the denization. If, on the other hand, the woman had been naturalized, she could claim her endowment from the purchaser. The buyer had "consented" to the abridgment of his rights, for the act of naturalization virtually included his acknowledgment of the woman's "natural" birth. Sir John Comyns, *A Digest of the Laws of England*, I (London, 1762), 321; Viner, *General Abridgment of Law*, II, 259. Viner observed that "the *King by his Letters Patents cannot make the Son Heir to his Father*, nor to any other, for he *cannot alter the Law by his Letters Patents*, nor otherwise but by Parliament, for he cannot disinherit the right Heir, nor disappoint the Lord of his Escheat." Naturalization took "*Effect from the Birth of the Party*," but *Denization takes Effect from the Date of the Patent*." *Ibid.*, 269, 266. For a discussion of the development and significance of the theory that Parliament could transfer property by the implied consent of the subject, see Edward T. Lampson, "Some New Light on the Growth of Parliamentary Sovereignty: Wimbish versus Taillebois," *American Political Science Review*, XXXV (1941), 952–960.

mission could bestow a higher status and more extensive privileges than could denization. The parliamentary act operated retrospectively to the birth of the party, enabled him to inherit as well as to take lands by descent, purchase, or devise, and apparently naturalized his alien-born children. In denization, the law continued to acknowledge the party's alien birth and merely accorded him the future rights of a subject; in naturalization, the law deemed the alien actually to have been born within the protection of the king. Consequently, the children of a naturalized subject also had to have been born subjects.[16]

Many Scottish *antenati* obtained denization and then later sought the larger grant of naturalization, which suggests that this distinction concerning retrospectivity was well understood.[17] Presumably, the main motive for the second grant was to insure that children could inherit the lands that their parents acquired in England. Denization would have enabled the father to purchase and hold lands in England, but these would have descended only to *postnati* children born after his denization.[18] *Antenati* children, however, could not even purchase lands unless included by name in their father's denization. In no case could they inherit, for they were either aliens or merely denizens. Since a subsequent naturalization made the father a subject "from his birth," it followed logically that all his issue were subjects as well, capable of taking by descent from him.[19]

16. Parry, *British Nationality Law*, 55–58, discusses this whole issue, and though he denies that naturalization was inherently retrospective—mistakenly, in my opinion—he admits that the wording of the acts commonly provided for the children.

17. *Ibid.*, 54, 58.

18. All *postnati* were personally capable of inheriting, for, like Robert Calvin, they were native subjects. But *postnati* born before the father's denization could not take his lands, because his alienage barred him from transmitting to them. The defect was in the father, not the child. See above, n. 12.

19. See Bacon v. Bacon, chap. 1, n. 8. Children, like alien wives, could also be considered subordinate to the father and, through him, "*quasi* under the Allegiance." In Collingwood v. Pace, 1 Ventris 413, 419 (1661–1664), Chief Baron Matthew Hale illustrated the distinction here between retrospective and retroactive operation. If a man had two sons, the elder alien and the younger natural-born, the younger would inherit his father's estate. If the older son was naturalized after his father's death, this would not normally divest the younger brother of lands already descended to him, although the "Act of Parliament, may by a strange and unusual retrospect direct it so, if penn'd accordingly." The usual naturalization, Hale noted, "hath only respect to what shall be hereafter." A specific clause would be required to make it retro*active*, giving the older son the right to claim to have had a capacity to inherit at the moment of the father's death and thus to take the estate already vested in the younger son. In another report of the same case (O. Bridg. 410, 458), Justice Bridgman added a further refinement. He considered the case in which an alien had an alien

English law discriminated between denizens and naturalized subjects in other areas as well. Statutes of 1485 and 1540, for example, regularized the monarchs' practice by providing that all denizens should continue to pay aliens' duties unless specifically exempted by the king.[20] At the time of this legislation the differences between the two modes of admission were still blurred; the acts may have been intended to include aliens admitted by Parliament also. Yet once the distinction hardened in law, only denizens and not naturalized subjects had to "pay Aliens Customs, and divers other Things as Aliens."[21]

By the early seventeenth century naturalized subjects apparently enjoyed full political rights along with native Englishmen. Coke in his *Fourth Institutes* noted that aliens and denizens were ineligible to sit in Parliament but that this disability was removed by naturalization. "An alien," he observed,

> cannot be elected of the parliament, because he is not the king's liege subject, and so it is albeit he be made denizen by letters patent, etc. for thereby he is made *quasi, seu tanquam ligeus*: but that will not serve, for he must be made *ligeus revera*, and not *quasi*, etc. And we have had such an one chosen and disallowed by the house of commons, because such a person can hold no place of judicature: but if an alien be naturalized by parliament, then he is eligible to this or any other place of judicature.[22]

---

son, came to England and was endenized, had two more sons in England, then died. The older of the two natural-born sons would inherit, and he would not be divested of the property by an ordinary naturalization of the eldest son—the point made by Hale. However, if the youngest son bought lands and died after the oldest son's naturalization, the latter would now inherit in preference to the brother who had taken the father's estate. The naturalization act of Parliament made one an "heir at one time, and the other at another time." The son who was "naturalized after his father's death, and so had not a civil birth till then, [would] draw and derive a legal and inheritable blood from his father." This "hypothetical" case closely followed the real case of Godfrey v. Dixon, Cro. Jac. 539, also reported Godbolt 275 (1619). In its ordinary form, naturalization meant that in all subsequent actions the party would be considered to have been born a subject (retrospectivity), though it would not invariably allow the party to overturn actions completed when he had been an alien (retroactivity). The point was difficult, and judges did not always follow a consistent policy here. Compare, e.g., the case of the widow's dower mentioned above, n. 15, and the decision in Fish v. Klein, 2 Merivale 431 (1817). The important point is that though parliamentary naturalization was always "retrospective to the birth of the party" and could be retroactive "if penn'd accordingly," royal denization could only grant rights prospectively. The courts remembered the denizen's alien birth and judged his rights with reference to the date of the denization.

20. 1 Hen. VII, c. 2 (1485), and 32 Hen. VIII, c. 16 (1540), discussed in Parry, *British Nationality Law*, 36–38.

21. John Lilly, *The Practical Register; or, a general abridgment of the law* . . . , 2d ed., I ([London], 1735), 606; Tucker, ed., *Blackstone's Commentaries*, I:2, 374.

22. Coke, *Fourth Institutes*, chap. 1, 47. In denization, the party's alien birth still affected

The influx of William's Dutch followers after 1688, however, led to a restriction on the political rights of naturalized aliens, reducing them in this respect to the level of denizens. The Act of Settlement (1701) declared that

no person born out of the dominions of the kingdoms of England, Scotland, and Ireland or of the dominions thereunto belonging (although he be naturalized or made a denizen) except such as are born of English parents shall be capable to be of the Privy Council, or a Member of either House of Parliament, or to enjoy any office or place of trust, either civil or military, or to have any grant of lands, tenements or hereditaments from the Crown to himself or to any others in trust for him.[23]

This policy was reaffirmed in 1714, this time to exclude the German adherents of the Hanoverian George I.[24] The act of 1714 confirmed the rights of persons naturalized before 1700, but it established that for the future no bill of naturalization could be received for consideration unless it contained a special clause repeating the prohibitions of the Act of Settlement.[25]

While the precise scope of the rights conferred by naturalization remained subject to regulation, it was clear that only Parliament was capable in theory of placing an alien "in exactly the same state as if he had been born in the king's ligeance."[26] The ordinary presumption was that the privileges granted were those enjoyed by native subjects, and any regulation or restriction of those privileges had to be specified, as in the area of political rights. And naturalization was permanent. Denization could be granted upon conditions, or the patent voided for noncompliance.[27] But one could not "be naturalized, either with limitations for life, or in taile, or upon condition: for that is against the absolutenesse, puritie, and indebility of naturall allegiance."[28]

---

his rights. He was not a "true" liege subject (*ligeus revera*), but was only treated "as though" he were such while the patent remained in effect (*quasi, seu tanquam ligeus*).

23. 12 & 13 Will. III, c. 2, sec. 3 (1701).

24. Shaw, ed., *Denization and Naturalization, 1603–1700*, x.

25. 1 Geo. I, stat. 2, c. 4 (1714). This restriction could be circumvented by first passing a public act permitting the introduction of a private naturalization bill without the required clause. The procedure was used primarily for naturalizing relatives of the royal family. See, e.g., 7 Geo. II, c. 3 & 4 (1734), passed on the occasion of the marriage of the prince of Orange to the eldest daughter of George I. Jones, *British Nationality*, 77–78.

26. Tucker, ed., *Blackstone's Commentaries*, I:2, 373.

27. Worselin Manning's Case, Lane 58 (1609). The court here admitted that denization was conditional, but held that the patentee's failure to do legal homage as specified was not a sufficient breach of conditions to void his patent.

28. Coke, *First Institutes*, ed. Hargrave and Butler, I, 129a.

Whether a denizen obtained privileges outside of the realm—indeed, whether he was to be a denizen everywhere within England—depended upon the precise terms of his grant;[29] so, too, did the transmittability of the status to his descendants born abroad.[30] But naturalization created a permanent and irrevocable bond that made the alien an Englishman wherever Parliament was supreme.

The diverse principles and precedents concerning the adoption of aliens into the community were not drawn into a comprehensive theory until the mid-seventeenth century, after *Calvin's Case* had formulated the authoritative doctrine of natural allegiance. Although Coke had occasionally alluded in that case to denizens and naturalized subjects and had briefly described acquired allegiance (*ligeantia acquisita*), his discussion of these matters was desultory.[31] It was left to others to explore these issues in depth and to draw the detailed connections between naturalization and Coke's doctrine of natural, personal, and perpetual allegiance.

A series of intricate legal cases between 1656 and 1670 involving the estate of John Ramsey, earl of Holderness, prompted an extended analysis of acquired allegiance.[32] The earl had died childless in 1625, and the courts were called upon to decide which of his relatives should inherit his English landholdings.[33] Holderness and

29. In 1677 the *James* of New York, commanded by Jacob Mauritts, was seized as being in violation of the navigation acts. It was argued in justification of the seizure that Mauritts lost the rights granted in his English denization when he removed to the colonies and was endenized in New York. The case was dismissed due to "extenuating circumstances," and the lord treasurer avoided the central issues. However, the principle seemed to be that denization privileges could be limited in space as well as time, depending on the precise wording of the patent. Shaw, ed., *Denization and Naturalization, 1603–1700*, xxvii.

30. Jones, *British Nationality*, 30.

31. See above, chap. 1, n. 18.

32. Three separate cases were involved—Foster v. Ramsey (1656), Collingwood v. Pace (1661–1664), and Craw v. Ramsey (1669/1670)—and the numerous reports vary in the details presented. For full citations, see the Table of Cases, p. 357.

33. Holderness held lands in Surrey, Lincolnshire, and Norfolk. Craw v. Ramsey, Vaughan 275. As part of his marriage contract, the property in Surrey and Lincolnshire was to go to his widow for her life, then to his children. *Ibid.*, 2 Ventris 2. In a will drawn up several weeks before his death, the earl devised the property in Lincolnshire "unto the heir of my brother Nicholas." Collingwood v. Pace, O. Bridg. 415, and 1 Keble 174; Foster v. Ramsey, 2 Sid. 23. However, the court invalidated this provision of the will on the grounds that it did not clearly specify the earl's intent. Nicholas was still alive when Holderness died, and, strictly speaking, he had no "heir" but only an "heir apparent." Collingwood v. Pace, O. Bridg. 412. The whole court agreed on this point, and it was only because the judges split evenly on the question whether naturalized brothers could inherit each other that the case was adjourned to the Exchequer-Chamber. *Ibid.*, 1 Levinz 59.

his three brothers—Robert, Nicholas, and George Ramsey—were *antenati* Scots, aliens by the principles of *Calvin's Case*. But the earl and his younger brother George had been naturalized by the English parliament, and George's son John (the earl's nephew) had been born in England. Another nephew—Patrick, son of the earl's older brother Nicholas—was also an English subject by birth.

The question of which nephew should inherit was complicated by two additional facts. First, an official inquest of office held in 1631 found that the earl had died without any legal heirs, and in consequence part of his estate escheated to the king.[34] In 1634 the king granted the escheated property to William Murray, the grant to take effect upon the death of the earl's widow (which occurred in 1641). Second, the earl's older brother Nicholas had been included in a general Irish statute of 1634 that naturalized all Scottish *antenati* in Ireland. This raised the question whether an act of the Irish parliament could have a legal effect in England, making naturalized Irishmen into English subjects. The various ramifications of the cases demanded a thorough examination of the essential character of naturalization.

The first issue examined in the *Ramsey* cases involved the legal effect of the English naturalization of the earl and his brother George, for if George's son John were to inherit the estate he had to trace the title through his father. The point was hotly debated, but eventually the judges agreed that the earl's estate could pass to George Ramsey and thence to his son.[35] As one of the counsel observed, "Naturalizations are acts of grace, and so to be taken liberally, being but a restitution to those capacities which [in aliens] are restrained for reasons of state. . . . That they shall, to all purposes, be made *natural liege people*, are operative words to this purpose, and [the earl and George Ramsey] may do any thing that two brothers in England might."[36] Naturalization was a legal act,

---

34. The inquest was dated 1631 in Craw v. Ramsey, Vaughan 275, and Carter 185; but Collingwood v. Pace, O. Bridg. 415, dated it 1634. There is no explanation why only the "rectory of Kingston"—part of the Surrey property—escheated. *Ibid.*; also Craw v. Ramsey, Vaughan 275.

35. See generally Collingwood v. Pace, 1 Ventris 422–427. The disagreement centered on the way descent between two brothers was to be traced, not on the effects of naturalization.

36. John Archer, for the plaintiff, in Collingwood v. Pace, 1 Keble 266, my emphasis. Hale noted that Calvin's Case had been founded upon a "gentle interpretation" of alien disabilities, and he suggested that this policy should be observed here, since the issues in

but it equated a man's status in the eyes of the law with that of a man made a subject by God and nature.

By this process of reasoning, it seemed clear that the earl's nephew John was entitled to the estate, which descended to him through his father, George Ramsey. But before the courts could affirm John's title it was necessary to dismiss the arguments of other claimants. The royal inquest of office had found that Holderness had died without legal heirs, and if John were to inherit the estate he had to traverse (that is, overturn) this finding and the later transfer of title (through escheat and regrant) to William Murray.[37] He also was obligated to contest the claims of the other nephew, Patrick, who argued that the estate should descend to him through his father, Nicholas (Holderness's older brother).

Justice Orlando Bridgman thought that the court should defend the decision of the royal inquest of 1631. Escheats provided the king with an important source of revenue and were a recognized part of his prerogative: "To hold up the prerogative of the King in point of revenue . . . I have always held is the great interest of the people, who are necessitated, for their own safety, to supply what the King's revenue falls short of to answer the public charge. And, therefore, those rights which concern the King and people in general are to be preferred before the interests of particular subjects."[38] On one side here were the rights of "aliens, or those whose ancestors" were "wholly of alien extraction." On the other side stood the royal prerogative and the "*bonum publicum.*" Since "in his allegiance every man ought to favour the King more than the party," and since part of the oath taken by judges stated "that we shall do and procure the profit of the King and of his Crown, in all things where we may rationally do the same," Bridgman felt obligated to side with the party who claimed "under the King's title."[39]

The other judges were not swayed by these considerations. The king had already regranted the property in question, and his interests were no longer directly involved.[40] In any case, the royal

---

question might involve the claims of "very considerable and noble families of Scottish extract . . . that [now] enjoy their inheritance in peace." *Ibid.*, 1 Ventris 428.

37. Murray conveyed the property in question to the earl of Elgin and to Sir Edward Sydenham, who in turn leased to Perses Pace, the defendant in Collingwood v. Pace.

38. Collingwood v. Pace, O. Bridg. 459.

39. *Ibid.*, 461.

40. See [Sir Wadham?] Windham's comment, *ibid.*, 1 Keble 581, and Serjeant John Maynard's argument in Craw v. Ramsey, Carter 189.

prerogative could not abridge the subject's right of inheritance. The earl of Holderness and his younger brother deserved the same rights as natives, for Parliament had naturalized them. Naturalization, even more than the king's right to escheats, was "a great point of State-interest," involving the consent of the whole nation.[41] If the law protected the native Englishman against the force of royal power, then it must also protect the naturalized subject.

These two decisions—that John could inherit and that he could protect his inheritance even against the king—were significant statements of principle: the law envisioned a fundamental equality of status and rights among naturalized and native-born subjects. Perhaps even more important and revealing, however, was the court's decision that John should inherit in preference to his cousin Patrick. In this determination the judges articulated the most complete analysis of the essential character and the constitutional limitations of naturalization.

In order for Patrick to prove that he had the best claim to the estate, he had to show that his father, Nicholas Ramsey, should have taken the property in preference to the earl's younger brother. The problem was that Nicholas had been born an alien (an *antenatus* Scot) and had never been naturalized by England's parliament. If he remained an alien, then Patrick could not claim through him.[42] Patrick thus was required to convince the court that Nicholas had become a subject, capable of serving as the medium of descent.

Patrick's lawyers sought to demonstrate this point by calling into play an Irish statute of 1634. By this act of the Irish parliament all Scottish *antenati* and "all and whatsoever person or persons of the Scottish Bloud and Nation hereafter, whensoever, and wheresoever, to be born, within any [of] your Highness['s] . . . Realms and Dominions" were naturalized and "adjudged natural subjects of Ireland with all priviledges."[43] Since Nicholas Ramsey had not died until 1638, he had been included in this general act; however, the crucial question was whether the act of the Irish parliament had effect in England. Natural-born Irishmen were surely English subjects. Was the same true for naturalized Irishmen, or were the two categories of subjects different in some essential way?

41. John Vaughan's opinion, *ibid.*, 2 Ventris 7.
42. The situation would have been different after 1699, after the statute 11 & 12 Will. III, c. 6 (1699). See above, Prologue, n. 8.
43. 10 Car. I, c. 4 [Ireland] (1634).

Ireland was subordinate to England, and ordinarily a subordinate kingdom could not bind its superior by law. But according to Patrick Ramsey's counsel, King John in Parliament had conferred upon Ireland the right to govern itself under the general supervision of the English parliament. When the king-in-Parliament invested his Irish subjects "with a power Parliamentary, he gave them the power to naturalize; and if he gave the substance, he gave the consequence of it."[44] Naturalization was the "adoption of one to be entitled by birth, to be entitled to what an English man may claim." It created the same personal relationship with the king that Coke had defined: "Allegiance and natural subjection relate to the King in his natural capacity, and follow the person of the King; therefore, *when by the law of England*, the Parliament in Ireland had power to naturalize, it cannot be restrained to that kingdom, for it follows the person of the King, not as he is King of that kingdom, but as he is King. Naturalization is a new birth, and virtually here is the consent of the Parliament of England; and what they [the Irish] do, within their limits, is good here."[45] Since the Irish parliament "had original power from that of England," and since it was "not held without the King," there was in fact one "fountain of naturalization," although there were "two streams."[46]

Of the four judges who heard this argument, Justice Thomas Tyrrel alone agreed with its historical analysis and its conclusion that persons naturalized by the Irish parliament could inherit as subjects in England. This was not because Irish acts of themselves were "obligative to England." Rather it was the "law of England co-operating with the Act, that gives the naturalization an effect here." Although the Irish statute was, in Tyrrel's opinion, the "*causa remota*, or *sine qua non*; the law of England is the *causa proxima*, and this of naturalization was one of the wonders of the powers and privileges of Parliament."[47] The efficacy of an Irish act of natural-

44. Craw v. Ramsey, Carter 186–187.
45. *Ibid.*, 187–188, my emphasis.
46. *Ibid.*, 188.
47. *Ibid.*, 2 Ventris 4. McIlwain, *American Revolution*, 96–99, argues that two of the judges affirmed the efficacy of an Irish naturalization statute in England and sees this as a "concession of considerable importance" for the history of constitutional thought. However, McIlwain misread the report here, placing Vaughan with Tyrrel on the central issue. Vaughan did side with Tyrrel on several minor points, but he explicitly denied Ireland's power to naturalize in England. McIlwain's misreading weakens his overall argument about the "validity" of American constitutional claims concerning the limits of authority in the empire.

ization was derived from England's grant of that power to Ireland and Parliament's implied consent to the admission of aliens into the community of allegiance.

Justices John Wylde and John Archer and Chief Justice John Vaughan disagreed with this analysis. Following Coke's view of Irish history, they admitted that kingdom's dependence as well as its right to its own parliament, but rejected the notion that Ireland's form of government stemmed from an act of the English parliament.[48] From this starting point it was difficult to see any original English consent to Irish naturalizations. The king might personally agree to accept aliens as his Irish subjects, and Irishmen might adopt outsiders through their parliament; but Englishmen were not bound to honor an Irish naturalization without their own consent. As Justice Wylde observed, "If this naturalization should be good, King James might have made the Scots *antenati* inheritable here without any difficulty."[49]

The law clearly held that naturalization equated an alien and a born subject. Yet as Chief Justice Vaughan noted, native Irishmen were natural English subjects, although aliens naturalized in Ireland were not. "The reason is, that naturalization is but a *fiction of law*, and can have effect but upon those consenting to that fiction: therefore it hath the like effect that a man's birth hath, where the law-makers have power, but not in other places where they have not. Naturalizing in Ireland gives the same effect in Ireland as being born there, so in Scotland as being born there, but not in England, which consents not to the fiction of Ireland or Scotland, nor to any but her own." A legal fiction could not in any absolute sense make an alien a natural-born subject, for this would mean that he would have "two natural princes, one where he was born and the other where naturalized."[50] The idea was as absurd as the supposition that a man could have "two natural fathers, or two natural mothers."[51]

The conclusion that naturalization rested upon a legal fiction made it possible to distinguish among the various classes of subjects. Native Englishmen, *postnati* Scotsmen, and natural-born Irishmen were natural subjects. "Natural legitimation respecteth actual obedience to the Sovereign at the time of the birth," and these persons

48. Craw v. Ramsey, T. Jones 11, 2 Ventris 4–5.
49. *Ibid.*
50. *Ibid.*, Vaughan 280.
51. *Ibid.*, 283.

were born into the king's protection.[52] Naturalized Englishmen—
that is, aliens adopted by act of the English parliament—were
legally the same as natural-born Englishmen in that realm and in all
subordinate kingdoms. The reason was quite clear: "The people of
England now do, and always did, consist of native persons, natu-
raliz'd persons, and denizen'd persons; and no people, of what
consistence soever they be, can be aliens to that they have conquer'd
by arms, or otherwise subjected to themselves, (for it is a contradiction to be a stranger to that which is a man's own, and against
common reason and publique practise)."[53]

Where the legal systems were distinct and independent, however,
the effects of naturalization were limited. The constitutional relationship between England and Scotland meant that aliens naturalized in
one kingdom remained aliens in the other, for neither parliament
had authority in the jurisdiction of the other. A stranger adopted as
an Irishman by Irish statutes, like Nicholas Ramsey, was also
excluded as an alien in England, but for the different reason that it
was "a contradiction that the inferior, which is civilly the lesser
power, should compel the superior, which is [the] greater power."[54]
Only where a parliament's authority held good did its legal fictions
control a man's status.

This theory of naturalization as a legal process conferring a
"fictional" status was subordinated to Coke's earlier doctrine of
natural allegiance. Significantly, English judges did not extend their
analysis of the process of admission to new concepts of the character of allegiance in general. While conceding that the naturalized
alien had to be deemed a subject only within the specific dominion
that admitted him and within its dependencies, they still insisted
that within these affected jurisdictions the allegiance of the new
member must be considered as perfect and complete as that of a
native subject. In actuality, his status depended on and derived from
a specific legal act and not from nature; but in law, the fact of his
alien birth was obliterated.

The very terminology of admission—"naturalization"—led to
the conclusion that the alien must be considered reborn as a natural
subject. Thus all the attributes that Coke had ascribed to the alle-

52. *Ibid.*
53. *Ibid.*, 291.
54. *Ibid.*, 300.

giance owed by native Englishmen could be transferred to the acquired allegiance of the adopted member. Although English law overrode the true natural obligation that every adopted alien owed to his former sovereign, it would not accept in principle that an English subject—natural or naturalized—could relinquish the allegiance owed to the English king. Coke had defined allegiance and subjectship as perpetual, and his successors insisted that this principle be maintained, even though the obligations of allegiance originated not in nature, but in legal fiction.

Naturalization merely augmented the inner community of allegiance established by nature. That inner community had existed before legal systems and political boundaries were created; laws and kingdoms fashioned by men could only acknowledge the natural community and expand it by adopting outsiders. But within those kingdoms and legal systems, allegiance and subjectship remained as Coke had defined them—natural, perpetual, personal, and immutable.

CHAPTER 3

Coke, Locke, and the Theory of Perpetual Allegiance

The seventeenth century was for England a time of constitutional crisis and fundamental political change. The clash between crown and Commons developed and intensified in the early years until it exploded into civil war. The Restoration of Charles II brought temporary peace after a troubled decade of parliamentary rule, but the attempts of James II to restore the supremacy of the monarchy revitalized political opposition and ultimately produced the Glorious Revolution. By the end of the century the English Constitution had been fundamentally altered. Parliament emerged as the embodiment of sovereignty, and the power of the monarchy would henceforth be limited and constrained.

This fundamental shift in the structure of political authority was accompanied by a major intellectual revolution, symbolized by the constitutional theories of John Locke. Rejecting old notions of the divine or patriarchal right of kings and the natural, hierarchical principles of political and social order, Locke explained the structure of society and government in terms of a primal social compact in which free individuals voluntarily joined together to form communities. Thus part of their natural independence was relinquished in order to protect their most essential liberties. Individual men then submitted to majority rule and delegated power to government in order that they might better protect and enjoy the liberty that was their inherent, natural, and inalienable right.

The revolution in political concepts was important—but incomplete. Lockean theories of contract and consent had only a superficial impact on the practical applications of the law in matters of subjectship, for here the British courts continued to acknowledge the authority of *Calvin's Case*. Indeed, well into the nineteenth century a citation of Coke's report of the case was virtually mandatory in any argument, opinion, commentary, or treatise that involved questions of allegiance, alienage, naturalization, or subject status. Coke was not cited merely to be explained away or "distinguished" into irrelevance. Rather the maxims of *Calvin's Case* and the authority of Coke shaped the outcome in cases that quite literally involved matters of life and death.

Some adjustments and refinements in Coke's doctrines were made, of course. Subtle and often unperceived shifts in the use of words distorted Coke's original meaning. The emergence of Parliament, the formal union of Scotland and England, and the rapid diffusion of Lockean ideas of contract and consent all challenged old ideas and changed the context within which *Calvin's Case* exerted its influence. Yet as a quick glance at the working law will show, the established doctrines of subjectship survived these constitutional and intellectual changes. By the mid-eighteenth century English thinking in matters of allegiance was inconsistent, self-contradictory, and riddled with ambiguities.

Narrowly construed, *Calvin's Case* involved the status of Scotsmen, and Coke's conclusion that the *postnati* were natural-born subjects survived the seventeenth-century upheavals and challenges unimpaired. To be sure, subject status did not protect Scotsmen from all legal discrimination. Particularly after the Restoration of Charles II, subjects of the northern kingdom were denied commercial equality with "Englishmen"—defined in this context as "his Majesty's Subjects of England, Ireland, and the plantations"—in the burgeoning colonial empire.[1] The comprehensive "Act for preventing Frauds and regulating Abuses in the Plantation Trade" (1696) not only repeated the commercial discriminations of the earlier navigation acts but also excluded Scotsmen from "all Places of Trust in the Courts of Law, or what relates to the Treasury of the

1. Statute of Frauds, 13 & 14 Car. II, c. 11, sec. 6 (1661/1662), discussed in Andrews, *Colonial Period of American History*, IV, 65. Earlier, Scotsmen could generally trade as Englishmen, and at least one Aberdeen merchant was licensed to trade with America. See Theodora Keith, *Commercial Relations of England and Scotland, 1603–1707* (Cambridge, 1910), 18, 45–46.

said Islands [that is, colonies]."² To certain political factions across the Atlantic in East Jersey, this clause seemed to imply that Scotsmen were aliens, and politicians seized upon the law to dismiss their Scottish-born governor, Andrew Hamilton.³ When Hamilton appealed his case to England, however, Attorney General Thomas Trevor reaffirmed Coke's conclusion that Scotsmen were subjects: "A Scotchman borne is by Law capable of being appointed Governor to any of the Plantations, he being a natural born-Subject of England in Judgment and Construction of Law, as much as if he had been born in England."⁴

The primary issue in the matter of commercial privileges was not the subject status of Scotsmen, but rather their relationship to the English parliament. In contrast to Englishmen and Irishmen, merchants operating from Scotland were outside the English legislature's jurisdiction. In view of Scotland's traditional commercial connections with the Dutch and the French—whose trade with the colonies the navigation acts aimed to destroy—it was unrealistic to suppose that the Scottish parliament or merchants within that kingdom would voluntarily follow trading patterns designed in London.⁵ Practical considerations and constitutional realities thus dictated that jurisdictional boundaries between the two kingdoms —and not subject status—would determine the distribution of commercial privileges.

Until the early eighteenth century questions involving the rights and obligations of Scotsmen were complicated, and judges were forced to consider carefully the complex interplay of the Scotsman's unconfined allegiance and of his constitutional autonomy vis-à-vis Parliament. In 1704 the English Court of King's Bench was faced with the question whether John Lindsay, a *postnatus* Scot, could be convicted of treason for violating a penal statute passed in 1697

2. 7 & 8 Will. III, c. 22, secs. 2, 10, 12 (1696). For the earlier navigation acts, see Barrow, *Trade and Empire*, 5–19.
3. Proprietors in England to Gov. Hamilton and council, Oct. 12, 1697, William A. Whitehead *et al.*, eds., *Documents Relating to the Colonial History of the State of New Jersey* (*Archives of the State of New Jersey*, 1st Ser., I–XXXIII [Newark, Paterson, Trenton, N.J., etc., 1880–1928]), II, 176, hereafter cited as *N.J. Archives*, 1st Ser.
4. *Ibid.*, 250–251. I have revised several archaic spellings and contractions here. For the controversy in East Jersey, see generally Ian Charles Cargill Graham, *Colonists from Scotland: Emigration to North America, 1707–1783* (Ithaca, N.Y., 1956), 142–143, and George S. Pryde, "The Scots in East New Jersey," New Jersey Historical Society, *Proceedings*, N.S., XV (1930), 24–30.
5. Keith, *Commercial Relations*, 87–94.

when he resided in England. Two facts complicated the case: the act had since expired, and Lindsay had received a pardon from Queen Anne under her Scottish seal.[6] Counsel tried to argue that Lindsay "was the late king's subject, as king of Scotland, but not as king of England," thus reviving an argument rejected by Coke in 1608. They agreed that when Scotsmen resided in England they were technically obliged to obey the laws defining the duties of English subjects; "but as soon as they are gone out of that kingdom, their [English] allegiance, which was but local, ceases, and they are no longer obligated by the laws of England."[7]

The prosecution responded by warning Lindsay's counsel that they "would do little service to the subjects of Scotland, if they should endeavour to overthrow Calvin's case, which was so solemnly determined near an hundred years ago." Noting that "we are not now putting in execution this act in Scotland, but putting it in execution here in England on a Scotchman that had long been an inhabitant here before," the prosecuting counsel insisted that Lindsay still owed whatever obligations English law required of subjects.[8] Queen Anne's pardon, issued under her Scottish seal, removed any possibility of procedures against him in the northern kingdom; but a Scottish pardon, like a Scottish naturalization, could not reach into England.[9] Lindsay was a natural-born subject, and if he violated his allegiance to the sovereign, he deserved condign punishment. His Scottish birth and Scottish pardon did not prevent the English court from sentencing him to death.[10]

The *Lindsay* case was filled with difficult technical questions, and even the basic facts of Lindsay's behavior were disputed; what was significant about the case was the court's preservation of Coke's doctrines about the obligations of natural allegiance and simultaneous recognition of the constitutional independence of Scotland and England. Such cases required hard thought and subtle distinctions between the community of allegiance and the various lines of

6. Regina v. Lindsay, 14 Howell *State Trials* 987 (1704). The act of 1697 forbade subjects to go to France or return from there to England without license on pain of punishment for treason. Lindsay went to France without license, but returned to Scotland, where he was allowed the benefit of a general pardon proclaimed by Queen Anne under the Scottish seal. When Lindsay left Scotland and returned to England, he was imprisoned and charged with treason. *Ibid.*, 992, 1000.
7. *Ibid.*, 1008, 1013.
8. *Ibid.*, 1017, 1018.
9. *Ibid.*, 1026.
10. Lindsay was later reprieved by the queen. *Ibid.*, 1029, 1035.

political and legal authority in the several dominions under the king.

The Act of Union of 1707 ended the possibility of Scotsmen claiming exemptions from Parliament's acts as well as England's rationale for treating Scotsmen as aliens for commercial purposes. The merger of the two kingdoms under one parliament centralized and unified the lawmaking authority and extended a single jurisdiction over English, Irish, and Scottish subjects. Once the separate dominions came together to form Great Britain, all Scotsmen were "to be looked upon for the future as Englishmen to all intents and purposes whatsoever."[11] In short, the Union brought the community of allegiance into closer alignment with the structure of political and constitutional authority, and the careful, complicated distinctions required in the seventeenth-century context would seem increasingly unnecessary. Not until the 1760s would similar issues arise in the course of disputes between Britain and America. By then the lines between the obligations of subjectship and the jurisdiction of Parliament would be even more difficult to draw.

The practical effect of the Union was to subordinate those aspects of *Calvin's Case* that required a sensitivity to boundaries between different political jurisdictions, but Coke's conclusions that allegiance and subjectship were natural, perpetual, and immutable still occupied a central position in legal thinking. Although the political condition of Scotsmen was now free of major ambiguities and their status as subjects was unassailable, the broader discussions and implications of *Calvin's Case* remained both useful and authoritative for other purposes. Nowhere was the continuity of Coke's influence more evident than in the analysis of the law of treason.

The essence of the crime of treason was "a renunciation of that allegiance . . . which is due from every man, who lives under the

11. Board of Trade to governors of Rhode Island, Connecticut, and Pennsylvania, John Russell Bartlett, ed., *Records of the Colony of Rhode Island and Providence Plantations, in New England* (Providence, R.I., 1856–1865), IV, 23, hereafter cited as *R.I. Col. Recs.* The attorney and solicitor generals, Thomas Trevor and Sir John Hawles, advised that Scots were subjects within the meaning of the navigation acts in an opinion submitted in June 1701; but the Scots' right to trade was still sometimes challenged before the Union. See George Chalmers, *Opinions of Eminent Lawyers, on Various Points of English Jurisprudence . . .* , II (London, 1814), 361–363, and W. Noel Sainsbury *et al.*, eds., *Calendar of State Papers, Colonial Series, America and West Indies . . .* (London, 1860–1953), XIX, 279, hereafter cited as *Cal. State Papers, Col.*

King's protection."[12] An act of 1350 had given the basic statutory definition of the crime, dividing the actions that constituted the offense into seven main categories; subsequent acts extended the range of treasonable behavior by interpreting those categories.[13] Coke used England's treason law as part of his proof that allegiance was owed to the natural person who was king. His argument that only a natural person (not a political construct) could be killed or harmed led to the conclusion that the definition of such actions as treason was meaningful only if the law assumed a necessary connection between the monarch's natural and political capacities.[14]

By analyzing the various categories of allegiance and by discussing the different kinds of treason that persons could commit against the king, Coke made *Calvin's Case* a guiding judicial authority in treason cases. He showed that even aliens temporarily resident in England owed a local allegiance and had a limited capacity to commit treason, though the technicalities of pleading had to reflect the exact nature of the allegiance owed.[15] Temporary allegiance, he argued, "ceaseth whenever he [the resident alien] withdraweth with his Family and Effects," but an absolute obedience was required of a subject born into the allegiance of the king of England, in all places and at all times.[16]

12. Kelyng, "A Treatise upon Treason," 1, in *Kelyng's Report of Crown Cases*, ed. Loveland. Kelyng cites Coke as authority throughout his work.

13. 25 Edw. III, stat. 5, c. 2 (1350). Bradley Chapin, "Colonial and Revolutionary Origins of the American Law of Treason," *William and Mary Quarterly*, 3d Ser., XVII (1960), 3; and see generally Willard Hurst, "English Sources of the American Law of Treason," *Wisconsin Law Review*, MCMXLV (1945), 315–356. The most important categories of action involving treason were compassing or imagining the death of the king, adhering to the king's enemies or giving them aid and comfort, and levying war against the king. An example of statutory expansion of the crime is 3 Jac. I, c. 4, secs. 22–23 (1605), which specified that persuading subjects to withdraw their allegiance or to promise obedience to the "pretended" authority of the See of Rome constituted adherence to the king's enemies. Piggott, *Nationality*, I, 159.

14. Calvin's Case, 10a–10b.

15. A resident alien could only be indicted for treason "*contra ligeant[iae] suae debitum*" (against the allegiance that he owed); if the indictment read "*naturalis ligeantiae suae debitum*" (against his natural allegiance), then it was invalid. Aliens were best defined as persons born "*extra ligeantiam domini regis, &c. et infra ligeantiam alterius regis*" (out of the allegiance of the lord king, and under the allegiance of another king), and the indictment had to reflect this. See Calvin's Case, 6a, 16b, and Coke, *Third Institutes*, chap. 1, 4–5. In Cranburn's Case, 2 Salkeld 633 (1696), the court held that either plea was good against a native subject. King v. Tucker, Skinner 338, 442 (1694), noted that some form of the clause "against his allegiance" was necessary, for the breach of allegiance, rather than the overt act, constituted the crime.

16. Sir Michael Foster, *A Report of some proceedings on the Commission of Oyer and Terminer and Goal Delivery for the trial of the Rebels in the year 1746 in the County of Surry, and of other*

The most significant contribution of *Calvin's Case* to seventeenth-
and eighteenth-century treason law was its conclusion that English
subjects could never give up their allegiance or lose their capacity to
commit treason. Earlier precedents were ambiguous on this issue,
but by linking subjectship with immutable principles of natural
order, Coke firmly established the rule, "Once a subject always a
subject."[17] He insisted that allegiance could not be ended either by
foreign conquest or by expatriation. His maxim that no man could
abjure his native country or his allegiance ("*Nemo patriam, in qua
natus est, exuere, nec ligeantiae debitum ejurare possit*") was strictly
applied throughout the period, even though it could lead to individual hardship or logical inconsistency.[18]

Manasses Gillingham had settled on St. Thomas and had been
naturalized by the king of Denmark, but when the question of his
status arose in 1704, he was held to his native allegiance. His
participation in trade with the Spanish, who at the time were at
peace with Denmark but at war with England, theoretically might
have been punished as treason, for naturalization by another sovereign "will not discharge him from the natural allegiance he owes to
her Majesty [Queen Anne]."[19]

In 1747 the principle was again invoked when Aeneas Macdonald,

---

Crown Cases. To which are added Discourses upon a few branches of the Crown Law (Oxford,
1762), "Discourse I: On High Treason," 183, hereafter cited as Foster, *Crown Cases*. Foster
referred his readers to Coke, noting that Coke's maxim, "*Nemo potest exuere Patriam*,
comprehendeth the whole Doctrine of Natural Allegiance, and expresseth My Sense of it."
Ibid., 184.

17. Story's Case, 3 Dyer 300b (1570), implied that subjects could never expatriate
themselves. On the other hand, the king's claim to the escheat of Norman lands in 1324
(above, Prologue, at n. 5) could sustain the inference that the inhabitants lost in war became
aliens, and a statute of 1522/1523 that imposed aliens' customs on Englishmen sworn to
foreign princes actually declared such persons aliens. For the latter, see 14 & 15 Hen. VIII,
c. 4, discussed in Parry, *British Nationality Law*, 37. George Hansard, *A treatise on the law
relating to aliens, and denization and naturalization* (London, 1844), 10, notes that such persons
could be restored to their subject status on returning to England. "Alienage" here—as in
the act 5 Geo. I, *c.* 27 (1718)—can be seen as a shorthand for a set of disabilities imposed as a
penalty on disloyal subjects, an interpretation that would allow such acts to be reconciled
with the theory of perpetual allegiance.

18. Coke, *First Institutes*, ed. Hargrave and Butler, I, 129a. The maxim was usually
shortened to "*Nemo potest exuere Patriam*." I-Mien Tsiang, *The Question of Expatriation in
America Prior to 1907*, Johns Hopkins University Studies in Historical and Political Science,
LX (Baltimore, 1942), 11.

19. Attorney General Edward Northey to Lords of Trade, Mar. 22, 1703/1704, Chalmers,
Opinions of Eminent Lawyers, II, 363–364. Northey advised against criminal proceedings,
noting that Gillingham had not been commanded to return to the realm at the outbreak of
the war and implying that trading with the enemy was high treason only when the "stores
of war" were involved.

born in Scotland but raised in France from infancy, was convicted of high treason for his part in the rebellion of 1745. His counsel attacked the "slavish principle" of perpetual allegiance, arguing that it "seemed to derogate from the principles of the Revolution." But the court refused to listen to such arguments and admonished the lawyer for trying to use the Glorious Revolution to justify treason. In a reaffirmation of the rules of established law, the court declared, "It is not within the power of any private subject to shake off his allegiance, and to transfer it to a foreign prince. Nor is it in the power of any foreign prince by naturalizing or employing a subject of Great Britain to dissolve the bond of allegiance between the subject and the crown."[20] Macdonald had been born under the king's protection, and he was thus perpetually bound to give the allegiance required of a subject.

Given Coke's original theoretical premises, the doctrine of perpetual allegiance was logical enough; so, too, was the corollary that a man could never relinquish his native English subjectship. To be sure, these principles were somewhat at odds with other established principles and ideas. For example, while denying Englishmen the right to expatriate themselves under any circumstances England continued to naturalize foreigners and to hold them to an absolute and unconditional allegiance to their new king. Similarly, though jurists insisted that English subjects conquered by a foreign sovereign retained their old allegiance as well as acquired new obligations to the conqueror—being now *ad fidem utriusque regis*—they considered aliens conquered by England "newly born" into a pure and indivisible English allegiance.[21] Still, for most of the seventeenth century these contradictions did not really seem to strike at the heart of Coke's theory of perpetual allegiance. They occurred in areas of law that dealt primarily with acquired subjects, and one could argue that the individuals who might be inconvenienced by the king's claim to their absolute obedience either had chosen that obligation by seeking naturalization or had forfeited the right to exercise their native loyalty by being conquered. As the Ramsey litigation illustrated, the ambiguities here could in any case be dismissed by invoking the legal fiction that such persons had been born in England.

20. The Case of Aeneas Macdonald (alias Angus Macdonald), Foster 59, 60 (1747).
21. See Calvin's Case, 6a, 17a–18a; Tucker, ed., *Blackstone's Commentaries*, I:1, 94; and above, chap. 1 at n. 6.

The Glorious Revolution and the political doctrines associated with it constituted a far more serious challenge to Coke's ideas, rendering them less congruent with England's constitutional arrangements and increasingly Lockean proclivities. Although the court in 1747 refused to listen to the claim of Aeneas Macdonald's counsel that the concept of perpetual allegiance derogated from the principles of 1688, that claim was indeed perceptive. Doctrines of consent and parliamentary sovereignty subtly eroded the original premises of the dicta still reflexively applied by the courts. Some modifications of _Calvin's Case_ theories gradually appeared, and Coke's conclusions and new Lockean assumptions were at least superficially integrated, but the configuration of ideas about allegiance, community, and authority present in English law increasingly lost coherence and logical integrity.

Coke had begun his analysis of subjectship with a state of nature in which kings commanded allegiance by virtue of their natural superiority and power. This allegiance provided the obligations necessary for the creation of a state of man-made laws and political institutions. Once such a state emerged, the king to whom allegiance was owed protected his subjects through the means provided by law; he then consisted of an inseparable combination of a natural person and a political construct. Still, even in the real state of England, the principles of natural hierarchy and subordination remained the source of the reciprocal obligations of the sovereign and the subject.

John Locke rejected Coke's ideas about the structure of authority in the state of nature, but by building upon the idea of the king's political capacity, he could at least partly integrate Coke's doctrines and his own. Locke agreed that allegiance was owed to the person who wore the crown and who thus embodied and controlled the legal means of protection. He did not adopt the heresy, damned as treason in _Calvin's Case_, that allegiance could be owed to "disembodied law" alone.[22] In contrast to Coke, however, Locke insisted

22. Calvin's Case, 11a–11b. For the revival in the 17th century of the notion that one could oppose the "king" (person) in the name of the "King" (the crown) without committing treason, see Kantorowicz, _The King's Two Bodies_, 20–23. See also Nathaniel Bacon, _An Historical and Political Discourse of the Laws and Government of England, from the First Times to the End of the Reign of Queen Elizabeth. With a Vindication of the Antient Way of Parliaments in England_, 5th ed. (London, 1760 [orig. publ. 1651]), pt. II, 45–53. Bacon denied that the natural person was necessarily involved in the concept of the crown. Locke disagreed.

that the political capacity was necessary for there to be any allegiance at all. Allegiance was a binding tie only in political society and could not exist in a lawless state of nature. While the king in real society remained the object of the subject's allegiance, the laws giving the king his political capacity—not nature—created the obligation to obey.

Oaths of allegiance were sworn to the king, and Coke and Locke both recognized the monarch as the necessary focal point of political obligation. Yet although Locke admitted that allegiance went to the king,

'tis not to him as Supream Legislator, but as *Supream Executor* of the Law, made by a joint power of him with others; *Allegiance* being nothing but an *Obedience according to Law*, which when he violates, he has no right to Obedience, nor can claim it otherwise than as the publick Person vested with the Power of the Law, and so is to be consider'd as the Image, Phantom, or Representative of the Commonwealth, acted by the Will of the Society, declared in its Laws; and thus he has no Will, no Power, but that of Law.[23]

Locke contended that the removal of a king who "quits this Representation, this publick Will, and acts by his own private Will" did not necessarily destroy the binding force of the law that created the obligation of allegiance and defined its object.[24] He cautioned that one had to "distinguish between the *Dissolution of the Society, and the Dissolution of the Government.*"[25] When society dissolved, men returned to the state of nature, and all political obligation ceased. The dissolution of government, however, did not require the total disintegration of the community and, indeed, could transpire within an essentially unchanged structure of obligation. The dethronement of an individual king did not necessarily mean even a change in the forms of government: in England "whatever provocations have made the Crown be taken from some of our Princes Heads, they never carried the People so far, as to place it in another Line."[26]

Lockean concepts about the origins of government and political obligation clashed with the traditional idea of perpetual allegiance at the fundamental theoretical level. The latter ultimately depended

23. John Locke, *Two Treatises of Government*, ed. Peter Laslett, II (Cambridge, 1960), sec. 151.
24. *Ibid.*
25. *Ibid.*, sec. 211.
26. *Ibid.*, sec. 223.

upon a state of nature in which some men were bound to obey and others were bound to protect; the former posited instead a primal state in which all men were essentially equal or, if not equal, at least autonomous. Where Coke found allegiance rooted in the immutable principles of natural order, in the Lockean scheme allegiance to the king followed, rather than preceded, the agreement to form a civil state and to establish written laws. Yet once men did agree to form a society and a government of a specific kind, Locke and his successors could agree with Coke that allegiance was binding. As long as the society and government functioned correctly, individual members could not of their own accord break the contract or renounce their allegiance. Resistance to good kings was still treason. Within an established society, allegiance and subjectship remained perpetual, despite alterations or even revolutions in the forms of government.[27]

No one undertook the task of completely reassessing the legal position of subjects in the light of the new theories of consent. Had this been done, Locke's argument that political obligation originated in the consent of autonomous individuals to form a society might have been extended to its logical conclusion that individuals should be permitted to end their obligations through expatriation or foreign naturalization. This step was not taken. Instead, Locke's arguments remained more significant as theory than as a source of major change in the practical workings of the law of subjectship. While it became possible to conceive of a dissolution of society that would end all political obligation, in practice as long as society— if not a specific government—remained intact, Coke's dicta requiring perpetual allegiance of individuals could continue to be applied.

Lockean doctrines of consent did modify the framework of premises within which Coke's dicta were enforced, and by the mid-eighteenth century English ideas about subjectship incorporated some new Lockean assumptions. Sir William Blackstone's definition of natural allegiance illustrates both the continuity and the changes in the law:

Natural allegiance is such as is due from all men born within the king's dominions immediately upon their birth. For, immediately upon their birth, they are under the king's protection; at a time, too, when (during

27. This point is discussed in further detail below, chap. 6.

their infancy) they are incapable of protecting themselves. Natural allegiance is therefore a debt of gratitude; which cannot be forfeited, cancelled or altered by any change of time, place, or circumstance, nor by any thing but the united concurrence of the legislature. . . . For it is a principle of universal law, that the natural-born subject of one prince cannot by any act of his own, no, not by swearing allegiance to another, put off or discharge his natural allegiance to the former; for this natural allegiance was intrinsic, and primitive, and antecedent to the other; and cannot be devested without the concurrent act of the prince to whom it was first due.[28]

For the most part, this definition reflected the traditional rules controlling the obligations of the natural-born subject. Yet there is one significant alteration that reveals the shift in underlying premises. Without reference to precedent and without explanation, Blackstone added to the standard formulations the proviso that the bond of allegiance could be sundered by "the united concurrence of the legislature." Such an admission would have been impossible for Coke, who found the source of obligation in the immutable laws of nature. Allegiance to him was antecedent to man-made laws and not dependent on consent or contract.

To Blackstone and his contemporaries, however, government and political obligation were ultimately grounded in consent. Even while they repeated Coke, reiterating that allegiance was intrinsic and primitive—that it was a moral obligation of gratitude—they found it inconceivable that an act of Parliament could not alter the tie between the subject and his sovereign. Perhaps intellectual conservatism, respect for established legal authority, and a disinclination to work out the implications of consent led eighteenth-century Englishmen to accept this logical inconsistency as the price of preserving both the established law and the principles of 1688. In the absence of parliamentary acts to the contrary, they found it easy to affirm the old rule, "Once a subject always a subject."[29]

The concession that Parliament, embodying the consent of the nation, might theoretically release a subject from his allegiance is one example of how Lockean ideas required modifications of the

28. Tucker, ed., *Blackstone's Commentaries*, I:2, 369–370.
29. As late as 1869, it was argued that no such acts had been passed. See Cockburn, *Nationality*, 63–64. After the American Revolution, some Englishmen contended that Parliament's ratification of the peace constituted "national consent" to the expatriation of the former colonists. The question remained unsettled at law until at least 1824. I have discussed this in some detail in "Subjects or Citizens? A Note on British Views Respecting the Legal Effects of American Independence," *Virginia Law Review*, LXII (1976), 945–967.

principles of *Calvin's Case*, at least in terms of abstract specula-
tions. More important is the way in which Locke's theories—
combined after 1688 with real constitutional innovations—forced
changes in Coke's conception of the relationship between the community of allegiance and the political state. Coke, of course, had
stressed natural allegiance as the tie that bound together the subjects of the various dominions of the crown. He had envisioned a
multi-kingdom empire centered on and united by the king, who was
the focus of all allegiance and was the "hieroglyphic" of the separate legal systems that constituted the subjects' protection. Within
this empire the authority of the English parliament was extensive
but not absolute. Kingdoms gained by conquest were under Parliament's supervisory power, but those descending to the crown by the
operation of non-English laws were not. Consequently, Coke could
maintain that English subjectship did not necessarily imply the individual's subordination to Parliament everywhere in the dominions.

To eighteenth-century English thinkers, this idea was anomalous.
The Act of Union of 1707 abolished Scottish independence and the
one clear-cut example of Coke's logic. Developing assumptions of
parliamentary sovereignty, buttressed by Locke's vision of Parliament as a mirror of the people, made it increasingly difficult to
conceive of dominions and subjects under the king but not under
the authority of Parliament. *Calvin's Case* was still useful for explaining the dependence of some of the dominions, of course. For
others—particularly the American plantations—the task of legitimization was more complicated.

Coke's doctrine of conquest remained the simplest and surest explanation for dependence. His analysis of the grounds of Ireland's
subordination to England could easily be extended to other posses-
sions won from foreign powers. The inhabitants of Jamaica, for
example, continued under their old laws as modified by the king;
but Parliament could bind them if it chose to do so: "The laws by
which the people were governed before the conquest of the island,
do bind them till new laws are given, and Acts of Parliament made
here since the conquest do not bind them unless particularly named.
The reason is, because though a conqueror may make new laws, yet
there is a necessity that the former should be in force till new are
obtained, and even then some of the old customs may remain."[30]

30. Blankard v. Galdy, 4 Modern 222, 225 (1693); also reported in 2 Salkeld 411.

Grenada also could be controlled by Parliament, provided that "express words, shewing the intention of the Legislature" to do so were included in the statute.[31] Lord Mansfield cited Coke as late as 1774 to prove that any "country conquered by British arms becomes a dominion of the King in the right of his Crown; and, therefore, necessarily subject to the Legislature, the Parliament of Great Britain." While the king, as conqueror, could alter the laws of the vanquished country, he could not exempt the dominion from the authority of Parliament, for his local legislative prerogatives as conqueror remained subject to his authority in Parliament.[32]

To men influenced by the Lockean idea that political authority ought to rest on consent, it was more satisfying to disguise the reliance on power implied by the *jus conquesta*. Blackstone attempted to do this in his modification of Coke's version of Irish history:

The original and true ground of this superiority, in the present case, is what we usually call, though somewhat improperly, the right of conquest: a right allowed by the law of nations, if not by that of nature; but which in reason and civil policy can mean nothing more, than that, in order to put an end to hostilities, a compact is either expressly or tacitly made between the conqueror and the conquered, that if they will acknowledge the victor for their master, he will treat them for the future as subjects and not as enemies.[33]

The myth or mask of implied consent could not hide the fact of conquest and the continuing superiority of force. When the Irish disputed their dependence and subordination, the British parliament, not the Irish people, decided the issue.[34]

Not all dominions had been gained by conquest, however, and Coke had declared that kingdoms descending to the crown by the operation of foreign laws were not within Parliament's jurisdiction. Scotland had proved the case. It was feasible to argue that the status of "vacant" territories acquired by settlement or colonization more

31. Rex v. Vaughan, 4 Burrow 2494, 2500 (1769). Coke's argument that conquest extended Parliament's authority but did not automatically introduce English laws was followed in Collett v. Keith, 2 East 260 (1802), a case relating to the conquest of the Cape of Good Hope, and in Attorney General v. Stewart, 2 Merivale 143 (1816–1817), another case from Grenada.

32. Campbell v. Hall, 1 Cowper 204, 208, 209 (1774). Mansfield differed from Coke with respect to the automatic voiding of existing laws in the conquest of pagan countries, which he thought was "absurd." *Ibid.*, 209.

33. Tucker, ed., *Blackstone's Commentaries*, I:1, 103.

34. See Blackstone's comments on the Irish Declaratory Act, 6 Geo. I, c. 5 (1719), *ibid.* See also Schuyler, *Parliament and the British Empire*, 89–91.

nearly resembled the Scottish model of descent than the Irish model of conquest in this respect. The possibility, at least, was implied by the reaction of some members to a parliamentary bill of 1621 that would have regulated fishing in Virginia. John Guy questioned whether "this House have jurisdiction to meddle with this bill," and Sir George Calvert declared the bill "not proper for this House, because [it] concerneth America."[35]

The argument that America was outside Parliament's jurisdiction was not inconceivable within the framework of early seventeenth-century thought. The infant colonies were largely settled by private companies chartered by the king, and it could be argued that Englishmen transporting themselves to America left Parliament's immediate jurisdiction. They were still subjects, of course. But it could easily appear that they were like Englishmen who settled in Scotland (or, indeed, in France): they could demand the rights of subjectship when in England and could claim the king's protection. But as long as they resided abroad, they were under the day-to-day authority of a government that could not be controlled by the English parliament.

35. Leo Francis Stock, ed., *Proceedings and Debates of the British Parliaments respecting North America*, Carnegie Institution of Washington, Publication No. 338 (Washington, D.C., 1924–1941), I, 36, 39. More detail on this issue can be found in Wallace Notestein *et al.*, eds., *Commons Debates, 1621*, I–V (New Haven, Conn., 1935). A number of arguments were used in favor of Parliament's right to intervene. Sir Edwin Sandys contended that "Virginia is holden of East Greenwich and so may be bound by the parliament." *Ibid.*, II, 320, V, 99. Christopher Brooke argued that the House "hath power to binde mens persons and transitories in another kingdom," and though he agreed that Virginia was to be ruled by the king's prerogative, he insisted that "his greatest prerogative is in parliament." *Ibid.*, V, 99, II, 320, III, 82. Serjeant Francis Ashley agreed that acts of Parliament were also acts of the king, while Sir Edward Giles upheld Parliament's jurisdiction on the grounds that the bill involved "mariners" and "moneys." *Ibid.*, III, 82, II, 386, III, 298. Opponents of the bill rejected these claims. John Guy would have left all regulations to the king, acting by letters patent. *Ibid.*, II, 386. Sir George Calvert, secretary of state, rejected the bill on the grounds that the king had the sole right to "governe the countries he discovers and conquers"; he added that the House could not act because Virginia was not represented. *Ibid.*, V, 98, II, 386, III, 298. Although Calvert termed Virginia a "conquest," he clearly did not use the description in Coke's sense, that is, as a dominion under Parliament's supervisory authority. In fact, James I and Charles I succeeded in maintaining their exclusive right of control over the colonies until the civil war. Stock, ed., *Proceedings and Debates*, I, xi. Note that Sandys's attempt to introduce Parliament's authority via the charter clause stating the mode of tenure in fact invested the "manor of East Greenwich" formula with a significance not intended by the drafters. By the 17th century this formula was commonly used in royal grants within the realm, and its insertion in colonial grants originally had no significance respecting the question of parliamentary jurisdiction. See Edward P. Cheyney, "The Manor of East Greenwich in the County of Kent," *AHR*, XI (1905–1906), 29–35; Andrews, *Colonial Period of American History*, I, 86.

Such doubts about Parliament's jurisdiction did not arise for eighteenth-century English theorists. Men like Blackstone apparently began with the assumption of Parliament's authority, then sought its justification. Blackstone himself simply declared that the American colonies had been obtained "either by right of conquest and driving out the natives (with what natural justice I shall not at present enquire) or by treaties."[36] Of course, this clearly brought Parliament into the picture. Others argued that "if there be a new and uninhabited country found out by *English* subjects, as the law is the birthright of every subject, so, wherever they go, they carry their laws with them, and therefore such new found country is to be governed by the laws of *England*; though, after such country is inhabited by the *English*, acts of parliament made in *England*, without naming the foreign plantations, will not bind them."[37] Here one was not obliged to see the colonists themselves as a conquered population. Rather the authority of Parliament was explained as part of the subject's birthright, carried over with the laws of England.

Whatever specific explanation was given, it was clear that eighteenth-century Englishmen automatically assumed that subjectship implied subordination to Parliament. Lockean doctrine made a considerable contribution to this assumption, for the concept of the social contract did seem to suggest that membership in the community meant subordination to the will of the majority and to the government established by that majority.[38] The implication was logical when one's attention focused on England, where the king-in-Parliament seemed to represent or embody the interests of all Englishmen. The link between membership, representation, and subordination to Parliament continued to hold when Scottish representatives were added to form the imperial Parliament of Great Britain. How far Locke's theories could justify Parliament's jurisdiction over Englishmen who emigrated to the colonies, however, was a question not directly posed until later. Until that question was raised, Englishmen would look to Locke to explain the connection between membership in the community of allegiance and subordi-

36. Tucker, ed., *Blackstone's Commentaries*, I:1, 109, and see below, chap. 6.
37. [Anonymous] 2 Peere Williams 75 (1722). The passage implies that acts naming the plantations will bind them. The case here is one of a number of authorities from which the doctrine of "discovery" emerged. This is discussed in some detail below, chap. 6.
38. For a more detailed discussion of this, see below, chap. 6.

nation to Parliament, and they would look to Coke to define the duration and extent of the rights and duties of the subject.

The emergence of political theories that placed the origins of allegiance in consent did not destroy the effectiveness of Coke's doctrines. As long as the social contract continued in force, individuals could be held to a perpetual allegiance. Their membership in society might even be seen as a sufficient reason for their unalterable subordination to Parliament. Although Englishmen might move away from the notion that their obligations as subjects stemmed from natural principles of hierarchical order and toward the concept that those obligations in theory originated in consent, the practical conclusion remained the same: no subject could of his own independent volition give up his membership in the community of allegiance.

The seeds of a different kind of community were present in English law, but they failed to flower in England itself. The practice of naturalization might have suggested that allegiance in general was the result of the individual subject's choice, and the logic of that process might have been extended to imply the possibility of expatriation. But naturalization in England was subordinated to the concept of perpetual natural allegiance; the adopted alien was by legal fiction deemed to owe a pure and permanent birthright obligation of loyalty. Lockean doctrine, too, might have suggested that all subjects ought to be able to choose to leave society as well as to join it, thus placing membership on an effective volitional basis. However, Lockean doctrines about the origins of government were not extended to new perspectives on the operation of subjectship. Coke's old doctrines, though somewhat modified, could still be applied. As long as society remained intact, the courts could insist that Englishmen owed their king an allegiance that was personal, perpetual, and immutable.

Across the Atlantic the consensual and contractual elements implicit in naturalization and in the new political theories of the later seventeenth century would slowly emerge to dominate ideas of subjectship and allegiance. Faced with the need to stimulate population growth, Americans would welcome newcomers from diverse lands. Naturalization would become a crucial yet familiar process, shaping colonial assumptions about the origins and meaning of membership. Beginning with a common legal heritage, but confronting new problems and conditions, Americans would center their attention on the legal basis and contractual aspects of allegiance and undercut the personal, natural elements that had made English allegiance perpetual. Approaching questions of allegiance from the starting point of naturalization, Americans ultimately would evolve a new concept of citizenship.

PART II

The Colonial Experience

CHAPTER 4

Naturalization and the Colonies

Englishmen who left their native country to settle on the far shores of the Atlantic remained subjects of the king. Their children, too, could claim subjectship and the liberties of Englishmen as their birthright. A bill was introduced in the House of Lords in 1648 "for making the planters that are born in New England free denizens of England," but no action was taken, for indeed such explicit legislation was unnecessary.[1] The same common law principles that made subjects of the Scottish *postnati* applied equally well to persons born in America. Moreover, the colonial charters commonly guaranteed that "all and every the Persons being our Subjects, which shall dwell and inhabit within every or any the said several Colonies and Plantations, and every of their children, which shall happen to be born within any of the Limits and Precincts of the said several Colonies and Plantations, shall HAVE and enjoy all Liberties, Franchises, and Immunities, within any of our other Dominions, to all Intents and Purposes, as if they had been abiding and born, within this our Realm of *England*, or any other of our said Dominions."[2] English emigrants lost neither their allegiance nor their status when they left the mother country, and all children born under the king's protection were natural-born subjects in all the dominions.

Not all American immigrants were Englishmen, however, and it

1. Stock, ed., *Proceedings and Debates*, I, 204; Parry, *British Nationality Law*, 49; Shaw, ed., *Denization and Naturalization, 1603–1700*, xxvii.
2. Virginia Charter of 1606, Francis Newton Thorpe, ed. and comp., *The Federal and State Constitutions, Colonial Charters, and Other Organic Laws* ... (Washington, D.C., 1909), VII, 3788. Smith, *Appeals to the Privy Council*, 313, notes that only the Pennsyl-

was primarily the case of non-English settlers that raised questions of allegiance and subjectship. The colonial charters customarily permitted the grantees to transport to America "strangers not prohibited or under restraint that will become Our Loving subjects and live under Our Allegiance," and local colonial authorities quickly assumed that such clauses gave them the right to make such "strangers" subjects, at least within their own jurisdiction; but the initial expectation of the London government may well have been that aliens who wished to be subjects would first obtain naturalization or denization in England.[3]

Throughout the colonial period many aliens did seek admission to subjectship in England prior to emigrating to America. As early as 1621 a group of Walloons and French Protestants initially associated with the Leyden Pilgrims negotiated with the Virginia Company of London for settlement in the company's territory, and though most of the group finally obtained better terms from the Dutch and went to New Netherlands, some may have received an English naturalization or denization before sailing to Virginia.[4] In 1625 Giles de Bomont requested and received denization for "England and America, upon his humble petition to furnish himself and some number of persons into Virginia at his own charge."[5] Others sought an English grant after locating in the colonies, as did John Michael "of the county of Northampton in New England [Virginia]," whose name was included in a parliamentary act of naturalization of 1663.[6]

Parliamentary naturalization gave the prospective non-English settler a higher status and more extensive rights than royal denization. However, naturalization through most of the seventeenth and

vania charter of 1681 lacked such a clause, and even that document included a provision "saving the allegiance" of the settlers to the king.

3. See, e.g., the grant of New Netherlands to the duke of York, Mar. 12, 1663/1664, E. B. O'Callaghan and Berthold Fernow, eds., *Documents Relative to the Colonial History of the State of New York* (Albany, N.Y., 1856–1887), II, 297, hereafter cited as *N.Y. Col. Docs.*

4. Charles W. Baird, *History of the Huguenot Emigration to America* (New York, 1885), I, 162; Susan M. Kingsbury, ed., *Records of the Virginia Company of London*, III (Washington, D.C., 1933), 491.

5. Entry dated Jan. 5, 1624/1625, Shaw, ed., *Denization and Naturalization, 1603–1700*, 37.

6. Stock, ed., *Proceedings and Debates*, I, 314. Shaw, ed., *Denization and Naturalization, 1603–1700*, 90, lists Michael as being born in Holland. Apparently, he preferred parliamentary naturalization to naturalization in Virginia, for the latter was already practiced by 1663.

eighteenth centuries was an expensive and cumbersome process, and certain groups were statutorily barred from seeking its benefits.[7] An act of 1609 declared naturalization and the "restoration to Blood" of attainted persons to be "Matters of mere Grace and Favour, which are not fit to be bestowed upon any others than such as are of the Religion now established in this Realm." The statute proceeded to declare that no person "shall be naturalized or restored in Blood unless the said Person or Persons have received the Sacrament of the Lord's Supper within one Month next before any Bill exhibited for that Purpose, and also shall take the Oath of Supremacy, and the Oath of Allegiance, in the Parliament-House, before his or her Bill be twice read."[8] The aim of this policy was to exclude Catholics, but it effectively discriminated against professing Jews and other non-Christians as well. Although several later acts contained loopholes through which members of such groups might enter the community, it was impossible for them to gain access to the rights of natural-born subjects by the ordinary means of private legislative acts.[9]

The king was not similarly restricted in granting denizations, nor did the English monarchs prove to be as xenophobic as many members of Parliament regarding the admission of outsiders into the community of allegiance. Despite public and parliamentary opposition to the admission of Jews, the later Stuart monarchs proved liberal in granting them denizations, giving them access to the colonial trading system they otherwise could not have obtained and frequently exempting them from the usual burden of paying

7. Although it is difficult to find precise figures for any particular time, the costs for denization or naturalization could be quite high. Caroline Robbins, "A Note on General Naturalization under the Later Stuarts and a Speech in the House of Commons on the Subject in 1664," *Journal of Modern History*, XXXIV (1962), 169n, cites a pamphlet of 1673 to the effect that naturalization cost £50 to £60. Thomas W. Perry, *Public Opinion, Propaganda, and Politics in Eighteenth-Century England: A Study of the Jew Bill of 1753*, Harvard Historical Monographs, LI (Cambridge, Mass., 1962), 15, 79n, hereafter cited as Perry, *Jew Bill*, describes denization as a "rather costly privilege" as a rule (although it was often granted without fee as a mark of special favor), and he notes that naturalization at mid-century cost £20 to £30 per person. By 1843 a Select Committee of the House of Commons reported that "the cost of letters patent of denization is not less than 120 l.," and termed the cost of a naturalizing act "considerable." Hansard, *A treatise on aliens*, 207.

8. 7 Jac. I, c. 2 (1609).

9. Perry, *Jew Bill*, 15. 15 Car. II, c. 15 (1663), established special admission procedures for foreigners engaged in making linen cloth and tapestries. This act (and those cited below, n. 19) omitted the Sacrament requirement, technically allowing Jews to benefit, though Perry denies that any of these statutes were of "practical importance" for this purpose.

aliens' customs.[10] A number of the Jews so favored settled in the American plantations, among them Rowland Gideon of Boston and Joseph Bueno, Abraham Desosamendes, and Luis Gomes of New York.[11] The London merchant Manuel Henriques also sought letters patent from the king when he planned to transfer to the colonies, having been "advised that he could not inhabit there without being endenized."[12]

Although persons excluded from naturalization by the sacramental test or by Protestant declarations in the required oaths were forced to rely on denization, others simply found this mode of admission more accessible than parliamentary legislation.[13] When Louis XIV moved against the French Huguenots, Charles II, not Parliament, opened the dominions to the Protestant refugees. By an order-in-council of July 28, 1681, Charles declared that he held himself "obliged in honour and conscience to comfort and support all such afflicted Protestants, who, by reasons of the rigours and severitys which are used towards them upon the account of their religion, shall be forced to quitt their native country, and shall desire to shelter themselves under his Majestys Royall protection for the

10. Perry, *Jew Bill*, 16; Cecil Roth, *A History of the Jews in England*, 3d ed. (Oxford, 1964), 182. Samuel Oppenheim, "A List of Jews made Denizens in the Reigns of Charles II and James II, 1661–1687," American Jewish Historical Society, *Publications*, No. 20 (1911), 109–113, is useful but incomplete.

11. Gideon's name appears on the Boston tax list for 1674, and he was endenized five years later. Lee M. Friedman, "Early Jewish Residents in Massachusetts," Am. Jewish Hist. Soc., *Pubs.*, No. 23 (1915), 80; Shaw, ed., *Denization and Naturalization, 1603–1700*, 122. Bueno and Desosamendes were licensed to "trade and traffique" in New York in 1683, having been endenized in England in 1662 and 1670, respectively. Max J. Kohler, "Civil Status of the Jews in Colonial New York," Am. Jewish Hist. Soc., *Pubs.*, No. 6 (1897), 104; Oppenheim, "A List of Jews made Denizens," Am. Jewish Hist. Soc., *Pubs.*, No. 20 (1911), 110, 111. Luis Gomes received his denization in London in 1705 and then moved to New York. He was involved in a mercantile suit in Boston in 1706. W. A. Shaw, ed., *Letters of Denization and Acts of Naturalization for Aliens in England and Ireland, 1701–1800* (Hug. Soc. of London, *Pubs.*, XXVII [Manchester, 1923]), 47, hereafter cited as Shaw, ed., *Denization and Naturalization, 1701–1800*; Friedman, "Early Jewish Residents in Massachusetts," Am. Jewish Hist. Soc., *Pubs.*, No. 23 (1915), 81.

12. Feb. 25, 1687/1688, in W. L. Grant and James Munro, eds., *Acts of the Privy Council of England, Colonial Series* (London, 1908–1912), II, 95–96, hereafter cited as *Acts of Privy Council, Col.*

13. Mary Winter, "a papist," was included, then dropped, from a naturalization bill in 1661/1662. Shaw, ed., *Denization and Naturalization, 1603–1700*, 84–85. It is probable that some Catholics did receive letters of denization, but it is difficult to tell from Shaw's lists. The numerous Frenchmen, Spaniards, and Portuguese may have included some Catholics (as well as Jews), and several Greeks and Italians also obtained these grants. See, e.g., the entries for Nicholas George, "a Grecian born"; Francis Brunetti, born in Florence; and Charles Salviatti, a native Italian. *Ibid.*, 89, 96, 108. National origins, of course, are not conclusive evidence of religion.

preservacon and free exercise of their religion." Charles promised to grant the distressed refugees letters of denization without charge, adding that all who took advantage of the offer should pay the same customs and duties as native subjects. Moreover, he declared that he would request a general act of naturalization from Parliament that would fully adopt the refugees as English subjects.[14]

Hundreds of French Protestants took advantage of the offer of royal denization after 1681, and scores eventually found their way to the American plantations.[15] Others sought full naturalization in England before coming to the colonies, for they, unlike the Jews, could pass the religious tests. Upon arriving in America, these refugees often sought to have their names and the fact of their admission recorded by the local authorities. Gabriel Bernon, for example, asked the clerk of the Suffolk County office for the registry of deeds to record the letters patent of denization of more than four hundred Huguenots and their families, even though only a few actually removed to Massachusetts.[16] One who did come to Boston advised that others "who might wish to come to this country, should become naturalized in London, in order to be at liberty to engage in traffic of all kinds, and to voyage among the English islands; without this, it cannot be done."[17] Admission to subject-ship in England gave these Frenchmen the freedom to settle and to enjoy rights throughout the colonies in America.[18]

Parliament remained conservative in its approach to naturalization throughout most of the seventeenth and eighteenth centuries. Traditional xenophobia, jealousy of English commercial privileges, religious prejudices, and a fear of alien political views all militated against easy and open admission policies. For the most part, Parliament preferred to examine each applicant for naturalization, evaluating individual merit and maintaining a strict control over

14. *Ibid.*, 124–125.
15. *Ibid.*, 126–214, and *passim*. The footnotes of Baird, *Huguenot Emigration*, are replete with references to Huguenots admitted in England who later settled in the American colonies.
16. Baird, *Huguenot Emigration*, II, 204n.
17. *Ibid.*, App., 387–389, from Baird's translation of the "Narrative of a French Protestant Refugee in Boston" (1687).
18. Herbert L. Osgood, *The American Colonies in the Eighteenth Century*, II (New York, 1924), 488–489, claims that the largest groups settled in Massachusetts, New York, and South Carolina. Baird, *Huguenot Emigration*, I, 173, claims that New York, South Carolina, and Virginia received "the greatest portion of the refugees," and he notes that many were naturalized locally rather than in England.

admissions. A series of statutes did open the possibility of naturalization without special individual acts to limited and definable
groups making clear contributions to England's economic prosperity and military well-being. Among them were people engaged
in making linen cloth and tapestries and foreigners who served on
English men-of-war or merchant ships in wartime. Yet not until
1709 (and then only briefly) did Parliament provide a quick and
inexpensive procedure for admitting large numbers of immigrants
into the allegiance.[19]

For a half-century after 1664 groups who favored a liberal immigration policy made numerous attempts to pass bills to attract
foreigners to England and ease their adoption into the community,
but no general naturalization act succeeded until 1709.[20] In that
year Parliament finally approved "An Act for naturalizing Foreign
Protestants," which established a simple administrative procedure
for admitting aliens to subjectship. Applicants were to take and
subscribe the oaths of allegiance and supremacy and disavow the
Catholic doctrine of transubstantiation in open court, proving at
that time that they had taken the Sacrament within the preceding
three months. Their names were to be enrolled in the court records, and they were thereafter to be deemed natural-born subjects
throughout the empire. The fee was only one shilling.[21]

The statute passed despite strenuous objections from the Tory
minority. Opponents of the bill argued that the refugees owed a
foreign allegiance and would be a threat to established religion.
They feared that the newcomers would stimulate existing animosi-

19. For the clothmakers, see the statute cited above, n. 9. For mariners, see 6 Anne, c. 37,
sec. 20 (1707); renewed 13 Geo. II, c. 3, secs. 2–3 (1740); declared still in force, 20 Geo. III, c.
20 (1780). These acts required neither the oaths nor the Sacrament, in contrast to the act for
naturalizing foreign Protestants serving in the whale fisheries: 22 Geo. II, c. 45 (1749);
renewed 28 Geo. II, c. 20 (1755). An unusual feature here was the provision that persons
would lose the benefits of this act if they left Great Britain, Ireland, or the colonies for more
than one year at a time. This seems to go against the notion of perpetual allegiance, but
perhaps the assumption was that this was a penalty imposed on disobedient subjects rather
than a deprivation of a usually immutable status. Compare above, chap. 3, n. 17.
20. Robbins, "A Note on General Naturalization," *Jour. Mod. Hist.*, XXXIV (1962),
170–176, discusses proposals in 1664, 1667, 1672/1673, 1673, 1680, 1685, 1693/1694, and
1696/1697. Shaw, ed., *Denization and Naturalization, 1603–1700*, ix, claims that the numerous proposals made in the 1680s and 1690s had "reference entirely to the Huguenot
immigrations." For the politics of these proposals, see generally Geoffrey Holmes, *British
Politics in the Age of Anne* (New York, 1967), 67–69, and [Cobbett and Wright, eds.],
Cobbett's Parliamentary History, VI, 437–438.
21. 7 Anne, c. 5 (1709). The oaths and declarations taken followed the form established
by 6 Anne, c. 23 (1707).

ties against foreigners and increase popular commotion. Ultimately, the immigrants would vote, take office, intermarry and "extinguish the English race." The Tories argued that naturalization had always been and should remain a rarely granted privilege, bestowed by special acts after investigations of individual merit. Financial ruin would result from competition between immigrants and the native poor. The statute would defeat the purposes of the navigation acts by diluting the British monopoly of the colonial trade and reduce the revenue from aliens' duties.[22] For the moment, such protests were unavailing. The act of 1709 with its novel provisions for naturalization by enrollment passed by a "great majority" in the Commons and with "very little opposition" in the Lords.[23]

The general naturalization act remained in force for little over three years, long enough for great numbers of foreign Protestants to acquire British subjectship under its provisions.[24] Among those taking advantage of the statute were refugees from the war-ravaged German Palatinate, led by a small advance party of 41 immigrants under the Reverend Joshua Kochertal. Upon their arrival in 1708 these refugees had been welcomed by the government, which granted them free denization, gave them financial and other material aid, and arranged for their transportation to New York, where they were to settle at government expense.[25] The English authorities anticipated further arrivals, yet they were not prepared for the scale of the immigration that followed. Ship after ship cleared the Dutch ports, bringing more than 13,500 refugees to England between May and October 1709.[26] The Palatines crowded into London, requesting food and shelter from the government and when

22. [Cobbett and Wright, eds.], *Cobbett's Parliamentary History*, VI, 780–783.

23. *Ibid.*, 783. The bill passed the Commons on Mar. 7, by a vote of 203 to 77; passed the Lords on Mar. 15, 65 to 20; and received the royal assent on Mar. 23, 1708/1709. Walter Allen Knittle, *Early Eighteenth Century Palatine Emigration: A British Government Redemptioner Project to Manufacture Naval Stores* (Philadelphia, 1937), 27.

24. Shaw, ed., *Denization and Naturalization, 1701–1800*, 72–77ff. Note that Shaw's lists include persons admitted only by the High Courts in London and Ireland, though others undoubtedly were admitted by the Quarter Sessions in the country.

25. For the history of the Kochertal group, see Knittle, *Palatine Emigration*, 32–46.

26. The official correspondence lists 13,146 names, but the total probably exceeded this figure. More than 3,500 (mostly Catholics) were sent back. *Ibid.*, 66–67. About half of those who remained settled in the British Isles (especially in southern Ireland) or found employment in the whale fisheries. At least 650 went to North Carolina as part of a colonizing venture under Christoph von Graffenried and François Louis Michel, and over 3,000 were sent to New York in an abortive scheme to establish a colony to produce naval stores. Osgood, *American Colonies in the 18th Century*, II, 494–495; Knittle, *Palatine Emigration*, chaps. 4–5.

that proved inadequate, begging in the streets. The initial curiosity of the Londoners gave way to resentment and fear. Refugee encampments were visited not only by fever, plague, and starvation but by angry London mobs.

The Tories, always the strongest opponents of open immigration, quickly moved to overturn the naturalization act of 1709 after they had captured the ministry and the Commons in the 1710 elections.[27] Early in 1711 the Commons undertook an investigation of the Palatine immigration. Finding that the government had spent over one hundred thousand pounds on behalf of the refugees, the House resolved—

1. That the inviting and bringing over into this kingdom of the Palatines, of all religions, at the public expense, was an extravagant and unreasonable charge to the kingdom, and a scandalous misapplication of the public money, tending to the increase and oppression of the poor to this kingdom and of dangerous consequence to the constitution in church and state;
2. That whoever advised the bringing over the poor Palatines into this kingdom was an enemy to the Queen and kingdom.[28]

A repeal bill was rejected by the House of Lords in 1711, but continued pressure by the Tories finally brought success. In February 1711/1712 the general naturalization act was repealed with the observation that "divers Mischiefs and Inconveniencies have been found by Experience to follow from the same, to the Discouragement of the natural-born Subjects of this Kingdom, and to the Detriment of the Trade and Wealth thereof."[29]

After 1712 immigrants desiring a subject status valid throughout the empire were once again forced to seek private naturalization acts. Conservative, restrictive procedures involving case-by-case investigation and high fees replaced the brief liberal policy of admission by courts applying standardized qualifications. Several attempts were made at mid-century to revive the concept of general naturalization, but memories of the Palatinate episode of 1709

27. Holmes, *British Politics in the Age of Anne*, 69.
28. Quoted in Knittle, *Palatine Emigration*, 183. See also [Cobbett and Wright, eds.], *Cobbett's Parliamentary History*, VI, 100, and Holmes, *British Politics in the Age of Anne*, 142.
29. Preamble, 10 Anne, c. 5 (1712). Queen Anne "packed" the upper house by creating 12 new peers in Jan. 1711/1712, and though her aim was to overcome Whig opposition to the ratification of the peace treaty, it may also have provided the margin for this repeal act. David L. Keir, *The Constitutional History of Modern Britain since 1485*, 8th ed. (New York, 1966), 287; Keith Feiling, *A History of the Tory Party, 1640–1714* (Oxford, 1924), 445–446; [Cobbett and Wright, eds.], *Cobbett's Parliamentary History*, VI, 1088.

helped defeat the bills proposed in 1747 and 1751.[30] Supporters of
these proposals pointed in vain to the later history of the Palatines,
noting that many had gone to Pennsylvania, where their kind reception had convinced "Numbers of their Countrymen to join them."
Pennsylvania had been so enriched by the German immigrants,
argued Josiah Tucker, "that an Estate in Land, which might be
purchased for 100 £. Sterling, before their Arrival, cannot now be
had for *Three Times* that Sum; so greatly have they encreased the
Wealth and Property of the Landed Interest."[31] But despite appeals
to economic self-interest and Christian charity, Parliament continued to reject bills proposing inexpensive and administratively
simple adoption of aliens.

For one brief moment Parliament did consider easing the religious restrictions imposed by the sacramental test and by the Christian professions in the required oaths. In the spring of 1753 a new
act exempted Jews from these requirements, making them eligible
for private acts of naturalization.[32] The "Jew-Bill" passed casually,
with little fanfare, and the restrictionists were caught off guard. But
passage of the bill stirred a vigorous counterattack. Building on the
ever-present hostility to foreigners, opponents of the act organized
public sentiment against it, and on December 20, 1753, the statute
was repealed. No one gained subjectship under its provisions.[33]

Opposition to liberal naturalization policies reflected fears about
the effects of massive immigration into England itself; however,
opinions on restrictive admissions procedures altered when Englishmen considered the advantages of attracting aliens to the colonies. As early as 1700 promoters like William Penn argued in favor
of a general naturalization act designed specifically for the plantations. Penn suggested that Parliament provide "that such foreigners
that come to inhabit in any of the King's Colonies that are by Act of
[the local] Assembly declared freemen in the said Provinces, shall

30. [Cobbett and Wright, eds.], *Cobbett's Parliamentary History*, XIV, 133–148, 970–
971; Robbins, "A Note on General Naturalization," *Jour. Mod. Hist.*, XXXIV (1962), 171.
31. Josiah Tucker, *Reflections on the expediency of a law for the Naturalization of Foreign Protestants* (London, 1751), pt. i, 64.
32. 26 Geo. II, c. 26 (1753); [Cobbett and Wright, eds.], *Cobbett's Parliamentary History*,
XIV, 1365–1432. For the history of the episode, see generally Perry, *Jew Bill*, and Roth,
History of the Jews in England, 212–223.
33. Perry, *Jew Bill*, 177. The preamble observed that "occasion has been taken from the
said Act to raise Discontents, and to disquiet the Minds of many of his Majesty's Subjects,"
and the act proceeded to repeal the earlier statute "to all Intents and Purposes whatsoever."
27 Geo. II, c. 1 (1753).

enjoy the rights and liberties of English subjects, except being masters or commanders of vessells and ships of trade."[34] The delegation to colonial authorities of the power to admit aliens would obviate the difficulties inherent in the existing system, for as things stood (even under the general act of Anne's reign), the actual process of admission had to take place in the British Isles.

Not until 1740 did Parliament follow Penn's suggestion and establish a mechanism by which aliens who wished to settle in America could be naturalized as full British subjects without having to seek a special act in London. In that year Parliament finally approved a general enabling act for the colonies, declaring that "the Increase of People is a Means of advancing the Wealth and Strength of any Nation or Country: And . . . many Foreigners and Strangers, from the Lenity of our Government, the Purity of our Religion, the Benefit of our Laws, the Advantages of our Trade, and the Security of our Property, might be induced to come and settle in some of his Majesty's Colonies, if they were made Partakers of the Advantages and Privileges which the natural born Subjects of this Realm do enjoy."[35] The act required applicants to reside seven years or more, without being absent more than two consecutive months, in "any of His Majesty's Colonies in America." They were to take the oaths of allegiance and to subscribe the profession of Christian belief before the chief justice or some other colonial judge in open court. At the time of this ceremony the applicant had to submit a certificate, signed by two witnesses, proving that within the preceding three months he had taken the Sacrament "in some Protestant and Reformed Congregation within this Kingdom of *Great Britain*, or within some of the said Colonies in America." Quakers and Jews were exempted from the latter provision, and the wording of the required oaths was modified to their benefit.

The name of each person naturalized under this statute was to be entered in the local court records (for a maximum fee of two shillings) and in the official books of the colony's secretary; lists of

34. *N.Y. Col. Docs.*, IV, 757. This was the sixth of a number of proposals made by Penn in a paper endorsed, "Heads of Severall things proper for the Plant[atio]ns." The paper was received by the Council of Trade and Plantations, Dec. 6, 1700, and read Jan. 10 following. *Cal. State Papers, Col.*, XVIII, 599.

35. Preamble to "An Act for naturalizing such foreign Protestants, and others therein mentioned, as are settled, or shall settle, in any of his Majesty's Colonies in America," 13 Geo. II, c. 7 (1740). For passage of the act, see Stock, ed., *Proceedings and Debates*, V, 15, 17–18n.

these names were then to be transmitted to the Lords Commissioners of Trade. Failure to enter the names in the record made the
judge or secretary liable to a fine of ten pounds and any secretary
who neglected to send the yearly lists to London could be fined fifty
pounds.[36] Most significant, the certificates of naturalization issued
under this statute were to be recognized in all courts throughout the
British empire. The person so naturalized thus became a British
subject not only in the local colony but in all the dominions of the
king.

The statute of 1740 was Parliament's most significant attempt
during the colonial period to provide an easy method for the assimi-
lation of foreign immigrants in America. Despite the inconvenience
of the seven-year residence requirement, the general procedure was
inexpensive and administratively simple. Catholics were still excluded, of course, but the benefits of the act were available to Jews
and to most Protestants. An amending statute of 1747 extended the
concessions already made to Quakers to other groups like the
Moravians who had conscientious scruples against taking oaths,
and thereafter they, too, could be naturalized under the authority of
the 1740 law.[37]

The liberality of the provisions for naturalization in America
under parliamentary auspices contrasted sharply with existing practices in the mother country. English Jews commented on the anomaly
and the unfairness of the government's policy when they sought
passage of the act of 1753. One prominent Jewish merchant complained that "as the Law at present stands, the Principal Jews suffer
a great Hardship, they having encouraged and sent several of their
Profession to the American Plantations, some of whom are returned and Naturalized, or capable of being so, while those who
protect them cannot enjoy the like privilege."[38] One way to remove the discrepancy would have been to tighten the policy in the
colonies, a move favored by restrictionists. During the debates on

---

36. For lists of persons naturalized under this act, insofar as the names have been
preserved in the British Public Record Office, see M. S. Giuseppi, ed., *Naturalizations of
Foreign Protestants in the American and West Indian Colonies* . . . (Hug. Soc. of London,
Pubs., XXIV [Manchester, 1921]), hereafter cited as Giuseppi, ed., *Naturalizations*. The lists
are incomplete, but there is no evidence that the penalties for noncompliance with the
registration provisions were ever enforced. *Ibid.*, xiv.

37. 20 Geo. II, c. 44 (1747).

38. Joseph Salvador to the duke of Newcastle, London, Jan. 14, 1753, Roth, ed., *Anglo-
Jewish Letters, 1158–1917* (London, 1938), 129–130.

the "Jew-Bill," the duke of Bedford argued that the provision for the naturalization of Jews in the plantation act "ought to be repealed. We know how artfully that part of the act was introduced: we know that it was passed by surprise, or rather, I may say, by stealth; for nothing relating to the Jews ever appeared in the votes, nor does now appear in the title of the act."[39]

However, this effort was beaten back. Noting that the statute "has been in force for many years, and many Christians as well as Jews are concerned in its preservation," Lord Chancellor Hardwicke argued that repeal, "even with respect to the Jews would be a breach of the public faith, and would prevent any Protestant Christians from trusting to it for the future; which would put an end to that increase of inhabitants our plantations receive yearly from almost every Protestant country in Europe." The earl of Grenville doubted Parliament's right to repeal the act unilaterally: "When the public offers terms to private men by act of parliament, and the latter accept of those terms, and perform their part of the conditions required, such an act becomes a *pactum conventum* between the public and those private men, and to them the public faith is engaged, that such an act shall never be repealed or altered without their consent."[40] The restrictionists' effort to modify the act failed by a wide margin.[41] The act of 1740 remained as originally passed: a broad invitation to foreign immigrants to settle in the American colonies and to enter the community of allegiance.

Far from further restricting naturalization in the colonies, Parliament, in response to the exigencies of war, established a second method for admitting aliens to subjectship in America. Citing the need for officers who could assist with the "manners and language" of foreign-born recruits, especially in Maryland and Pennsylvania, Parliament in 1756 enabled the king to commission a limited number of foreigners as officers and engineers in his colonial regiments. The men were to take the customary oaths of allegiance and the Sacrament and then were allowed to serve only in America.[42] Five

39. Speech in House of Lords, Nov. 14, 1753, Stock, ed., *Proceedings and Debates*, V, 572–573. The clauses relating to Jews in the 1740 statute were introduced in Commons after the bill was reported from the Committee of the Whole and after amendments made there were read and approved, Jan. 23, 1740. *Ibid.*, 22.

40. Hardwicke, *ibid.*, 571; Grenville, *ibid.*, 573. See also [Cobbett and Wright, eds.], *Cobbett's Parliamentary History*, XV, 102–103, 107–110, 113–114.

41. The motion for leave to bring in a repeal bill was defeated 208 to 88. Stock, ed., *Proceedings and Debates*, V, 575.

42. 29 Geo. II, c. 5 (1756). The colonel of the regiment was to be "a natural-born Sub-

years later these officers and the common soldiers under them in the Royal American Regiment and Engineers were permitted to obtain naturalization on special terms. Observing that many of the commissioned officers had "given the strongest Assurances and Fidelity to his Majesty's Government," not only in their faithful service but also in their purchase of estates in the colonies, and hoping to increase the recruitment of foreign-born settlers, Parliament eased their admission to the allegiance, a concession sanctioned by justice and good policy alike. All foreign Protestants who had served or would serve for two years in the British forces in North America, who would take the oaths and declarations, and who could certify that they had taken the Sacrament within the six months preceding admission, were deemed natural-born subjects. All estates purchased by the parties since the act of 1756 were confirmed.[43]

Both the act of 1740 and the act of 1761 included the customary prohibitions established by the Act of Settlement concerning political offices, crown grants, and places of trust and profit—but with one significant alteration.[44] Naturalized subjects were still barred from the Privy Council, Parliament, and offices in the kingdoms of Great Britain and Ireland. However, the usual addition, "and in the dominions thereunto belonging," was dropped. Legally, persons who took advantage of either of these acts were qualified to enjoy full political rights within the colonies, including the right to seek and hold civil and military offices. Questions did arise on this issue until Parliament finally clarified its policy in 1773. An explanatory act of that year declared all persons naturalized under the statutes of 1740 and 1761 "capable of taking and holding any Office or Place of Trust, either Civil or Military, and of taking and holding any Grant of Lands, Tenements, and Hereditaments, from the Crown to himself or themselves, or to any other or others in Trust for him or them, as well under the Great Seal of *Great Britain*, as otherwise (other than and except . . . within the Kingdoms of *Great Britain* and *Ireland*); any Law and Act of Parliament to the contrary notwithstanding."[45]

The system was now complete. Foreigners could still approach

---

ject, and not any Person naturalized or made a Denizen." Officers were to take the Sacrament within six months prior to receiving their commissions.

43. 2 Geo. III, c. 25 (1761).
44. See above, chap. 2, at nn. 23–25.
45. 13 Geo. III, c. 25 (1773).

Parliament directly, but they could also be admitted as full members of the community of allegiance by colonial authorities under the parliamentary statutes of 1740 and 1761. Although subjects adopted in this manner remained under some disabilities in the British Isles, they could demand full equality with natural-born subjects in America.

In fact, the American colonists had not waited for Parliament's formal delegation of authority, but had adopted aliens as fellow subjects almost from the beginnings of settlement. If the isolated communities scattered along the edge of the continent were to become militarily secure and economically viable, they had to attract newcomers. In the early years survival demanded growth, and the desirability of an ever-increasing population remained clear even after the physical security of the initial plantations was assured. The need for labor to exploit the magnificent resources of the new land remained constant and pressing; hence the invitation extended to foreign settlers broadened with time. By the mid-eighteenth century the first trickles of non-English immigrants had swelled to a flood of foreign newcomers.

England alone could not supply the numbers needed to settle the colonies, and both private and official promoters saw the value of inviting foreigners to people the king's new dominions. To force such immigrants to seek admission in England—which may have been London's original expectation—would have been difficult. By the end of the seventeenth century the colonial governments, acting on dubious legal authority, had already established a variety of procedures for incorporating aliens into the local communities. In contrast to the restrictive policies favored in London, the acts passed by colonial legislators granted aliens extensive rights and benefits. The American governments gave little attention to theoretical limitations on naturalization and denization—indeed, their actions often displayed either an extensive ignorance of or a blatant disregard for those limitations. Survival, population growth, and economic expansion—not doctrinal consistency—dictated the course of colonial policy.

Neither the royal charters, nor parliamentary statutes, nor common law principles explicitly conferred upon colonial authorities the right to adopt aliens as subjects. Yet it was possible to find sanctions for the exercise of that power. The Virginia Company charter of 1612 empowered the company to admit to its membership "any Person or Persons, as well Strangers and Aliens . . . being in Amity with us, as any our natural Liege Subjects born in any our Realms and Dominions." Company officers were authorized to administer the oaths of allegiance and supremacy to all who wished to "go or pass to the said colony in Virginia."[46] The fundamental grants of the other colonizing companies and of chartered colonies as well commonly allowed the membership (governor, assistants, and freemen) to admit persons to the freemanship of the corporation, never definitely limiting the candidates to those who already were subjects.[47] Such clauses were not necessarily designed to delegate the responsibility for naturalization, but the transformation of companies into colonies and the removal of company government to America (as in the case of Massachusetts Bay) made it difficult to distinguish between admission to the status of a freeman and naturalization or denization as an English subject.[48]

Other provisions in the colonial charters could also be interpreted as proof that the plantation governments had the "power parliamentary" of naturalization. The right to transport "strangers" who would "become Our Loving subjects" was included in most of the early grants. Since the place of admission was not specified, it was easy to argue that the operation could be performed in the colonies.[49] Moreover, if aliens could be made subjects by local action, clauses guaranteeing that all "present" and "future" subjects

46. Virginia Charter of 1611/1612, in Thorpe, ed. and comp., *Constitutions, Charters, and Laws*, VII, 3806, 3807. Cora Start, "Naturalization in the English Colonies of America," American Historical Association, *Annual Report . . . for the Year 1893* (1894), 324, sees this as a distinct recognition of the power to naturalize, though in fact the clause provided only for the admission of aliens to company membership.

47. Massachusetts, Connecticut, and Rhode Island all enjoyed this power. Joseph Willard, *Naturalization in the American Colonies, with more Particular Reference to Massachusetts* (Boston, 1859), 10–12.

48. Massachusetts (Aug. 3, 1664) and New Hampshire (1680) required by statute that freemen be English. Frank Hayden Miller, "Legal Qualifications for Office in America, 1619–1899," A.H.A., *Annual Report . . . for the Year 1899*, I (1900), 94. For the texts of the laws, see William H. Whitmore, ed., *The Colonial Laws of Massachusetts. Reprinted from the Edition of 1660, with the Supplements to 1672* (Boston, 1889), 229, and Albert S. Batchellor, comp., *Laws of New Hampshire* (Manchester, Concord, N.H., etc., 1904–1922), I, 25–26.

49. See above, n. 4. Most of the charters and patents—up to and including Georgia's—included this or a similar clause.

in America would be considered subjects in all the king's dominions implied that colonial naturalization had an imperial, and not merely a local, effect.[50]

Whether the colonial authorities could lawfully confer a subject status valid throughout the empire was a question not formally answered until the end of the century, but the charters undoubtedly permitted the grantees to confer certain local benefits upon whomever they wished. London officials showed little interest in the distribution of purely local political privileges for most of the seventeenth century; the recipients of colonial charters were explicitly given power to bestow real property rights at their discretion. The Maryland charter of 1632, for example, empowered Lord Baltimore and his heirs to "assign, alien, grant, demise, or enfeoff so many, such, and proportionate parts and parcels of the premises, to any person or persons willing to purchase the same," any English laws to the contrary notwithstanding.[51] The general authority to make laws and ordinances, "whether relating to the public state of the said province, or the private utility of individuals," was circumscribed by the boundaries of the particular colony, but nevertheless seemed to legitimate the granting of local rights to persons regardless of their status in English law.[52]

Ultimately, the question of colonial jurisdiction over naturalization was only part of a much larger problem of the legal relationship between the mother country and the new plantations. Royal patents and charters provided the clearest link between London and the American settlements. Since these patents had their primary operation outside the realm, it was not clear to what extent English law and England's parliament should control legal developments within the boundaries of the American grants. The general understanding in England, at least in the early decades of colonization,

50. See, e.g., the grants of Pennsylvania (1682) and Maryland (1632), in Samuel Hazard, ed., *Minutes of the Provincial Council of Pennsylvania . . . [Colonial Records of Pennsylvania]* (Philadelphia and Harrisburg, Pa., 1852–1853), I, 20, hereafter cited as *Col. Recs. Pa.*; Thorpe, ed. and comp., *Constitutions, Charters, and Laws*, III, 1681 (Art. 9). A unique provision in Charles I's grant of Maine to Sir Ferdinando Gorges (1639) specified that emigrant subjects and "the children and posteritie discending of English Scottish or Irish parents" born in the colonies would be deemed natural-born subjects, apparently excluding children born in Maine of alien parents. *Ibid.*, III, 1635.
51. Charles I to George Calvert, 1st Lord Baltimore, June 20, 1632, Virgil Maxcy, ed., *The Laws of Maryland . . .* (Baltimore, 1811), I, 9. See also the Carolina charter, Thorpe, ed. and comp., *Constitutions, Charters, and Laws*, V, 2749–2750 (Art. 12).
52. Maxcy, ed., *Laws of Md.*, I, 3.

seemed to be that the crown retained a supervisory jurisdiction over legal practices in the new settlements.[53] Colonial governments sometimes disputed the right of crown officials to intervene in local affairs, as did Massachusetts Bay in 1632, 1637, and most notably in 1646 during the Robert Child controversy. Not until the 1664 patent to the duke of York was there an explicit provision for appeals to the king in all cases decided in an American colony.[54]

The source and content of the colonial charters affirmed the existence of a fundamental link between the king and the local governments; no one was prepared to deny that the colonists remained connected to England in some fashion by virtue of their allegiance to the same king. What part Parliament and English law played in shaping and maintaining this connection was less clear. Colonial charters frequently declared that local laws should not be repugnant or contrary to the "laws, statutes, customs, and rights" of England, and these were enacted or authoritatively interpreted by Parliament and the English courts in the first instance. Yet conformity to England's laws was often required only "so far as conveniently may be," and no charter specified a parliamentary right to determine "convenience" or to intervene directly in colonial affairs.[55] Efforts to justify the enforcement of parliamentary acts adopted after the charters had passed the seals were even more questionable. In any event, none of these problems arose in the seventeenth century in connection with colonial naturalizations. Whatever later claims might be made for its right to intervene, Parliament neither acknowledged, nor rejected, nor attempted to regulate the incorporation of aliens by the colonial governments in these early years.

Even the common law failed to provide clear guidelines with respect to naturalization in the colonies. Existing precedents—

---

53. Smith, *Appeals to the Privy Council*, 42, and above, chap. 3, n. 35.

54. Smith, *Appeals to the Privy Council*, 44–49, 53. Harold D. Hazeltine, "Appeals from Colonial Courts to the King in Council, with Especial Reference to Rhode Island," A.H.A., *Annual Report . . . for the Year 1894* (1895), 308, notes that there was no general regulation of colonial appeals until an order-in-council of Jan. 23, 1683/1684.

55. See, e.g., the Maryland Charter of 1632/1633 to Cecilius Calvert, in Maxcy, ed., *Laws of Md.*, I, 4 (Art. 7). The charters of Massachusetts Bay (1629) and Connecticut (1663) included the requirement without an explicit proviso regarding "convenience." Thorpe, ed. and comp., *Constitutions, Charters, and Laws*, III, 1853, I, 533. Rhode Island's laws were to "bee not contrary and repugnant unto, butt, as neare as may bee, agreeable to the lawes of this our realme of England, considering the nature and constitutione of the place and people there." *Ibid.*, VI, 3215.

most notably the *Ramsey* cases—related exclusively to the English realm and to previously independent governments acquired by conquest or descent. The authority of new governments established under the king in the course of colonization was, as John Adams would later claim, *"casus omissus* at common law."[56] New colonies might be seen as coordinate dominions like Scotland, having independent legal systems and operating outside the control of Parliament, though acknowledging the appellate jurisdiction of the king-in-council. Alternatively, they might be deemed subordinate kingdoms like Ireland, capable of being bound by acts of Parliament if expressly named. The American colonists' acceptance of much of the common law and many English statutes as binding within their own legal systems and, more important, their acknowledgment of the validity of parliamentary naturalizations in the plantations would lend some plausibility to later claims of English jurists that the colonies were dependent "conquered" kingdoms.[57]

The colonists themselves would resent the contention that they were a conquered people within the imperial structure. They preferred to justify their reception of written and unwritten English laws on the grounds of birthright and consent, citing charter guarantees to affirm their right to the "rights of Englishmen."[58] The colonists valued English laws as bulwarks to their liberty, and they accepted as fellow subjects aliens naturalized by Parliament because population growth was of paramount importance; the subtler im-

56. Eighth letter of "Novanglus," Mar. 13, 1775, Charles Francis Adams, ed., *The Works of John Adams* (Boston, 1850–1856), IV, 121.

57. Although there is some controversy over the extent of the reception of English common and statute law in the colonies in the 17th century, there is no doubt that Americans considered both—especially the common law—to be part of their heritage. For a concise review of the issue, see Zechariah Chafee, Jr., "Colonial Courts and the Common Law," in David H. Flaherty, ed., *Essays in the History of Early American Law* (Chapel Hill, N.C., 1969), 53–82. Smith, *Appeals to the Privy Council*, 472–474, 486, observes that works like Coke's *Institutes* and *Reports* "were well disseminated along the seaboard" by 1700. "In the immune zone beneath the fixed amount of civil appeals," he continues, "the colonial judicial record shows a general and widespread practice of using applicable English acts passed after colonization in which the dominions were not named."

58. The theoretical claims were explored most extensively in the 1760s, but the basic argument appeared much earlier. When in 1684 the Maryland proprietor supported his prerogative on the grounds that "the King had power to dispose of his conquests as he pleased," the lower house objected to the implication that they were a conquered people. They based their privileges on "their birthright by the words of the Charter." St. George Leakin Sioussat, "The Theory of the Extension of English Statutes to the Plantations," in Association of American Law Schools, *Select Essays in Anglo-American Legal History*, I (Boston, 1907), 424.

plications of the Americans' acknowledgment of the authority of English law and of the binding force of parliamentary acts would not be revealed until late in the colonial period.

Although the legal authority of the colonial governments to admit foreigners to the status of English subjects was questionable, the colonies quickly began to exercise this power, receiving no challenge from London until the late seventeenth century. Methods varied from colony to colony, but generally bore some resemblance to the English practices of executive denization and legislative naturalization and reflected some familiarity with established principles of allegiance and subjectship.[59]

At the outset little uniformity of procedure existed among the various colonies, and in some cases admission practices varied within a single province. Several colonies permitted naturalization by enrollment, establishing general requirements for admission to be administered by local courts. Elsewhere, admission to freemanship served as the analogue of naturalization, particularly in New England, where both the towns and the central government were involved. Royal governors and lords proprietary issued patents of denization, and local assemblies passed both general and special acts of naturalization.

For a time Virginia and the Carolinas allowed denization or naturalization by enrollment, actually preceding England's brief experiment with this method.[60] A Virginia law passed during the commonwealth period permitted "all aliens and strangers" who had resided in the colony four years and who had a "firme resolution to make this countrey their place of residence" to become "free denisons." They were obliged to "take the oath of Fidelite to be true to the government of this countrey," the oath to be "administered by the severall courts respectively in the counties where anie such aliens do dwell."[61]

The Virginia law of 1658 placed responsibility for admitting

---

59. There were some practical divergences, and it is probable that colonial officials were not abreast of the finer legal aspects of the theory of allegiance discussed in Part I, above. Access to English treatises and law books improved in time, and by the later 18th century American lawyers could build their arguments on Coke and Hale, as well as Blackstone.

60. Above at n. 21.

61. William Waller Hening, ed., *The Statutes at Large; Being a Collection of all the Laws of Virginia, from the First Session of the Legislature in the Year 1619* (Richmond, New York, and Philadelphia, 1809–1823), I, 486.

"free denisons" in the courts, but the procedural details were not spelled out; the House of Burgesses itself from time to time adopted foreigners under the authority of this law. On April 1, 1658, the House declared the "Dutchman" William Westerhouse a free denizen, "giving thereby and granting unto the said Westerhouse full power and privilege to purchase, hold and dispose of Lands. To trade and traffique and all other law[ful] priviledges and Imunities to be invested with and enjoy, in as full and ample manner to all intents and purposes as if he had been an Englishman born (The bearing of publique offices and imployments Exempted), with which Denizacon his Children may also be invested with." The Burgesses granted four other identical patents the same day and gave commissions of naturalization to two men "in the forme above, onely that they and their issue are capeable of bearing office, they being borne of English parents."[62]

Fragmentary records and the vagueness of the procedural requirements in the 1658 law make it impossible to say whether this was truly naturalization by enrollment or a modified form of admission by special act. That is, it is not clear that the assembly necessarily had to be involved in the process by ordering the final issuance of the patents after the other requirements were satisfied. Evidently the House of Burgesses felt free not only to issue both limited denizations and full naturalizations but also to modify the statutory requirements as they saw fit. Although there was no explicit revision of the general law until 1671, the Restoration seems to have caused some alterations in procedure. When Nicholas Boot petitioned for a confirmation of his 1658 patent, asking that it be renewed "in his majesties name," the assembly ordered him to take the oaths of allegiance and supremacy and continue to reside in the colony. After two years additional residence he was to be "admitted to enjoy all the priviledges an Englisman enjoyes in Virginia."[63]

62. "Extracts from Proceedings of the House of Burgesses of Virginia, 1652–1661," *Virginia Magazine of History and Biography*, VIII (1900–1901), 393–394. Lambert Grooten, John Abraham, Minor Dowdas, and George Hacke were also endenized. William and John Custis, the two persons naturalized, were the sons of John Custis of Rotterdam, formerly of Baltimore, Ireland. John's petition of Mar. 15 noted that he was of foreign birth though of English descent, and he requested that the assembly "restore him to the freedom of his parents." *Ibid.*, 391. Technically, both might have claimed subjectship under the statute *De natis* (1350).

63. Assembly Resolutions, Oct. 11, 1660, and Mar. 23, 1660/1661, Hening, ed., *Statutes of Va.*, II, 16, 34.

The basic law in the Carolinas was much clearer. The Articles of Agreement between the proprietors and the expedition of 1665 under Sir John Yeamans authorized the establishment of a local assembly with full power to "give unto all strangers as to them shall seeme meete a Naturalizion," and instructions of 1667 to the governor of the Albemarle settlement confirmed that these naturalized aliens were to be "accompted the King's Naturall Subjects" within the colony.[64] Articles 117 and 118 of the Fundamental Constitutions, drafted by John Locke in 1669, provided a simple enrollment procedure for incorporating foreigners. Applicants merely subscribed a copy of the Constitutions before any precinct register, promising to be "true and faithful to the Palatine and Lords Proprietors," and they were "thereby naturalized."[65] This procedure was used for at least twenty years, and there is some evidence that naturalization continued to be performed at the county level in North Carolina through most of the eighteenth century.[66]

The unusual characteristic of naturalization by enrollment was its availability to anyone meeting certain minimum standard requirements.[67] It was far more common, both in England and America, to assume that the grant of the extensive privileges entailed by denization or naturalization required a scrutiny of individual cases. Because of this assumption, most English jurists, at least, considered "group grants" (even those in which the parties affected were potentially identifiable when the acts were passed) irregular and of doubtful propriety.[68]

64. Articles of Agreement (Jan. 7, 1664/1665) and "Instructions to the Governors of the County of Albemarle" (1667), William L. Saunders, ed., *The Colonial Records of North Carolina* (Raleigh, N.C., 1886–1890), I, 83, 169, hereafter cited as *N.C. Col. Recs.*

65. Mattie Erma Edwards Parker, ed., *North Carolina Charters and Constitutions, 1578–1698* in Mattie Erma Edwards Parker et al., eds., *The Colonial Records of North Carolina*, N.S., I (Raleigh, N.C., 1963), 151–152. These provisions were retained in the revisions of Mar. 1, 1669/1670, of Jan. 12, 1681/1682, and of Aug. 17, 1682. They were omitted in the version of Apr. 11, 1698. *Ibid.*, 184, 206, 231, 234–240.

66. Edward A. Hoyt, "Naturalization under the American Colonies: Signs of a New Community," *Political Science Quarterly*, LXVII (1952), 250. Arthur Henry Hirsch, *The Huguenots of Colonial South Carolina* (Durham, N.C., 1928), 114–115, refers to a list of 30 names of signatories that included several Huguenots. The records of the Rowan County Court, Sept. 24, 1766, refer to several naturalizations. *N.C. Col. Recs.*, VII, 255–256. These may have been performed under the parliamentary statute of 1740, but if so, they were not reported as such to London.

67. The nearest equivalent to group naturalization at the time in England was the act of 15 Car. II, c. 15 (1663), mentioned above, n. 9. Being limited to a narrowly defined occupational group, that act was not as indiscriminate as some of the American examples.

68. See the opinion of Attorney General Edward Northey on the New York act of 1715, delivered Jan. 2, 1717/1718, *N.Y. Col. Docs.*, V, 495–497.

Group naturalizations were enacted in several of the colonies before 1700, however. New York naturalized resident foreigners "professing Christianity" who took and subscribed the oath of allegiance by an act of November 1, 1683.[69] Pennsylvania in 1682 allowed all "Strangers and Foreigners" resident in the colony and the lower counties of Newcastle, Jones, and Whoreskill to become subjects by swearing allegiance and fidelity to the king and the proprietor within three months and by paying a maximum fee of twenty shillings.[70] South Carolina passed an act in 1691 that would have admitted all French and Swiss inhabitants to the rights of subjectship, asking only that they register their names with the clerk or secretary of the assembly within six months. However, this generous proposal met with political opposition and was apparently annulled by the proprietors.[71] Instead, a more limited statute of 1697 bestowed the privilege of subjectship on a group of sixty-three persons (who had earlier petitioned the assembly for the favor). All others who petitioned the governor within three months and who swore allegiance to the king were allowed to take advantage of the act.[72]

Naturalization practices in the New England colonies are more obscure than elsewhere, for non-English immigration to that area was of "relatively little importance" in the seventeenth century.[73]

69. *The Colonial Laws of New York from the Year 1664 to the Revolution* (Albany, N.Y., 1894–1896), I, 123–124, hereafter cited as *Col. Laws N.Y.* Foreigners arriving after this date were to apply to the legislature, which was hereby authorized to pass special acts of naturalization.

70. Gertrude MacKinney and Charles F. Hoban, eds., *Pennsylvania Archives*, 8th Ser. (Philadelphia, 1931–1935), I, App., 328–330, hereafter cited as *Pa. Archives*, 8th Ser. This was the Act of Union, Dec. 7, 1682, which incorporated the counties later known as Delaware. Cornelius Plockhoy was naturalized under this act on May 18, 1683. Leland Harder, "Plockhoy and His Settlement at Zwaanendael, 1663," *Delaware History*, III (1948–1949), 152. Several French Huguenots also were admitted under its provisions. See, e.g., Baird, *Huguenot Emigration*, I, 308n, II, 113n.

71. Thomas Cooper and David J. McCord, eds., *The Statutes at Large of South Carolina* (Columbia, S.C., 1836–1841), II, 58–60, hereafter cited as *S.C. Statutes*. Hirsch, *Huguenots of Colonial S.C.*, 118–119, claims that the act was annulled, although there is some indication that a few Huguenots were admitted under its provisions. Thomas Gaillard, "Copious Extracts by the Committee on Publication from the History of the Huguenots of South Carolina, and Their Descendants," Huguenot Society of South Carolina, *Transactions*, No. 5 (Charleston, S.C., 1897), 19.

72. *S.C. Statutes*, II, 131–133. Lists of French Huguenots who petitioned for the benefits of this act can be found in Gaillard, "Copious Extracts," Hug. Soc. of S.C., *Trans.*, No. 5, 24–48.

73. Clifford K. Shipton, "Immigration to New England, 1680–1740," *Journal of Political Economy*, XLIV (1936), 225. For a brief survey of New England laws relating to immigra-

Massachusetts permitted a group of French Protestants to locate in the colony by a resolve of the General Court in 1662,[74] and a number of Huguenots already granted subjectship in England settled there at the end of the century.[75] Under the Dominion of New England, several aliens (and at least one Scotsman) received patents of denization, but for the most part, no formal procedures for naturalization appeared in these settlements until the eighteenth century.[76] The only unmistakable naturalization in New England before 1700 was a unique act passed in Connecticut in 1695, whereby the Indian Abimelech, grandson of Uncas, was declared a subject of the king and granted "the privilege and protection of his Majesties lawes this Colony alowes his subjects here, provided he takes the oath of alegiance."[77]

Admission to freemanship seems to have replaced the practices of naturalization and denization in the corporate colonies of New England. Massachusetts and New Hampshire limited freemanship to Englishmen in 1664 and 1680, respectively, but Connecticut and Rhode Island did not.[78] The General Court of Connecticut in 1657

---

tion, see Emberson Edward Proper, *Colonial Immigration Laws: A Study of the Regulation of Immigration by the English Colonies in America* (New York, 1900), chap. 4.

74. A. H. Carpenter, "Naturalization in England and the American Colonies," *AHR*, IX (1903–1904), 296. Among these Frenchmen was Jean Touton, who was residing at Rehoboth, Mass., in 1675. On June 29, 1687, Touton petitioned the General Court for a grant of letters representing him as an Englishman, claiming that he had been an inhabitant of the king's territories since 1662 and a free denizen of Virginia "by my Lord Effingham's favour." Baird, *Huguenot Emigration*, I, 270–271.

75. Baird, *Huguenot Emigration*, esp. II, 209–214, lists a number of these refugees. One group attempted to settle in Rhode Island, but many left because of the discriminatory treatment they received. See generally Elisha R. Potter, *Memoir concerning the French Settlements and French Settlers in the Colony of Rhode Island* (Providence, R.I., 1879), 1–9.

76. A group of Huguenots from St. Christopher was admitted July 12, 1686. They were to take the oath of allegiance and were thereafter allowed to reside in and "to proceed from hence and return hither as freely as any other of his Ma'tys Subjects." The order was to extend to all French Protestants who might arrive later. Batchellor, comp., *Laws of N.H.*, I, 121. Mungo Craford, a Scot, was given a certificate under the public seal on July 20, 1686, declaring that "he is allowed to trade, and deal and enjoy Liberties and Priviledges as other his Ma'tys Subjects here." See "Records of the Council of Massachusetts, under Joseph Dudley," Massachusetts Historical Society, *Proceedings*, 2d Ser., XIII (1899–1900), 258. Another group of Frenchmen was admitted into the colony by the governor and council on Feb. 1, 1691/1692. *Report of the Record Commissioners of the City of Boston*, X (Boston, 1886), 62.

77. J. Hammond Trumbull and Charles J. Hoadly, eds., *The Public Records of the Colony of Connecticut . . .* (Hartford, Conn., 1850–1890), IV, 153, hereafter cited as *Conn. Col. Recs.* The motive for this unusual act seems to have been to clarify and settle a land-title dispute. Start, "Naturalization in the English Colonies," A.H.A., *Annual Report 1893*, 327.

78. See above, n. 48. "Englishmen" apparently included English subjects, born or naturalized. The Huguenots, e.g., were qualified for freemanship after they acquired subjectship.

confirmed the action of the town of Pequot in admitting "Mr. Laurence Cornelius, Dutchman," as an inhabitant with the right to engage in trade. In the future, however, all persons wishing to "bee made free men" had to submit a certificate from the "major part of the deputies in their severall townes, of their peaceable and honest conversation." Only after the central government had registered its approval were such persons thereafter to be given rights.[79] Rhode Island, too, required "the generall consent of our Collonie" before any "foriner, Dutch, French, or of any other nation" could be received as a free inhabitant.[80]

Although there was some central control over entry into the freemanship of the New England colonies, the local authorities occasionally may have proceeded on their own. As long as the foreign-born settler behaved peaceably and was of "honest conversation," long residence and local acceptance were perhaps enough to overcome any initial discrimination.[81] Subordinate officials or governing bodies from time to time clearly disregarded the distinction between grants of purely local rights and grants of wider significance. The town meeting of Greenwich, Rhode Island, for example, voted to bestow patents of denization upon Daniel Aryault and a number of others in 1701.[82] Although the English charter of New York City would later require that those admitted to the freedom of the corporation already be subjects, the mayor and aldermen did not initially observe that restriction.[83] On No-

79. *Conn. Col. Recs.*, I, 290.

80. Order of the General Assembly at Providence, Oct. 18, 1652, *R.I. Col. Recs.*, I, 245–246.

81. Freemanship admissions rarely indicate national origins, and I have not examined local town archives. It is apparent that aliens did settle in New England, and there are no records of naturalization for most of them. See generally Ethel Stanwood Bolton, "Immigrants to New England, 1700–1775," Essex Institute, *Historical Collections*, LXIII–LXVII (1927–1931). Most of the immigrants were from the British Isles, but there were also some Germans and Frenchmen. See, e.g., listings for Dr. Frederick Ambrey, Claudius Bartheleme, Joseph Bas, and William Blazo, *ibid.*, LXIII, 180, 186, 187, 191.

82. Potter, *Memoir concerning the French*, 105; Sidney S. Rider, *The History of Denization and Naturalization in the Colony of Rhode Island, 1636–1790* (Providence, R.I., [1905?]), 8–9. My thanks to the Rhode Island Historical Society for making a copy of this pamphlet available.

83. The English permitted the Dutch "burgher-right" to continue after the conquest. The Dongan Charter of Apr. 20, 1686, provided for the admission of freemen but required that they be "his Majestys natural born Subjects or Such as Shall first be naturalized by an Act of general Assembly or Shall have Obtained Letters of Denization." Beverly McAnear, "The Place of the Freeman in Old New York," *New York History*, XXI (1940), 418–419; *The Burghers of New Amsterdam and the Freemen of New York* (New-York Historical Society, *Collections . . . for the Year 1885*, XVIII [New York, 1886]), 49, hereafter cited as *Burghers of*

vember 9, 1676, David Jochamse swore fidelity to the duke of York and "was made a free Burger of this Citty and taken to bee an English Man within this Citty and Collony and hath the same Priviledges and Libertyes as any other of his Majesties Subjects within this Citty and Collony." Several similar grants were made in 1678.[84]

Whatever the local variations, by far the most common procedures used to adopt foreigners in America were individual acts of legislative naturalization or executive denization. These modes permitted a tighter control over entry (the authorities could examine the personal merits of each applicant), and they probably produced a larger income in fees. The New York act of 1683, referred to above, empowered the legislature to issue special naturalizations; Sir George Carteret and John, Lord Berkeley, authorized the New Jersey assembly to do likewise.[85] Maryland used this method after 1666, and Virginia adopted it between 1671 and 1680.[86]

Colonial governors frequently issued patents of denization until the practice was banned in 1700. Royal instructions to Governor Richard Nicolls respecting the surrender of New Netherlands after the English conquest authorized him to give letters patent to those Dutchmen who "entirely submitt to Our Government," signifying by a "Publicqe Declaracon" that "Wee take them into Our Protection."[87] Later royal governors of New York exercised this power without the express consent of the crown. In the private colonies the lords proprietors generally did permit their lieutenants to endenize deserving foreigners, though their right to do so was questionable. The governors of Maryland issued patents in the name of the Calverts to more than fifty people between 1661 and 1675.[88]

New Amsterdam. The practices used in creating "citizens" generally followed procedures long established in England, though there were a few modifications. See generally Robert Francis Seybolt, *The Colonial Citizen of New York City: A Comparative Study of Certain Aspects of Citizenship Practice in Fourteenth-Century England and Colonial New York City* (Madison, Wis., 1918).

84. Grant to David Jochamse, Nov. 9, 1676. See also grants to Cornelius Jacobson and Matthias van der Heathen, Nov. 4, 1678, *Burghers of New Amsterdam*, 41–42.

85. For New York, see above, n. 69. For New Jersey, see Willard, *Naturalization in the American Colonies*, 13, and Hoyt, "Naturalization," *Pol. Sci. Qtly.*, LXVII (1952), 248n.

86. See, e.g., the act of Apr. 10, 1666, William Hand Browne *et al.*, eds., *Archives of Maryland* (Baltimore, 1883–   ), II, 144–145, hereafter cited as *Md. Archives*. The Virginia procedure was established Sept. 20, 1671. Hening, ed., *Statutes of Va.*, II, 289–290.

87. The instructions were quoted in a letter from Nicolls to the governor and council of Maryland, Jan. 24, 1664/1665. *Md. Archives*, XLIX, 388–392.

88. See, e.g., the denization of Augustine Herman, Jan. 14, 1660/1661. *Ibid.*, III, 398–399.

After 1680 Virginia combined the traditionally separate legislative and executive procedures when the House of Burgesses passed an act empowering the governor "by a publique instrument under the broad seale" of the colony to declare any alien "to be to all intents and purposes fully and completely naturalized."[89]

The Virginia act of 1680 is particularly noteworthy, for it was sent over from England with Thomas, Lord Culpeper, and presumably represents a model of local naturalization acceptable in London.[90] The act centered authority in the royal governor, who could be controlled from England more easily than the assembly. The act explicitly stated that the rights conveyed by naturalization were only local ones, being "of and unto" the laws and privileges "of this colony." Furthermore, the act expressly forbade any interpretation of its provisions that would extend privileges contrary to English laws concerning the plantations. The act thus dealt with issues of the scope of local authority and potential conflicts between colonial and imperial laws, issues that by the late seventeenth century were raising difficult legal and political questions involving both imperial and intercolonial relationships.

The first naturalization policies were developed in America without interference from England. Although the imperial government claimed the power to review colonial legislation and to prevent objectionable acts by instructions to royal governors, no systematic attention was paid to local laws until after 1660.[91] Indeed, the first major indication that London was aware of colonial naturalization practices is the Virginia act of 1680 described above. The absence of

89. Hening, ed., *Statutes of Va.*, II, 464–465. After 1728 settlers could take the oath locally instead of before the governor. This modification was designed for the convenience of settlers on the southern border of Virginia. *Ibid.*, V, 57–58. The same practice was instituted in Maryland in 1692 when Governor Lionel Copley arrived from England. Apparently, the act expired when Copley died in 1694, for special assembly acts resume that year. *Md. Archives*, XIII, 440–441, 424.

90. *Cal. State Papers, Col.*, X, 353, 452. Culpeper described the motive for the naturalization act as being "to invite persons to come to this place by makeing the Same as Ready and easy as possible" in his speech to the assembly on June 8, 1680. "Virginia Colonial Records. Culpeper's Administration," *VMHB*, XIV (1906–1907), 363. Passage by the House was accomplished easily. H. R. McIlwaine and John Pendleton Kennedy, eds., *Journals of the House of Burgesses of Virginia, 1619–1776* (Richmond, Va., 1905–1915), *1659/60–1693*, 120–126.

91. Elmer Beecher Russell, *The Review of American Colonial Legislation by the King in Council*, Columbia University Studies in History, Economics, and Public Law, No. 155 (New York, 1915), 18.

central direction from England undoubtedly contributed to the confused and uncertain character of the policies by which plantation officials admitted aliens to the rights of Englishmen in the seventeenth century.

English jurists had developed fairly fixed ideas about the distinctions between legislative naturalization and executive denization by the time serious colonization got underway, but even basic principles about the two modes of admission were sometimes blurred in the colonies. Colonial legislatures endenized and governors naturalized, reversing established English procedures, and at times the two kinds of grants appeared indistinguishable. Between 1665 and 1671 in Maryland, for example, six persons who had already obtained patents of denization later applied for and received acts of naturalization, although the texts of the grants were virtually identical.[92] Assemblies naturalized children born in America; however, by English law and explicit charter guarantees they should have been deemed natural-born subjects.[93]

Some of the complexity of colonial practices is illustrated by the case of Dr. George Hacke, a German-born immigrant who came with his Dutch wife, Anna, to Virginia in the early 1650s.[94] On March 28, 1653, the Northampton County Court declared "Dr. George Hacke Practitioner of Physic . . . to be a German," but in the July following he was granted four hundred acres of land in the county.[95] A patent of denization was issued to "George Hacke, Chirurgeon, being a German borne, now resident in the County of Northampton," on April 1, 1658, and the grant was confirmed and renewed to "himselfe, his Brother and Children" in March 1660/1661.[96] Between the original grant and its renewal, the doctor

92. See, e.g., Augustine Herman's denization (Jan. 14, 1660/1661), followed by his naturalization during the assembly session beginning Apr. 10, 1666. *Md. Archives*, III, 398–399, II, 144–145.

93. In 1671 Maryland passed an act naturalizing Cornelius Comegys and his family. Cornelius, Jr. (born in Virginia), and Elizabeth, William, and Hannah Comegys (all born in Maryland) were included in the act by name. *Md. Archives*, II, 319, 331–333. Peter Mills and his children (born or to be born) were endenized on Mar. 23, 1668/1669. Mills himself was naturalized in 1671, and his daughter Mary was granted letters of denization on July 12, 1672. *Ibid.*, V, 36–38, II, 282–283, V, 112.

94. "Tithables of Lancaster County, Va., 1654," *VMHB*, V (1897–1898), 256.

95. "Northampton County Records in 17th Century," *ibid.*, 37.

96. Hacke's patent was in the same form as that granted to William Westerhouse, quoted above at n. 62.

received an additional 1,350 acres in Northampton County for transporting twenty-seven persons to the colony.[97]

By 1663 Dr. Hacke had moved from Virginia to Maryland, perhaps to join his brother-in-law Augustine Herman, himself a recent immigrant to that colony.[98] On September 15 of that year, the Maryland assembly ordered that an "Acte of Naturalizacon be prepared for Augustine Herman, and his Children and his brother in lawe George Hack and his wife and children."[99] For some reason this act did not pass, and before a second attempt could be made, the doctor died. Nevertheless, by an act of April 1666, Maryland naturalized George's widow, Anna, and their two sons, George Nicholas and Peter.[100] Meanwhile, the Virginia legislature regranted one thousand acres in Northampton County to Dr. Hacke's widow and children, land "which he had patented, but which escheated at his death as he was an alien."[101]

The case points up some of the confusion that characterized colonial naturalization policies. Dr. Hacke was granted land by public authorities long before he was legally qualified to own real property.[102] The denization of 1658 and renewal of 1661 bestowed this right, of course, but Hacke was still deemed an alien at his death, and part of his property escheated. This could indicate a strict adherence to English law: denizens could own land, but their children could not inherit from them, even if they were included in the patent (as Hacke's children were). Yet Hacke's denization had given him the power to "hold and dispose of Lands . . . in as full and ample manner to all intents and purposes as if he had been an Englishman born," and apparently only part of his property had to be regranted.[103]

97. "Land Certificates for Northampton County," *VMHB*, XXVIII (1920–1921), 148.

98. Herman was appointed by Peter Stuyvesant to deal with Governor Josias Fendall of Maryland on the problems of absconding debtors and runaway servants in 1659. *Md. Archives*, III, 366–369. He apparently left Delaware for Maryland shortly thereafter, for he was endenized in the latter on Jan. 14, 1660/1661.

99. *Ibid.*, I, 461–462.

100. *Ibid.*, II, 144–145.

101. "Tithables of Lancaster County," *VMHB*, V (1897–1898), 257; O. A. Keach, "The Hack Family," *Tyler's Quarterly Historical and Genealogical Magazine*, VII (1925–1926), 253.

102. Hacke apparently owned land in Maryland as well, for he sold 400 acres "called Anne Cattrins Weeke" to Abraham Morgan on Sept. 18, 1660. This was before the confirmation of his Virginia denization. *Md. Archives*, XLI, 492.

103. See above, n. 96 and text at n. 62.

It has been argued that the Maryland naturalization operated as a form of expatriation and that the privileges granted in Virginia were annulled when the family was accepted in the neighboring colony.[104] This could not explain Dr. Hacke's "alien" status, however, for he died before the Maryland naturalization was completed. Anna Hacke had never been explicitly included in the Virginia denizations, yet both she and her children were obviously considered capable of holding land, for they received the regrant in 1666. As for the sons, both had been born at Accomack, Virginia, and their inclusion in the Virginia denization and the Maryland naturalization was legally unnecessary.

Confusion about the jurisdiction of the colonial governments and the extent of the rights they could grant also appeared in controversies involving England's navigation acts. The ban on alien participation in colonial shipping was the starting point for several intercolonial conflicts. In 1664 Maryland officials seized the sloop *Red Sterne*, commanded by Jacob Backer, a Dutchman who had been made a denizen by the governor of New York after the conquest of New Netherlands. It was argued that Backer was not an English subject and that his ship, therefore, was liable to seizure and condemnation as an illegal trader. The court finally dismissed the case, but only after an exchange of letters with Governor Nicolls, who upheld the legitimacy and efficacy of Backer's denization. Veiled threats regarding Maryland's own dubious record of compliance with the navigation acts and the possible consequences if Nicolls were to bring this lapse to the attention of the English authorities probably influenced this decision.[105]

104. Frank George Franklin, *The Legislative History of Naturalization in the United States, from the Revolutionary War to 1861* (Chicago, 1906), 17. Franklin erred in thinking that the initial bill of 1663 was successful. But the privileges of both denization and naturalization could be lost in the colonies. Andrew Dupuy petitioned Governor Cornbury for "redenization, having lost, by shipwreck, his denization papers." Entry of Oct. 15, 1703, E. B. O'Callaghan, ed., *Calendar of Historical Manuscripts in the Office of the Secretary of State, Albany, N.Y.* (Albany, N.Y., 1865–1866), II, 317, hereafter cited as *Cal. Hist. MSS, N.Y.* In this case, the physical loss of the patent meant that Dupuy had no proof of his claim to rights. As late as 1737 a New York act naturalizing Johannes Carstens provided that he would lose his status if he "Shall Afterwards Remove himself and Family out of this Colony, and Continue out of the Same, for the Space of one year at any one time." *Col. Laws, N.Y.*, II, 945–946.

105. *Md. Archives*, XLIX, xxii, 388–392. While the case against Backer was in progress, the attorney general filed an information against six prominent Marylanders for illegally trading with the Dutch. Included in the charge was Alexander D'hinoyossa, the last Dutch governor of the Delaware settlements, now resident in Maryland, and soon to be naturalized

The Backer case, as far as can be judged, did not reach the attention of London, but similar cases did. In 1682 Governor William Stapleton of Nevis seized a ship belonging to Henry Brunett, who had been naturalized by Lord Culpeper in Virginia. The Lords of Trade asked Chief Justice Francis North's opinion on the legality of the seizure, specifically desiring to know whether a naturalization under the Virginia act of 1680 made one an "Englishman" within the meaning of the Navigation Act of 1660 (12 Car. II, c. 18). North replied that a colonial grant could convey local privileges only and that the seizure was therefore valid.[106] This position came to be generally accepted in London, although many of the colonies continued to phrase their acts in broad terms well into the eighteenth century.

More important than either of the cases above in its effects upon colonial practices was the controversy involving Arnold Nodine, a Frenchman who had received a patent of denization from Governor Benjamin Fletcher of New York in 1697.[107] According to the Lords of Trade, writing to Fletcher's successor, Nodine's ship had been seized in Maryland as an illegal trader, but the charge was dismissed on the grounds that his patent of denization had been phrased "in such extensive terms" that "he was adjudged there to be qualified to trade as an Englishman."[108] The case made its way from the Maryland courts (via the customs commissioners, the Treasury, and the Lords Justices) to the Lords of Trade. There it only compounded

---

there (1671). This case was dropped shortly after the dismissal of the Backer case. *Ibid.*, 299, 341–342, II, 282–283 (for D'hinoyossa's naturalization).

106. *Cal. State Papers, Col.*, XI, 198, 211, 243, 250, 258, 346. England's policy was far from consistent. On May 19, 1691, the Treasury Lords ordered customs officials not to collect aliens' duties from Dutch New Yorkers, being "of opinion that they [the Dutch] should have the like privilege in point of duties with their Majesties' natural born subjects and should pay no other or greater duties than if they were natives of New York." William A. Shaw, ed., *Calendar of Treasury Books . . . Preserved in the Public Record Office* (London, 1904–1957), IX, Pt. vii, 1159. A South Carolina Huguenot endenized in England won his case when he appealed the seizure of his ship to England. Hirsch, *Huguenots of Colonial S.C.*, 122–123.

107. Baird, *Huguenot Emigration*, II, 35n, notes that Nodine was naturalized [actually, endenized] twice in England before obtaining his third grant from Fletcher. Elias Naudin and his children (Arnauld, Mary, and Elye) received the first patent on Mar. 8, 1681/1682. Elias apparently died in England. His widow married Jacob Ratier, and they were endenized with "Arnald Naudin" on May 8, 1697. They came that year to New York, where Arnold was granted his third denization, Nov. 12, 1697. For the English grants, see Shaw, ed., *Denization and Naturalization, 1603–1700*, 151, 249.

108. Lords of Trade to earl of Bellomont, Jan. 5, 1698/1699, *N.Y. Col. Docs.*, IV, 454. See also *Md. Archives*, XXIII, 418–420.

Fletcher's troubles. Nodine's denization already formed one of the "heads of complaints" against the governor, for it was charged that he had acted without authority and against the acts of trade. Fletcher defended his actions as a necessary concession to the need of the American plantations "for an increase of settlers" and argued that he was following the example set by his predecessors. In fact, he thought that he deserved commendation for ruling that the standard five-pound fees not be taken from "the poor French Protestants."[109]

London rejected Fletcher's arguments. The Lords of Trade could not agree that "Governor Fletcher or any other Governor in America had or have any authority by their commissions to endenize foreigners; and though in some cases this power has been conferred on Governors by their Assemblies, yet it has been so limited as not to extend to any advantage to any persons denized beyond the bounds of the Government where the grant was made." The letters of denization granted by Fletcher were "not only grounded on no authority, but of most pernicious consequence and directly contrary to the intent of the Acts of Trade."[110]

The Nodine case led to an order-in-council explicitly restricting colonial authority; issued on January 18, 1699/1700, the order forbade governors to issue letters of denization unless "expressly authorized to do so by their commissions." The matter of imperial trade was specifically resolved in the declaration that "no Act of denization or naturalization in any of the Plantations will qualify any person to be Master of a ship within any of the statutes made in this Kingdom, which require masters of ships to be Englishmen."[111]

The order-in-council of 1700 effectively halted the practice of colonial denization and virtually settled the question of the extensiveness of local naturalizations. Although assembly acts might still purport to transform aliens into "his Majesties subjects," the phrase was now more often qualified by the addition of "within this

109. Fletcher to Lords of Trade, Dec. 24, 1698, *N.Y. Col. Docs.*, IV, 450. Bellomont cast doubt on this claim of self-restraint, *ibid.*, 520–521. Fletcher was at least correct in alleging that his predecessors had granted numerous denizations. See, e.g., *Cal. Hist. MSS, N.Y.*, II, 143–147.

110. Lords of Trade to the Lords Justices, Oct. 27, 1698, *Cal. State Papers, Col.*, XVI, 510–511.

111. *Ibid.*, XVIII, 34; Leonard Woods Labaree, ed., *Royal Instructions to the British Colonial Governors, 1670–1776* (New York, 1935), I, 84.

colony."[112] Crown lawyers certainly assumed this local efficacy only, and when in 1736 the Board of Trade raised the question "whether a foreigner naturalized by an Act of Assembly in any of the plantations, can thereby claim the priviledges of natural born subjects in this kingdom," the secretary referred it to an opinion of 1703 denying such a right as authoritative.[113] Aliens naturalized in a particular colony were henceforth considered Englishmen only in that province. They retained their alien status elsewhere.

The order-in-council of 1700 was an explicit statement of a policy that had sometimes been acknowledged by the colonists themselves. Jacob Peterson had "obtained a Free Denization under the Seale" of Maryland on November 2, 1677; yet after removing to North Carolina and living there seventeen years, he felt the need to petition the governor and council there for "the Life Liberty and Priviledge as His Majestys Subjects of Maryland hath donne and to signify the Same under the Seale of this province, etc."[114] Dr. Hacke had also sought grants from two colonies, and neither Maryland nor Virginia seemed to recognize the status conferred by the other's authority in that case. Prior to 1700, however, the extraterritorial effects of specific admissions had been uncertain. Virginia considered a patent of denization given by King James to Jacob Coutanceau "better than anything they could give" to his son, but South Carolina's attorney general "questioned the Kings Authority of Denizeing" in the colonies.[115] The Carolina proprietors encour-

112. Compare, e.g., the New York naturalization acts of July 6, 1723, and July 24, 1724. The latter was the first in this colony to add the qualifying clause. *Col. Laws N.Y.*, II, 164–167, 240–242. The texts of the Maryland acts vary, but the phrase, "within this province," appears regularly from the 1720s on.

113. *Journals of the Commissioners for Trade and Plantations . . . Preserved in the Public Record Office . . .* (London, 1920–1938), *Jan. 1734/35–Dec. 1741*, 92. The secretary referred to an opinion of 1702/1703 by Attorney General Northey. Northey commented on an act of the Leeward Islands naturalizing Col. Walter Hamilton of Nevis, advising the Board that the effect of the act would be to make Hamilton a natural-born subject only there, that it would not allow him to claim the rights of a natural-born subject in England. *Cal. State Papers, Col.*, XXI, 251.

114. Undated petition. "From Court Records of Albemarle County at Edenton, N.C.," *North Carolina Historical and Genealogical Register*, III (1903), 143. Peterson's will was dated Jan. 13, 1696/1697, and was probated July 1698. J. Bryan Grimes, comp., *Abstract of North Carolina Wills* (Raleigh, N.C., 1910), 285.

115. Entry dated Oct. 1669, "Some Extracts from Northumberland County Records," *WMQ*, 1st Ser., XXI (1912), 100–101; A. S. Salley, Jr., ed., *Records in the British Public Record Office Relating to South Carolina* (Atlanta, Ga., and Columbia, S.C., 1928–1947), III, 166. Coutanceau's denization is listed in Shaw, ed., *Denization and Naturalization, 1603–1700*, 47.

aged Governor John Archdale to naturalize the Huguenots in the province, "both because it's as valid as if it were done here [in London] and much more Difficult to Obtaine it here."[116] It is likely that aliens removing from one colony to another sought the security of multiple local grants; those who merely engaged in intercolonial trade from a fixed base probably found one grant enough.[117]

At almost the same time that denization in the colonies was banned, the government in London moved to block indiscriminate group naturalizations. In November 1700 the Pennsylvania assembly passed an act empowering "the proprietary and governor and his heirs, or his or their lieutenant and governor for the time being, by a public instrument under his or their broad seal," to naturalize aliens, thereby establishing a mode of executive naturalization similar to that approved in Virginia in 1680. The third section of the act provided that all "Swedes, Dutch, and other foreigners" settled in the territory prior to Penn's charter "shall be deemed and by this act are declared to be fully and completely naturalized."[118] Objections to the act arose in London, and upon the recommendation of the attorney general—who observed that the proprietor had no power by his charter to naturalize and referred especially to the provisions for admitting the Swedes and the Dutch—the law was repealed by an order-in-council on February 7, 1705/1706.[119]

Only one similar group naturalization can be found after 1700, and its validity was upheld only because of extenuating circumstances. German Palatines immigrated to New York in large numbers during the first decade of the century, when there was pressure

116. Lords Proprietors to Archdale, Sept. 10, 1696, Salley, Jr., ed., *Recs. Rel. S.C.*, III, 177.

117. Colonial grants should not have been enough to qualify aliens under the navigation acts in any case, though local denizations seem sometimes to have sufficed for this purpose. See above, n. 106.

118. James T. Mitchell and Henry Flanders, eds., *Statutes at Large of Pennsylvania from 1682 to 1801* (Harrisburg, Pa., 1896–1911), II, 29–31, hereafter cited as *Pa. Statutes*.

119. *Ibid.*, App. I, sec. ii, 492. The act apparently remained in force in Delaware. The first separate Delaware assembly met Nov. 1704, and it immediately continued all acts then in force. This apparently included the naturalization statute (not yet annulled in England), for an act was passed to "supplement" it in 1788. *Laws of the State of Delaware, from the Fourteenth Day of October, One Thousand Seven Hundred, to the Eighteenth Day of August, One Thousand Seven Hundred and Ninety-Seven* (New-Castle, Del., 1797), I, 52–54, II, 921–923. See also Richard S. Rodney, "Early Relations of Delaware and Pennsylvania," *Pennsylvania Magazine of History and Biography*, LIV (1930), 238–240, and Walter A. Powell, *A History of Delaware* (Boston, 1928), 94–95.

to naturalize the newcomers as well as to regularize land titles.[120] Internal political conflicts between the executive and the assembly blocked initial efforts to meet these needs. The assembly entertained a bill in 1710, but then allowed it to drop. When Governor Robert Hunter reminded the legislators that it was royal policy to show favor to the Palatines by naturalizing the newcomers without fee, they declined to revive the bill—probably, according to Hunter, because the action was now recommended.[121] The governor considered bypassing the assembly by issuing patents of denization to the Palatines, but when he found letters to his predecessor, Governor Bellomont, prohibiting the practice, he could only request further instructions from London.[122]

By 1713 the situation was reversed. Now the assembly was pressing for a bill, and Hunter adamantly refused his assent. The governor cited the shift in policy in England, exemplified by the repeal there of the general naturalization act of 1709. He now "judged it advisable and for her Majesty's service" to veto the New York bill.[123]

On July 5, 1715, a general naturalization and land titles bill finally passed the assembly and received the governor's assent. The law naturalized many aliens by fiat while establishing enrollment procedures for others.[124] Hunter would have preferred that the act have included a clause suspending its operation until "his Majesty's pleasure be known," but he feared that the assembly planned to use such a veto as the excuse for refusing financial support for Hunter's administration for yet another year.[125] After negotiations with legislative leaders, the governor agreed not to insist on the suspending clause in return for the grant of a five-year revenue. By concluding this bargain, Hunter thought that he had "laid a foundation for

120. For an account of the act and of the Palatine experience generally, see Knittle, *Palatine Emigration*, 212–215, and chaps. 5–7.
121. Hunter to Lords of Trade, Nov. 28, 1710, *N.Y. Col. Docs.*, V, 183–186.
122. Hunter to Lords of Trade, May 7, 1711, *Cal. State Papers, Col.*, XXV, 485.
123. Hunter to Lords of Trade, Mar. 14, 1712/1713, *N.Y. Col. Docs.*, V, 356–358.
124. The act declared that all aliens resident in New York before the act of 1683 (above, n. 69), whether still living or since deceased, should be deemed to have been naturalized (thus confirming their land titles). Foreigners arriving after 1683 and since deceased were included, and those now living could be naturalized by taking the usual oaths in any court of record within nine months. *Col. Laws N.Y.*, I, 858–863. A list of 125 persons who qualified themselves under this law in the Mayor's Court of New York City is given in "The Oath of Abjuration, 1715–1716," *New-York Historical Society Quarterly Bulletin*, III (1919), 35–40.
125. Hunter to Lords of Trade, May 21, 1715, *N.Y. Col. Docs.*, V, 402–405.

a lasting settlement on this hitherto unsettled and ungovernable Province."[126] The act was transmitted to London for a final decision.

The New York naturalization act stood despite the objections raised by Attorney General Edward Northey, who condemned the clauses retrospectively naturalizing foreigners as bad law and prejudicial to the interests of the crown. Northey contended that the earlier New York act of 1683 had provided a mechanism for obtaining special acts of naturalization; if aliens had been negligent in applying under the terms of that act, it was their own fault. Their lands should remain liable to forfeiture to the crown. It "would be a great goodness in his Majesty," suggested Northey, "to depart with the advantage that may accrue to him" and to confirm titles that his subjects had acquired from persons not naturalized. The king might also "direct that purchases made by such Aliens as shall be thought fit to be naturalized, should be confirmed by letters patent under the Seal of that Colony." But Northey did not think it wise or proper to "naturalize in the lump all Foreign protestants within that Colony, for that in Naturalizations the particular circumstances of the persons naturalized should be considered."[127] Northey was overruled, but his recommendations may nevertheless have had an effect on subsequent colonial practices. The New York act of 1715 was the last indiscriminate group naturalization of the colonial period.

The decisions made early in the eighteenth century helped standardize American naturalization procedures; the methods and limits of colonial grants now seemed fairly clear. Most colonies admitted foreigners by special acts in which the persons benefited were mentioned by name. Virginia, Delaware, and (for a time) Maryland put the administration of the procedure in the hands of the governor, although his power ultimately derived from the local assembly and was not seen as the analogue of the king's prerogative right to make denizens.[128] New York naturalized at least 135 foreigners by

126. Hunter to Lords of Trade, July 25, 1715, *ibid.*, 416–418.
127. Attorney General Edward Northey to Lords of Trade, Jan. 2, 1717/1718, *ibid.*, V, 495–497.
128. Virginia had used this method since the enabling act of 1680 (above, n. 90). Delaware established the procedure in 1700 (above, n. 119), but records of its use "are unfortunately not known to exist." Hoyt, "Naturalization," *Pol. Sci. Qtly.*, LXVII (1952), 251n. Maryland adopted the procedure briefly after 1692 (above, n. 89), and an act of 1735 again empowered the governor to issue public instruments naturalizing foreigners. The act ex-

special acts before 1740; Maryland admitted over 83; and Pennsylvania incorporated over 552 in the same period.[129] New Jersey passed special naturalization acts throughout the century, and North Carolina apparently did likewise.[130] South Carolina permitted naturalization by enrollment after 1704, with the justices of the peace certifying that the required oaths had been taken.[131]

In New England naturalization remained a minor part of public policy, for these colonies did little to attract non-English immigration.[132] Massachusetts admitted a number of French Protestants in 1731 and established a general procedure available to others. But the statute does not appear to have been used after 1732.[133] Connecticut passed no laws on the matter until the 1770s; Rhode Island adopted about twenty aliens by private act after 1750.[134] New Hampshire alone failed to legislate at all in this area, although some aliens settled there and perhaps were locally accepted as fellow subjects.[135]

pired after three years, and repeated attempts to revive it failed because of contentions between the two houses. *Md. Archives*, XXIX, 287–288, XL, 154–155, and *passim*.

129. These figures are all approximate. Hoyt, "Naturalization," *Pol. Sci. Qtly.*, LXVII (1952), 248–250, gives other figures. For a partial list for Maryland, see "Early Maryland Naturalizations, Etc., from Kilty's Laws," in Gaius Marcus Brumbaugh, ed., *Maryland Records: Colonial, Revolutionary, County and Church from Original Sources*, II (Lancaster, Pa., 1928), 311–313.

130. John R. Stevenson, "Persons Naturalized in New Jersey between 1702 and 1776," *New York Genealogical and Biographical Record*, XXVIII (1897), 86–89, is incomplete. Other acts can be found in the New Jersey Historical Records Survey Program, *Guide to Naturalization Records in New Jersey* (Newark, N.J., 1941), and in the *N.J. Archives*, 1st Ser. N.C. *Col. Recs.*, II, 463, lists a special act of naturalization (Council Journal, entry of Oct. 29, 1722), and it is possible that the procedure was used throughout the century. However, "no significant figures are available as to the total number of acts." Hoyt, "Naturalization," *Pol. Sci. Qtly.*, LXVII (1952), 250n.

131. *S.C. Statutes*, II, 251–253. Such persons were not qualified to be elected to the assembly, but they could vote if they were over 21 and could meet the other property and residence requirements.

132. See generally Proper, *Colonial Immigration Laws*, chap. 4.

133. *The Acts and Resolves, Public and Private, of the Province of Massachusetts Bay* . . . (Boston, 1869–1922), II, 586–587. Willard, *Naturalization in the American Colonies*, 22, suggests that the law may have been disallowed or may have died "an untimely death," for he sees no use of it after 1732.

134. Connecticut received and distributed among the towns a large number of "French neutrals" from Nova Scotia by an act of 1756, but it is not clear whether these people were naturalized. *Conn. Col. Recs.*, X, 452–453. Several special acts of naturalization were passed in the 1770s, after the king had forbidden the practice. *Ibid.*, XIX, 94, 309–310; see below, n. 155. For Rhode Island, see generally Rider, *Denization and Naturalization in R.I.*, 10–11; Samuel G. Arnold, *History of the State of Rhode Island and Providence Plantations* . . . , II (New York, 1860), 494–495; and Hoyt, "Naturalization," *Pol. Sci. Qtly.*, LXVII (1952), 249.

135. *Ibid.*, 248, 251. Bolton, "Immigrants to New England," Essex Inst., *Hist. Colls.*,

The most unusual procedure for adopting foreigners occurred in the new colony of Georgia. The charter granted to the Trustees in 1732 did not explicitly mention naturalization.[136] Nevertheless, in negotiating with the Society for the Propagation of Christian Knowledge for settling a group of "persecuted Saltzburghers" in the colony, the Trustees promised that the Germans "shall become Denizens, and have all the Rights and Priviledges of Englishmen."[137] The negotiations were made with the king's knowledge and approval, but the actual admission of the immigrants was neither by his denization nor by any act of Parliament.[138] Rather the refugees were apparently taken into the king's allegiance in a ceremony reminiscent of feudal rites of homage.

Martin Bolzius and Israel Gronau, pastors to the first group of Lutheran Salzburgers settling in Georgia, described the ceremony in their travel diary:

On December 21st [1733], on which day our Saltzburgers were bound by oath and had to promise with hand and mouth to be subject to the English government, their present authority, and, as subjects, to show obedience in their enjoyment of the rights and freedoms of the land. On this occasion the following ceremony took place: There appeared before us Captain [Thomas] Coram, deputy for the Trustees, and also the captain of our ship [Tobias Fry] and an English merchant [William Sale]. In their presence Commissioner [Philip Georg Friedrich] von Reck [who led the first group of emigrants] gave a brief address in which he praised the good deeds done for the Saltzburgers and urged upon them gratitude to God and to their benefactors. After they had promised obedience with a loud *yes*, a proclamation, written in German, was read to them in the name of the Trustees, which told them about the freedom and privileges they were to enjoy in this land and also about their duties. Hereafter the names of the Saltzburg-

---

LXIII–LXVII (1927–1931), lists a number of non-English immigrants who settled in New Hampshire. See, e.g., the entry for William Blazo, *ibid.*, LXIII, 191.

136. Thorpe, ed. and comp., *Constitutions, Charters, and Laws,* II, 773.

137. Trustees' Journal entry, Oct. 12, 1732, Allen D. Candler, comp., *The Colonial Records of the State of Georgia* (Atlanta, Ga., 1904–1916), I, 79, hereafter cited as *Col. Recs. Ga.*

138. Henry Newman to Samuel Urlsperger, London, Oct. 13, 1732, and July 3, 1733, George Fenwick Jones, ed., *Henry Newman's Salzburger Letterbooks* (Athens, Ga., [1966]), 29, 47. I have found none of the Salzburgers in Shaw's lists of persons naturalized and endenized in England, nor do the colony's published records contain references to grants by the Trustees, the royal governors, or the assembly. A unique act of Mar. 25, 1765, authorized the naturalization of "all Persons male and Female of what Nation or Color soever being born of free parents," aiming specifically to encourage the immigration of "Mulattoes or Mestizo's [*sic*]"; but I have seen no evidence that this authority was ever used. *Col. Recs. Ga.*, XVIII, 659.

ers were written on the bottom of the proclamation. Then the Saltzburgers had to touch the paper and were asked whether they meant to honor all
of this. They confirmed it with a yes and then shook the deputy's hand.[139]

Just what effect this ceremony had in law is uncertain, but it
seemed sufficient to protect the Salzburgers' rights. Bolzius reported to a correspondent in Augsburg in 1751 that the immigrants
enjoyed full equality. Asked whether "a Protestant stranger, from
whatever nation he may be, may hold public office in the government, or whether that kind of prerogative is enjoyed preferably by
the citizens," the pastor replied: "I have never yet noticed that a
discrimination was made against nationals who had sworn allegiance to the King of England; indeed I know that there is in the
secret council at Charlestown a Frenchman and a Dutchman. . . .
The deputies to Parliament in Charlestown and in Georgia are not
only English men, but also Frenchmen and Germans, provided
they know the English language."[140] To the question whether an
immigrant who "has lived for a certain time in America, owns
property there, and afterwards turned to England and settled there"
could enjoy rights in the mother country, Bolzius answered that
such a person "also is, in America and England, an English subject
at all times, and enjoys all the privileges of the kingdom like a native
Englishman."[141]

Pastor Bolzius may have erred in thinking that the status enjoyed
within the colony held good throughout the British dominions—
his reply certainly conflicts with the law stated in the order-in-
council of 1700—but he was probably right in reporting the local
situation. A suffrage law passed in Georgia in 1761 permitted
"every free White Man and no other who has attained to the Age of
Twenty One Years and hath been Resident in the Province Six
Months and is legally possessed in his own Right of Fifty Acres of

139. George Fenwick Jones, ed., *Detailed Reports on the Salzburger Emigrants Who Settled
in America*, trans. Hermann J. Lacher, I (Athens, Ga., 1968), 35–36; see also Jones, ed.,
Salzburger Letterbooks, 365–366, 408–409.
140. Klaus G. Loewald *et al.*, eds. and trans., "Johann Martin Bolzius Answers a Ques-
tionnaire on Carolina and Georgia," *WMQ*, 3d Ser., XIV (1957), 254. Bolzius thought the
existing status of persons still technically aliens by English law so satisfactory that he
refused "to approve the recent request of a German jeweler in Charlestown, Joh. Paul
Grimke, for a testimonial from me that he had received Holy Communion from my
colleague in Charlestown and was therefore a Protestant, so as to enable him to be naturalized. The Englishman with whom I talked about it could not accept the idea either." *Ibid.*,
255.
141. *Ibid.*

Land" to vote in local elections. Only free-born subjects or naturalized Christians could hold office, however. It is not clear whether aliens incorporated by the moving shipboard ceremony were included or excluded by this requirement.[142]

In the eyes of English officials, all colonial acts making aliens subjects were purely local "fictions," limited in their effect to the specific province concerned. The parliamentary act of 1740 discussed above, however, validated an alternative admission procedure to be administered in the colonies that made it possible for aliens to acquire a subject status good throughout the empire.[143] In essence, Parliament had delegated its authority to bring strangers into the community of allegiance to the local courts, maintaining only a loose supervisory function by requiring that the names of those adopted as subjects be sent yearly to the Board of Trade.

Lists in the British Public Record Office show that at least 6,911 persons in the mainland colonies were given subjectship under this statute between 1740 and 1773, almost 92 percent of them in Pennsylvania.[144] A number of Jews gained rights in this manner, including some who already had been admitted to local privileges. One Jewish merchant from New York sought the benefits of the act even though he claimed to have been born in the colonies.[145] A few of the American governments apparently neglected or refused to administer the act, for some colonial secretaries never returned lists to London. Yet the procedure was still available to all alien immigrants. One merely had to travel to a neighboring colony where the act was administered—admission in one province was effective in all others.[146]

Although the parliamentary procedure was both inexpensive and convenient, the colonial assemblies continued to pass their own acts

142. Act of June 9, 1761, *Col. Recs. Ga.*, XVIII, 464–472.

143. Above, at n. 35.

144. Giuseppi, ed., *Naturalizations*, table, xii, corrected to exclude admissions in Jamaica. More than one-third of the Pennsylvania admissions were at one session of the Superior Court, Sept. 24–Oct. 26, 1765. Chilton Williamson, *American Suffrage from Property to Democracy, 1760–1860* (Princeton, N.J., 1960), 52, suggests that the wave of naturalizations was probably related to the elections of that year.

145. Isaac Levy claimed to have been born in New York, but after his removal to London in 1752, he was naturalized under the 1740 statute (Nov. 14, 1752). Herbert Friedenwald, "Isaac Levy's Claim to Property in Georgia," Am. Jewish Hist. Soc., *Pubs.*, No. 9 (1901), 57.

146. Giuseppi, ed., *Naturalizations*, xiii, gives a table of residents of one colony naturalized in another.

until the practice was prohibited in 1773.[147] It is easy to understand why a man might seek qualification under the English act though already naturalized locally, as did Colonel Henry Bouquet in 1765.[148] The persistence of purely local admission is more difficult to explain. Fees for naturalization under colonial acts were often considerably higher than the maximum two shillings charged under the parliamentary statute of 1740; moreover, the imperial status available under the English statute should have been more attractive than the limited privileges conferred locally. Perhaps the seven-year residence requirement established by Parliament discouraged some alien settlers.[149] Whatever the reason, foreign immigrants still sought grants from the colonial governments.[150]

The propriety of continuing to allow local naturalization acts was questioned in London in light of Parliament's authorized admission procedure.[151] In 1764, Attorney General Fletcher Norton expressed the opinion that unless aliens were naturalized under the act of 1740, they could have no right to acquire and hold lands.[152] Six years later the Board of Trade discussed with Richard Jackson, king's counsel, "whether the naturalization of foreigners by Acts of Assembly of New York . . . is consonant to the laws of this Kingdom," and the Board agreed to refer a "case and question thereupon" to the attorney and solicitor generals.[153]

147. The rough figures for local and locally administered parliamentary naturalizations are, respectively, 5 and 127 for Maryland; 855 and 324 for New York; and 20 and 6,406 for Pennsylvania. Only these colonies and Massachusetts (1), South Carolina (24), and Virginia (24) reported names to London, though the 1740 procedure may have been used in other colonies as well. Even the lists from the colonies reporting admissions are incomplete. Willard, *Naturalization in the American Colonies*, 9–10, e.g., gives the names of three persons admitted in Massachusetts not listed by Giuseppi. The figures decline rapidly after 1765, and the last reported lists are from 1773.
148. Bouquet was naturalized by Maryland on Apr. 22, 1762. *Md. Archives*, LVIII, 206–207. He qualified under the parliamentary act in Pennsylvania, Apr. 10, 1765. Giuseppi, ed., *Naturalizations*, 98.
149. See the comments of Daniel Dulany, discussed below, chap. 5, at n. 59.
150. On Sept. 24, 1767, William Hemble and Lewis Farmer petitioned the Pennsylvania assembly for admission. Farmer was given leave to bring in a bill on Jan. 9, 1769, but "finding that the Circumstances of the said Hemble do not exclude him from Naturalization in the usual way by the Supreme Court," the assembly "referred him to the said Court." *Pa. Archives*, 8th Ser., VII, 6040, 6302. Hemble petitioned again and was finally naturalized by an act of Mar. 21, 1772. On May 19, 1773, this act was annulled in England. *Ibid.*, VIII, 6847, 7034–7036; *Pa. Statutes*, VIII, 257–259. Farmer qualified under the parliamentary statute on Apr. 11, 1771. Giuseppi, ed., *Naturalizations*, 156.
151. See, e.g., *Jour. of Comm. Trade, 1759–1763*, 345.
152. Opinion of July 27, 1764, Chalmers, *Opinions of Eminent Lawyers*, II, 365–366.
153. *Jour. of Comm. Trade, 1768–1775*, 194–197.

In February 1772 the issue of local naturalizations came up again when a Pennsylvania act naturalizing Peter Mierkin, a sugar refiner from Hamburg, was reviewed. Jackson expressed doubts about clauses in the act giving Mierkin trading rights that he thought might be repugnant to the navigation acts. Yet the legal issue was not clear:

And though I am humbly of opinion that the said act of Parliament [the navigation act 12 Car. II, c. 18] might probably mean to include a provincial naturalization, within the excepted cases, more especially as such naturalization, passing under the control of his Majesty in council seems at least equivalent to letters of denization, yet I cannot but remark that such determination seems more properly altogether left to the decision of a court of justice. I am, however, to remark to your Lordships that this clause is to be found in many acts of assembly confirmed by His Majesty, and does not exclude the power of the proper court to decide against it, and that [this and two other] laws appear to me to be in other respects proper in point of law.[154]

The English authorities finally banned local admissions in 1773. Naturalization acts from Pennsylvania (May 19) and New Jersey (September 1) were disallowed. On November 19 an order-in-council fixed the new policy, requiring that colonial governors be instructed not to assent to any more naturalization acts.[155] Although one or two acts were confirmed thereafter due to extenuating circumstances, the order was generally effective in blocking the further exercise of this power by the American assemblies.

The colonists reacted to the order-in-council with anger. In the context of a deepening imperial crisis, the denial of the right to determine the membership of the community appeared as another sinister stroke at the liberty and prosperity of Americans. A few short years later, the Declaration of Independence would include in its indictment of George III the charge that he had conspired "to prevent the population of these States; for that purpose obstructing the laws for the naturalization of foreigners."

154. *Pa. Statutes*, VIII, 116–117, App. XXIX, sec. i, 575–576.
155. Labaree, ed., *Royal Instructions*, I, 154–155. A Pennsylvania act of 1773 naturalizing six German Protestants was confirmed because it had passed before the order-in-council. *Pa. Statutes*, VIII, 337–338, App. XXI, sec. i, 613–615, 617–620. Connecticut passed several acts after the ban. *Conn. Col. Recs.*, XIV, 94, 309–310. On the other hand, at least three New Jersey acts were disallowed as contrary to the new policy. *N.J. Archives*, 1st Ser., XVIII, 371, 477; *Acts of Privy Council, Col.*, V, 379–381.

CHAPTER 5

Privileges and Problems:
The Significance of Colonial
Naturalization

The restrictive naturalization policies that had developed in England could not withstand the demands of the New World. Although the processes of admission and the details of legislation varied from colony to colony, common problems and pressures underscored the importance of attracting alien-born settlers to America. The desire for military security, the persistent need for labor, and the generally acknowledged benefits of population growth led the colonists to grant extensive inducements to foreign immigrants by way of naturalization.

The tendency toward generous naturalization policies was the outgrowth of preeminently practical concerns but resulted in systematic deviations from English patterns that carried significant theoretical implications. Despite intermittent resistance from the imperial authorities, the practices of the colonial governments increasingly obliterated the formal legal distinctions that still divided subjectship in English law. England's hierarchical ranking of natives, naturalized aliens, and denizens collapsed in America, and subjectship in the New World tended in practice to become a simplified and more uniform status. Emergent characteristics of naturalization could thus be easily extended to new perceptions about the attributes of subject status generally. The experience of the colonists in dealing with naturalization would ultimately provide both a base and a legitimization—evidence and proof—for seeing subjectship as a contractual, quid pro quo relationship in which the privileges of membership could be claimed as a right by the person who chose to contribute his efforts and talents to the welfare of the community.

Americans did not fully articulate new theories about the character and meaning of membership in the community until the imperial crisis of the 1760s. New assumptions and emergent attitudes are nevertheless apparent both in the substance of naturalization laws —that is, in the detailed rights and obligations involved in the admission process—and in the controversies that attended the creation and operation of those laws. When Americans clashed over such questions as eligibility for admission, the extent of the status granted, and the legal effects of naturalization—in short, when they confronted the privileges and problems resulting from the adoption of aliens into the community—they revealed some of the forces that were pushing them away from British conceptions and toward a new understanding of allegiance.

Americans frequently debated the issue of naturalization because it was a matter of general importance involving the interests of immigrants and native subjects alike. Alien settlers were understandably anxious to acquire the privileges of subjectship. Denization or naturalization was necessary if the foreigner was to gain security in his possession and enjoyment of real property. Moreover, subjectship was ordinarily the first (though not the only) step toward the acquisition of political rights.[1] But naturalization was not just a matter of concern for the newcomer. Natural-born subjects had much at stake in the ability of their governments to attract and to assimilate alien immigrants. A steady growth in population enhanced land values generally, and the use of land as a medium of exchange required that all titles be secure and easily transferable. The chronic labor shortage characteristic of the American economies meant that every new pair of willing hands was welcomed. Support for liberal naturalization laws thus was usually popular, a fact that many colonial politicians were quick to note.[2]

1. See generally Miller, "Legal Qualifications for Office," A.H.A., *Annual Report 1899*, I, 87–105.
2. See, e.g., governor's message to the assembly, May 16, 1742, *Col. Recs. Pa.*, IV, 542. Hirsch, *Huguenots of Colonial S.C.*, 103–105, discusses the political importance of the

There were occasional attempts to control immigration in order to exclude "undesirables," but a number of factors operated against truly restrictive practices. During the seventeenth century New England tried to discourage settlers who did not share the locally dominant religious views; yet success was elusive as long as the mother country itself disputed the propriety of the local orthodoxy.[3] Opposition from London also frustrated efforts to prevent the influx of indigents and others considered unfit. Rhode Island required shipmasters to post bond so that their immigrant passengers would not become burdens on the local community; New Haven forced importers to carry away any newcomers rejected by the towns; and other colonies tried tactics ranging from outright prohibition to discriminatory taxation in order to prevent the transportation of convicts and vagabonds to America. But for the most part, these laws were disallowed in England.[4]

From time to time the colonists exhibited attitudes reminiscent of English xenophobia. A bill submitted to the Connecticut assembly in 1713 would have levied special duties on strangers generally, and an "Act providing Relief against the evil and dangerous Designs of Foreigners and Suspected Persons" was specifically aimed against the Moravians.[5] French Huguenots in Rhode Island were harshly treated in the 1690s, and their compatriots in South Carolina were sometimes harassed by local officials.[6] New York's ultimate treatment of the first Palatine immigrants of 1709 proved so ungenerous that many moved away and advised their countrymen to shun the colony in the future.[7]

Pennsylvania attracted huge numbers of foreigners, especially Germans, in the eighteenth century.[8] Although the reception there

Huguenots. For the Germans, see Andreas Dorpalen, "The Political Influence of the German Element in Colonial America," *Pennsylvania History*, VI (1939), 147–158.

3. Proper, *Colonial Immigration Laws*, 17–18.

4. *Ibid.*, 35 (Rhode Island law of 1700, reenacted 1729), 33 (New Haven law of 1657), 20 (disallowance policy). See also Graham, *Colonists from Scotland*, 9–10.

5. The first bill failed; the second passed in May 1743 and was amended in Jan. 1756. *Conn. Col. Recs.*, V, 405–406, VII, 521, X, 450–451.

6. Above, chap. 4, nn. 75, 106.

7. Dorpalen, "Political Influence of the German Element," *Pa. Hist.*, VI (1939), 150; Knittle, *Palatine Emigration*, 199–212.

8. See, e.g., Israel Daniel Rupp, *A Collection of Upwards of Thirty Thousand Names of German, Swiss, Dutch, French, and Other Immigrants in Pennsylvania from 1727 to 1776 . . .*, 2d ed. rev. (Baltimore, 1965 [orig. publ. Philadelphia, 1876]).

was largely favorable, there were outbursts of antiforeign sentiment. In 1717, for example, Deputy Governor William Keith

> observ'd to the Board that great numbers of Foreigners from Germany,
> strangers to our Language and Constitutions, having lately been imported
> into this Province daily dispersed themselves immediately after Landing,
> without producing any Certificates, from whence they came or what they
> were; and as they seemed to have first Landed in Britain, and afterwards to
> have left it Without any License from the Government, or so much as their
> knowledge, so in the same manner they behaved here, without making the
> least application to himself or to any of the magistrates.

The governor and council feared that alien enemies might slip in
unnoticed and weaken the province from within. To prevent this
they ordered that in the future shipmasters must provide lists of all
passengers and that all newcomers must appear and publicly "take
such Oaths appointed by Law as are necessary to give assurances of
their being well affected to his Majesty and his Government."[9]

During the 1720s attempts to secure acts of naturalization for the
Pennsylvania Germans were received with indifference. A bill was
proposed in 1725 that would have required petitioners for naturalization to submit a certificate from a justice of the peace attesting to
the value of their property and to the nature of their religious
beliefs. The governor vetoed the measure, claiming that it was
"dangerous and unjust" to inquire into private faiths and estates.[10]
An act naturalizing a number of Palatines passed in 1730, but only
after a brief experiment with what has been called "the most comprehensive anti-immigration act ever passed in America."[11] The
short-lived act of 1729 had attempted to discourage the importation
of "lewd, idle and ill-affected persons" by imposing a forty-shilling
per capita tax on all alien immigrants and by charging importers of
Irish servants and redemptioners twenty shillings per person.[12]

For the most part, these policies reflected not so much a desire to
eliminate immigration as a wish to control its character and to
regulate its flow. At times a concern for public health and safety

9. Council Minutes, Sept. 17, 1717, *Col. Recs. Pa.*, III, 29.

10. William Thomas Johnson, "Some Aspects of the Relations of the Government and
German Settlers in Colonial Pennsylvania, 1683–1754," *Pa. Hist.*, XI (1944), 95.

11. *Ibid.* For the text of the 1730 act and the governor's message favoring naturalization,
see respectively *Pa. Statutes*, IV, 147–150, and *Col. Recs. Pa.*, III, 374–375. The characterization of the act is from Proper, *Colonial Immigration Laws*, 19.

12. The act was adopted May 10, 1729, and repealed Feb. 14, 1729/1730. *Pa. Statutes*,
IV, 135–140, 164–171.

dictated a restrictive policy; conditions on board the ships carrying persons to the colonies were often abysmal, and too often fever and disease heralded the arrival of the immigrant transports. Massachusetts had the health of newcomers and natives alike in mind in an act of 1751 "to regulate the importation of Germans and other passengers coming to settle in this Province." A series of quarantine measures enacted in Pennsylvania after 1754 also aimed at protecting both residents and immigrants.[13] Some legislators may have supported such policies out of a desire to restrict immigration generally, but most local authorities welcomed a controlled inward flow of foreign settlers.

Restrictive policies proved difficult to maintain. English officials frowned upon laws that attempted to prevent the transportation of convicts and paupers to the plantations, and pressure from London also weakened colonial laws barring or harassing Quakers and other undesirables.[14] Internal conditions fostered official leniency; the need for labor and the desire to increase land values by continued settlement and improvement encouraged favorable immigration legislation.[15] Furthermore, competition among the colonies promoted the development of liberal immigration and naturalization laws. As Lieutenant Governor Cadwallader Colden of New York noted in 1761, "Should we in this Province refuse such acts of naturalization, which can easily be obtained in the neighbouring colonies, it would draw all foreigners, who are willing to settle and improve lands, from this Colony to the others."[16]

Despite occasional restrictive acts, then, the majority of colonial policies encouraged foreign immigration. Inducements varied, but in general the local governments tried to mitigate the disabilities of alienage and to facilitate the process of admission. Both public and private promoters stressed the advantages of the New World and offered attractive conditions for settlement.

13. *Acts and Resolves, Mass. Bay*, III, 536–537. *Col. Recs. Pa.*, VI, 169, 170–173, 226, 344–351, and *passim*; *Pa. Statutes*, VI, 432–440. See also Frank Ried Diffenderffer, *The German Immigration into Pennsylvania Through the Port of Philadelphia, 1700 to 1775*, II (Lancaster, Pa., 1900), 78–89.

14. See generally Richard Hofstadter, *America at 1750: A Social Portrait* (New York, 1971), 46–49, 208–209, and Abbot Emerson Smith, *Colonists in Bondage: White Servitude and Convict Labor in America, 1607–1776* (Chapel Hill, N.C., 1947), 120–122.

15. See, e.g., Deputy Governor George Thomas's message to the assembly, Jan. 5, 1741/1742, *Col. Recs. Pa.*, IV, 508.

16. Lieutenant Governor Colden to the Board of Trade, New York, Sept. 25, 1761, *N.Y. Col. Docs.*, VII, 469–470.

Although the New England colonies preferred immigration from the British Isles, their policies also involved some relaxation of traditional alien disabilities. Massachusetts guaranteed to "every person within this Jurisdiction, whether Inhabitant or forreiner, . . . the same justice and law, that is generall for the plantation," and aliens were even allowed in town meetings to "move any lawfull, seasonable, and materiall question, or to present any necessary motion, complaint, petition, Bill or information, . . . so it be done in convenient time, due order, and respective manner."[17] A special oath sufficed to insure the obedience of "divers strangers of foreign parts [who] do repaire to us of whose fidelity we have not that Assurance which is Commonly required of all Governments."[18] Rhode Island, too, provided that "all men of what nation soever they bee" who were received as inhabitants by the towns "shall have equall libertie to buy, sell, or trade amongst us as well as any Englishman, any lawe or order to the contrary notwithstandinge."[19]

Outside New England the invitations to foreigners were more open and official. Even though its relations with the Palatines quickly deteriorated, the New York government initially worked with imperial authorities to sponsor the German immigration. Pennsylvania carried out extensive publicity campaigns on the Continent, and the land agents, or *Neuländer*, often tried to suppress negative reports about the colonies that might inhibit further migrations.[20] Swiss emigrants heading for Virginia went on condition that "they may be treated and regarded as the subjects of your Majesty."[21] In the Carolinas the proprietors forswore their right to escheats, guaranteeing the descent of lands acquired by aliens to their heirs or to assignees on payment of the usual fees for title transfers.[22]

The Trustees of the new colony of Georgia offered excellent terms to foreign settlers, including payment of transportation charges, a supply of tools and provisions until the first harvest, and land grants

17. Body of Liberties (1641), Arts. 2, 12, Whitmore, ed., *Col. Laws Mass.*, 33, 35.
18. Act of 1652, included in the Body of Laws and Liberties, *ibid.*, 182–183.
19. *R.I. Col. Recs.*, I, 256. A special oath was required of the Frenchmen at Narragansett to insure their allegiance during the war with France, Mar. 3, 1689/1690, *ibid.*, II, 264.
20. See generally Knittle, *Palatine Emigration*, esp. 12–22, 128–135, 216–217.
21. William J. Hinke, ed. and trans., "Report of the Journey of Francis Louis Michel from Berne, Switzerland, to Virginia, October 2, 1701–December 1, 1702," *VMHB*, XXIV (1916), 298.
22. Declaration of Apr. 12, 1693, Salley, Jr., ed., *Recs. Rel. S.C.*, III, 81–83.

"in Perpetuum free from all Vassalage and Servitude, liable to no
Rent for the first Ten Years, and then only to the small acknowledgment of Ten Shillings per Annum, for every hundred Acres."[23]
Later statutes promised protection against creditors and even offered immigrants temporary economic monopolies.[24] Immigration
was also stimulated by the availability of land, by the growing
toleration of diverse religious beliefs, and by the frequent policy of
granting bounties to those who transported foreigners to the colonies.[25]

Although aliens often enjoyed more extensive rights in America
than they would have been granted in England, they still bore
certain disabilities. In 1658 Virginia put "all aliens" on the same
footing as "Irish servants without indentures," demanding that
they serve six years if over sixteen and to age twenty-four if under
sixteen when they arrived.[26] Alien land titles in the Old Dominion
and in royal colonies generally remained defeasible, escheating to
the king upon the alien's death.[27] This hardship was sometimes
mitigated in proprietary or charter colonies; but whether strictly
observed or not, the legal discriminations against non-subjects
remained worrisome enough. They were best overcome by naturalization.[28]

Promoters and developers in the plantations frequently used the
promise of subjectship as a lure to foreign settlers. William Fitzhugh of Virginia claimed enough acreage in 1686 to seat 150 to 200
families. He offered to lease or sell the land on easy terms and to

23. H. Newman to S. Urlsperger, London, Dec. 29, 1732, Jones, ed., *Salzburger Letterbooks*, 35–36. For later terms, including a sliding scale of land grants based on age and
social status, see entry of May 11, 1738, *Cal. State Papers, Col.*, XLIV, 82.
24. An act of July 19, 1757, "protected, freed, exempted and discharged" settlers from
debts incurred before their arrival, except those owed to the inhabitants of Great Britain,
Ireland, Georgia, or South Carolina north of the Savannah River, for seven years. An act of
Mar. 15, 1758, noted that the use of slave labor had discouraged the immigration of white
tradesmen, and it forbade the use of the former except when whites refused to work at rates
established yearly by special commissioners. Certain trades were not included in the act,
which was to last seven years. *Col. Recs. Ga.*, XVII, 191–196, 277–282.
25. Proper, *Colonial Immigration Laws*, 11–15.
26. Act of Mar. 1657/1658, basically reenacting a law of Mar. 1654/1655. Hening, ed.,
Statutes of Va., I, 471, 411.
27. See, e.g., the petition of Christopher Robinson, 1660, relating to the escheat of lands
belonging to his alien father-in-law, in Wm. P. Palmer *et al.*, eds., *Calendar of Virginia State
Papers and Other Manuscripts* . . . (Richmond, Va., 1875–1893), I, 3.
28. See the Carolina proprietors' declaration, above, n. 22, and the Pennsylvania dispute
discussed below, at n. 56.

supply bread and meat for the first year. Moreover, Fitzhugh promised to "engage to naturalize every Soul of them at £3 p. head
without any more or other matter of charge or trouble to them,
whereby the heirs will be capacitated to inherit the father's purchase."[29] The Carolina proprietors urged Deputy Governor Joseph
Blake to recommend an act of naturalization to the assembly after
receiving an application for settlement from several Vaudois versed
in silk manufacture.[30] William Byrd II had both economic gain and
military security in mind when he suggested proposals for facilitat-
ing the peopling of the backcountry:

In the mean time it may be necessary to encourage Foreign Protestants
to come over and seat themselves in the vallys of those Mountains which
are exceedingly rich and the air perfectly wholesome, and the better to
tempt them to it, it would be worth while to pass an act of Naturalization
for all such and suffer them to enjoy a certain Portion of Land for each
Family free from Quitrents for ten years, and if this could be transported
without charge it would be an effectual Temptation to them and no loss to
Great Britain by any means.[31]

Restrictions that ordinarily limited access to subjectship in England—the sacramental test and Protestant oaths or the high fees
for admission—were often attenuated in the American colonies.
Only in Rhode Island were the costs of naturalization consistently
high, amounting to as much as seven pounds in the colony's currency. Most of the provinces kept the fees low, often charging poor
immigrants nothing at all.[32] Massachusetts asked those persons
admitted under the act of 1731 for merely a sum of seven shillings
and sixpence.[33] Several colonies statutorily limited the fees charged
for naturalization. Maryland tried to insure enforcement of its fee
schedule by setting a high penalty of two thousand pounds of
tobacco for officers who attempted to exact more than the law

29. Quoted in Fairfax Harrison, "Brent Town, Ravensworth, and the Huguenots in
Stafford," *Tyler's Qtly. Hist. and Geneal. Mag.*, V (1923–1924), 175.
30. Lords Proprietors to Deputy Governor Blake, London, Oct. 19, 1699, Salley, Jr.,
ed., *Recs. Rel. S.C.*, IV, 114.
31. William Byrd II to Mr. Ochs, [ca. 1735], "Letters of William Byrd, 2d, of Westover,
Va.," *VMHB*, IX (1901–1902), 226–227.
32. Hoyt, "Naturalization," *Pol. Sci. Qtly.*, LXVII (1952), 258–260, gives a sampling
of the fees, which varied considerably among and within the colonies. Note that the apparent high cost of naturalization in Rhode Island may have merely reflected the chronic
inflation in that colony's currency.
33. Act of Apr. 2, 1731, *Acts and Resolves, Mass. Bay*, II, 586–587.

allowed, and half of the fine could be claimed by the aggrieved party.[34]

As in England, foreign Protestants were considered the most desirable candidates for naturalization in the colonies, though some of the more radical sects were prohibited or persecuted in the seventeenth century. Requiring oaths of various kinds from all those who sought to enter the allegiance often excluded groups like the Quakers or Moravians, but the passage of time brought a general relaxation of these restrictions. New York and Massachusetts enacted laws in 1734 and 1744 respectively that permitted Quakers to substitute an affirmation or declaration for oaths.[35] Pennsylvania anticipated parliamentary action by four years when in 1743 the assembly allowed all who had conscientious scruples against oaths to enjoy the exemption from oath requirements granted Quakers only by the English statute of 1740.[36]

Unlike the mother country, the colonies frequently admitted members of non-Protestant religious persuasions. New York, Pennsylvania, Virginia, and Maryland deliberately allowed Catholics to acquire subjectship under various seventeenth-century laws, although the extension of Protestant tests and oaths officially ended this policy after 1689.[37] Yet it was still possible for some of this faith to slip by. Onorio Rasolini, a Venetian and probably a Catholic, was naturalized in Maryland in 1732 and even received a commission as "Master Gunner and Store Keeper" from Governor Samuel Ogle a few years later.[38] Rhode Island adopted several members of the Roman faith after 1750.[39]

The parliamentary statute of 1740 excluded Catholics from its benefits by imposing the sacramental test, but permitted the natu-

---

34. Hoyt, "Naturalization," *Pol. Sci. Qtly.*, LXVII (1952), 259. For the Maryland act of 1704, see James Bisset, ed., *Abridgment and Collection of the Acts of Assembly Of the Province of Maryland, At present in Force . . .* (Philadelphia, 1759), 37.

35. For the New York act of June 22, 1734, see *Col. Laws N.Y.*, ·II, 828–830, and Governor William Cosby to Lords of Trade, June 10, 1735, *Cal. State Papers, Col.*, XLI, 450. The Massachusetts act of Mar. 1, 1743/1744, is in *Acts and Resolves, Mass. Bay*, III, 126–127.

36. Act of Feb. 3, 1742/1743, *Pa. Statutes*, IV, 391–394.

37. Hoyt, "Naturalization," *Pol. Sci. Qtly.*, LXVII (1952), 256–257.

38. *Ibid.*, 257n; *Md. Archives*, XXXVII, 442, XXVIII, 69.

39. Stephen Decatur, a Catholic, was naturalized in Feb. 1752/1753. *R.I. Col. Recs.*, V, 367; Arnold, *History of R.I.*, II, 185, 494. Francis Ferrari and Ami Decotay, both from Genoa and probably Catholics, were naturalized June 1751 and Feb. 1754, respectively. *R.I. Col. Recs.*, V, 340, 403.

ralization of Jews.[40] Here the English authorities merely recognized a policy that had been long established at the local level. Virginia had made John Abraham a denizen as early as 1658, and Maryland admitted Dr. Jacob Lumbrozo five years later.[41] Other colonies allowed Jews to settle within their bounds and to enjoy at least partial subjectship on the strength of English denizations.[42] If it was sometimes deemed more discreet to keep silent about the faith of non-Protestant applicants, or if Jews sometimes converted or swore falsely "upon the true faith of a Christian," such subterfuges were not always necessary.[43] New York, for example, made its divergence from English policy explicit when it added this clause to a special act of naturalization in 1727:

AND WHEREAS the following words are contained in the latter part of the Oath of Abjuration vizt [upon the true faith of a Christian] be it farther Enacted by the Authority aforesaid that when ever any of his Majestys Subjects professing the Jewish religion Shall present himself to take the Said Oath of Abjuration in pursuance of this present Act the Said Words [upon the true faith of a Christian] Shall be omitted out of the said oath . . . and the taking the said oath . . . without the words aforesaid in like manner as Jews are to be admitted to be Sworn to give evidence in Courts of Justice Shall be deemed to be A Sufficient taking of the Abjuration Oath within the meaning of this Act.[44]

40. Above, chap. 4, at n. 35. For lists of Jews naturalized under this act, see J. H. Hollander, "The Naturalization of Jews in the American Colonies under the Act of 1740," Am. Jewish Hist. Soc., *Pubs.*, No. 5 (1897), 111–117; Leon Hühner, "Naturalization of Jews in New York under the Act of 1740," *ibid.*, No. 13 (1905), 6, and Giuseppi, ed., *Naturalizations*, under heading "Jews" in the "Index of Subjects."

41. According to Leon Hühner, "The Jews of Virginia from the Earliest Times to the Close of the Eighteenth Century," Am. Jewish Hist. Soc., *Pubs.*, No. 20 (1911), 89, John Abraham was a Jew although described as a "Dutchman" in his denization. For Dr. Lumbrozo, see J. H. Hollander, "Some Unpublished Material Relating to Dr. Jacob Lumbrozo, of Maryland," *ibid.*, No. 1 (1893), 29, and *Md. Archives*, III, 488.

42. See above, chap. 4, at nn. 11, 12.

43. No explicit reference was made to the religion of Rasolini, Abraham, or Lumbrozo, referred to above. James Lucena, a Portuguese Jew, was naturalized on the Christian oath in Rhode Island in Feb. 1761. It is not clear whether he converted or swore falsely. *R.I. Col. Recs.*, VI, 262; Arnold, *History of R.I.*, II, 228; David C. Adelman, "Strangers. Civil Rights of Jews in the Colony of Rhode Island," *Rhode Island Jewish Historical Notes*, I, No. 2 (1954), 110.

44. Act of Nov. 25, 1727, *Col. Laws N.Y.*, II, 418–419. A number of Jews had already been naturalized by an act of July 6, 1723. *Ibid.*, 164–167. At least six of those men included in the 1723 act also received naturalization under the parliamentary statute of 1740. Max J. Kohler, "Civil Status of the Jews in Colonial New York," Am. Jewish Hist. Soc., *Pubs.*, No. 6 (1897), 105–106.

Permission for naturalization did not end all discrimination against Jews; however, their occasional exclusion in law did not always hold in practice. Maryland denied rights to persons of this profession de jure, but they were nevertheless permitted undisturbed domicile and allowed to exercise "undefined rights" de facto.[45] Surveyor General William Dyer attempted to seize the property of Newport Jews in 1685 on the grounds that they were aliens, yet after the failure of his suit the Rhode Island Jewish community was allowed to engage freely in trade and commerce. Despite the grant of this prerogative, they were excluded from freemanship and denied full political rights, even though they might be naturalized.[46] The same situation obtained in New York, where a disputed election in 1737 led to the decision that Jews could not vote.[47]

Since the parliamentary act of 1740 allowed the admission of Jews to the rights of subjectship, it was difficult for any of the colonies to exclude them entirely. The case of Aaron Lopez and Isaac Elizur is illustrative. The two Newport merchants applied to the Rhode Island Superior Court in March 1761, seeking naturalization under the English statute of 1740. The court sent the petitioners to the legislature "on the grounds that the Naturalization Act of 1740 referred to in the petition, was not in the Court and that only the General Assembly could act upon this petition as it had in other cases." The lower house offered to grant the petition, provided that Lopez and Elizur were excluded from office and denied the vote. The upper house, however, refused; since Parliament had provided an authorized procedure to be administered by the colonial courts, the assembly's involvement in the matter was illegitimate.[48]

Their petition rejected by the assembly, the two men returned to the superior court in Newport. In March 1762 their request for admission was again denied. The court observed that in passing the 1740 statute, Parliament had cited the desirability of an increasing population as the motive for easing naturalization. Since Rhode Island was "already so full of people that many of his Majesty's

45. J. H. Hollander, "The Civil Status of the Jews in Maryland, 1634–1776," *ibid.*, No. 2 (1894), 41.
46. Adelman, "Civil Rights of Jews in R.I.," *R.I. Jewish Hist. Notes*, I, No. 2 (1954), 106.
47. *N.Y. Col. Docs.*, VI, 56n; Kohler, "Jews in Colonial N.Y.," Am. Jewish Hist. Soc., *Pubs.*, No. 6 (1897), 98.
48. Adelman, "Civil Rights of Jews in R.I.," *R.I. Jewish Hist. Notes*, I, No. 2 (1954), 110. For a brief biographical sketch, see Bruce M. Bigelow, "Aaron Lopez: Colonial Merchant of Newport," *ibid.*, II, No. 1 (1956), 4–17.

good subjects born within the same have removed and settled in Nova Scotia, and other places, [the colony] cannot come within the intention of the said act." Moreover, said the judges, the adoption of Jews as fellow subjects was "wholly inconsistent with the first principles upon which the colony was formed."[49]

Although Lopez and Elizur met with failure in Rhode Island, they had an alternative course available to them. The statute of 1740 conferred a status that had to be recognized throughout the dominions, and the two merely sought admission elsewhere. Elizur went to New York, where he qualified himself according to law on July 23, 1763;[50] Lopez removed to Swansea, Massachusetts, and on October 15, 1762, was naturalized in the superior court at Boston.[51] Both men returned to Newport, having effectively circumvented local opposition to their admission.

The Lopez-Elizur incident illustrates the stiff opposition to the naturalization of Jews in the colonies, although special political overtones heightened this particular controversy.[52] Ezra Stiles had been disgusted by the performance of the Rhode Island authorities. He noted that there was considerable "Tumult at New York in procuring the Taking place of [Jewish] natural[ization] there." Yet his conclusion was mistaken: "The Jews will never become incorporated with the p[eo]ple of America, any more than in Europe, Asia and Africa."[53] As long as the statute of 1740 remained in effect, and as long as the colonies themselves competed with each other for settlers, purely local opposition could not effectively exclude Jews or other groups from naturalization.

In the eyes of both alien and native settlers, the crucial benefit conferred by naturalization was security of property. Whenever the

49. Max J. Kohler, "The Jews in Newport," Am. Jewish Hist. Soc., *Pubs.*, No. 6 (1897), 71.
50. Giuseppi, ed., *Naturalizations*, 37.
51. Willard, *Naturalization in the American Colonies*, 9; Leon Hühner, "The Jews of New England (Other than Rhode Island) prior to 1800," Am. Jewish Hist. Soc., *Pubs.*, No. 11 (1903), 81.
52. Arnold, *History of R.I.*, II, 494–496. Lopez was closely associated with the Browns of Providence, and like them he supported the political faction led by Stephen Hopkins. The court and the upper house were under the influence of Samuel Ward. For the continuous struggle between these two factions, see Mack E. Thompson, "The Ward-Hopkins Controversy and the American Revolution in Rhode Island: An Interpretation," *WMQ*, 3d Ser., XVI (1959), 363–375.
53. W. Willner, "Ezra Stiles and the Jews," Am. Jewish Hist. Soc., *Pubs.*, No. 8 (1900), 126.

rights granted by naturalization acts were enumerated, the ability "to hold lands" figured prominently. The common law allowed aliens to acquire defeasible titles only, and even if such titles were subsequently transferred to native subjects, they could be challenged by the crown or by the lords proprietors in private colonies. When an alien died, his property escheated to the government authorities.

The potential for misery and exploitation under these provisions can be seen in a Maryland case of the late 1750s. Valerius Duchart, a French Protestant from Strasbourg, arrived in the colony in late 1753 or 1754. During the next two years he purchased about four hundred acres of land in Baltimore County. This property he assiduously improved, constructing three "tenements," sinking a well, and clearing, fencing, and draining over one hundred acres. In 1756 he learned that his property was open to challenge because he was an alien, and he immediately sought counsel and aid from a neighbor, Dr. William Lyon. Duchart prepared to apply for naturalization, but he died before he could carry out his intention.

In May 1756 Daniel Chamier was appointed to administer Duchart's estate. But Dr. Lyon moved first. Secretly lodging a preemption of escheat in the land office, he obtained a patent for the Frenchman's land. Chamier petitioned for relief, pleading that Lyon's action deprived Duchart's widow and seven children of their inheritance; moreover, generosity in this case would encourage other settlers to come to Maryland. Chamier himself promised to reimburse Lyon for the fee the doctor had paid for the escheat warrant. He proved his own disinterested motives by suggesting public auction of the land, the proceeds to be deposited with the commissary general for the benefit of Duchart's heirs. On August 20, 1757, Chamier's petition was rejected.[54]

The implications of the Duchart case touched the interests of native subjects as well as those of other unnaturalized aliens, since land changed hands frequently in the colonies. Anyone who might have purchased Duchart's estate from him would have been vulnerable to the machinations of schemers like Dr. Lyon, for any title acquired from an alien remained insecure. Naturalization altered defeasible titles and made them unchallengeable, and much of the

54. The petition is given in full in *Md. Archives*, LVI, App. IV, 517–519. The case is also discussed in the preface, *ibid.*, lxv.

popular interest in generous admission policies clearly derived from the widely shared desire to make all private property secure.[55]

In view of their deeply rooted interest in security of property, the colonists were particularly frustrated when higher authorities obstructed local naturalization legislation. One related clash occurred in 1759 when the Pennsylvania assembly passed an act "for the Relief of the Heirs and Devisees, and Assigns of Persons born out of the King's Liegance," which would have confirmed the titles of lands conveyed by aliens who had died before being naturalized. The act was annulled in London after the proprietors convinced English officials that this was an "infamous" attempt to suggest their exploitation of widows and orphans. Admitting that "the estates of persons dying unnaturalized do by law escheat to the proprietaries, yet there is no instance to be found and the proprietaries do challenge the assembly to produce one, wherever the proprietaries have refused to grant the lands of the deceased to his heirs or devisees."[56] The proprietors did not specify the fees charged for such regrants.

The Pennsylvania act of 1759 was not the only law of this type to suffer defeat. In 1772 the English government disallowed a New Jersey act of October 1770 on the grounds that, although founded on "principles of Humanity and Good Policy," it materially affected the king's rights and should not have been passed without prior permission.[57] Other acts were blocked locally. A New York bill passed the assembly in 1769, but was suspended by the governor until the king's approval could be obtained. However, the approval was not granted, which fixed the suspension permanently.[58] The Maryland assembly repeatedly failed to pass such a law between 1758 and 1767. In this province the anti-Catholicism of the lower house combined with the upper house's concern for the proprie-

55. The New York act of 1715 (above, chap. 4, n. 124), e.g., was designed in part "to render His Majesties Subjects Secure in the quiet and peaceable enjoyment of their Several Estates, Rights and Properties, and to prevent any doubts, controversies or disputes that may hereafter arise." *Col. Laws N.Y.*, I, 861. See also the Pennsylvania act of Nov. 24, 1700, repealed in 1706 by the queen-in-council, *Pa. Statutes*, II, 122, App. I, sec. ii, 496.

56. *Ibid.*, V, 443–445, App. XXIII, sec. i, 669–670.

57. *N.J. Archives*, 1st Ser., X, 300, 324–327, 337–338; *Acts of Privy Council, Col.*, V, 320–321. An act with the same title passed Sept. 26, 1772, and was allowed to stand. *N.J. Archives*, 1st Ser., XVIII, 350, 370–371.

58. Governor Henry Moore to the earl of Hillsborough, May 29, 1769, *N.Y. Col. Docs.*, VIII, 169–170. The act was considered in London the following year and was ordered to lie for further consideration. *Jour. of Comm. Trade, 1768–1775*, 150, 187, 191.

tor's escheat rights to frustrate the passage of the desired legislation.

The act to naturalize aliens and to confirm land titles introduced in Maryland in 1758 led to heated debates that reveal how such acts could be complicated by their connection with broader issues. Daniel Dulany pushed for the bill against the opposition of his colleagues in the upper house, and when the bill was defeated Dulany entered his protests in the record. He argued that the bill ought to have been passed because, in the first place, aliens had been invited to the colony, "and the Faith of this Government which ought to be religiously observed, hath been in the most solemn and explecet Terms that they should be secure and protected in the enjoyment of their property." Claims that the bill would reduce the proprietor's revenue from escheats were "Derogatory to his Lordship's Honour" and beneath "the Dignity of the Middle Branch of the Legislature." In fact, Dulany argued, if the rights of aliens were not protected, many families would leave the colony and others would not come, leading to "the real Demunition of his Lordship's Revenue, the Disgrace of his Government and the Impoverishment of his Province." Dulany reminded his colleagues that aliens who sought naturalization under the parliamentary statute of 1740 had to reside in America seven years. Since the circumstances in America were such that, except for a few "mechanics," inhabitants could not subsist "without the Allowance of some Portion of real Property," failure to pass a liberal bill in Maryland would divert immigration to those colonies where aliens' titles were secure.[59]

But more was involved than public honor and the colony's prosperity. Dulany warned that rejection of the bill would set an evil and dangerous precedent for rejecting "any Bill securitative of the rights of the People." Already the public controversy attending the bill made it necessary to "quiet the minds of the Alien Inhabitants," who might now be "intimidated into the surrender of their rights upon the Issuing of Escheat warrants." Unscrupulous operators who "may be tempted by the Bait of Escheat warrants would be ensnared by the alluring Prospects of gain or Acts of Power the most dangerous in their Nature exercised to vindicate and Support those oppressive Escheats." Failure to pass the bill, in short, would threaten liberty by promoting corruption and by rewarding acts of arbitrary power.[60]

59. *Md. Archives*, LVI, 56–59.
60. *Ibid.*, and preface, lxiii–lxvi.

Actually, the Maryland proprietor was willing to forgo his profits if Catholics, excluded from the benefits of the 1758 bill, were
included in a revised naturalization program. A new bill in accord
with his views was proposed in the upper house in 1760. This time
the lower house proved obstinate, refusing to accept the bill unless
it was amended to exclude Catholics.[61] Although the two houses
deadlocked and the bill was defeated, the assembly ordered it published along with several other rejected bills. Broader political
conflicts and constitutional controversies had overwhelmed the
original issue, with the result that land titles involving aliens remained insecure. By 1767, after numerous attempts to legislate on
the matter had failed, the proprietor and the governor decided to
bypass the assembly and simply to favor alien heirs who applied for
a reissuance of their parents' titles. The solution did not completely
solve the problem of insecurity, but at least prevented the recurrence of instances such as the Duchart case.[62]

A generous proprietor might forgo escheats and perhaps even
fees in order to dampen political strife and ease the minds of alien
settlers, but the king proved more jealous of his royal rights. Local
acts confirming defeasible titles doubly abridged his prerogatives:
first, the colonial laws presumed to undercut and in effect to deny
his traditional claim to escheats; second, they involved a loss of the
revenue that he might otherwise receive from expropriating or
legitimizing lands held by defective titles. In calmer times the royal
advisers had often urged the king to accept his losses in the interests
of public tranquility. By 1773, however, the monarch could no
longer tolerate such affronts to his sovereignty. The order-in-
council issued in that year to ban local naturalization acts included
instructions to colonial governors to refuse assent to any bills
"establishing a title in any persons to lands, tenements, or real
estates in our said province originally granted to or purchased by
aliens antecedent to naturalization."[63]

The colonists not only diverged from English patterns in controversies over the interconnected issues of naturalization and prop-

61. *Ibid.*, 209, 217–218, 220.
62. [Hugh] Hamersley [secretary to the proprietor] to Governor Horatio Sharpe, London, Nov. 10, 1767, *ibid.*, XIV, 431. Sharpe had informed the proprietor of the Duchart
case and had suggested this policy in a letter of June 9, 1767. *Ibid.*, 393.
63. Labaree, ed., *Royal Instructions*, I, 155.

erty rights but also moved away from English laws restricting political participation to natural-born subjects. It is likely that the colonists were never overly scrupulous about the participation of aliens, though English law on this point was clear. In a close election every vote counted, and if one was willing to run the risk of disqualification, aliens could be persuaded to vote illegally. A parliamentary address to Queen Anne in 1706, relative to recent elections in North Carolina, complained that "all sorts of people, even servants, Negroes, Aliens, Jews and Common sailors were admitted to vote."[64] In Maryland, Mathias Vanderheyden held local office for over two years before he was naturalized by an act of 1692.[65] Pennsylvania Germans evidently voted and held office without the benefit of naturalization acts.[66] It has been said that success at the polls in Philadelphia "for a number of years after 1738 depended upon control of the staircase of the building in which the poll was taken." Sailors hired to block the way claimed "that they 'had as much a right to be there as the damned Dutchmen.' "[67]

The distinctions in English law separating naturalized aliens and denizens from the native-born blurred in America, but English statutes regulating personal rights according to the old rankings could still be invoked to delay or destroy the political careers of ambitious naturalized subjects. An early example occurred in Virginia in 1698. John Keeton, naturalized by an assembly act in April 1679, was elected to the House of Burgesses in 1698. The Committee of Elections and Privileges challenged his capacity to serve, but when his local naturalization came to light, it was resolved that Keeton "(notwithstanding he is a forreigner born)" was "by Virtue of the Said Act of Naturalization duely qualified to Serve as a Member in this Assembly." Despite this decision, Governor Edmund Andros declared Keeton's election illegal and forthwith dissolved the assembly.[68] Andros justified his action by citing the parliamentary statute of 1696 for the prevention of frauds and abuses in the plantation trade, which required that "all Places of

64. *N.C. Col. Recs.*, I, 639.
65. *Md. Archives*, XIII, 245, 536–537.
66. Williamson, *American Suffrage*, 50.
67. *Ibid.*, 56.
68. McIlwaine and Kennedy, eds., *Jours. of Va. Burgesses, 1695–1702*, preface, ix, xxviii–xxix, 122, 124, 127.

Trust in the Courts of Law, or what relates to the Treasury of the said Islands" be entrusted only to natural-born subjects.[69]

England's fixed policy after the Act of Settlement (1701) was to exclude naturalized subjects from high political office.[70] It was unclear whether the provisions of this statute were to extend to the colonies as well. Whatever the intention, many of the local governments did not follow England's lead. A Pennsylvania election law of 1706 permitted persons "naturalized in England or in this province and territories" to elect and to be elected.[71] Peter Bard, "a very worthy and ingenuous man," was naturalized in New Jersey in 1714 and became a member of the provincial council.[72] The New York agent, urging confirmation of the naturalization and land titles act of 1715, noted that "some of the most considerable persons there, and such as have been of the Council, have not been natural born subjects of the Crown of Great Britain."[73] In Georgia, propertied aliens could vote, and naturalized Christians could hold office.[74]

A few colonies did incorporate the English restrictions into local laws. The general act of 1704 establishing South Carolina's procedure for naturalization excluded from the assembly those admitted under its provisions, though they could vote if they met the property and residence requirements.[75] Maryland's election laws em-

69. See 7 & 8 Will. III, c. 22 (1696), sec. 12, discussed above, chap. 3, n. 2; and H. R. McIlwaine, ed., *Executive Journals of the Council of Colonial Virginia*, I (Richmond, Va., 1925), 389. H. R. McIlwaine calls Andros's claim "far-fetched," since the House of Burgesses was neither a court of law nor directly concerned with the revenue service. He suspects that this was an excuse used by Andros to end what promised to be a long session. The governor's successor had already been appointed, he himself was ill, and there was no pressing business. McIlwaine and Kennedy, eds., *Jours. of Va. Burgesses, 1695–1702*, preface, xxviii–xxix.

70. See above, chap. 2, at n. 23.

71. *Pa. Statutes*, II, 212–221. The act was originally passed in 1700 and disallowed on technical grounds. *Ibid.*, 24–27, App. I, sec. ii, 465.

72. Governor Hunter to the Lords of Trade, Aug. 22, 1714, *Cal. State Papers, Col.*, XXVIII, 18; *N.J. Archives*, 1st Ser., XIII, 513n, 541.

73. Report of John Champante to the Lords of Trade, Dec. 1, 1715, *Cal. State Papers, Col.*, XXVIII, 354. Champante may have had in mind the French-born Gabriel Minvielle, alderman and mayor of New York City and a member of the council under four governors. Baird, *Huguenot Emigration*, II, 140n. Shaw, ed., *Denization and Naturalization, 1603–1700*, lists a Gabriel Minviele as being endenized Aug. 19, 1688. If this was the same man, he received his denization four years after becoming mayor. See also *Cal. Hist. MSS, N.Y.*, II, 132.

74. See the act of June 9, 1761, cited above, chap. 4, n. 142.

75. See the act of Nov. 4, 1704, above, chap. 4, n. 131; but compare the comments of J. M. Bolzius quoted in the text, chap. 4, at n. 140.

bodied the English rules, and Connecticut may also have denied naturalized subjects full political rights.[76] Royal instructions to Governor Benning Wentworth of New Hampshire reminded him that only native-born subjects were qualified to sit on juries or to hold high offices in that province.[77]

Enforcement of restrictions on the political rights of adopted subjects led to several controversies in Maryland. In 1744 an act of naturalization passed the assembly, granting James Richard of Baltimore County the rights of a natural-born subject within that province. Sometime within the next two years Richard was appointed sheriff of the county, an "office of trust" within the meaning of the law. The Committee of Aggrievances subsequently reported in May 1747 that Richard "hath not been an Inhabitant within any of his Majesty's Plantations of America, for seven years, nor Naturalized under the Statute of the 13th of Geo: 2d; . . . therefore your Committee humbly conceive, that by the Laws and Statutes of England, the said James Richard, though naturalized by any Act of this province, is not qualified for such Office." The committee cited the parliamentary statutes excluding naturalized subjects from office and called for Richard's dismissal. Two days later Governor Ogle promised to replace Richard, pledging on all occasions to "be very careful of the rights and privileges of his lordship's Tenants."[78]

A more important case arose in the same province in 1771. In October of that year Jonathan Hagar was elected as a delegate to the assembly from Frederick County. Although Hagar had been natu-

---

76. The Maryland case is discussed below. The Connecticut act naturalizing Don Gabriel Sistera, May 1773, declared him to be "entitled to all the privileges, immunities and advantages of his Majesty's English subjects born within this Colony . . . excepting only such privileges and immunities as by law are not competent to foreigners who have been or are naturalized." *Conn. Col. Recs.*, XIV, 94. See also Hoyt, "Naturalization," *Pol. Sci. Qtly.*, LXVII (1952), 253n.

77. Instructions of June 30, 1761, Batchellor, comp., *Laws of N.H.*, III, 297.

78. For the text of Richard's naturalization, see *Md. Archives*, XLII, 602–603. The report of the committee and the governor's reply are given *ibid.*, XLIV, 457, 508–513. It is likely that motives other than legal punctiliousness were involved in the dismissal. Complaints filed with the council in Dec. 1746 charged that the sheriff "has repeatedly cursed and damned the King for an Hanover Dog and a Turnep Man, and wished himself in the French or Pretenders Army that he might drive that Hanover Dog home again." He also allegedly cursed and damned "the Young Princesses for a Parcel of damned Bitches and Whores," called the duke of Cumberland "a Beefheaded Son of a Bitch and a Bull headed Dog," and praised the Pretender. It was decided that these allegations were the fruit of personal animosity on the part of the deponents, but the charges certainly indicate some opposition to the sheriff that may have stood behind later proceedings. *Ibid.*, XXVIII, 370–376.

ralized in 1747 (apparently under the parliamentary statute of 1740), his eligibility for the office was challenged.[79] Hagar appeared in the House with his counsel, but after extensive debate the assembly declared him ineligible by a narrow vote of twenty-four to twenty-three.[80] Three days later a bill was introduced that allowed naturalized subjects all the rights and privileges of native Marylanders, notwithstanding any laws to the contrary. The bill became law on October 16—only eight days after the vote dismissing Hagar—and a month later he was reelected and duly seated.[81]

The incident did not go unnoticed in England. In 1772 Lord Dartmouth wrote to Governor Robert Eden asking him about the act, which "upon the Genl. Provisions of it, appears to extend the benefits of naturalization beyond what the British Parliament have allowed, and to set aside the limitation contained in the [1740] Statute of the 13th of Geo: the 2d." Eden quickly responded that the act was not designed to contravene the British law. He pointed to the large numbers of German immigrants in Maryland and emphasized their "usefulness." Hagar's ineligibility, he declared, stemmed not from the parliamentary statutes (which, in his estimation, referred only to offices in Great Britain and Ireland), but from local Maryland laws: "The Effect of this Act is merely local, the Design of it was in no degree to set aside the limitation contained in the [English] Statute, and the provisions of it are almost necessary on

79. Basil Sollers, "Jonathan Hagar, the Founder of Hagarstown," Society for the History of Germans in Maryland, *Second Annual Report* (1887–1888), 21, gives this date for Hagar's naturalization. I have found no local act in his benefit. Giuseppi, ed., *Naturalizations*, xvi, refers to the case but says that Hagar's name does not appear on any of the lists returned under the 1740 statute. However, a "Jonathan Isagar" is named among those naturalized in Maryland in 1747, and this is probably "Hagar," misspelled or mistakenly copied.

80. *Md. Archives*, LXIII, 89–93. During the debate, the lower house examined the English statutes 12 & 13 Will. III, c. 2 (1701); 1 Geo. I, stat. 2, c. 4 (1714); 13 Geo. II, c. 7 (1740); and 22 Geo. II, c. 45 (1749). Also read were the Maryland election act of July 17, 1716—which excluded anyone from the assembly who was disabled from sitting in Parliament by English laws—and the lower house resolves of Oct. 18, 1753—which declared English statutes regulating elections and office qualifications to be in force in Maryland. *Ibid.*, XXX, 616–622, L, 177–178.

81. *Ibid.*, LXIII, 239, 175–177. Hagar's problems were not yet over, for in Oct. 1773 his case was reconsidered. It was now argued that because the proprietor had died in Sept. 1771, the Oct. elections (when Hagar was first chosen) were not valid. The act of Oct. 16 was declared void because it had not been passed by a legal body. Hagar was again declared ineligible, and a new election was ordered. Governor Eden, already exasperated by political opposition, found the argument both ridiculous and offensive, and he promptly prorogued the assembly. *Ibid.*, LXIV, 22–23, 434–436.

account of the Privilege enjoyed by Foreigners naturalized in Pensylvania."[82]

Eden's defense of the Maryland act was both accurate and satisfactory, and the law was permitted to stand. Indeed, the British authorities acknowledged the accuracy of Eden's reading of the 1740 parliamentary act by passing the explanatory statute of 1773 that expressly confirmed the right of aliens naturalized under parliamentary auspices to enjoy full equality in local politics. The limitations imposed by the Act of Settlement now remained in force only with respect to offices and places in the kingdoms of Great Britain and Ireland.[83]

The orthodox English theory of allegiance had been formulated in relation to problems concerning the natural-born subject, and the status of adopted members was subsequently explained within the framework of ideas articulated in *Calvin's Case*. In the colonies, on the other hand, naturalization most often served as the starting point for considerations of allegiance and subjectship. The patterns of policy that emerged there were well defined, but the new patterns of thought remained largely implicit, half-hidden in intermittent, complicated controversies. Despite all the conflicts surrounding naturalization in the colonial period, there was no coherent or far-reaching analysis of its theoretical import; debates centered on the surface facts and the practical effects rather than on the underlying reason of the law. Still, as American circumstances altered the facts of the law, new assumptions were created that would help shape the colonists' response when forced to define and defend their ideas of allegiance and their vision of community membership.

Imperial directives and colonial needs blurred the traditional legal distinctions between different types of subjects. After 1700 the status of denizen disappeared as a separate order of membership in the colonies. Generous inducements designed to entice foreign settlers expanded the benefits conferred by naturalization and made it difficult to consider natives and adopted aliens distinct types of members. While liberal naturalization policies accelerated the trend toward ethnic, social, and cultural diversity by luring ever-increas-

82. "The Correspondence of Governor Eden," *Maryland Historical Magazine*, II (1907), 299, 301–303.
83. The act of 1740 had in fact omitted the political disability with respect to the colonies, but, as Dartmouth's comments indicate, the point was not clear. See above, chap. 4, at n. 44.

ing numbers of foreigners, these same policies contributed to a growing assumption that membership status was and ought to be undifferentiated.

The circumstances of life in America not only reinforced the tendency toward a uniform subject status but also played into an emergent belief in equality of rights. Admission to the community in England remained a matter of grace and favor, and there was no doubt that adopted aliens could legitimately be denied privileges that natives claimed as their birthright. In America the foreign immigrant's contribution to the welfare of the community—its military security, its economic prosperity, its rapid and sustained growth—was obvious and highly valued. To limit his rights seemed senseless on grounds both of self-interest and of abstract justice. Native subjects knew that their own interests benefited when immigrants were naturalized quickly and on easy terms, an awareness abundantly illustrated in the statutes linking naturalization and the confirmation of land titles. More generally, debates over both property and political rights revealed an increasing sense that aliens who chose to commit their efforts and resources to the common good justly deserved an equal share of the rights of membership.

The colonists favored foreign immigration, and they cared little about how the alien became a member. From the beginnings of settlement until the eve of the Revolution, natives accepted as fellow subjects persons admitted by a variety of agencies.[84] Local grants had at times and for some purposes been accorded an extra-territorial effect, though the colonies did not invariably feel bound by the local naturalizations performed in other provinces;[85] but every government at least recognized the validity of parliamentary admissions as well as its own, and the status acquired by the locally

84. As discussed in chap. 2 above, political relationships had been crucial in determining the status of persons naturalized in England, Scotland, and Ireland when they were out of the immediate jurisdiction of the naturalizing body. It is true that the 1740 act might still be squared with traditional theory by emphasizing that persons admitted by its provisions were admitted ultimately by parliamentary authority. In practice, however, the adopted alien dealt solely with local institutions and proved his status by a certificate under colonial seals.

85. See, e.g., the Backer case discussed above, chap. 4, at n. 105. Herbert Osgood thought that the colonies probably gave "practical recognition" to each other's naturalizations. He admitted that he was "not aware that a test case of this kind ever arose, but the course indicated would have been in harmony with the vague consciousness of a common citizenship which was gradually growing up in the colonies by the middle of the eighteenth century." Osgood, *American Colonies in the 18th Century*, II, 527.

administered English statute of 1740 was by law binding on all the dominions. English theorists might see the colonies' acceptance of English naturalizations as proof of colonial dependency, for in law parliamentary naturalization was valid only in the mother country and in other kingdoms under Parliament's control. Americans would reject this contention and move toward a notion of a community of allegiance that encompassed separate governments with concurrent jurisdiction over admission. In effect, the colonists experienced and came to accept a kind of federal distribution of power in their naturalization practices long before the idea took full shape in theory.

Whatever agency admitted them, aliens became subjects by a legal process involving choice, consent, and contract. The kind of volitional relationship between member and community that naturalization implied and familiarized gradually came to dominate Americans' assumptions about subjectship generally. This tendency was logically reinforced by the colonists' overall view of the historical origins of their societies: had not the original English emigrants chosen to cross the Atlantic to establish new communities, and had they not constructed their governments on consent-based charters, covenants, and contracts?[86] If native and adopted subjects shared the same status and the same rights, could not one conclude that their allegiance, too, was the same—contractual, volitional, and legal rather than natural and immutable?

These theoretical implications embedded in the patterns and processes of naturalization were not fully perceived until the mid-eighteenth century. As the imperial crisis that was to culminate in revolution developed, however, Americans examined more closely their notions of allegiance. The debates that began in the 1760s would reveal how far they had moved from the principles of English law, for the colonial experience had already initiated the transformation of Americans from subjects to citizens.

---

86. See generally Michael Kammen, "The Meaning of Colonization in American Revolutionary Thought," *Journal of the History of Ideas*, XXXI (1970), 337–358.

PART III

Revolution

CHAPTER 6

The Pre-Revolutionary Debate

The imperial crisis of the 1760s forced Americans to articulate their notions of allegiance and political obligation. In resisting the new British policies at the end of the Seven Years' War, the colonists began to give logical form and consistency to hitherto vague and disconnected assumptions concerning their rights and duties as British subjects. As the character of the bond between the colonies and the mother country became a topic of reasoned debate, disputants on both sides "discovered" the principles that defined, or ought to define, that relationship. Initially, the claims made by apologists for the new British programs determined the course of the debate. Yet the concepts formulated in reaction to these claims had a logic and a momentum of their own.[1] Basic principles established in the pre-Revolutionary years would help move Americans toward and then beyond independence, operating in unforeseen ways to create a new concept of citizenship.

The theoretical confrontation between Great Britain and America embraced a number of separate controversies occurring over a span of years and involving many participants. The logical stages of the debate did not always follow in strict chronological fashion, for the major arguments appeared in exchanges that varied widely in timing, aim, and emphasis. Some protagonists moved farther and faster, thought more deeply, than others. At times, tactical consid-

---

1. See generally Bernard Bailyn, *The Ideological Origins of the American Revolution* (Cambridge, Mass., 1967), esp. chaps. 4–6.

erations obscured underlying principles or directed discussion away from the central areas of contention. Taken as a whole, however, the individual exchanges formed a coherent and logical pattern that may be analyzed as a two-sided debate.

The essential conclusion of British arguments remained remarkably consistent throughout the years of controversy. This central contention was expressed most succinctly in the Declaratory Act of March 18, 1766:

> That the said colonies and plantations in *America* have been, are, and of right ought to be, subordinate unto, and dependent upon the imperial crown and parliament of *Great Britain*; and that the King's majesty, by and with the advice and consent of the lords spiritual and temporal, and commons of *Great Britain*, in parliament assembled, had, hath, and of right ought to have, full power and authority to make laws and statutes of sufficient force and validity to bind the colonies and people of *America*, subjects of the crown of *Great Britain*, in all cases whatsoever.[2]

Parliament's claim to absolute authority over the colonies remained the core of the British argument long after American thought had shifted to new grounds. Even as late as 1778, the point could not be compromised in theory.[3] The political-constitutional structure of Great Britain itself stood on the foundation of parliamentary sovereignty, and to retreat on the principle in the interest of appeasing the Americans would have had unacceptable implications for the structure of authority at home.[4]

Apologists for British authority kept their eyes fixed on the central tenet of Parliament's sovereignty, developing a series of arguments and adducing a variety of proofs to support their position. From the outset they pointed to the fact that Parliament had enacted laws and regulations affecting America. No one could dispute the existence of the navigation acts, for example, or deny their profound impact on colonial economic life. The legitimacy of statutes providing for naturalization or establishing a colonial postal system had been accepted without question; yet it was obvious that such statutes, useful as they were to British polemicists, could not

2. 6 Geo. III, c. 12 (1766).

3. Bailyn, *Ideological Origins*, 227. In 1778 the North ministry was still prepared only to compromise the point in practice, not in theory.

4. G. H. Guttridge, *English Whiggism and the American Revolution* (Berkeley and Los Angeles, Cal., 1942), 61, and *passim*. This remains one of the best accounts of the potential political ramifications in England itself of theoretical concessions on the issue of parliamentary sovereignty.

alone be expected to persuade the colonists to accept Parliament's broad claims. Most of the laws before the 1760s had been acts of "general and external policy," and to argue that they constituted badges of absolute subordination was not convincing. The colonists certainly were not prepared to see their historical acceptance of parliamentary intervention to promote and protect trade and internal communications or to stimulate immigration as a concession that "America's dependency" was unlimited.[5]

Imperial policies adopted in the 1760s went beyond existing legislative precedents and threatened to introduce "government in depth."[6] When Parliament claimed absolute authority "in all cases whatsoever," the colonists demanded a theoretical justification of its right. Admittedly, they had acknowledged and submitted to previous legislation, but fact did not prove right. "Our ancestors," observed Thomas Jefferson, "were farmers, not lawyers." Their acceptance of parliamentary legislation stemmed from ignorance and did not preclude more cautious and knowledgeable men from searching out the fundamental principles underlying and limiting the authority of the mother country.[7] Because Americans resisted the translation of the fact of legislation into the right of complete authority, defenders of the new British policies were forced to articulate the theoretical premises behind their central claim.

The arguments put forward in support of Britain's authority fell into two general categories that are of special interest here. The first centered on the implications of subjectship: in essence, British polemicists contended that Americans were subjects, that all subjects were under Parliament, and that therefore Americans were under Parliament. The second focused on the attributes of sovereignty and presupposed a certain fusion of the ideas of the empire and the community of allegiance. Building on the premise that two sovereign powers could not exist within the same state, British spokesmen argued that the empire was a state, that Parliament was its sovereign power, and that as members of the empire the colonies were of necessity under Parliament's sovereign authority. The two sets of arguments merged easily at a number of points, and elements

---

5. R. A. Humphreys, "The Rule of Law and the American Revolution," *Law Quarterly Review*, LIII (1937), 80.

6. Bailyn, *Ideological Origins*, 203.

7. [Thomas Jefferson], *A Summary View of the Rights of British America . . .* (Williamsburg, Va., 1774), ed. Thomas P. Abernethy (New York, 1943), 20.

of both appeared side by side throughout the long controversy. At the expense of doing some violence to the complexity and the chronology of the debate, however, the two arguments may be considered as separate and consecutive.

The argument from subjectship began with an uncontested premise, namely, that Americans were British subjects. Among other available proofs, both sides cited the guarantees embodied in the early grants and charters to substantiate the claim. Both also found support in the naturalization act of 1740, which plainly assumed that Americans were entitled to the rights of natural-born Englishmen.[8] The colonists' right to the benefits of the common law—a right virtually unquestioned by the mid-eighteenth century —provided additional corroborative evidence of their status as British subjects, although this particular proof was double-edged.[9] For Americans, their enjoyment of the common law was both a proof of their subjectship and a source of principles limiting Parliament's authority; in the hands of British polemicists, Americans' reception of the common law could be used as proof of Parliament's right to absolute sovereignty.

The use of the common law as evidence of Parliament's jurisdiction emerged largely in connection with the second (and crucial) premise of the argument from subjectship, the premise linking subject status and subordination to Parliament. British spokesmen at first expressed this premise in qualified form, drawing on established legal precedents and maxims rather than on broader principles of political and constitutional theory and arguing that certain categories of subjects, at least, were under Parliament. Initially, the British attempted to prove that the colonists were a class of subjects

8. The charter guarantees are discussed above, chap. 4, at n. 2. For arguments from the statute 13 Geo. II, c. 7 (1740), see James Otis, *A Vindication of the Conduct of the House of Representatives in the Province of Massachusetts-Bay* . . . (Boston, 1762), in Charles F. Mullett, ed., *Some Political Writings of James Otis*, University of Missouri Studies, IV (Columbia, Mo., 1929), 43; James Otis, *The Rights of the British Colonies Asserted and Proved* (Boston, 1764), in Bernard Bailyn, ed., *Pamphlets of the American Revolution, 1750–1776*, I (Cambridge, Mass., 1965), 475. See also [Stephen Hopkins], *The Rights of Colonies Examined* (Providence, R.I., 1765), *ibid.*, 511. The contrasting inferences that could be drawn from the 1740 statute can be seen by comparing the following: [Martin Howard, Jr.], *A Letter from a Gentleman at Halifax, to His Friend in Rhode-Island, Containing Remarks upon a Pamphlet, Entitled, The Rights of the Colonies Examined* (Newport, R.I., 1765), *ibid.*, 541; [Samuel Adams], the House of Representatives of Massachusetts to the earl of Shelburne, Jan. 15, 1768, in Harry Alonzo Cushing, ed., *The Writings of Samuel Adams* (New York, 1904–1908), I, 155.

9. Blackstone's denial of the colonists' right to the common law—discussed above, chap. 3, n. 36—was unusual.

subordinate to Parliament according to Coke's analysis in *Calvin's Case*. Eventually, however, Britain's defenders would move to a broader, more inclusive argument. Leaving Coke's subtle classifications—which left subjects in kingdoms like Scotland outside Parliament's jurisdiction—and turning instead to Lockean concepts, they would ultimately contend that all subjects, regardless of their particular condition or laws, were under Parliament's authority.

By the late seventeenth century English jurists had worked out three historical-constitutional paradigms to explain the relationships between the various dominions in the community of allegiance. Coke had defined two of these models, distinguishing between kingdoms acquired by descent and those gained by conquest and using Scotland and Ireland, respectively, to illustrate his arguments.[10] Dominions descending to the English king maintained their separate laws and governments; neither the laws of England nor the jurisdiction of Parliament extended to them. Territories won by force of arms were under the immediate control of the king, who could impose whatever laws he wished upon the subjugated population. In addition to its unquestioned authority over subjects in the realm of England, Parliament retained an ultimate supervisory jurisdiction over conquered kingdoms as well. When its laws named the conquered dominion particularly, according to Coke, they extended in full force.

Neither of Coke's models seemed to apply completely to lands acquired by discovery and colonization, and in the late seventeenth century English jurists devised a third model of imperial relations.[11] Responding to the question whether the laws of England

10. See above, chap. 1, at n. 35.
11. The starting point for this development was Blankard v. Galdy, 2 Salk. 411, 412 (1693). Chief Justice John Holt here commented that in uninhabited lands newly found by Englishmen, all English laws then in force prevailed. Holt's dictum was picked up and used by the counsel in Dutton v. Howell, Shower's Parl. Cases 24 (1693). This was the appeal of Wytham v. Dutton, 3 Mod. 159 (1687). In the original action, involving an incident in Barbados, the court had relied on the familiar doctrine of conquest. On appeal, Richard Howell's counsel contended that Barbados was a discovered colony or plantation, not a conquest, and that the laws of England prevailed there. In Smith v. Brown and Cooper, 2 Salk. 666 (1702?), Holt termed Virginia a conquest, denying that English laws extended to that colony. Richard West, counsel to the Board of Trade, rejected this classification in an opinion of 1720, claiming that "the common law of England is the common law of the plantations, and all statutes in affirmance of the common law passed in England, antecedent to the settlement of a colony, are in force in that colony, unless there is some private act to the contrary." William Forsyth, *Cases and Opinions on Constitutional Law, and Various Points of English Jurisprudence* . . . (London, 1869), 1. A memorandum by the master of

applied in "vacant" territories settled by emigrant Englishmen, jurists concluded that settlers from the mother country carried with them the common law and the existing English statutes that were "applicable to their own situation and the condition of an infant colony." The identification of applicable law was to be made in the first instance "by their own provincial judicature, subject to the revision and control of the king in council."[12] In contrast to the conquered countries, where English law extended only if and to the extent that the conqueror chose to impose it, the colonies to which the discovery model applied could claim the benefits of the common law as their birthright.

With these limitations, the discovery model would not have fully suited Great Britain's needs in the 1760s, for it merely provided the colonies concerned with a strong claim to rights while eliminating the possible implication of conquest in their reception of English law. But the initial formulation of the doctrine implied that those "discovered" colonies could be bound by Parliament when they were particularly named.[13] By mid-century Blackstone would go so far as to say that the very constitutions of such colonies were "liable to be new-modelled and reformed by the general superintending power of the legislature in the mother country."[14] In the 1760s British polemicists would stress this aspect of the doctrine and insist that Americans had to accept all the consequences of being "discovered colonies"—namely, the legitimate supervisory jurisdiction of Parliament as well as the benefits of the common law.

Early discussions of the discovery doctrine had centered on its divergence from the model of conquest concerning the extension of English laws; the similarity of the two paradigms concerning the extension of Parliament's authority went virtually unnoticed. Indeed, the proviso that discovered colonies could be bound by Parliament appeared in the doctrine without any explanation or theoretical justification. The intellectual trends and constitutional

the rolls, Aug. 9, 1722, reported in 2 Peere Williams 75, elaborated the doctrine of discovery, accepting Holt's original dictum as an authoritative statement of the law. Attorney General Sir Philip Yorke's opinion of 1729 that Maryland enjoyed the status of a discovered colony included both elements of what was now a fixed legal model or paradigm—namely, the extension of the common law and of Parliament's jurisdiction. Forsyth, *Cases and Opinions*, 2.

12. Tucker, ed., *Blackstone's Commentaries*, I:1, 108.

13. See the opinions of West (1720) and Yorke (1729) and the anonymous case in 2 Peere Williams (1722) cited in n. 11 above.

14. Tucker, ed., *Blackstone's Commentaries*, I:1, 108.

changes of the late seventeenth century were moving toward a concept of parliamentary sovereignty, and the judges seemingly included this proviso reflexively, assuming that existing precedents required modification only in order to fit the circumstances of the new colonies. The idea that only those statutes specifically naming the discovered and newly colonized lands extended to them seems to have been carried over from Coke's analysis of Ireland and other conquered dominions. An association of ideas and precedents on this point certainly appeared in the 1760s. Supporters of the Declaratory Act often assumed an analogy between Ireland and America in their arguments, even when they did not contend that the latter had been conquered.[15] In any event, whether the unquestioned fact of America's reception of English law was explained on the grounds of conquest or of discovery, British polemicists could point to that reception as evidence of the colonies' legal obligation to obey parliamentary acts.

Americans had initially accepted the doctrine of discovery as applicable to their situation, ignoring or failing to recognize its assumptions concerning Parliament's authority, and this made them vulnerable in the imperial debate of the 1760s. Judge Martin Howard, Jr., of Newport was among the first to exploit the weakness created by the colonists' appropriation of the doctrine. He reminded —or perhaps informed—his readers that "the common law has established it as a rule or maxim that the plantations are bound by British acts of Parliament if particularly named; and surely," he added pointedly, "no Englishman in his senses will deny the force of a common law maxim."[16] In short, if the colonists claimed to enjoy the common law according to the doctrine of discovery, they

15. Americans seemed more sensitive than the British to the initial connection between Ireland's dependence on Parliament and its acquisition by conquest. Coke had drawn this connection in Calvin's Case, and Americans constantly cited him—and argued against their own conquered status—when they were compared with Ireland. For one of many examples, see [Richard Bland], *The Colonel Dismounted: Or The Rector Vindicated . . .* (Williamsburg, Va., 1764), in Bailyn, ed., *Pamphlets of Am. Rev.*, I, 319, 323. Owen Dudley Edwards, "The American Image of Ireland: A Study of Its Early Phases," *Perspectives in American History*, IV (1970), 199–241, discusses the colonists' understanding of Ireland in the Revolutionary era, but he does not concentrate on the "constitutional image." For the Americans' use of Calvin's Case in distinguishing their situation from Ireland's, see Randolph Greenfield Adams, *Political Ideas of the American Revolution: Britannic-American Contributions to the Problem of Imperial Organization, 1765 to 1775* (Durham, N.C., 1922), 43–48, and Charles F. Mullett, "Coke and the American Revolution," *Economica*, XII (1932), esp. 468–470.

16. [Howard, Jr.], *Letter from Halifax*, in Bailyn, ed., *Pamphlets of Am. Rev.*, I, 536.

were bound by the maxim that placed discovered colonies under Parliament.

Howard did not merely rely on a particular maxim to embarrass the colonies. He argued that Parliament's authority was inherent in the very nature of the laws Americans claimed as their birthright and as the chief guarantor of their liberties, however those laws had been extended. Liberty and subjection proceeded from the same source, and to divide the two was impossible: "Can we claim the common law as an inheritance, and at the same time be at liberty to adopt one part of it and reject the other? Indeed we cannot. The common law, pure and indivisible in its nature and essence, cleaves to us during our lives and follows us from Nova Zembla to Cape Horn; and therefore, as the jurisdiction of Parliament arises out of and is supported by it, we may as well renounce our allegiance or change our nature as to be exempt from the jurisdiction of Parliament."[17] Howard thus cleverly confronted Americans with two distinct arguments. First, if the colonists claimed the common law as their birthright according to the discovery model, they were also obligated to accept that model's proviso for the extension of Parliament's authority. Second, whatever the reasons for the colonists' reception of the common law, they could not claim its benefits without also admitting the authority of the British legislature. The latter argument in particular was to be repeated many times during the imperial debate.[18]

Howard's arguments were powerful, but they left several loopholes through which Americans might escape his conclusions. Insofar as he relied on specific precedents associated with the doctrine of discovery—that is, as long as he argued from traditional maxims defining the status of emigrant subjects—he could be outmaneuvered by the contentions that the doctrine itself was wrong or that it did not apply to the American situation. The colonists, for example, could argue that the discovery model illegitimately included too

17. *Ibid.*, 537.
18. See, e.g., [William Knox], *The Controversy Between Great Britain and Her Colonies Reviewed* . . . (London, 1769), in Samuel E. Morison, ed., *William Knox on American Taxation, 1769*, Old South Association, Old South Leaflets, No. 210 (Boston, 1917?), 4–5. See also the opening speech of Thomas Hutchinson to the Massachusetts General Assembly, Jan. 6, 1773, [Massachusetts General Court], *The Speeches of His Excellency Governor Hutchinson, to the General Assembly of the Massachusetts-Bay. At a Session begun and held on the Sixth of January, 1773. With the Answers of His Majesty's Council and the House of Representatives Respectively* (Boston, 1773), 9, hereafter cited as Hutchinson, *Speeches and Answers.*

much of the earlier conquest doctrine or contend that their status more nearly resembled that of the seventeenth-century Scots: subject to the king, but not to Parliament. To refute Howard's more general argument that the law was the source of both individual rights and parliamentary power, his opponents could insist that the law ought therefore to control and limit Parliament, thus using the law and the rights of Englishmen as a powerful weapon against the doctrine of absolute parliamentary authority.[19] Americans did develop such arguments, forcing British polemicists to find more fundamental explanations for America's dependence than could be derived either from traditional maxims about specific classes of subjects or from the colonists' reception of the common law. Ultimately, defenders of Parliament's absolute power found their best justification in a fourth model, the doctrine of consent.

Consent, indeed, was both more potent and more fundamental than the traditional historical-constitutional paradigms of conquest and discovery. When linked with the status of subjectship generally, it could produce a complete warrant for parliamentary power that cut across the old divisions and classifications. The impulse to forge this link was clearly manifest in the debates of the pre-Revolutionary years.

Blackstone's analysis of Ireland had introduced the concept of consent into the traditional doctrine of conquest. Parliament's legitimate right to bind Irish subjects, he asserted, flowed not from the *jus conquesta*, but rather from an express or tacit compact to end hostilities. Without such a compact, the Irish would have remained enemies ruled by force, not subjects ruled by consent.[20] Analogously, Blackstone's declaration that the American plantations had been obtained "either by right of conquest and driving out the natives or by treaties," along with his acknowledgment that Americans were subjects and not enemies, equally implied the existence of a primal compact legitimizing Parliament's authority.[21] This consent explained America's dependence on the British legislature.

There were obvious tactical advantages to the notion of conquest as conceived by Blackstone, namely, as a rule by force leading to a compact in which the conquered submitted to the conqueror. By

19. Hopkins and Otis attacked Howard specifically on these grounds. Bailyn, ed., *Pamphlets of Am. Rev.*, I, 734n.

20. See above, chap. 3, at n. 33.

21. Tucker, ed., *Blackstone's Commentaries*, I:1, 109.

assuming a necessary compact ending hostilities, one could argue that the subsequent relationship rested on consent and was governed by law. Moreover, it would be possible both to explain the colonists' reception of much of England's law and to justify specific disparities between English and American laws and rights if the concept could be applied to America's situation. The latter was crucial, for the specific "rights of Englishmen" could be invoked as a defense against arbitrary power. Blackstone himself saw a "very remarkable case" in which those rights had legitimized opposition to established authority—England's own Glorious Revolution.[22] By denying, in essence, that the particular rights of Englishmen were held by Americans—who had nevertheless consented to Parliament's authority—Blackstone's doctrine limited the precedent of the revolution undertaken in defense of those rights in 1688.

Blackstone could not invalidate the precedent of the Glorious Revolution with this technicality or destroy its relevance for Americans. According to his argument, the rights of the colonists differed from those of other subjects, and an American revolution would not be justified under circumstances similar to those in England in 1688; however, there could be circumstances "which a fertile imagination might furnish, since both law and history are silent," to legitimate "the exertion of those inherent (though latent) powers of society, which no climate, no time, no constitution, no contract, can ever destroy or diminish."[23] Blackstone still admitted a theoretical limit to all legitimate authority, even the authority Britain exercised over its "conquests."[24] Yet by denying the inherent birthright of Americans to the common law—by choosing to stress an undefined postconquest consent to dependency rather than a specific compact fully embodying all the rights inherent in England's law —Blackstone deprived the colonists of an appeal to the "rights of Englishmen" as a challenge to the legitimacy of Parliament's American policies.

Blackstone himself did not explicitly connect his analysis of Ire-

22. For an analysis of Blackstone's treatment of the Glorious Revolution and its resonance in the colonies, see Gerald Stourzh, "William Blackstone: Teacher of Revolution," *Jahrbuch für Amerikastudien*, XV (1970), 186–187, and *passim*.

23. The full passage is quoted *ibid.*, 187n.

24. For Blackstone (as for Locke), "absolute" authority was never "arbitrary." Positive law—law-as-will or as command of the sovereign—was always limited by higher principles of legitimacy. See Gerald Stourzh, *Alexander Hamilton and the Idea of Republican Government* (Stanford, Cal., 1970), 12–13, 21–22, and 216n.

land's dependence, his declaration that America was "conquered," and the potentially explosive implications of England's Glorious Revolution. Others more directly involved in the imperial controversy did seem to see the logic of the doctrine. In particular, British polemicists tended to avoid arguments centering on America's enjoyment of the common law and to stress the Blackstonian implication of colonial consent to parliamentary authority. They were apt to accept and, indeed, to justify the absence of certain "English rights" in the colonies on the grounds of different circumstances, simultaneously maintaining that this in no way lessened or altered the dependence flowing from original consent.

Lieutenant Governor Thomas Hutchinson's debates with the Massachusetts General Court in 1773 contained arguments in this vein. Although Hutchinson accepted the notion that the first settlers had carried over the common law when they emigrated from England, he did not build his argument on the traditional model of discovery.[25] Rather he emphasized that when the first emigrants left England, "it was their Sense, and it was the Sense of the Kingdom, that they were to remain subject to the supreme Authority of Parliament. This appears from the Charter itself and from other irresistable Evidence." The imperfect transmission of the "Rights of English Subjects" destroyed neither the colonists' status as subjects nor the power of the government to which they had consented: "Does it follow that the Government, by their Removal from one Part of the Dominions to another, loses it's Authority over that Part to which they remove, and that they are freed from the Subjection they were under before; or do they expect that Government should relinquish its Authority because they cannot enjoy this particular Right?"[26] The Americans remained British subjects, part of the community of allegiance, and they remained bound by their own consent to accept the absolute authority of the government of that community.

The argument from subjectship was completed when British theorists focused on the idea of consent. The initial premise of that argument remained unchanged: Americans were subjects. But the

25. See Hutchinson's charge to the grand jury, Mar. term, 8 Geo. III (1768), in Josiah Quincy, Jr., *Reports of Cases Argued and Adjudged in the Superior Court of Judicature of the Province of Massachusetts Bay, between 1761 and 1772* (Boston, 1865), 258–260, hereafter cited as Quincy, *Mass. Reports*.
26. Opening speech, Jan. 6, 1773, in Hutchinson, *Speeches and Answers*, 10.

second premise had been altered and strengthened. Instead of classi-
fying Americans in a category of subjects whose subordination to
Parliament could be explained by traditional maxims, models, or
precedents, the defenders of British policies now insisted that subjectship implied consent to Parliament's authority. Whether Americans were subjects by birthright or by conquest, whether they
inherited the common law or not, they were bound by their own
consent to obey Parliament.

Shifting from arguments about both the origins of the colonial
settlements and the implications of the colonists' reception of the
common law and moving instead to the broader notion of consent
to subordination, British polemicists forged a solid link between
the concept of subjectship and the Lockean notion of a fundamental
compact creating a community of men under one government. If
all Englishmen shared in such a primal contract, then even those
who left the mother country to settle in America could be presumed
to remain within the jurisdiction of the government established for
the community: "They went out subjects of Great Britain, and
unless they can shew a new compact made between them and the
parliament of Great Britain (for the king alone could not make a
new compact with them) they are still subjects to all intents and
purposes whatsoever. If they are subjects, they are liable to the laws
of the country. . . . If the colonies are subjects of Great Britain, they
are represented and consent to all statutes."[27]

In arguing that American subjects remained under Parliament by
virtue of an original compact, British thinkers merely extended to
imperial problems a set of theories already adopted to explain the
structure of authority in the mother country. As noted earlier,
Englishmen in the late seventeenth century had combined Lockean
ideas of the contractual basis of government with Coke's theory of
perpetual allegiance and subjection.[28] The logic of this combination
seemed to work well as long as analysis focused on the realm of
England. By the 1760s, however, it was no longer England but the
constitutional structure of an empire that was at stake, and the shift
in perspective threatened the conflation of Cokean and Lockean
ideas. Although British theorists remained oblivious to the significance of this altered context, assuming that ideas persuasive at

27. Speech of Lord George Lyttelton, House of Lords debate on repeal of the Stamp Act,
Feb. 10, 1766, in [Cobbett and Wright, eds.], *Cobbett's Parliamentary History*, XVI, 167.
28. See above, chap. 3, at n. 22.

home were equally valid for the empire as a whole, Americans who felt the force of the theoretical contradictions in the shape of objectionable policies would be driven to reassess the foundations of their imperial connection.

For Coke, the community of allegiance—the empire—was a by-product of the personal ties between individual men and the king. Internal political divisions within that community grew as new realms were acquired by the king, and the relationships between those realms and the mother country were determined by the mode of acquisition. The separate dominions might well display different legal and governmental systems. Although the laws of God and nature provided some uniformity, dissimilar customs and constitutional histories insured considerable local diversity; the precise duties and rights of subjects thus varied within the whole community. What held the community together, what enabled men to conceive of it as a whole, was not the extension of English law or the superintending power of Parliament, but rather the primal natural relationship that each member shared with the king.

The emergence of the contract theory of government and society subtly altered this concept. Locke reversed Coke's notion that the subject-king relationship preceded and defined the community. Rather than seeing the origins of subjection in the natural dependence of the inferior on the superior, he placed his emphasis squarely upon the individual's consent to join with other men in forming a society. The social compact defined the community and obliged its members to submit to the will of the majority. The community as a whole instituted government and set the metes and bounds of its authority.[29] For Locke, the social contract established the obligation of allegiance; the community merely defined its object in establishing government.[30]

Much of the traditional law of allegiance was applicable within this Lockean framework. While the community itself remained intact the allegiance and subjectship of individual members remained perpetual. As long as government continued to operate

29. The separate agreements were later defined as the "social contract" and the "government contract," though for the most part Locke himself saw the relationship between society and government as a trusteeship relation rather than a contractual one. Ernest Barker, *Essays on Government*, 2d ed. (Oxford, 1951), 91, 98–101. Obligation to government stemmed not from a contract with government, but rather from the prior social contract.

30. See above, chap. 3, at n. 22.

legitimately, protecting life, liberty, and property, individual subjects were bound. Even when events forced the "dissolution of government," the obligation of allegiance remained unchanged, although focused, perhaps, on a new government.[31] Only the dissolution of society itself destroyed that bond.

The theory was beautifully adapted for those who wished to legitimize alterations and revolutions in government without sanctioning as a necessary first step the obliteration of all authority and all obligation. When applied to the Glorious Revolution, the persistence of the fundamental social contract legitimized the Convention Parliament and gave its acts a binding force; it explained and justified the transference of allegiance from James II to William and Mary. Moreover, the theory sanctioned not only the dethronement of princes who became tyrants but also the limitation of all government. The people—the community as a whole—could even dissolve the supreme legislative power when it transgressed its lawful bounds.[32]

Locke did not hesitate to declare that "the People shall be Judge" when the legitimacy of either Prince or Legislative was challenged.[33] Yet he paid little attention to the mechanisms by which the people could make their decisions known.[34] Indeed, Locke's analysis failed to clarify the role of Parliament in its relation to the community as a whole. As the "Legislative," Parliament was part of the government—the dominant, supreme part—exercising an absolute authority over the governed within the framework of the fundamental contract.[35] As the representative embodiment of the community as a whole, however, it was in a sense the "people," capable of judging the legitimacy of the government. This dual character of both ruler and ruled, resting on the assumption that the community of allegiance was truly represented at Westminster, underlay the notion that Parliament was adequately limited by its own self-control. Extraordinary oppressions and usurpations might require resistance outside this institution, but Englishmen could

31. Locke, *Two Treatises*, ed. Laslett, II, esp. secs. 211–212, 243.
32. *Ibid.*, secs. 221–223. For Locke's general statement of the limits on "absolute" government, see secs. 135–139.
33. *Ibid.*, sec. 240.
34. J. R. Pole, *Political Representation in England and the Origins of the American Republic* (London, 1966), 22.
35. Pole notes Locke's tentative but undeveloped sense of the distinction between positive and fundamental law. *Ibid.*, 18–19. Fundamental law limited what Parliament could do by positive law. See also above, n. 24.

rely for the most part on the common sense and political virtue of their chosen representatives to prevent Parliament from becoming arbitrary and hence illegitimate.

In Great Britain this trust seemed persuasive, for there was convincing evidence that this parliamentary self-restraint could work. In 1765 (the same year that the Stamp Act was passed) Parliament proposed a bill to annex the Isle of Man to the home realm, a measure dictated by the general desire to tighten up the commercial system and by the specific wish to eliminate the rampant smuggling centered in this little "independent kingdom." Parliament's right to effect this annexation rested on the contention that Manxmen were subjects, even though both royal patent and parliamentary charter had solemnly delegated independent governmental authority to the proprietors.[36]

Counsel for the Manx proprietors protested Parliament's right to take private property without the owner's consent and compensation, even while affirming its power to do so: "I do not presume to set the bounds of legislative power; they are, and perhaps ought to be, invisible: but I venture to say, that it is bounded, not only by its own moderation and equity, but by the trust reposed in it by society, and by the laws of God and nature. Even absolute power, where it is necessary, is not arbitrary by being absolute, but it is still limited by that reason, and confined to those ends, for which it was made absolute."[37] Even tyrants who observed no other rule of morality—Tiberius, Domitian, Henry VIII, and the French kings —expropriated private property only upon the condition of compensation: "What Parliament can do, I presume not to say: but I think I know what it will not do: it will not take away private property without imminent necessity and just compensation."[38] And Parliament agreed. Persuaded of its mistake, reminded of the dictates of reason and justice, it resolved to annex the Isle of Man only after consultation with and payment to the proprietors.[39]

Incidents such as this reinforced the assumption that Parliament represented all subjects and could be relied upon to rule with self-

36. Adams, *Political Ideas of Am. Rev.*, 45, sees this as a precedent for the argument that allegiance could be owed to the crown, not the realm. Details of the status of the Isle of Man and of the proposed annexation can be found in [Cobbett and Wright, eds.], *Cobbett's Parliamentary History*, XVI, 15–20.

37. Argument of Mr. [Grey?] Cooper, counsel for the proprietors, *ibid.*, 24.

38. *Ibid.*

39. *Ibid.*, 34.

restraint. The idea was inherent in Locke's vision of Parliament as the embodiment of the people and was made even more persuasive by constitutional changes after the Glorious Revolution that attenuated the sense that there were subjects who were beyond Parliament's control. The Act of Union ended the autonomy of Scottish subjects, giving them representatives in the new British parliament and bringing them under its authority. Others who might have claimed to enjoy the status of pre-Union Scotsmen—the Dutch born during the reign of William III and Hanoverians born after 1714—apparently made no effort to do so. British jurists and theorists accepted that anomaly simply by ignoring it.[40] Conquered subjects had never posed a problem, for traditional legal authority put them under Parliament's control. The imputation of consent to subjugated peoples neatly aligned the doctrine of conquest with the more recent constitutional theories.

British thinkers saw no reason for excluding the American colonists from this paradigm. By combining the established rule against expatriation (*"Nemo potest exuere patriam"*) with the newer idea of an original contract, they reached the obvious conclusion that emigrant subjects remained within the allegiance and the jurisdiction of the government erected by the original community. American subjects continued under the authority of Parliament until the community as a whole decided otherwise or until society itself dissolved. Barring such a dissolution, the community of allegiance formed a single political unit with a single sovereign, and wherever subjects resided, they remained represented in and bound by the parliament embodying that community.

The idea that the community of allegiance formed a single political unit was essential to the "argument from sovereignty" used by British writers to counter American claims to exemption from parliamentary acts. That argument drew its compelling force from the generalized belief that *"imperium in imperio"* (a state within a

40. The status of Hanoverians was finally considered in Isaacson v. Durant, 17 Q.B.D. 54 (1886), when it was decided that they had been subjects until the accession of Queen Victoria. As for the Dutch, their status was apparently never judicially considered. I have found no treatment of the question, and Professor Thomas Broun Smith of the University of Edinburgh has informed me that he knows of no consideration of the issue in the Scottish materials. The status of Dutchmen may have been considered a separate case, falling outside the normal doctrine of allegiance and subjectship, since William was not "king" of the United Provinces. Americans did see and comment on the discrepancy between the status of Hanoverians and the theory of parliamentary sovereignty as it was linked with subjectship.

state) was a political absurdity, but it necessarily presupposed the validity of the empire as a single state. Until Americans challenged this presupposition, the British insistence that "there must reside somewhere in every political unit a single, undivided, final power, higher in legal authority than any other power," caused them tremendous intellectual difficulties.[41] The rapidity and ease with which defenders of Parliament adopted this argument underscore its power in mid-eighteenth-century British thought.

Governor Francis Bernard was perhaps the first to give explicit constitutional meaning to the concept of the "British Empire," proclaiming that "the King in Parliament is the sole and absolute sovereign of the whole British Empire."[42] Lord Chancellor Northington assumed the point when opposing repeal of the Stamp Act: "Every government can arbitrarily inpose [*sic*] laws on all its subjects; there must be a supreme dominion in every state; whether monarchical, aristocratical, democratical or mixed. And all subjects of each state are bound by the laws made of government."[43] The Declaratory Act itself, in a "stylistic innovation of constitutional significance," proclaimed the colonies dependent upon the "imperial crown *and parliament* of Great Britain," altering the formula adopted earlier with respect to Ireland that had stressed dependence on the "Imperial Crown" alone and had ultimately relied on the doctrine of conquest.[44]

Instances of the use of the sovereignty argument, linked with the concept of a unitary state formed by the community of allegiance, became commonplace after 1765. Both concepts had become a part of the established theoretical orthodoxy, requiring little explicit justification for their use. To state them was to justify them, for their validity seemed self-evident. William Knox's *The Controversy Between Great Britain and Her Colonies Reviewed* (1769) reflects the tone, the confidence, the force of this argument:

41. Bailyn, *Ideological Origins*, 198, 198–229.

42. Richard Koebner, *Empire* (Cambridge, 1961), 134, 135, 145. Bernard's claim was made as the tenth thesis of his *Principles of Law and Policy, applied to the British Colonies in America*, written and circulated in 1764, though not published until 1774.

43. House of Lords debate on repeal of the Stamp Act, Feb. 10, 1766, [Cobbett and Wright, eds.], *Cobbett's Parliamentary History*, XVI, 170. Compare Lord Mansfield's assertion that "the British legislature . . . represents the whole British empire, and has authority to bind every part and every subject without the least distinction, whether such subjects have the right to vote or not, or whether the law binds places within the realm or without." *Ibid.*, 173.

44. My emphasis. The point is made in Koebner, *Empire*, 154, 157.

For if the authority of the legislative be not in one instance equally supreme over the colonies as it is over the people of England, then are not the colonies of the same community with the people of England. All distinctions destroy this union; and if it can be shown in any particular to be dissolved, it must be so in all instances whatever. There is no alternative: either the colonies are a part of the community of Great Britain or they are in a state of nature with respect to her, and in no case can be subject to the jurisdiction of that legislative power which represents her community, which is the British Parliament.[45]

American attempts to justify exemption from certain kinds of parliamentary acts were fruitless as long as the linkage of one community, one empire, one sovereign was accepted. Until they restated the nature of the community of allegiance, challenged the equation of empire and state, and turned to a reexamination of sovereignty, the colonists faced an unwanted choice between absolute dependence and total independence. No one expressed the point better than Thomas Hutchinson:

I know of no line that can be drawn between the supreme Authority of Parliament and the total Independence of the Colonies: It is impossible there should be two independent Legislatures in one and the same State, for although there may be but one Head, the King, yet the two legislative Bodies will make two Governments as distinct as the Kingdoms of England and Scotland before the Union. If we might be suffered to be altogether independent of Great Britain, could we have any claim to the Protection of the Government of which we are no longer a Part?[46]

Forgetting that Scotsmen had been subjects before the Union, assuming the connection between allegiance and protection, and relying on a concept of community that embodied subordination to the sovereign power of the king-in-Parliament, Hutchinson symbolized perfectly the intellectual position of the British in the imperial debate.

Americans constructed reasoned arguments against parliamentary claims, for the most part drawing on the same heritage of law and theory as the British. Yet the colonists joined the elements of that heritage in different ways, ways more consonant with their own experience and needs. In the process, they moved toward new principles of political obedience and constitutional thought. A va-

45. [Knox], *The Controversy Reviewed*, in Morison, ed., *Knox on Am. Taxation*, 10–11.
46. Opening speech, Jan. 6, 1773, Hutchinson, *Speeches and Answers*, 11.

riety of real interests and frustrations, perceived through a lens of radical ideology, motivated individuals to undertake this opposition and drove them toward the final breach. Law and logic alone were not enough to mobilize a widespread resistance or to impel men to take up the sword against their brothers.[47] But the ideas used to advance colonial claims were more than mere expedients, more than temporarily useful weapons to be dropped when the war of words was over. They would continue to shape both thought and action in the years after 1776.

Although the Declaratory Act expressed what was to remain the central British position throughout the imperial debate, it served as the symbolic focus of American opposition for only a time. The colonists first examined the nature and extent of Parliament's authority over them, but the thrust of their arguments soon carried them beyond this issue. Starting with responses to specific British claims, the Americans moved inexorably toward new views of the community of allegiance, the empire, and the location and limits of sovereignty.

In the opening stages of the debate, many colonists acknowledged that they owed "all due Subordination to that August Body, the Parliament of *Great-Britain*."[48] Some admitted that the British legislature had "a general authority, a supreme jurisdiction over all His Majesty's subjects," assuming (for the moment, at least) the connection between subjectship and parliamentary power.[49] James Otis proclaimed that "every lawyer, nay every tyro" knew that "the Parliament of Great Britain hath a just, clear, equitable, and constitutional right, power and authority to bind the colonies by all acts wherein they are named."[50]

Yet the colonists insisted from the beginning on the limitation of this "due Subordination." It was limited first by the rights inherent in the status of subjectship, rights embodied in and defined most clearly by the common law that Americans claimed as their birth-

---

47. See generally Bailyn, *Ideological Origins*, esp. "A Note on Conspiracy," 144–159.

48. "The Declarations of the Stamp Act Congress," Article I (Oct. 7–24, 1765), in Edmund S. Morgan, ed., *Prologue to Revolution: Sources and Documents on the Stamp Act Crisis, 1764–1766* (Chapel Hill, N.C., 1959), 62.

49. [Thomas Fitch et al.], *Reasons Why the British Colonies, in America, Should Not be Charged with Internal Taxes . . .* (New Haven, Conn., 1764), in Bailyn, ed., *Pamphlets of Am. Rev.*, I, 387.

50. [James Otis], *A Vindication of the British Colonies, against the Aspersions of the Halifax Gentleman, in His Letter to a Rhode-Island Friend* (Boston, 1765), *ibid.*, 555.

right. It was determined and bounded as well by the universally recognized principle that allegiance was owed in return for protection. And, ultimately, this dependence rested on the consent of the colonists to England's exercise of power.

The notion that the rights of Englishmen restricted Parliament was not new, nor was it confined to one side of the Atlantic. As early as 1721 Jeremiah Dummer had distinguished between Parliament's power—which was "absolute and unaccountable"—and its right to legislate on certain matters with respect to the plantations: "One may say, that what the parliament can't do justly they can't do at all. *In maximis minima est licentia.* The higher the power is, the greater caution is to be used in the execution of it, because the sufferer is helpless, and without resort."[51] Although the "omnipotence of the Legislature" was "a favourite doctrine," declared Lord Camden in 1766, "there are some things they cannot do."[52] Throughout the controversy Americans and their allies would insist that the rights they claimed as Englishmen—indeed, the rights they claimed as men—ought to keep Parliament within the bounds of legitimacy.

The brilliant but often tortured arguments of James Otis had this firm belief at their core. Otis accepted much of the British position. He acknowledged America's rightful subjection to Parliament, resting this belief on the "natural relation" existing between the mother country and the colonies and on the notion that "*imperium in imperio*" was "the greatest of all political solecisms."[53] Yet to accept Parliament as the absolute sovereign was not to concede that it was all-powerful: "The Parliament cannot make 2 and 2, 5: omnipotency cannot do it."[54] Sovereign power was, by definition, legitimate

51. Jer[emiah] Dummer, *A Defence of the New-England Charters* (London, 1765 [orig. publ. 1721]), 85. Henry Campbell Black, *Black's Law Dictionary: Definitions of the Terms and Phrases of American and English Jurisprudence, Ancient and Modern,* 4th ed. rev. (St. Paul, Minn., 1968), 897, states the maxim, "*In maxima potentia minima licentia*" (in the greatest power there is the least freedom), citing the Commendam Case, Hobart 140, 159 (1612). In its original context, the maxim directly follows the observation that "there is nothing more contrary to liberty, than licentiousness, nor to discretion, than foolishness."

52. House of Lords debate on repeal of the Stamp Act, Feb. 10, 1766, [Cobbett and Wright, eds.], *Cobbett's Parliamentary History,* XVI, 168.

53. [Otis], *Vindication of the British Colonies,* in Bailyn, ed., *Pamphlets of Am. Rev.,* I, 555. Otis discussed the imperial relationship in his "Postscript" to this pamphlet. He linked the natural allegiance of the colonists to their imperial situation, using the same parent-child metaphor Coke had used in describing subjectship: "As there is a natural relation between father and son, so is there between a mother state and its colonies." Like Coke, Otis contended that "political relations are but modifications of those which are founded in nature, and from whence rise duties of universal obligation." *Ibid.,* 578.

54. Otis, *Rights Asserted and Proved, ibid.,* 454.

power, exercised within a framework of rights. Just as the allegiance owed by American subjects was "natural, perpetual, and inseparable from their persons, let them be in what country they may, their rights" were "also natural, inherent, and perpetual."[55] To deny these rights was to destroy sovereignty, leaving no recourse but revolution, namely, appeal "to the Law of Nature." For Otis, authority exercised illegitimately, in disregard of rights and justice, was tantamount to "an Abdication, a total Dissolution of Government."[56]

This general claim that rights limited Parliament's authority raised two crucial questions, the first involving the nature of those rights and the second concerning enforcement. What were the rights Americans could use to draw the line between legitimate and illegitimate power? How could clashes between power and right be prevented or resolved? In dealing with these issues, the colonists slowly shifted their attention from the specifics of parliamentary authority to broader questions concerning the constitutional structure of the empire. The shift was accomplished within the context of debates over the character and meaning of subjectship.

The colonists' concern over the nature of their subjectship had always involved the question of rights. Long before the 1760s Americans had rejected attempts to place them in the category of conquered subjects, for the rights of conquered peoples depended upon the will of the conqueror. As early as 1651 Virginia had carefully declared that its surrender to the Commonwealth commissioners was "a voluntary act not forced nor constrained by a conquest upon the country."[57] Opposition reappeared whenever royal governors or proprietorial representatives tried to claim the conqueror's power to alter or create local law, or whenever the suggestion was made that Americans, in the position of a con-

55. *Ibid.*, App. II, 474.

56. Argument before the Massachusetts council, Dec. 21, 1765, Quincy, *Mass. Reports*, 204. Otis argued here with reference to the shutting up of courts of justice during the Stamp Act controversy. His point was that when the courts were closed, there were no legal remedies for infringements of rights. This amounted to a default of protection by which the king "un-kings himself in the most essential Point." Although Otis thus focused on the king—a "dissolution of government" reminiscent of 1689, not necessarily affecting Parliament's power—John Adams centered his attention on the parliamentary act at the root of the controversy. Adams specifically declared that "a Parliament of Great Britain can have no more Right to tax the Colonies than a Parliament of Paris." *Ibid.*, 205, 201.

57. Quoted in St. George Leakin Sioussat, *The English Statutes in Maryland*, Johns Hopkins University Studies in Historical and Political Science, XXI (Baltimore, 1903), 24.

quered people, could not claim the rights inherent in the common law.[58]

During the pre-Revolutionary years Americans rejected outright the British argument—explicit in Blackstone's analysis, implicit in the frequent analogies with Ireland—that parliamentary authority extended to the colonies by conquest. Fully aware of the legal and political implications of the traditional doctrine, Richard Bland stoutly denied that Virginians were "a people conquered by British arms." In phrases already familiar from earlier disputes over the extension of English law, Bland maintained that the colonists were "the descendants of Englishmen, who by their own consent and at the expense of their own blood and treasure undertook to settle this new region for the benefit and aggrandizement of the parent kingdom," concluding that "the native privileges our progenitors enjoyed must be derived to us from them, as they could not be forfeited by their migration to America."[59]

The Maryland lower house struck the same chord when it resolved that the province was "not under the circumstances of a conquered country; that if it were, the present Christian inhabitants thereof, would be in the circumstances, not of the conquered, but of the conqueror."[60] James Otis ridiculed the British legal writers who considered the colonies "as a parcel of *little insignificant conquered islands.*" According to James Wilson, the principle of conquest, "so far as it can operate, will operate in favour of the colonists, and not against them." John Dickinson rejected Blackstone's assertion that America was conquered because it involved a "confusion of ideas," while James Iredell saw it as an "extraordinary" error. John Adams and Thomas Jefferson also deemed the first settlers emigrant subjects and not a subjected people.[61]

58. See *ibid.*, App. II, 80–104, for the pamphlet by Daniel Dulany, Sr., *The Right of the Inhabitants of Maryland to the Benefit of the English Laws* (Annapolis, Md., 1728). The pamphlet was written during a controversy over the extension of English laws that embittered politics in Maryland for over a decade. In the course of the dispute (1722), the lower house resolved that the province was "not under the Circumstances of a Conquered Country," and declared that whoever said otherwise "are ill Wishers to the Country and mistake its Constitution." *Ibid.*, App. I, 74. The resolutions were repeated in almost the same form in May 1768.

59. [Bland], *The Colonel Dismounted*, in Bailyn, ed., *Pamphlets of Am. Rev.*, I, 319. Bland cited Coke, Bacon, and Holt in the course of his argument.

60. Resolution of May 26, 1768, *Md. Archives*, LXI, 330.

61. Otis, *Rights Asserted and Proved*, in Bailyn, ed., *Pamphlets of Am. Rev.*, I, 435. [James Wilson], *Considerations on the Nature and Extent of the Legislative Authority of the British Parliament* (Philadelphia, 1774), in Robert Green McCloskey, ed., *The Works of James Wilson*,

Although Americans' main impulse was to defend their birth-right to the liberties of Englishmen by rejecting the status of con-quered subjects, they did not hesitate to challenge the traditional doctrine of conquest more generally. Even conquered subjects, "upon submission and good behavior," were "entitled to the essen-tial rights of men and citizens."[62] The idea that "the conqueror is absolute master of his conquest" was a "monstrous principle" and "one of the sources of despotic government." The conqueror's right proceeded from "the just defense of himself," and although he could apportion praise and blame according to the origins of the dispute, seek reparations for his expenses and damages, and impose exemplary penalties to forestall further conflict, he was limited by the law of nature in his relations with the conquered.[63] Americans also questioned Parliament's claim to absolute authority over Ire-land and other conquered dominions. Benjamin Franklin thought that the British legislature had "*usurped* a dominion" over Ireland.[64] James Wilson found it foreign to his central purpose to "inquire into the reasonableness of founding the authority of the British parliament over Ireland, upon the title of conquest," although "it would be somewhat difficult to deduce it satisfactorily in this manner."[65] The Massachusetts House actually reinterpreted Coke's classic explanation of Irish dependency to correspond with its own notions of the proper foundations of political obligation: "The Opinion of Lord Coke that Ireland was bound by Statutes of England wherein they *were named*, if compared with his other Writings, appears manifestly to be grounded upon a Supposition, that Ireland had by an Act of their own, in the Reign of King John,

II (Cambridge, Mass., 1967), 740; [John Dickinson], *An Essay on the Constitutional Power of Great-Britain over the Colonies in America; with the Resolves of the Committee for the Province of Pennsylvania, and their Instructions To their Representatives in Assembly* (Philadelphia, 1774), in *The Political Writings of John Dickinson . . .* (Wilmington, Del., 1801), I, 389n; James Iredell, "Address to the Inhabitants of Great Britain," Sept. 1774, in Griffith J. McRee, ed., *Life and Correspondence of James Iredell . . .* , I (New York, 1857), 216. For Adams, see generally, "Novanglus IX," in Adams, ed., *Works of John Adams*, IV, 141–151. For Jefferson, see *A Summary View*, ed. Abernethy, esp. 6. The point was canvassed in Congress in the debate of Sept. 8, 1774. See John Adams, "Notes of Debates," [Sept. 8, 1774], in Edmund C. Burnett, ed., *Letters of Members of the Continental Congress* (Washington, D.C., 1921–1936), I, 20–22.
62. Otis, *Rights Asserted and Proved*, in Bailyn, ed., *Pamphlets of Am. Rev.*, I, 452, 460.
63. *Ibid.*, App. II, 477n.
64. John Bigelow, ed. and comp., *The Complete Works of Benjamin Franklin . . .* (New York and London, 1887–1888), IV, 309.
65. [Wilson], *Considerations on Parliament*, in McCloskey, ed., *Works of James Wilson*, II, 739.

consented to be thus bound, and upon any other Supposition this Opinion would be against *Reason*; for *Consent only* gives human Laws their Force."[66]

John Adams, writing as "Novanglus," undertook the most complete examination of the legal foundations of Ireland's subordination and the traditional formulation of the doctrine of conquest. He concluded that Parliament's authority to rule Ireland was "founded on the consent and compact of the Irish by Poyning's [*sic*] law to be so governed, if it have any foundation at all; and this consent was given, and compact made, in consequence of a conquest." The only valid source of any parliamentary right to bind countries by specifically naming them in legislation lay not in the common law or in conquest per se, but in compact and statute:

These are the principles upon which the dependence and subordination of Ireland are founded. Whether they are just or not is not necessary for us to inquire. . . . But this much is certain, that none of these principles take place in the case of America. She never was conquered by Britain. She never consented to be a state dependent upon, or subordinate to the British parliament, excepting only in the regulation of her commerce; and therefore the reasonings of British writers upon the case of Ireland are not applicable to the case of the colonies, any more than those upon the case of Wales.[67]

American polemicists thus countered the "argument from conquest" not only by denying that the colonies were analogous to Ireland but also by affirming that Parliament's power over conquered dominions was limited by compact and natural law. Since the colonists had not been conquered, however, they did not need to rely upon nature or upon an undefined original contract to discover their detailed prerogatives. As emigrant subjects, proclaimed James Otis, Americans knew from England's history as well as from their own the rights they were entitled to "by the common law, by their several charters, by the law of nature and nations, and by the law of God."[68]

66. House response to second Hutchinson speech, Mar. 2, 1773, Hutchinson, *Speeches and Answers*, 46.

67. [Adams], "Novanglus X," in Adams, ed., *Works of John Adams*, IV, 151, 158. For a more detailed analysis of Adams's views on Ireland, see Edwards, "American Image of Ireland," *Perspectives Am. Hist.*, IV (1970), 220–229. For a brief explanation of Poynings's Law, see Keir, *Constitutional History of Modern Britain*, 434.

68. Otis, *Vindication of the Conduct of the House*, in Mullett, ed., *Pol. Writings of James Otis*, 43.

Perceiving the dangers inherent in the doctrine of conquest and intent on affirming their birthright to the laws and liberties of Englishmen, Americans had at first claimed the benefit of the doctrine of discovery, insisting that their relationship with England be discussed in terms of colonization rather than conquest.[69] Yet the inadequacies of that doctrine were revealed once attention shifted from its guarantee of both the transmission of the law and the retention of English rights to its provision for Parliament's ultimate superintending power over colonized lands. By the 1760s this provision was being justified by defining subjectship as participation in a primal social compact that bound men to obey the government established by the community, regardless of whether they remained in the home realm or not. This raised the difficult problem of how the individual rights guaranteed by the doctrine were to be protected against the power of the government whose authority the doctrine also purported to extend.

Some Americans were still convinced by the prevailing British idea that self-control would prevent Parliament from infringing the rights of subjects; the Isle of Man incident showed that parliamentary self-restraint was not necessarily an illusion. Other examples, too, confirmed this trust. Although the British legislature claimed absolute power over Ireland, James Otis observed, it had never presumed to tax that dominion.[70] Within the mother country itself, Parliament had sometimes passed unjust laws that sparked popular resistance and, consequently, self-correction. The representatives of the community had erred in the past—"they are not infallible; they have been refused to be submitted to."[71] Americans were "not the first People who have risen to prevent the Execution of a Law; the very People of England themselves rose in Opposition to the famous Jew-Bill, and got that immediately repealed."[72]

---

69. For a brief summary of this struggle, see Morton J. Horwitz, "The Emergence of an Instrumental Conception of American Law, 1780–1820," *Perspectives Am. Hist.*, V (1971), 293–294.

70. Otis, *Rights Asserted and Proved*, in Bailyn, ed., *Pamphlets of Am. Rev.*, I, 453; *Considerations on Behalf of the Colonies in a Letter to a Noble Lord* (Boston, 1765), in Mullett, ed., *Pol. Writings of James Otis*, 124.

71. J. Adams, speech before the Massachusetts council, Dec. 21, 1765, in Quincy, *Mass. Reports*, 200.

72. J. Otis, speech before the Massachusetts council, Dec. 21, 1765, *ibid.*, 205. Otis's reliance on the self-controlling character of Parliament stemmed not only from the Lockean notion of that body as the surrogate of the people, but also from the early 17th-century concept of Parliament as a High Court. For a discussion of the latter view, see Bailyn's

The principle of parliamentary self-control, though supported by such precedents, seemed inadequate to most Americans. They, like Englishmen, could petition and remonstrate, but there was no guarantee that they could convince Parliament of the rightness of their claims. Unlike Englishmen, the colonists were not represented at the center of government. Since Americans lacked the procedural safeguards associated with representation at Westminster, they did not have the institutional reinforcement that sustained the ordinary Englishman's intuitive confidence in Parliament's just exercise of power.

As long as Parliament's sovereignty was acknowledged, however, there was little Americans could do in the face of persistent clashes between parliamentary power and their rights. The stark choice seemed to be either submission or denial of all authority. English history legitimized dissolution of government in defense of subjects' rights, of course. But repudiating Parliament was much more serious than dethroning a tyrannical king, for many considered it tantamount to repudiating society itself. John Dickinson cautioned his countrymen to remember that "resistance, in the case of the colonies against their mother country, is extremely different from the resistance of a people against their prince." England had replaced the Stuart monarchs with the Hanoverians while "retaining their ancient form of government." Society had remained intact, embodied in Parliament, and individual subjects were still protected in their rights. "But if once *we* are separated from our mother country," asked Dickinson, "what new form of government shall we adopt, or where shall we find another *Britain*, to supply our loss?"[73]

The doctrine of discovery linked parliamentary authority and the rights of Englishmen, and as long as men like Otis—and, to some extent, Dickinson—accepted the traditional analysis of emigrant

introduction to Otis's *Rights Asserted and Proved*, in Bailyn, ed., *Pamphlets of Am. Rev.*, I, 411–413.

73. [John Dickinson], *The Farmer's Letters to the Inhabitants of the British Colonies*, "Letter III" (Virginia, 1769), in *Political Writings of John Dickinson*, I, 170, 171. Dickinson contended that "he, who considers these provinces as states distinct from the *British empire*, has very slender notions of *justice*, or of their *interests*. We are but parts of a *whole*; and therefore there must exist a power somewhere to preside, and preserve the connection in due order." See "Letter II," *ibid.*, 151. As the crisis deepened, Dickinson moved away from his initial acknowledgment of parliamentary sovereignty, though he continued to see separation as involving a dissolution of society.

subjects, they were caught in a theoretical impasse. The colonists had to break through the conceptual framework imposed by established precedents by undertaking a fresh examination of the status of dominions attached to Great Britain by the process of colonization. What was needed was a new look at the logic and validity of the doctrine of discovery.

When colonial thinkers challenged this doctrine, they found both a suspect ancestry and a debatable logic. James Iredell charged that the theory had emerged from decisions tainted by judicial reliance on earlier notions of conquest: "It is plainly from this title of conquest that in all the cases where the power of Parliament is extra-judicially recognized (as it is said that, though general laws do not take effect in the Plantations, because they are not supposed to be within the ordinary contemplation of the legislature, yet all wherein they are particularly named have authority there), that power is derived: of course, this source failing, it has from those cases no other support."[74] Although law books upheld Parliament's authority over the colonized dominions, such statements could be dismissed as *obiter dicta*—passing comments made by judges that were not essential to the final decision and hence not binding. According to James Wilson, the Scottish-born lawyer, Americans were in this case free to adopt the sentiments of "the very accurate Mr. Justice Foster" and assert that "general rules thrown out in argument, and carried farther than the true state of the case then in judgment requireth, have . . . no great weight."[75]

A close analysis of the genesis of the doctrine of discovery was not enough to refute the current claim that emigrant subjects remained under Parliament, for by the 1760s that contention no longer rested merely upon judicial authority. If they were to arrive at new conclusions respecting their status as subjects, Americans now had to cope with a more difficult argument: since the original settlers and their descendants remained within the community of

74. Iredell, "Address to the Inhabitants," in McRee, ed., *Life and Correspondence of Iredell*, I, 216.

75. [Wilson], *Considerations on Parliament*, in McCloskey, ed., *Works of James Wilson*, II, 738. Edwards, "American Image of Ireland," *Perspectives Am. Hist.*, IV (1970), 224–225, characterizes Wilson's statement as an evasion of sorts, "too legal and too cryptic" to command a wide audience. Wilson's argument seems neither cryptic nor idiosyncratic. He had to dismiss the "Irish argument" as British polemicists applied it to America, whether or not he found conquest adequate to explain Ireland's dependency. In fact, Wilson doubted that conquest ever gave absolute power over the conquered.

allegiance, they were bound by their own consent to obey Parliament.

To a large extent, colonial polemicists sought to combat this argument by going back to Coke's reasoning, stressing aspects of his thought that had been submerged by the rising sense of parliamentary sovereignty. Americans were especially struck by the relevance of much of *Calvin's Case* to their situation.[76] Coke's analysis of Scotland—his examination of the status of kingdoms acquired by descent—seemed to provide a better starting point for a consideration of the constitutional position of discovered colonies than did his irrelevant commentary on Ireland.

Calvin's Case held that Scotsmen were subjects despite their exemption from Parliament's extraterritorial jurisdiction. Their later consent to the authority of a new British parliament—in which they were represented—could not obscure their full membership in the community of allegiance before the Act of Union. Whatever the theoretical absurdity of *imperium in imperio*, declared the Massachusetts House in 1773, the union of Scottish and English subjects by allegiance to a common king had worked; the mutual independence of the two governments did not affect the status of individuals or the reality of the connection between the two realms.[77]

The notion that the colonies, like seventeenth-century Scotland, were bound to England only by a shared allegiance was enormously persuasive. The concept had been voiced from time to time long before the imperial debate, and with or without the authoritative theoretical support of Coke, it seemed to Americans to be a perfect explanation of their place in the British empire.[78] During his travels through the middle colonies in 1759 and 1760, the Reverend Andrew Burnaby noted that many Virginians "consider the colonies as independent states, not connected with Great Britain, otherwise than by having the same common king, and being bound to her with natural affection."[79] Governor Francis Bernard made the same

76. Mullett, "Coke and the American Revolution," *Economica*, XII (1932), 462, and *passim*.

77. House response to Hutchinson's opening speech, Jan. 26, 1773, Hutchinson, *Speeches and Answers*, 56. For the governor's initial claim that spurred this response, see above, n. 46.

78. For an early example of this argument of a connection through the king alone, see the Massachusetts General Court report on allegiance to the crown, June 10, 1661, in Michael G. Hall *et al.*, eds., *The Glorious Revolution in America: Documents on the Colonial Crisis of 1689* (Chapel Hill, N.C., 1964), 12–13, and Viola Florence Barnes, *The Dominion of New England: A Study in British Colonial Policy* (New Haven, Conn., 1923), 99, 119–120.

79. Andrew Burnaby, *Travels through the Middle Settlements in North America, in the Years*

observation of New Englanders when he informed Lord Barrington in 1765 that they "claim (I mean in public papers) to be perfect states, not otherwise dependent upon Great Britain than by having the same King."[80]

Coke's opinion in *Calvin's Case* was quoted to support the claim. The Massachusetts House rejected Hutchinson's contention that the Americans' subjectship proved the legitimacy of Parliament's authority, citing Coke to the effect that "every Man swears Allegiance for himself to his own King in his Natural Person." Subject status was defined with reference to the king in his natural, not in his political, capacity: "If then Homage and Allegiance is not to the Body politick of the King, then it is not to him as the Head or any Part of that Legislative Authority, which your Excellency says 'is equally extensive with the Authority of the Crown throughout every Part of the Dominion;' and your Excellency's Observations thereupon must fail."[81]

Hutchinson rejected this argument, though he would have passed over it "in Silence . . . if I had not been well informed that the artificial Reasoning of Lord Chief Justice Coke upon the Doctrine of Allegiance, in the noted Case of Calvin, as you have recited it, had great Weight with some of the Members of the House. But have you recited this Case truly?" As a discerning reader would observe, Coke had carefully asserted that the natural person must be accompanied by the political capacity. Parliament decided who was to bear the crown and fixed the law of succession; as the embodiment of the community, it determined the legitimate object of the subject's allegiance. Parliament thus created the political capacity and controlled its location. Was this not proof enough of its sovereign power to bind the subject?[82]

American polemicists did not think so. The king's role as part of Parliament did not extend the power of that body to the colonies, argued Moses Mather, for "when several rights or capacities meet and are vested in one and the same person they remain entire and distinct as though they were vested in different persons."[83] John

1759 and 1760. With Observations upon the State of the Colonies, 2d ed. (Ithaca, N.Y., 1968 [orig. publ. London, 1775]), 24.

80. Bernard to Lord Barrington, Nov. 23, 1765, quoted in Koebner, *Empire,* 151.

81. House response to Hutchinson's second speech, Mar. 2, 1773, Hutchinson, *Speeches and Answers,* 99.

82. Hutchinson's closing speech, Mar. 6, 1773, *ibid.,* 122–123.

83. [Moses Mather], *America's Appeal to the Impartial World* . . . (Hartford, Conn., 1775),

Adams agreed, refuting the Hutchinsonian argument when it was adopted by "Massachusettensis":

I beg leave to observe here that these words in the foregoing adjudication [*Calvin's Case*], that "the natural person of the king is ever accompanied with the politic capacity, and the politic capacity as it were appropriated to the natural capacity," neither imply nor infer allegiance or subjection to the politic capacity; because in the case of King James I, his natural person was "accompanied" with three politic capacities at least, as king of England, Scotland, and Ireland; yet the allegiance of an Englishman to him did not imply or infer subjection to his politic capacity as king of Scotland.[84]

When the king granted the first Massachusetts charter, argued Adams, he was both king of England and of Scotland. If his authority over America implied subordination to a political capacity, "had not the king as good a right to have governed the colonies by his Scottish, as by his English parliament, and to have granted our charters under the seal of Scotland, as well as that of England?" Even assuming a right in the English parliament to govern the colonies, where did it obtain the right, without America's consent, to share that authority with Scotland after the Act of Union? Adams concluded, "We owe no allegiance to any crown at all. We owe allegiance to the person of his majesty King George III., . . . to his natural, not his politic capacity."[85]

Admitting that "the King of Great-Britain was enthroned by virtue of an act of parliament, and that he is King of America, because he is King of Great Britain" was no admission of Parliament's authority, contended Alexander Hamilton: "The act of parliament is not the *efficient cause* of his being the King of America: It is only the *occasion* of it. He is King of America, by virtue of a compact between us and the Kings of Great-Britain. These colonies were

---

quoted in Bailyn, *Ideological Origins*, 224. Mather here used the "*Quando duo jura concurrunt*" maxim of civil law discussed above, chap. 1, at n. 25. Opposing counsel in Calvin's Case used the maxim to argue that James I and James VI were legally two different persons, and that Englishmen and Scotsmen were thus aliens to each other. Coke rejected the claim on the grounds that each political capacity was inseparably linked with the same natural person, and that the latter was the key to questions concerning allegiance. Mather did not deny this. Rather, he argued that the political capacities remained separate and could not interfere with each other, even though they converged in the same natural person. To argue differently would lead to the conclusion that George III as "King of Massachusetts," e.g., could act with the General Court to legislate for England.

84. [Adams], "Novanglus IX," in Adams, ed., *Works of John Adams*, IV, 143.
85. [Adams], "Novanglus VII," *ibid.*, 100, 114.

planted and settled by the Grants, and under the Protection of English Kings, who entered into covenants with us for themselves, their heirs and successors; and it is from these covenants, that the duty of protection on their part, and the duty of allegiance on ours arise." A denial of Parliament's power was no "dereliction of our allegiance to British Monarchs. Our compact takes no cognizance of the manner of their accession to the throne. It is sufficient for us, that they are Kings of England."[86]

Benjamin Franklin, too, found this argument persuasive. The American colonies were "extrinsic dominions of the King." Like pre-Union Scotland and contemporary Hanover, they were connected with England only by their common allegiance.[87] Not even the parliamentary law of succession bound the colonies without their consent: "Had the rebellion in 1745 succeeded so far as to settle the Stuart family again on the throne, by act of Parliament, I think the colonies would not have thought themselves bound by such an act. They would still have adhered to the present family, as long as they could."[88] The present allegiance of Massachusetts subjects, observed John Adams in the same vein, stemmed from a charter granted by William and Mary and from local statutes establishing oaths to the new monarchs: "So that our allegiance to his majesty is not due by virtue of any act of a British parliament. . . . It ought to be remembered that there was a revolution here, as well as in England, and that we, as well as the people of England, made an original, express contract with King William."[89]

The British argument was based on the false assumption that the community of allegiance was identical with the "state," an error embedded in the semantics of empire. "This language, 'the imperial crown of Great Britain,'" Adams declared, "is not the style of the common law, but of court sycophants. . . . The terms 'British Empire' are . . . the language of newspapers and political pamphlets; . . . the dominions of the king of Great Britain have no power coextensive with them."[90] There were neither legal nor logical

---

86. [Alexander Hamilton], *The Farmer Refuted: or A more impartial and comprehensive View of the Dispute between Great-Britain and the Colonies, Intended as a Further Vindication of the Congress* (New York, 1775), in Harold C. Syrett and Jacob E. Cooke, eds., *The Papers of Alexander Hamilton*, I (New York, 1961), 91.
87. Bigelow, ed. and comp., *Complete Works of Franklin*, IV, 310.
88. *Ibid.*, 301.
89. [Adams], "Novanglus VII," in Adams, ed., *Works of John Adams*, IV, 114.
90. [Adams], "Novanglus III," *ibid.*, 38, 37.

grounds for assuming that the body that represented part of the community of allegiance had jurisdiction over the whole. Franklin found it surprising "that a writer, who, in other respects, appears often very reasonable, should talk of our sovereignty over the colonies! As if every individual in England was part of a sovereign over America! The King is sovereign of all." The claim was ridiculous and even more offensive for its arrogance: "Our sovereignty again! This writer, like the Genoese queens of Corsica, deems himself a sprig of royalty."[91] Americans would never agree to the arguments of those who would make them the "subjects of *subjects*."[92]

Since the empire was not a true "state," as the term was commonly used, the accepted theory of sovereignty could not be used to sustain Parliament's authority over the colonies. True, the argument retained considerable force when the issue involved two sovereign legislatures within the same individual polity: "But what application does this make to the case of several distinct and independent legislatures, each engaged within a separate scale, and employed about different objects. The *imperium in imperio* argument is, therefore, not at all applicable to our case, though it has been so vainly and confidently relied on."[93]

With an increasing assurance leading American theorists adopted this response to the ultimate British argument. The idea of conflicting sovereignties was still unacceptable, but by separating the community of allegiance from the political community—by denying that the empire was a true "state"—the colonists turned the argument from sovereignty against the supporters of parliamentary power. The king in his legislature was the sovereign in each colony: "A supreme authority, in the Parliament, to make any special laws for this province, consistent with the internal legislature here claimed is impossible; and cannot be supposed, without falling into that solecism, in politics, of *imperium in imperio*."[94]

To the extent that the empire could be seen as a single state in some sense, one had to reconsider the nature and location of its sovereign power. It did not lie in any single legislature, surely, for the jurisdiction of each was restricted to those persons and places

91. Bigelow, ed. and comp., *Complete Works of Franklin*, IV, 311, 321.
92. Iredell, "Address to the Inhabitants," in McRee, ed., *Life and Correspondence of Iredell*, I, 209.
93. *Ibid.*, 219.
94. [Hamilton], *The Farmer Refuted*, in Syrett and Cooke, eds., *Papers of Hamilton*, I, 164.

each represented. Nor did it lie in the king alone, for he was a limited, not an absolute, monarch. Rather the "imperial sovereign" was the king in all his parliaments. The person and prerogative of George III was the "connecting and pervading principle" linking the individual members of the empire: "He it is that conjoins all these individual societies, into one great body politic. He it is, that is to preserve their mutual connexion and dependence, and make them all co-operate to one end the common good. His power is equal to the purpose, and his interest binds him to the due prosecution of it."[95]

Americans argued that all persons concerned should have a voice in deciding issues imperial in scope and effect. The king, sharing in the sovereignty of each subordinate unit, would mediate conflicts; his authority "over the whole will, like a central force, attract them all to the same point."[96] True, there might arise problems on which agreement proved impossible; but in theory, at least, this was nothing new. Even in England, where the sovereignty was in fact divided among king, Lords, and Commons, such an impasse could occur, despite the "*point of speculation*," the "narrow and pedantic rule" that required that "there shall always be a power in motion to regulate the concerns of the commonwealth, that they may never suffer by inaction or delay."[97] Inaction was tolerable—even necessary for the happiness of the governed—if it prevented the violation by any one member of the empire of the rights guaranteed to others.

This vision of empire—of a "body politic" composed of separate and independent sovereignties linked together by a common king —backed a number of proposals for the creation of some new institutional forum with representatives from all the dominions and jurisdiction over matters of common concern.[98] Imperial reorganization along these lines had been suggested as early as 1754 at the Albany Congress, and Joseph Galloway again proposed this solution to imperial problems at the Continental Congress of 1774.[99] Until such a supradominion legislature was established, however,

95. *Ibid.*, 98.
96. *Ibid.*, 99.
97. Iredell, "Address to the Inhabitants," in McRee, ed., *Life and Correspondence of Iredell*, I, 217–218.
98. See generally Adams, *Political Ideas of Am. Rev.*, chap. 4, and Koebner, *Empire*, 173–193.
99. For a discussion of the Galloway Plan, see David Ammerman, *In the Common Cause: American Response to the Coercive Acts of 1774* (Charlottesville, Va., 1974), 58–60.

and as long as Parliament persisted in attempting to exercise a self-proclaimed right of intervention, the colonists had to consider other means of protecting their liberties.

One of the modes of defense advocated by Americans on the eve of the Revolution was that the king revive his veto and use his royal prerogative more actively in England. Although the rejection of all inherent parliamentary authority in favor of a heightened royal prerogative did not gain widespread support among American theorists until the late 1760s and early 1770s, elements of this view appeared quite early in the controversy with the mother country. During the Stamp Act crisis Purdie and Dixon's *Virginia Gazette* reprinted the claim from a New York newspaper that "the Parliament which represents the people of England, who chose them, have no right of sovereignty over us; but the King has a constitutional right, and that we have always submitted to, and always shall." Implicit in this and similar statements was the possibility of arguing that the king, who had authority over the colonies, ought to curb Parliament, which had none.[100]

The king should restrain the British legislature when it unjustly attempted to intervene in affairs beyond its jurisdiction, argued Benjamin Franklin in 1770: "By our constitution he is, with his plantation parliaments, the sole legislator of his American subjects, and in that capacity is, and ought to be, free to exercise his own judgment, unrestrained and unlimited by his Parliament here [in England]."[101] The king should act as a Stuart monarch vis-à-vis England when American affairs were at issue, though he properly acted as a limited monarch, cooperating with the legislature, when dealing with individual dominions on matters legitimately within their respective jurisdictions.

Thomas Jefferson advised his countrymen in 1774 "earnestly [to] entreat his majesty, as yet the only mediatory power between the several states of the British empire, to recommend to his parliament of Great Britain the total revocation of these acts, which, however nugatory they be, may yet prove the cause of further discontents and jealousies among us." He charged that the king deviated from his duty as America's monarch when he permitted Parliament to

100. Purdie and Dixon's *Virginia Gazette*, Mar. 14, 1766, quoted in Stella F. Duff, "The Case against the King: The *Virginia Gazettes* Indict George III," *WMQ*, 3d Ser., VI (1949), 384.
101. Franklin to Samuel Cooper, June 8, 1770, Bigelow, ed. and comp., *Complete Works of Franklin*, IV, 345.

encroach upon American liberties. If mere recommendations failed, it was now "the great office of his majesty, to resume the exercise of his negative power, and to prevent the passage of laws by any one legislature of the empire, which might bear injuriously on the rights and interests of another."[102] As one of Jefferson's compatriots remarked, the king had authority and thus bore the ultimate responsibility for imperial harmony: "Your ministry I shall release, and charge on your majesty alone the execution of measures which promise to disgrace your government, and disturb your throne. . . . To *you* we look for protection; *you* are the sovereign and ruler, and not our fellow subjects in Parliament."[103]

American theorists found Coke's traditional interpretation of allegiance thoroughly useful insofar as it supported their claims of independence from Parliament, but the jurist's contention that allegiance was natural and perpetual was less to their liking. It would have been an unhappy bargain to escape from Parliament only to be immutably bound to the king. The question was how to use Coke's theory that allegiance focused on the king in order to avoid submission to the British legislature, and at the same time to leave some recourse in case the monarch himself infringed American rights. The solution to this dilemma was to be found in two doctrines: the ancient English assertion that allegiance was tied to protection and the more recent theories of John Locke concerning the contractual basis of society.

The colonists' initial response was a reflex incantation of the maxim that allegiance and protection were reciprocal: "As protection necessarily demands and binds to subjection and obedience to that authority and those laws whereby a people are protected, so subjection and obedience as necessarily and justly entitle to protection: these mutually imply, require, and support each other."[104] "Allegiance to the king and obedience to parliament are founded on very different principles," declared James Wilson. "The former is founded on protection: the latter on representation."[105] The connection between Great Britain and the colonies was formed, ac-

---

102. [Jefferson], *A Summary View*, ed. Abernethy, 16.
103. Letter of "Phocion" to Rind's *Virginia Gazette*, Sept. 14, 1774, quoted in Duff, "Case against the King," *WMQ*, 3d Ser., VI (1949), 396.
104. [Fitch *et al.*], *Reasons Why*, in Bailyn, ed., *Pamphlets of Am. Rev.*, I, 388.
105. [Wilson], *Considerations on Parliament*, in McCloskey, ed., *Works of James Wilson*, II, 736.

cording to Hamilton, "by the ties of blood, interest, and mutual protection."[106]

At this point the colonists blended Coke and Locke to their own ends. Coke was wrong, they argued, in seeing protection and allegiance as immutable and perpetual obligations stemming from nature and preceding law. Rather they were the quid pro quo of a contract, each given in return for the other according to the terms of an ongoing agreement. The colonial charters suggested the terms of the contract, guaranteeing the settlers the protection of as much of the English law as they chose to adopt and requiring in return allegiance to the king. If the charters were annulled, John Adams concluded, the king "would not be bound to protect the people, nor, that I can see, would the people here, who were born here, be, by any principle of common law, bound even to allegiance to the king. The connection would be broken between the crown and the natives of the country."[107] Colonial allegiance stood "upon no grounds, then, of law or policy, but what are found in the law of nature, and their express contracts in their charters, and their implied contracts in the commissions to governors and terms of settlement."[108]

Since allegiance and protection were contractual, neither party could default without releasing the other from his obligation: "The duties of the king and those of the subject are plainly reciprocal: they can be violated on neither side, unless they be performed on the other."[109] The nature of the protection that the king was bound to afford was defined most precisely by the laws of the particular dominion: "He possesses, indeed, the executive power of the laws in every state; but they are the laws of the particular state which he is to administer within that state, and not those of any one within the limits of another."[110] Americans had chosen to adopt the freedom-preserving principles of the English law when they formed their new societies, and thus they found English experience relevant in

---

106. [Alexander Hamilton], *A Full Vindication of the Measures of Congress, from the Calumnies of their Enemies* (New York, 1774), in Syrett and Cooke, eds., *Papers of Hamilton*, I, 51.

107. [Adams], "Novanglus VIII," in Adams, ed., *Works of John Adams*, IV, 122, 127. Adams thought that the original settlers, born under the king's protection in England, remained in his allegiance (though not under Parliament's power) after leaving the realm.

108. [Adams], "Novanglus XII," *ibid.*, 170.

109. J. Wilson, speech before the provincial convention of Pennsylvania, Philadelphia, Jan. 1775, in McCloskey, ed., *Works of James Wilson*, II, 753.

110. [Jefferson], *A Summary View*, ed. Abernethy, 22.

defining the circumstances that legitimized a withdrawal of allegiance: "We further observe, that the constitution has not expressly drawn the line beyond which, if a king, shall 'go,' resistance becomes *lawful*. . . . [Blackstone] has thought proper, when treating of this subject, to point out the 'precedent' of the revolution, as fixing the line."[111]

Allegiance, "when spoken of a subject with relation to his Sovereign," wrote one New Yorker in October 1775, "means the obligation the former is under to submit to and obey the latter in all things lawful; so that it is the legal faith and obedience which every subject owes to his Sovereign, immediately upon his being placed upon the throne, with the royal crown upon his head, accompanied with his coronation oath." The oath of allegiance and the coronation oath were counterparts—in essence, a "covenant between Prince and people." When the king added his sanction to illegitimate laws enacted by Parliament, he thereby violated his oath, and "the people in such cases" were "absolved from their obligations of obedience to the King." Resistance in this event was not rebellion. When the king ratified usurpations "and passed them into laws, when he might and could have negatived them," he in a sense deposed himself. "The person remains, but the constitutional King of *Great Britain* no longer exists in him."[112]

Americans hotly denied that they had defaulted on their obligations or forgotten their allegiance: "What allegiance is it that we forget? Allegiance to Parliament? We never owed—we never owned it. Allegiance to our King? Our words have ever avowed it,—our conduct has ever been consistent with it." The colonists had resisted only "in those cases, in which the right to resist is stipulated as expressly on our part, as the right to govern is, in other cases, stipulated on the part of the Crown. The breach of allegiance is removed from our resistance as far as tyranny is removed from legal government."[113]

111. [Dickinson], *Essay on the Constitutional Power*, in *Political Writings of John Dickinson*, I, 339.

112. [Anonymous], "Allegiance to Crowned Heads upon the British Throne" (New York, Oct. 19, 1775), in Peter Force, comp., *American Archives . . .* , 4th Ser. (Washington, D.C., 1837–1853), III, 1106–1107.

113. Response of the Second Continental Congress, Dec. 6, 1775, to the Royal Proclamation of Rebellion of Aug. 23, 1775, in Worthington Chauncey Ford *et al.*, eds., *Journals of the Continental Congress, 1774–1789* (Washington, D.C., 1904–1937), III, 410, hereafter cited as *Jours. Cont. Cong.*

After the clashes at Lexington and Concord had exploded in the spring of 1775, after the carnage had raged at Bunker Hill, and after the king had declared America in rebellion, rejected the Olive Branch petition, and closed the colonies to all commerce, it was clear that the last link with Great Britain had in fact been broken. Since the late 1760s Americans had rejected the authority of Parliament and had recognized allegiance to the king as their only connection with England. In their eyes, George III was responsible for the breach of that final tie. Sam Adams informed Dr. Samuel Cooper in April 1776 that "many of the leading Men see the absurdity of supposing that Allegiance is due to a Sovereign who has already thrown us out of his Protection."[114]

Royal government at the provincial level had ceased, according to Judge William Henry Drayton of South Carolina: "The king's judges in this country refused to administer justice; and the late governor, lord William Campbell, acting as the king's representative for him, and on his behalf, having endeavoured to subvert the constitution of this country, by breaking the original contract between king and people, attacking the people by force of arms; having violated the fundamental laws; having carried off the great seal, and having withdrawn himself out of this colony, he abdicated the government."[115] The remnant of the Virginia House of Burgesses agreed that the crisis had effected a "dissolution of government" in the Lockean sense, "it being their opinion that the people could not now be legally represented according to the ancient Constitution, which has now been subverted by the King, Lords and Commons of *Great Britain*, and consequently dissolved."[116]

At this juncture American leaders realized the need to take the final step—to declare their total independence of Great Britain.[117] They had to unite the home front, force the wavering to choose sides, and create the basis for a new loyalty not focused on the king.

114. Samuel Adams to Dr. Samuel Cooper, Apr. 30, 1776, in Erich Angermann, "Ständische Rechtstraditionen in der amerikanischen Unabhängigkeitserklärung," *Historische Zeitschrift*, CC (1965), 68.

115. Charge to the grand jury at Charleston, Apr. 23, 1776, William M. Dabney and Marion Dargan, *William Henry Drayton and the American Revolution* (Albuquerque, N.M., 1962), 183.

116. Resolution of 45 members of the House of Burgesses, at a meeting at Williamsburg after adjournment of the Burgesses, May 10, 1776, in Force, comp., *American Archives*, 4th Ser., V, 1206.

117. The following relies heavily on Angermann, "Ständische Rechtstraditionen," *Historische Zeitschrift*, CC (1965).

De facto independence was not enough to mobilize and justify widespread domestic support of the war, nor, as Silas Deane reported from France, was it adequate to legitimize overt aid from abroad.[118] The break with the mother country had to be formal, legal, and rightly motivated if it were to attract the active support of Americans and of "a candid world."

The justice of a formal withdrawal of allegiance was recognized in and out of Congress. For Thomas Jefferson, the question raised by the Virginia delegation's resolution for independence was not whether "we should make ourselves what we are not; but whether we should declare a fact which already exists":

That as to the people or parliament of England, we had always been independent of them, their restraints on our trade deriving efficacy from our acquiescence only and not from any rights they possessed of imposing them, and that so far our connection had been federal only, and was now dissolved by the commencement of hostilities:

That as to the king, we had been bound to him by allegiance, but that this bond was now dissolved by his assent to the late act of parliament, by which he declares us out of his protection, and by his levying war on us, a fact which had long ago proved us out of his protection; it being a certain position in law that allegiance and protection are reciprocal, the one ceasing when the other is withdrawn:

That James the IId. never declared the people of England out of his protection yet his actions proved it and the parliament declared it.[119]

An exact parallel was drawn between the circumstances that produced the English revolution and those that presently obtained in America, although the detailed usurpations of George III were judged even more heinous than those of James II. Judge Drayton compared the two "tyrants" item by item, to the detriment and dishonor of the current monarch:

King James broke the original contract by not affording due protection to his subjects, although he was not charged with having seized their towns and with having them held against the people—or with having laid them in ruins by his arms—or with having seized their vessels—or with having pursued the people with fire and sword—or with having declared them rebels, for resisting his arms levelled to destroy their lives, liberties and

118. *Ibid.*, 68–70.
119. Thomas Jefferson, "Notes of Proceedings in the Continental Congress," [June 7–Aug. 1, 1776], in Julian P. Boyd *et al.*, eds., *The Papers of Thomas Jefferson*, I (Princeton, N.J., 1950), 311.

properties—But George the third hath done all those things against America; and it is therefore undeniable that George the third had also broken the original contract between king and people; and that he made use of the most violent measures by which it could be done—Violences of which James was guiltless—Measures, carrying conflagration, massacre and open war amidst a people, whose subjection to the king of Great Britain, the law holds to be due only as a return for protection. And so tenacious and clear is the law upon this very principle, that it is laid down, subjection is not due even to a king, *de jure*, or of right, unless he be also king *de facto*, or in possession of the executive powers dispensing protection.[120]

The actions of George III perfectly matched what Erich Angermann has called the "tyrant-syndrome"—a closely structured, complete reverse image of the "Good Prince" made familiar by the history of the struggle between liberty and power.[121] Deeply embedded in the Western legal tradition, this history justified the withdrawal of allegiance from rulers who defaulted on their duties. The Dutch had declared their independence from Spain in these terms. Englishmen had found here legal sanction for their execution of Charles I and their deposition of James II.[122]

Americans firmly set their case within this tradition when they indicted George III for his misdeeds.[123] The Declaration of Independence rested not merely upon the "glittering generalities" of the Preamble, though the ideals stated there had the power to move men's souls and would profoundly affect later history. For many contemporaries, its legal force—its effective appeal to traditional

120. Dabney and Dargan, *William Henry Drayton*, 187. This is part of a long passage in which Drayton compared for the grand jury the actions of George III and James II, working from the grievances against the latter formally expressed in the House of Commons resolution of Feb. 1688/1689.
121. Angermann, "Ständische Rechtstraditionen," *Historische Zeitschrift*, CC (1965), 80.
122. *Ibid.*, 88–89. Angermann traces the development from the feudal relationship of man and lord and finds it surviving among the fundamental principles of the corporate state. He sees the theme in the writings of both Coke and Locke. I would argue that Coke twisted the development when he made the allegiance-protection relationship natural, for then it became immutable. Locke returned to the contractual concept when examining the link between the subject and the king, but he was influenced by Coke's dicta when considering the attributes of the bond between the individual subject and society as a whole.
123. Americans saw parallels to their situation in the Swiss revolt of 1291, Spain's loss of Holland in 1581, the sentencing of Charles I in 1649, and England's Glorious Revolution. Each could serve as a precedent for withdrawing allegiance after the king's default on protection. *Ibid.*, 82–85. Stourzh, "William Blackstone: Teacher of Revolution," *Jahrbuch für Amerikastudien*, XV (1970), 197n, is probably correct in stressing the special significance of 1689; but Americans saw a wider meaning in that event than did Locke or Blackstone. They had to justify secession from the community of allegiance as well as the deposition of a king.

conservatives as well as to philosophical radicals—lay in its familiar, formalized recital of the tyrannical acts of the king: the catalog of grievances, arranged in ascending order, culminating—almost exactly in the middle of the document—with the charge that George III had abdicated his government by withdrawing his protection.[124] He had broken the contract that made men subjects. They were therefore free to create a new allegiance.

Thus did Americans move from an acknowledgment of allegiance to the king and a due subordination to Parliament to an ultimate invocation of their right to be independent. Two crucial shifts—two critical denials of contemporary British assumptions —made this development possible. The first concerned the assumption that the same contracts of society and government explaining Parliament's sovereignty in Great Britain sanctioned its authority over all subjects in the empire. Americans rejected the notion that Locke's constitutional analysis of the state could be transposed intact to the political structure of the empire. Coke's vision of a community composed of autonomous dominions united by allegiance to a common king sustained their claim to freedom from parliamentary control. The second denial was a repudiation of the principle of natural and perpetual allegiance. Locke's insistence on the contractual, consensual basis of all political obligation shaped the colonists' conviction that there were recognizable limits to their duties as subjects, whether their obligations were to Parliament or to the king.

Before independence, Americans had quarreled only with the British claim that Locke's theories bound them to a parliament in which they were not actually represented. Locke still seemed appropriate enough to explain constitutional relationships within the individual colonial polities. Sovereign power emanated from the original consent to establish society, and Americans argued only that this power came to rest in their parochial assemblies, acting with the king, and not in Parliament. The authority of the provincial committees and congresses that supplanted the established assemblies in many colonies even before independence could also be explained in Lockean terms, for were they not the true represen-

---

124. Angermann, "Ständische Rechtstraditionen," *Historische Zeitschrift*, CC (1965), 79, 86–88, paraphrase, my translation.

tatives of coherent communities, voicing the views of "the people"? It was still the function of the community as a whole, embodied in a local parliament, to judge the legitimacy of government and, when necessary, to release the subjects from their allegiance.

But Americans were not in fact united. Many opposed the renunciation of Parliament's authority. Many denied that the king had acted illegitimately and had forfeited their loyalty. Many continued to affirm their membership in a society that extended beyond the bounds of a single colony. To these men, those who resisted established authorities and lusted after independence were rebels and traitors, guilty of that ultimate offense, a breach of their allegiance.

The formal break with England threw into sharp relief the problem of such dissenters. Could the community force them to reject their old allegiance against their will? Could the new governments, claiming to derive authority from the consent of the governed, demand their loyalty? The pre-Revolutionary debate, focused on the problem of allegiance as it pertained to groups within the empire, offered no clear answers to questions concerning the rights and duties of individuals and governments in a situation demanding a choice between conflicting loyalties. The need to confront this problem came with independence, and was to play a central role in shaping the concept of American citizenship.

CHAPTER 7

The Idea of Volitional Allegiance

The central purpose of American polemicists and pamphleteers in the years before independence was to defend the rights of the colonial communities against the encroaching power of the imperial authorities in London. As colonial spokesmen developed their arguments they steadily moved away from the traditional ideas of allegiance that still permeated British legal and constitutional thought. By 1776 American theorists had rejected the concept that the colonists were perpetually bound by their subjectship. Philosophy, law, and common sense had convinced them that subjects owed obedience to governments only in return for the protection of their fundamental rights. Allegiance was contractual, and contracts could be broken or annulled.

The framework and the dynamics of the imperial debate allowed —even forced—Americans to consider the problem of allegiance and subjectship as it pertained to whole communities within the empire and to evade questions concerning the relationship between individuals and the society of which they were a part. Although the rhetoric of discussion frequently and perhaps necessarily used an individualized vocabulary—men spoke of the relationship between the subject and his sovereign—the real point of the debate was to delineate and defend the prerogatives of the American colonies as though they were homogeneous entities. Massachusetts, New York, and Virginia were subjects writ large; it was their relationship with

England that American theorists had in mind when they considered the character and the limits of allegiance.

This perspective was no longer adequate once the colonies broke with the mother country. As thirteen sovereign and independent states supplanted the old colonial dependencies, Revolutionary leaders found themselves confronted with deeply divided societies. The loyalists—countrymen and quondam fellow subjects—refused to renounce their old allegiance, rejected the claim that the old contract had been abrogated, and resisted the imposition of a new citizenship.

The problem of the loyalists could neither be wished away nor be ignored, yet the principles articulated in the pre-Revolutionary polemics offered no clear guidelines for action. American leaders faced a dilemma. On the one hand, toleration of open disaffection and active opposition to the Revolution threatened the very survival of the cause; on the other hand, coercion of the unwilling to join the new republics seemed to violate the fundamental principle that legitimate government required the consent of the governed. Lockean contract theory assured Americans that once a society was formed, the majority could command the obedience of minorities. But what was to be done with those individuals—those neighbors —who refused from the beginning to accept the new contract?

The immediate practical problem of what to do with dissidents was more easily solved than the theoretical problems raised by their refusal to accept the new republican regimes. Congress and the states enacted a variety of measures to counter and control the threat of subversion from within, and theoretical niceties were frequently forgotten in the heated atmosphere of what was in many respects a civil war. But the fundamental issues involved in the competing claims for individual loyalty could not be evaded forever. Even during the war treason prosecutions necessarily involved questions of allegiance. With peace the problem became more acute. Diplomatic confrontations between Great Britain and the United States respecting treaty provisions for the recovery of prewar debts and for the compensation for wartime confiscations often hinged on the party's status as British subject or American citizen. In the process of facing such issues, Americans developed the idea of volitional allegiance.

The notion that individuals had the right to choose their own loyalty was perhaps embedded in the concept of contractual allegiance from the beginning; yet the transformation of the idea from a mythical construct to a human reality undeniably was the result of the situation created by the Revolution. It would take well into the nineteenth century for Americans to come to terms with this revolutionary legacy, to discover the ramifications and the limitations of the individual's right of election. Jurists, legislators, and theorists would often move slowly, with many a backward glance toward the old traditional doctrines of subjectship. But once the right was conceded, it could not be revoked. When subjects became citizens, they gained the right to choose their allegiance.

Americans repudiated the authority of Great Britain not as individuals, but as organized societies. They withdrew their allegiance from George III and severed the connection with England in formal, public, and communal acts passed by representative bodies purporting to speak for a united people. The process began even before Congress approved the Declaration of Independence on July 4, 1776. By legislative resolves and constitutional provisions, the provincial governments cut themselves loose from the royal authority and took steps tantamount to a general renunciation of allegiance.

Fundamental reform began as early as January 5, 1776, when New Hampshire formally adopted a new provisional constitution. In March, South Carolina required all its officers to swear an oath to "support, maintain, and defend" an interim constitution drawn up by the provincial congress, and although the drafters did not yet require a formal abjuration of the British king, they pointedly omitted the traditional oath of allegiance to the monarch.[1] In May, Connecticut and Rhode Island repealed their statutes defining and punishing treason, and both declared that writs, commissions, and public acts would no longer run in the king's name.[2] Virginia and New Jersey approved new constitutions on June 29 and July 2,

1. South Carolina constitution of Mar. 26, 1776, Art. XXXIII, Thorpe, ed. and comp., *Constitutions, Charters, and Laws*, VI, 3247, and see Willi Paul Adams, *Republikanische Verfassung und bürgerliche Freiheit: Die Verfassungen und politischen Ideen der amerikanischen Revolution* (Darmstadt, 1973), 73–74. New Hampshire was the first of the colonies to draft a provisional constitution (Jan. 5, 1776). *Ibid.*, 72–73; Jere R. Daniell, *Experiment in Republicanism: New Hampshire Politics and the American Revolution, 1741–1794* (Cambridge, Mass., 1970), 110–111.

2. Epaphroditus Peck, *The Loyalists of Connecticut* (New Haven, Conn., 1934), 11; *R.I. Col. Recs.*, VII, 522–526. Rhode Island established a test oath for inhabitants suspected of "being inimical to the United American Colonies," in June. *Ibid.*, 566–567.

respectively. Both preambles proclaimed the reciprocity of allegiance and protection, recounted the misdeeds of George III, and declared that his withdrawal of protection amounted to an abdication and a dissolution of government.[3]

The Declaration of Independence itself was the act of "the representatives of the United States of America, in general Congress assembled." The delegates in Philadelphia, "in the name, and by the authority of the good people of these colonies," declared those *colonies* "absolved from all allegiance to the British Crown." Copies of the official document were sent to each of the states, and between July and October state authorities formally approved the action of their representatives.[4] Throughout the entire proceeding it was assumed that the Revolutionary assemblies, committees, and conventions that chose the delegates to Philadelphia—as well as the congressional delegates themselves—truly represented and acted for the whole people. Dissidents were always considered to be a minority within legitimate and functioning societies, bound to obey the majority of their fellow members.

Long before the formal break with England the Continental Congress sanctioned the suppression of anti-Revolutionary activities, though it still refrained from direct attacks on the king. In proscribing or recommending the punishment of pro-British behavior before late June 1776, the American authorities maintained that their actions were consistent with their professed allegiance to George III. The British forces bloodied at Lexington and Bunker Hill could still be described as the "ministerial army"; anti-Revolutionary activity could still be defined as behavior against the welfare of the country rather than as loyal action in support of the king.

Congress did not hesitate to establish a code of discipline for the new Continental army organized in June 1775. The Articles of War

3. Virginia constitution (June 29, 1776), preamble. Thorpe, ed. and comp., *Constitutions, Charters, and Laws*, VII, 3815. New Jersey constitution (July 2, 1776), preamble. *Ibid.*, V, 2594.

4. Quotations from the final paragraph of the Declaration of Independence. John H. Hazelton, *The Declaration of Independence: Its History* (New York, 1906), 240–281, details the reception and approval of the document by the states, which occurred as follows: Delaware (council of safety), July 6; New York (convention), July 9; New Hampshire (assembly), ca. July 16; New Jersey (provincial congress), July 17; Rhode Island (assembly), July 18; Virginia (council), July 20; North Carolina (council of safety), July 22; Pennsylvania (convention), July 25; Georgia (president, council, assembly), Aug. 10; Maryland (convention), Aug. 17; Massachusetts (assembly), Aug. 28; South Carolina (lower house), Sept. 19; and Connecticut (assembly), Oct. 10.

provided for the punishment of soldiers who engaged in activities that, for civilians, would have fallen under one of the traditional categories of treason and thus would have raised the question of allegiance. Courts-martial were empowered to impose penalties short of execution on military men found guilty of mutiny and sedition (the equivalent of "levying war" against constituted authorities) or of supplying, harboring, or corresponding with the enemy (the equivalent of "adhering" or "giving aid and comfort" to the enemy). The discovery that Benjamin Church—a member of the Massachusetts Provincial Congress and surgeon general of the army—had engaged in "traitorous correspondence" with General Thomas Gage impelled Washington to seek a stiffening of the articles. On November 7, 1775, Congress empowered courts-martial to impose the death penalty on soldiers convicted of aiding the enemy.[5]

Congress moved more cautiously against disaffection among the civilian population. Not until January 11, 1776, did the delegates resolve that any person "so lost to all virtue and regard for his country" as to refuse to receive congressional bills of credit or otherwise to discourage their circulation should, on conviction by public committees or other authorities, be "deemed, published, and treated as an enemy of his country, and precluded from all trade or intercourse with the inhabitants of these colonies."[6] This public ostracism was to be enforced by local committees, for Congress was sensitive to the importance of showing a due respect for local and state authorities. The jurisdictional distinction between soldiers and civilians was intended to limit the actions of those working directly under Congress. After receiving complaints that General Charles Lee of the Continental army was improperly disregarding this distinction by using his troops to force suspected persons in Rhode Island and in New York to take test oaths, Congress on March 9 prohibited further similar actions by its military officers.[7]

By the spring of 1776 the internal threat seemed drastic enough to justify measures against civilians beyond formal public ostracism.[8] On March 14 Congress recommended that "the several assemblies,

5. Bradley Chapin, *The American Law of Treason: Revolutionary and Early National Origins* (Seattle, Wash., 1964), 29–32.
6. *Jours. Cont. Cong.*, IV, 49.
7. *Ibid.*, 195; Chapin, *American Law of Treason*, 33–34.
8. A large body of loyalists had already been defeated in armed battle at Moore's Creek Bridge in late Feb. 1776. For the participation of loyalists in early military operations, see

conventions, and councils or committees of safety of the United Colonies" immediately disarm all persons "who are notoriously disaffected to the cause of America, or who have not associated, and who shall refuse to associate, to defend, by arms, these United Colonies."[9] The suppression of the disaffected was to be carried out by public, not private, action. Congress reaffirmed its position on this point on June 18, when it resolved that "no man in these colonies, charged with being a tory, or unfriendly to the cause of American Liberty, be injured in his person or property, or in any manner whatsoever disturbed," unless the proceedings were sanctioned by Congress or by the local authorities.[10]

Since British law defined treason as opposition to the king, Revolutionary leaders found it difficult to take stern measures against dissidents as long as the colonies technically remained in allegiance to George III. Social pressure and mob action might effectively control the timid and the uncertain, but more drastic powers were needed to deal with the committed opponents of the American cause. Weak or vacillating civil authorities were not what the times demanded. America's enemies had to be controlled, and it was urgent that this be done in a regular and legitimate manner. The threat of anarchy was never far below the surface in the troubled months after Lexington; American leaders had to be concerned lest popular opposition to the "tories" get out of hand and destroy any semblance of order and legitimacy still held by the public authorities. Yet officials hesitated to act forcefully without a clear justification for demanding obedience and loyalty from persons who remained both Americans and British subjects.

The problem came to a head in early June with the discovery of an espionage and counterfeiting ring in New York. The conspirators allegedly distributed bogus congressional bills provided by the royal governor, William Tryon (who by now was safely aboard a British warship), to depreciate the Continental currency and to expedite the recruitment of pro-British forces in the province. The "tory plot" involved both soldiers and civilians, including Thomas Hickey, a member of Washington's personal guard, and David

---

Paul H. Smith, *Loyalists and Redcoats: A Study in British Revolutionary Policy* (New York, 1964), 10–31.

9. *Jours. Cont. Cong.*, IV, 205.

10. *Ibid.*, V, 464. This resolution was not to prevent the seizure for examination and trial of persons suspected of unfriendly acts.

Matthews, mayor of New York City. On June 26 a court-martial found Hickey guilty and ordered his execution under the authority of the Articles of War. Two days later Thomas Hickey became the first American to be hanged in the name of the Revolution.[11]

While the army took care of its own, the public authorities of New York hesitated to move against the civilian conspirators. On June 17 the provincial congress denied the authority of the colony's courts to deal with the plot, "being yet held by authority derived from the Crown of Great Britain."[12] The military had no power to punish civilians; the local government feared to act on its own. The situation demanded decisive measures, and the Continental Congress was forced to take the initiative.

On June 24, 1776, Congress moved to clarify the anomalous legal situation, taking the step that turned disaffection to treason. Recognizing the need to provide a clear legal basis for the suppression of the internal threat, the delegates resolved:

That all persons residing within any of the United Colonies, and deriving protection from the laws of the same, owe allegiance to the said laws, and are members of such colony; and that all persons passing through, visiting, or make [*sic*] a temporary stay in any of the said colonies, being entitled to the protection of the laws during the time of such passage, visitation, or temporary stay, owe, during the same time, allegiance thereto:
That all persons, members of, or owing allegiance to any of the United Colonies, as before described, who shall levy war against any of the said colonies within the same, or be adherents to the king of Great Britain, or other enemies of the said colonies, or any of them, within the same, giving to him or them aid and comfort, are guilty of treason against such colony.

Two additional resolves recommended that the legislatures of the individual colonies pass specific laws punishing counterfeiting and treason.[13]

The resolutions defining allegiance and treason, followed quickly by the Declaration of Independence, provided the individual states with authority to crush internal dissent. The ensuing torrent of legislation from the state legislatures would not cease until the end of the war. Every state established oaths and declarations to test the loyalty of its inhabitants. Non-jurors were subjected to penalties

11. Curtis P. Nettels, "A Link in the Chain of Events Leading to American Independence," *WMQ*, 3d Ser., III (1946), 39–40; Chapin, *American Law of Treason*, 35.
12. Nettels, "A Link in the Chain," *WMQ*, 3d Ser., III (1946), 43.
13. *Jours. Cont. Cong.*, V, 475–476. See also Nettels, "A Link in the Chain," *WMQ*, 3d Ser., III (1946), 38, and Chapin, *American Law of Treason*, 35–37.

ranging from imposition of punitive fines, disfranchisement, and deprivation of legal rights to confiscation of their property and banishment. State treason laws threatened execution for those who actively opposed the Revolution by waging war against the American forces or by overtly aiding the British.[14]

As long as the war continued, the demands of internal security took precedence over the consideration of individual rights, at least at the level of policy-making. State confiscation acts were designed to keep the wavering in line as well as to gain much-needed revenue at the expense of those who refused to support the cause. The Virginia House of Delegates contended that such acts were founded on firm principles of law and common justice, for "if virtuous citizens, in defence of their natural rights, risk their life, liberty and property on their success, vicious citizens, who side with tyranny and oppression, or cloak themselves under the mask of neutrality, should at least hazard their property and not enjoy the labors and dangers of those whose destruction they wished."[15]

Statutes providing for the seizure of property belonging to the disaffected seemed justified during the hostilities. At first the problem of identifying the accused's subject status was ignored; whether the property in question was that of a British subject or of a disloyal citizen seemed to make little difference. Sovereign states traditionally claimed the right to sequester the property of enemy aliens during periods of belligerency, and, of course, they had the power to punish their own citizens as they pleased. The distinction between "alien enemy" and "disloyal citizen" thus seemed unimportant as long as the fact of opposition was established; this differentiation became crucial only after the peace treaty had separated the two classes of persons for the assessment of compensation and reparations.

The issue of allegiance was less easily evaded when treason statutes were involved. Since the penalty for treason could be final, judges and juries generally acted with caution and discretion; confiscated property might be returned, but a hanging could not be

---

14. Claude Halstead Van Tyne, *The Loyalists in the American Revolution* (New York, 1902), chaps. 9, 10, 12, discusses the punitive laws; Appendixes B and C of his work conveniently summarize the major anti-loyalist acts. For a particular analysis of state treason provisions, see Chapin, *American Law of Treason*, 38–41, and J. Willard Hurst, "Treason in the United States," *Harvard Law Review*, LVIII (1944–1945), 248n, 256n.

15. Quoted in Van Tyne, *Loyalists in the American Revolution*, 280.

reversed. The desire to do justice in individual cases and the recognized danger of retaliation against American prisoners held by the British prevented frequent resorts to the gallows. Active loyalists unfortunate enough to fall into American hands might be executed for treason, but often they were dealt with as prisoners of war.[16] Whenever possible, prosecutors preferred to indict captured tories for murder, robbery, counterfeiting, or other felonies, thus avoiding the difficult problem of proving the obligation of allegiance and the fact of citizenship.[17]

Once a treason prosecution was begun, the question of the allegiance of the accused became unavoidable, for the essential quality of the crime lay not merely in the specific nature of the act but in the intent and status of the actor. A British soldier who "levied war" against the colonies obviously was no traitor. Nor did intent alone suffice to constitute the crime: Joseph Malin of Pennsylvania was acquitted of treason though he confessed to joining a corps of American soldiers, thinking they were British.[18] It was necessary to prove that the person accused had intentionally performed acts conflicting with his obligations as a member of the community. The law required proof of act, intent, and status before it would condemn a man for treason.

Treason indictments necessarily included a statement that the accused in fact owed allegiance to the state. Before specifying the

16. On Dec. 30, 1777, Congress ordered that loyalists captured while serving under British enlistment should be turned over to the states for punishment. Washington feared retaliatory executions and favored treating such persons as prisoners of war. Henry J. Young, "Treason and Its Punishment in Revolutionary Pennsylvania," *PMHB*, XC (1966), 299. In fact, the treatment varied. In one instance in New Jersey, of 35 persons convicted of treason and sentenced to death, only 2—William Iliff and John Mee—were hanged, while the others were handed over to Washington, who treated them as prisoners of war. [New Jersey v. Iliff] (1777–1778), William S. Stryker *et al.*, eds., *Documents Relating to the Revolutionary History of New Jersey* (*Archives of the State of New Jersey*, 2d Ser., I–V [Trenton, N.J., 1901–1917]), II, 11–14, 82, hereafter cited as *N.J. Archives*, 2d Ser. In Pennsylvania, George Spangler was hanged after General Benedict Arnold ordered his trial for treason: *PMHB*, LV (1931), 49. But Frederick Verner was exchanged for an American prisoner held by the British: Samuel Hazard, ed., *Pennsylvania Archives*, 1st Ser. (Philadelphia and Harrisburg, Pa., 1852–1856), VI, 704–705, 713, VII, 246, hereafter cited as *Pa. Archives*, 1st Ser.; *Col. Recs. Pa.*, XI, 561; *Jours. Cont. Cong.*, XI, 797–798.

17. In Pennsylvania, e.g., 48 men were hanged for crimes other than treason between 1778 and 1783, though only 84 had been executed during the whole period of settlement before the war. Young, "Treason and Its Punishment," *PMHB*, XC (1966), 297. In Virginia, Josiah Philips was attainted of treason, but when captured he was tried and executed for felonies he had committed as a guerrilla-outlaw, rather than for this crime. William P. Trent, "The Case of Josiah Philips," *AHR*, I (1895–1896), 444–454.

18. Respublica v. Malin, 1 Dall. 33 (Pa., 1778).

acts that one Pennsylvania prisoner had committed "against the Duty of his Allegiance," the state formally charged that

John Elwood, late of the County of Bucks, . . . being an inhabitant of and belonging to and residing within the State of Pennsylvania, and under the protection of its Laws, and owing Allegiance to the same State, as a false Traitor against the same, . . . the Fidelity which to the same State he owed, wholly with[drew], and with all his Might intend[ed] the Peace and Tranquillity of this Commonwealth of Pennsylvania, to disturb, and War and Rebellion against the same to raise and to move, and the Government and Independency thereof as by Law established, to subvert, and to raise again, and restore the Government and Tyranny of the King of Great Britain within the same Commonwealth.[19]

Elwood owed allegiance to Pennsylvania because he resided in the state and received the protection of its laws. When he acted against that obligation he was liable to charges of treason.

Hundreds of persons were indicted for treason during the war, but executions for that crime were fairly rare.[20] Many more persons were accused of the crime and forced to undergo the personal mortification of public obloquy or temporary detention than were ever tried, much less convicted, for this high offense. If the cases for which detailed reports are readily accessible are at all representative, the courts took great pains to observe procedural safeguards once the formal machinery of justice had been called into play.[21] Even those tried, convicted, and sentenced to death for treason usually escaped the gallows, for governors and legislatures liberally granted pardons or commuted sentences.[22] Convicted men were often given the "option" of accepting their sentence or of enlisting in state or Continental forces—a policy that showed perhaps a greater concern for the individual than for the morale and discipline of the

19. *Pa. Archives*, 1st Ser., VII, 59–60. Elwood was found guilty and sentenced to hang, but he was later reprieved. *Ibid.*, 61. He finally received a full pardon. *Col. Recs. Pa.*, XII, 48. This appears to have been the common form of a treason indictment in Pennsylvania. See, e.g., Respublica v. Carlisle, 1 Dall. 34 (Pa., 1778).

20. Chapin, *American Law of Treason*, 71. I have relied heavily on this work in my comments here. Where printed records have been accessible, I have examined the cases Chapin cites.

21. *Ibid.*, 63–80, and the cases therein cited.

22. E.g., the General Court at Richmond, Va., sentenced at least 10 men to hang for treason between Apr. and Oct. 1782, but all were pardoned. Palmer *et al.*, eds., *Cal. of Va. State Papers*, III, 120, 194, 361. New York tried a number of persons recruited for loyalist service by Jacob Rosa in 1777. Of these, 30 men were sentenced to hang, and 8 were acquitted. All except Rosa and his chief lieutenant, Jacob Middagh, were subsequently pardoned. Chapin, *American Law of Treason*, 52–53.

army.[23] Only one known execution for treason took place in New England during the war, and only four civilians met that fate in Pennsylvania.[24] Virginia did not carry out a single official execution for treason, and many of those sentenced to hang elsewhere in the middle and southern colonies apparently suffered lesser punishments.[25] The death penalty seems to have been carried out only when there was clear evidence of active disloyalty; even then the purpose was as much to warn other potential traitors as to satisfy a patriotic bloodlust.[26]

The circumspection with which courts handled cases of treason did not reflect doubts about the theoretical right of the states to punish the betrayal of obligations by those claimed as citizens. In American eyes, the Revolution had fragmented the old community of allegiance, dividing the onetime fellow subjects into three separate categories. On the one side were real British subjects, including all those whose continued loyalty to the king was uncontested. They had never become citizens of the new republics, and their status during the hostilities was that of alien enemies. On the other side were persons who resided in the states, supported the Revolution, and received the protection of the laws; they were deemed faithful citizens, entitled to the full privileges of membership. In the middle were the loyalists. They professed a continued allegiance to

23. See, e.g., [Pennsylvania v. Cassedy alias Thompson] (1779), *Col. Recs. Pa.*, XII, 222, 309; [New Jersey v. Bogart] (1777), *Minutes of the Council of Safety of the State of New Jersey* (Jersey City, N.J., 1872), 64, 170. Of seven men tried for treason in connection with a "tory plot" in Maryland, only the leader, Johan C. Frietschie, was hanged. At least one (and perhaps as many as four) was given the option of enlisting. Dorothy MacKay Quynn, "The Loyalist Plot in Frederick," *Md. Hist. Mag.*, XL (1945), 201–210.

24. Moses Dunbar was hanged at Hartford, Conn., in Mar. 1777. Peck, *Loyalists of Connecticut*, 22–27. The four Pennsylvanians were David Dawson, Abraham Carlisle, John Roberts, and Ralph Morden. I have found nothing on Dawson, but for the others see Young, "Treason and Its Punishment," *PMHB*, XC (1966), *passim*; Respublica v. Carlisle, 1 Dall. 34 (Pa., 1778); Respublica v. Roberts, 1 Dall. 39 (Pa., 1778); and John M. Coleman, "The Treason of Ralph Morden and Robert Land," *PMHB*, LXXIX (1955), 439–451. Samuel Ford and Samuel Lyons were hanged for deserting the provincial navy in 1778, and others may have met a traitor's fate under military authority. *Pa. Archives*, 1st Ser., VI, 697–699; *Col. Recs. Pa.*, XI, 565–566, 579, 625.

25. Isaac Samuel Harrell, *Loyalism in Virginia: Chapters in the Economic History of the Revolution* (Durham, N.C., 1926), 59; Robert O. DeMond, *The Loyalists in North Carolina during the Revolution* (Durham, N.C., 1940), 20. For New York, New Jersey, and Maryland, see Chapin, *American Law of Treason*, 48–54, 59–60, 77–78.

26. For example, George Hardy was convicted of treason in 1779 and sentenced to hang, but his friends, the jurors, and the judges agreed that he should be shown mercy. Since he was an unimportant man, wrote the judges to the Executive Council, there was no "exemplary" benefit in his execution. *Col. Recs. Pa.*, XI, 753–754, 761; *Pa. Archives*, 1st Ser., VII, 326–327.

the British monarch, but in the eyes of "patriot" authorities, the circumstances of their birth, residence, or behavior sufficed in law to prove them citizens of the new states. Their continued residence under the new republican governments after independence evinced their choice of allegiance, and adherence to Great Britain thereafter proved them not loyal subjects but disloyal citizens.

The American view of the Revolution's effect on the old community of allegiance was challenged by the British, but as long as the fate of the empire remained in the hands of contending armies, little could be done to reconcile conflicting claims for the loyalty of individuals. Nor did America's victory settle the issue. The treaty of peace insured that questions of status inherent in the punitive wartime laws would remain alive in other forums. Article IV provided that "creditors on either side" should meet with "no lawful impediments" to the recovery of bona fide prewar debts. Article V obligated Congress to recommend the restitution of rights and properties "belonging to real British subjects" and to persons "resident in districts in the possession of his Majesty's arms, and who have not borne arms against the said United States." Persons "of any other description" were allowed to return and reside in the country unmolested for twelve months in order to seek restitution and compensation for their losses. All persons with interests in confiscated lands were to meet with "no lawful impediment in the prosecution of their just rights." Finally, Article VI barred further confiscations and punishments and declared that no person should "suffer any future loss or damage" for the part he took in the war.[27]

Each of these provisions led to conflict in the postwar years. American lawyers quickly contended that Article IV comprehended only those debts belonging to acknowledged British subjects on the one side and loyal American citizens on the other. Persons considered by the states to be "disloyal citizens" could not claim to be British subjects without confessing to treason, and to make that admission automatically changed any confiscatory measure from a "lawful impediment" rendered nugatory by the treaty to a legitimate punishment for a domestic crime not affected by the agree-

27. John Bassett Moore, ed., *Arbitration of Claims for Compensation for Losses and Damages resulting from Lawful Impediments to the Recovery of Pre-War Debts*, in John Bassett Moore, ed., *International Adjudications, Ancient and Modern . . .* , Mod. Ser., III (New York, 1931), 1–4, hereafter cited as Moore, ed., *Int. Adjud.*

ment.[28] Justice James Iredell made the point in *Douglass* v. *Stirk*, a case that arose in Georgia and was brought before the United States Circuit Court in 1792: "Douglass was a citizen of this State; banished from it; and his estate and debts confiscated. This is a punishment by a state of one of its own citizens. There is no article in the treaty that can do away with a forfeiture actually incurred by a citizen actually named before the treaty took place, and with respect to which, no further inquiry is necessary than what property and debts he possessed."[29]

Articles V and VI of the treaty of 1783 clearly encompassed the loyalists, those persons whose status as "real British subjects" or "citizens" was open to dispute. Yet these provisions had little compulsory force on the states. Congress merely "recommended" the restitution of confiscated loyalist property, and the local governments complied at their own discretion. Although the ban on further prosecutions was stated more strongly, it, too, was frequently disregarded. North Carolina continued to sell confiscated tory estates until 1790. New York passed a number of discriminatory laws after learning of the treaty's provisions, and there was widespread popular retaliation against returning loyalists throughout the country. Discriminatory legislation tapered off through the 1790s, but many of the losses were irrecoverable, at least from American sources. After 1783 British claims commissioners did compensate some for the damages they had suffered; however, the recommendatory provisions of the treaty ultimately proved to be of little solace to many of those whom the American authorities had judged disloyal.[30]

28. Murray v. Marean (U.S.C.C., 1791) and Moore v. Patch (Mass., 1792) held that Massachusetts acts of attainder and confiscation barred recovery of prewar debts, despite Art. IV of the treaty. The cases are quoted and summarized, respectively, in Moore, ed., *Int. Adjud.*, III, 106, 173. The mixed commission established under Jay's Treaty divided on this issue. In the case of Bishop Charles Inglis, the commissioners unanimously agreed that a New York attainder that did not specifically claim that Inglis was a citizen was not proof of his citizenship and thus was a "lawful impediment." In the case of Andrew Allen, however, the American commissioners withdrew when their British colleagues insisted that a Pennsylvania attainder specifying Allen's citizenship constituted such an impediment. *Ibid.*, 98–165, 238–252. In Jackson v. Catlin, 2 Johns. Rep. 248, 260 (N.Y., 1807), James Kent denied that attainders were prima facie evidence of citizenship "because many of the persons attainted had never owed any allegiance to this state."

29. Douglass v. Stirk (U.S.C.C., 1792). Iredell's opinion was quoted before the mixed commission and can be found in Moore, ed., *Int. Adjud.*, III, 106–107, 174.

30. For general surveys of the treatment of the loyalists in relation to Arts. V–VI of the treaty, see Van Tyne, *Loyalists in the American Revolution*, 286–307; Wallace Brown, *The*

Although the British government proved willing to pay loyalists for losses incurred during the Revolution, it adamantly refused to take responsibility for the prewar debts owed to its own subjects. The American government had obligated itself to settle those debts in 1783, and until the obligation was met, Britain refused to comply with other treaty provisions. The question of the distinction between real subjects and disaffected citizens was thus not allowed to die, and indeed it flared anew after the negotiation of Jay's Treaty, signed November 19, 1794.

Article VI of Jay's Treaty established a mixed Anglo-American commission with authority to settle outstanding claims involving debts confiscated or otherwise abridged by the states during the Revolution.[31] The commission's proceedings began amicably enough, but the commissioners soon clashed over the question of who was eligible for compensation. The British representatives argued that until the peace treaty of 1783 the United States "were to be considered in a state of rebellion against Great Britain, and legally incapable of punishing in any case a person who was a natural-born British subject for acts of aid and support to his British sovereign in the use of armed force against the United States."[32] From this perspective all wartime acts punishing loyalty to the king were, without exception, "lawful impediments" to the recovery of prewar debts. A state's failure to remove these impediments— whether the sufferer was described as a "real subject" or as a "disloyal citizen"—left the United States responsible for compensating the creditor under Article IV of the peace treaty.

The American representatives could not accept this contention, for in their eyes, it not only obliterated the distinction made in 1783 between real subjects and loyalists but also impugned the sovereignty and independence of the states between 1776 and 1783.

Good Americans: The Loyalists in the American Revolution (New York, 1969), 171–179; Charles R. Ritcheson, *Aftermath of Revolution: British Policy toward the United States, 1783–1795* (Dallas, Tex., 1969), 49–62; and Merrill Jensen, *The New Nation: A History of the United States during the Confederation, 1781–1789* (New York, 1950), 268–281. For special studies, see DeMond, *Loyalists in North Carolina*, 153–169; Oscar Zeichner, "The Rehabilitation of Loyalists in Connecticut," *New England Quarterly*, XI (1938), 308–330; Oscar Zeichner, "The Loyalist Problem in New York after the Revolution," *N.Y. Hist.*, XXI (1940), 284–302; and Julius Goebel, Jr., ed., *The Law Practice of Alexander Hamilton: Documents and Commentary* (New York, 1964–1969), I, 197–202. Brown, *The Good Americans*, 181–190, discusses the work of the British Claims Commission.

31. Moore, ed., *Int. Adjud.*, III, 5–8, gives the relevant portions of the treaty.
32. *Ibid.*, 174–175.

Persons who were deemed disloyal citizens by the states and who had been punished for their breach of allegiance by a judgment of court, an attainder, or an act of confiscation had no standing before the commission. The Americans considered the position taken by the British to be derogatory to the nation's honor; the states were sovereign after July 4, 1776, and free to punish their citizens as they chose.[33]

The conflicting positions of the two parties deadlocked the proceedings of the mixed commission and led to its dissolution. The problem of the prewar debts was finally solved by a convention of settlement concluded January 2, 1802.[34] The United States made a lump payment of six hundred thousand pounds to the British government, extinguishing all claims under Article IV of the peace treaty. The compromise measure succeeded because it sidestepped the issue of individual status. Great Britain was free to disburse the money as it chose and to consider the loyalists as having always been British subjects.[35] The United States could continue to hold that they had been disobedient citizens rightfully punished for violating their allegiance.

America's wartime statutes defining treason and suppressing the loyalists initially rested on the assumption that the break with England was the action of a majority, binding the minority of dissenters. The Declaration of Independence, affirmed by the provisional local authorities, had justified the dissolution of the old allegiance on the grounds that George III had defaulted on his obligation to protect his subjects. The congressional resolves of June 24 and the state treason statutes that followed asserted that allegiance was now owed to the new republics. Citizenship supplanted subjectship as the source of protection shifted from George III to the independent states. Revolutionary leaders presumed that the will of the majority was clear authorization to extend jurisdiction over those who renounced independence and professed their continued loyalty to the king.

It was inevitable that this presumption would be challenged.

33. Thomas Fitzsimmons and Samuel Sitgreaves to Thomas Macdonald, Henry Pye Rich, and John Guillemard, Sept. 2, 1799, states the American commissioners' reasons for withdrawing. *Ibid.*, 277–307.

34. *Ibid.*, 8–10, for text of the convention.

35. For a more detailed discussion, see Kettner, "Subjects or Citizens? A Note on British Views," *Va. Law Rev.*, LXII (1976), 945–967.

Thoughtful loyalists and patriots alike questioned the legitimacy of demanding allegiance and coercing loyalty from individuals who were unwilling participants in the struggle for independence.

Few, perhaps, considered the question as carefully as did Peter Van Schaack, who retired to his New York farm in the winter of 1775–1776 to reread Locke, Vattel, Montesquieu, Grotius, Beccaria, and Pufendorf before taking his stand on independence. Van Schaack had supported the American cause when its main goal had been the redress of grievances within the old imperial system. Yet he was not convinced that the obnoxious British policies were signs of a conspiracy to establish tyranny and to reduce America to slavery.[36] He refused to impute illegitimate motives to the king. When Congress resolved to break the bonds with the mother country, Van Schaack insisted on his right to disagree.

Although Van Schaack accepted the ultimate right of revolution, he considered that in the absence of tyranny "society could not be dissolved, a state of nature did not exist, and a man could not take up arms against the government."[37] The decision whether such a tyranny existed had to be an individual matter: "Every man must exercise his own reason, and judge for himself; 'for he that appeals to Heaven, must be sure that he has right on his side,' according to Mr. Locke. It is a question of morality and religion, in which a man cannot conscientiously take an active part, without being convinced in his own mind of the justice of the cause; for obedience while government exists being clear on the one hand, the dissolution of government must be equally so, to justify an appeal to arms."[38]

No majority had the right to impose its opinions on individuals in questions such as this, according to Van Schaack. Even after New York had affirmed the Declaration of Independence and had actually assumed the authority and prerogatives of a sovereign state, it was "premature, to tender an oath of allegiance before the government to which it imposes subjection, the time it is to take the place of the present exceptionable one, and who are to be the rulers, as well as the mode of their appointment in future, are known."[39] Cutting to the heart of the matter, Van Schaack insisted that when

36. Henry C. Van Schaack, *The Life of Peter Van Schaack* . . . (New York, 1842), 56.
37. William H. Nelson, *The American Tory* (Boston, 1961), 122.
38. Van Schaack, *Life of Peter Van Schaack*, 57–58.
39. See Van Schaack to the Provincial Convention, Jan. 25, 1777, explaining Van Schaack's refusal to take the test oath (for which he was banished). *Ibid.*, 72.

new political communities were formed, individuals must have the right to choose or reject the new allegiance:

Admitting that a man is never so clear about the dissolution of the old government, I hold it that *every individual* has still a right to choose the State of which he will become a member; for before he surrenders any part of his natural liberty, he has a right to know what security he will have for the enjoyment of the residue, and "men being by nature free, equal, and independent," the subjection of any one to the political power of a State, can arise only from "his own consent." I speak of the formation of a society and of a man's initiating himself therein, so as to make himself a member of it; for I admit, that when once the society *is* formed, the majority of its members undoubtedly conclude the rest.[40]

Van Schaack's assertion that individual volition must determine ultimate allegiance in revolutionary situations pointed the direction in which American thought would move. The founders of the new republican states were aware of the inconsistency between advocating a doctrine of consent and requiring individuals to subject themselves to regimes that they condemned. Yet if allegiance was volitional as well as contractual, then difficult questions ensued with vaguely threatening implications for the stability and continuity of political obligation. Not until well after the Revolution would Americans follow those implications to the logical conclusion that individual men might legitimately choose to change their allegiance even after they had elected membership in and enjoyed the protection of an established society. But during the conflict with Great Britain, when governments fought over their competing claims to the obedience of the American people, the first real concessions were made to the right of the individual to decide his own loyalty.

Political theorists had founded political obligation on individual consent long before the American Revolution, of course. However, the political ramifications of the idea had never been deeply explored with respect to the character of allegiance and to the relationship between the individual and the community of which he was a member. In Locke's world, men lost the right of autonomous choice as soon as they left the state of nature and submitted to the rule of the majority. Thereafter they were bound by contracts—the

---

40. *Ibid.*, 73. Van Schaack finally became convinced that the English Constitution had been corrupted, renounced his allegiance, and returned to America after the war to become a citizen. *Ibid.*, 260–263.

social compact and the contract of government—over which they had no control as individuals.[41] Even the original act of volition— the individual's choice to join others to form a community—was more a theoretical construct than a human reality. Lockeans did not seriously consider that men in a "state of nature" might have alternative societies to choose among, nor did they explore in depth the validity of the concept of primal consent when applied to those born into already existing societies. Locke's theoretical scheme was thus ill equipped to deal with the difficult problems of choice raised by the American Revolution.

The colonies' separation from Great Britain did not create a state of nature in which free, autonomous individuals could consider the advantages and disadvantages of submitting to society and government. Supporters of Britain insisted that the old contracts remained unimpaired, that royal authority over the colonists was still legitimate despite its renunciation by individual rebels or by their pretended governments. Even among those who denied that contention, few considered government totally dissolved. In the colonies royal authorities were gradually replaced by ad hoc provisional governments that were in turn legitimized or superseded as new state constitutions were drafted and ratified. But there was no general perceptible break in the actual continuity of government. The Continental Congress defined (and thereby imposed) membership in the new states even before formalizing independence. And state governments easily and automatically claimed jurisdiction over the same inhabitants and territories that had constituted the colonial dependencies.[42]

There were several ways in which this assumption and presumption of jurisdiction could be defended in terms of traditional legal–constitutional theory. One argument stressed the validity of prior social compacts, despite the broken contract of government with George III. Proceeding from the idea propounded in the pre-Revolutionary debates that the old colonies had always been separate and complete communities merely sharing a common king, American lawyers could contend that the individual members of the colonial societies were still bound to follow the decisions made by the majority of their fellows. When that majority chose to declare the

41. See above, chap. 3, n. 28; chap. 6, at n. 29.
42. See generally Thad W. Tate, "The Social Contract in America, 1774–1787: Revolutionary Theory as a Conservative Instrument," *WMQ*, 3d Ser., XXII (1965), 375–391.

old government dissolved and a new one erected, minority dissenters were bound to submit. Just as William III had inherited the allegiance of English subjects once "the people" judged that James II had abdicated his throne, so did the new states fall heir to the obedience of all those who had once owed loyalty to George III as the king of their particular colony.[43]

Chief Justice Theophilus Parsons of the Massachusetts Supreme Judicial Court found this argument persuasive as late as 1812. Considering the question whether an infant born in Massachusetts in 1774, who left before independence and never returned thereafter, was a citizen or an alien, Parsons declared that the Revolution had worked just such an automatic transfer of allegiance:

This people, in union with the people of the other colonies, considered the several aggressions of their sovereign on their essential rights as amounting to an abdication of his sovereignty. The throne was then vacant; but the people, in their political character, did not look after another family to reign; nor did they establish a new dynasty; but assumed to themselves, as a nation, the sovereign power, with all its rights, privileges, and prerogatives. Thus the government became a republic, possessing all the rights vested in the former sovereign; among which was the right to the allegiance of persons born within the territory of the province of Massachusetts Bay.[44]

The court recognized the infant in question as a member of the Massachusetts community of allegiance, with all the rights and duties of a citizen.

Parsons personally thought that the bonds of allegiance could be broken when the sovereign defaulted on his obligations or when both parties consented to the dissolution of the contract.[45] The Massachusetts courts had already upheld the right of individuals caught up in the Revolution to change their allegiance with the consent of the government,[46] and they would later hold that persons born within the province could have "been expatriated volun-

---

43. See, e.g., Richard Stockton's argument for the defendant in error (Coxe) in McIlvaine v. Coxe, 2 Cranch 280, 317 (U.S., 1805).

44. Ainslie v. Martin, 9 Mass. 454, 457–458 (Mass., 1812).

45. *Ibid.*, 451. Justice Smith Thompson's later claim that Parsons adopted the doctrine of perpetual allegiance to its fullest extent is thus not strictly accurate. See Inglis v. Trustees of Sailor's Snug Harbor, 3 Pet. 99, 122–123 (U.S., 1830).

46. Palmer v. Downer, 2 Mass. 179n (Mass., 1801); Martin v. Commonwealth, 1 Mass. 347, 385 (Mass., 1805); Gardner v. Ward, 2 Mass. 244n (Mass., 1805); Kilham v. Ward, 2 Mass. 236, 239, 268 (Mass., 1806).

tarily, or by compulsion," during the conflict.[47] Yet, on the whole, the state's claim to obedience took precedence over the individual's right to determine his own loyalty. Massachusetts might consent to honor the individual's choice, but within the framework of the contract theory it had no obligation to do so.

An alternative justification of the states' assumption of authority over their inhabitants was found in a combination of the theory of the social contract and the traditional doctrine of conquest. The former readily explained the status of those who voluntarily accepted the new governments; the latter could be used to support the demands for obedience placed on American dissenters. Coke had claimed in *Calvin's Case* that the conqueror, holding the power of life and death over the conquered, was entitled to their allegiance.[48] By equating the "disaffected" with the "conquered," Coke's dictum could be applied to legitimize the authority that states exercised over the loyalists.

Justice Spencer Roane of Virginia denied that the Revolution involved a mere transfer of allegiance by which the states "inherited" or succeeded to the loyalty once owed to the king, and he would have disagreed with Parsons's contention that a person born in America who left before independence automatically acquired membership in the new republics. According to Roane, those who had been born in allegiance to George III became citizens only by choice or by conquest. The loyalists became citizens—albeit unwillingly—not because of their birth or residence in America, but because they had been conquered: "The people themselves who are conquered are legitimated [in the new states] by virtue of the implied compact only, and cannot claim such legitimation by the paramount title of having been, at the time of their birth, inheritable in that territory under another sovereign."[49] While the Virginia justice, like his Massachusetts colleague, acknowledged the "natural right" to withdraw allegiance from a tyrant, honoring "the memorable assertion of that right by the American people, who, sword in hand, expatriated themselves from the government which tyrannized over them," the two thus differed in how they justified the unwilling allegiance of the loyalists.[50]

47. Cummington v. Springfield, 2 Pickering 394, 395 (Mass., 1824), quoting an opinion of the Supreme Judicial Court to the Massachusetts Senate, June 1823, in the case of George Phipps.
48. Above, chap. 1, n. 36.
49. Read v. Read, 5 Call 160, 199 (Va., 1804).
50. *Ibid.*, 201–202.

If the conquest doctrine could reinforce claims to the allegiance of Americans who opposed independence, it had the additional advantage from the American point of view of allowing the courts to explain how persons who had once shared a common allegiance could now be divided into aliens and citizens. Roane used the theory that Virginia was a conquering sovereign to explain why after 1776 "real British subjects" could no longer claim the rights of membership they would have been entitled to enjoy had the state remained a colony:

> They do not become citizens of the conquering power and are not to be considered in that light; because they have not submitted to the conqueror, nor by any compact entitled themselves to the privileges of subjects; and yet they were once inheritable in the territories conquered, and can say as much as the present plaintiffs can say in respect of the territories of Virginia, viz. that, at the time of their birth [before 1776], they were legitimated here. . . . If, then, the territory of Virginia, had been conquered from Great Britain in the ordinary way, by an existing sovereign, there is no doubt but that, upon the foregoing principles of the common law, the residuary subjects of the British empire, not residing here, nor contracting an allegiance to the conquering power, would have remained aliens, as to the sovereignty established here by such conquest. . . . I see no difference in this respect between a change in the sovereignty of Virginia effected by an existing sovereign, and by a sovereign merely coeval with the change.[51]

Although traditional theory thus offered several ways of justifying the demands for loyalty placed on the reluctant citizens by the new governments, neither the idea of orderly succession nor the idea of conquest seemed to conform adequately to the spirit of the Revolution. Both concepts smacked too much of coercive power and seemed to contradict too blatantly the sense that the war was fought to protect and increase liberty. Somehow the Revolutionary leaders had to find a distinction between citizens and aliens that identified and suppressed the disloyal yet that legitimated America's cause and avoided measures closely resembling the arbitrary actions of the colonists' former sovereign.

Americans responded to the problem of conflicting loyalties by developing the doctrine of the right of election. The essence of the doctrine was that "in revolutions, every man has a right to take his part. He is excusable, if not bound in duty to take that which in his conscience he approves."[52] The personal choice of allegiance had to

---

51. *Ibid.*, 199.
52. William Tilghman (for McIlvaine), in McIlvaine v. Coxe, 2 Cranch 280, 281 (U.S.,

be made within a "reasonable" period of time and subsequently could be considered binding, but the initial concession was clear. Citizenship in the new republics was to begin with individual consent.

The states by no means moved in unison, but most began to adopt the idea of election during the war years. The general principle seemed fully consonant with the ideals of the Revolution, yet its application in practice sometimes proved harsh or disingenuous. Most states began with a fairly restrictive policy respecting the evidence for election and the time allowed for the exercise of the right. A few states initially assumed a claim to the allegiance of all their inhabitants at the moment of independence. If such persons chose to withdraw thereafter, or if they suffered "compulsory expatriation" on conviction or attainder for disloyalty, they could still be considered to have once been citizens. The disabilities of alienage incurred by this "election" thus could not be removed by later treaty provisions respecting "real British subjects."[53]

Other states were slightly more lenient. Defining citizenship as a contractual relationship in which allegiance was given in return for protection, such states viewed the period of governmental disorganization accompanying independence as the equivalent of a virtual state of nature. During this period individuals had some time to consider their choice of allegiance. Election occurred, explicitly, when they acknowledged the legitimacy of the new states or, implicitly, when they accepted the protection of the new constitutions and laws. The time limit for election thus depended upon when legitimate, protective laws came into being in the respective states.

The absence of treason prosecutions against civilians until after the states had passed treason laws—despite Congress's definition of the crime—suggests that individuals were generally allowed to choose sides before that time.[54] The assumptions behind this policy were articulated in the Pennsylvania case of *Respublica* v. *Chapman* (1781), a case worth examining in some detail both because of its

---

1805). Compare Caignet v. Pettit, 2 Dall. 234, 235 (Pa., 1795), where the court upheld the same right for French dissenters from the French Revolution.

53. See, e.g., the Massachusetts cases cited above, nn. 28, 44, and Apthorp v. Backus, Kirby 407 (Conn., 1788), where a British subject who acquired lands in the state before the Revolution was held to have once been a citizen.

54. Chapin, *American Law of Treason*, 72, 139n.

illustration of contemporary approaches to the problem of conflicting loyalties and because of its later relevance as a precedent in such
matters.[55]

Samuel Chapman had resided in Pennsylvania until December
26, 1776, when he departed and joined the British Legion. By a
proclamation of the Supreme Executive Council, June 15, 1778,
Chapman was required to surrender himself to the state authorities
before August 1, and when he ignored the order, he was attainted of
treason. Chapman was later captured at sea, taken to Massachusetts
(where he was treated as a prisoner of war), then extradited to
Pennsylvania. Although already convicted of treason by virtue of
his attainder, the prisoner was brought before the state supreme
court to give reasons against execution of the judgment.

The essential point of Chapman's argument was that since there
had been no legitimate government established in Pennsylvania at
the time of his departure from the state, he could have received no
protection and had owed no allegiance, and was thus not liable to
the penalties of treason. The old doctrine of perpetual allegiance, he
claimed, "applies only to established and settled governments; not
to the case of withdrawing from an old government, and erecting a
new one." When such an event took place, every member of the old
community had "a right of election." Chapman had signified his
choice by withdrawing from the state nearly a month before the
first legislative act had been passed under the new constitution and
nearly three months before all the branches of government had
been put into operation. A statute of January 28, 1777, revived all
the old laws, but admitted their suspension since May 14, 1776. The
state's treason law of February 11, 1777, was not, and could not be,
retroactive under the constitution. His attainder, therefore, was
illegitimate, unfounded, and utterly void.[56]

The state's attorney general countered this argument by contending that even before the new constitution was confirmed,
Pennsylvania had been governed by temporary yet legitimate bodies under the authority of the people. The constitution—"that
social compact under which the people of this State are now united"
—had been approved on September 8, 1776, before Chapman

55. Respublica v. Chapman, 1 Dall. 53 (Pa., 1781). For additional details, see Young,
"Treason and Its Punishment," *PMHB*, XC (1966), 301–302. For the use of the case as a
precedent, see McIlvaine v. Coxe, 2 Cranch 280, 284, 300 (U.S., 1805).
56. Respublica v. Chapman, 53–54.

withdrew, and a quorum of the new legislature had met as early as November. Chapman's continued residence in Pennsylvania until December signified his initial acceptance of the regime, regardless of his later actions.[57]

Chief Justice Thomas McKean saw some validity in both arguments, but his charge to the jury favored Chapman. Treason, claimed McKean, was "nothing more than a criminal attempt to destroy the existence of government," and it might certainly have been committed from the convening of the new legislature (November 18, 1776), before the different qualities of the crime were defined and its punishment declared by positive law. Yet extenuating circumstances tended to absolve the prisoner of this particular crime. The words of the statute reviving the old laws implied "that those who framed it, thought the separation from *Great Britain* worked a dissolution of all government, and that the force, not only of the Acts of Assembly, but of the common and statute law of *England*, was actually extinguished by that event."[58] Without the protection of the laws there evidently could be no allegiance.

All difficulty vanished from the case when one examined the treason act of February 11, 1777. With an evident intent to discriminate between those who owed allegiance and those who did not, the legislature claimed as citizens only those persons "then" or "hereafter" inhabiting the state. Although the policy was not explicitly stated, the jury thought "the desire and intention of the legislature . . . to have been, to allow a choice of his party to every man, until the 11th of February, 1777; and that no act savouring of treason, done before that period, should incur the penalties of the law." Samuel Chapman had made his choice and had done so within a "reasonable" period of time after independence. The jury found him not guilty of treason.[59]

Pennsylvania's definition of the time period in which individuals could choose or reject citizenship was perhaps the clearest of all the states', but its stress on the new constitution and on the treason statute was representative of a widespread policy. The New York state courts, for example, would hold that "every member of the old government must have the right to decide for himself, whether

57. *Ibid.*, 54–55.
58. *Ibid.*, 55–58.
59. *Ibid.*, 58–60. McKean here recapitulated and elaborated a position earlier stated in an advisory opinion to President Joseph Reed, July 1779. See Young, "Treason and Its Punishment," *PMHB*, XC (1966), 299–300.

he will continue with a society which has so fundamentally changed its condition." Since the Revolutionary government had been "imperfect and inchoate" before April 20, 1777—the date of the new constitution—it was a "very grave question" whether treason could have been committed earlier. Whatever precise time limits were established, clearly there had to be "some personal act, indicative of an assent to become a member of the new government, and without it, the rights of citizenship are not acquired."[60]

North Carolina permitted election even after the establishment of its new constitution in December 1776. A case in 1787 implied that the right to choose was inherent in the fact that the Revolution had created a "state of nature," throwing the inhabitants of the former colony "into a similar situation with a set of people shipwrecked and cast on a maroon'd island—without laws, without magistrates, without government, or any legal authority."[61] Another judge in 1796 thought that although the state could have claimed the allegiance of all persons resident at the moment of independence, "whatever were their sentiments or inclinations," it nevertheless had granted "the option of taking an oath of allegiance, or of departing the State" by an act of April 1777.[62] According to the new constitution, persons outside the state were aliens, but statutes allowed absentees to return and to be recognized as citizens as late as October 1778.[63] British subjects who had never lived in North Carolina and inhabitants who had preferred to leave rather than to swear allegiance within the time allotted by the act of April 1777 were deemed to have chosen the disabilities of alienage, but were not liable to the penalties of disloyalty.[64]

The states generally held that once a person had made his choice of citizenship by swearing allegiance or by accepting the protection of the laws, and once the state concerned had acknowledged his membership, he could not change his mind without risking punishment. This general rule admitted of some special exceptions, how-

60. Jackson v. White, 20 Johns. Rep. 313, 322, 323, 324 (N.Y., 1822).
61. Judge Samuel Ashe, on preliminary motion to dismiss, in Bayard v. Singleton, 1 N.C. 5, 6 (N.C., 1787).
62. Hamiltons v. Eaton, 1 N.C. 641, 688 (U.S.C.C., 1796), opinion delivered by Chief Justice Oliver Ellsworth.
63. Stringer v. Phillips, 2 Haywood 158, 159 (N.C., 1802). See also DeMond, *Loyalists in North Carolina*, 171.
64. Bayard v. Singleton, 9, ruled that a confiscation was as legally valid as an inquest of office for taking the property of an alien by escheat, but Ellsworth noted that special considerations might be warranted in cases of forced rather than voluntary exile.

ever. Infants might go into exile with their parents without losing the right to claim citizenship at a later date, for they could not be considered capable of making an independent choice during infancy. A child would usually be considered to adopt his father's choice, subject to the "right of disaffirmation, in a reasonable time after the termination of his minority."[65]

The dependent status of a *feme covert* (married woman) could also temper the prima facie evidence of election:

In the relation of husband and wife, the law makes, in her behalf, such an allowance for the authority of her husband, and her duty of obedience [to him], that guilt is not imputed to her for actions performed jointly by them, unless of the most heinous and aggravated nature. . . . A *wife* who left the country in the company of her husband did not *withdraw* herself; but was, if I may so express it, withdrawn by him. She did not deprive the government of the benefit of her personal services; she had none to render; none were exacted of her.[66]

Women could commit treason, of course: Esther Marsh was accused of that crime, for example, for helping to supply the British on Staten Island.[67] And women could make individual choices that made them incapable of rights in the new country: the widow of an Irish immigrant who refused to join her husband in New York became an alien after July 4, 1776, and she could take her dower only of lands he had acquired before, not after, independence.[68] But a woman's status as citizen or alien often depended upon the will of another. Here, as elsewhere, her freedom was limited.

Despite allowances for married women and infants, all states stoutly defended their right to define the criteria of membership and to punish persons whose election of citizenship they deemed clear. Public officials and courts regularly imposed penalties for the crime of disloyalty, and they accepted wartime statutes specifically claiming the allegiance of named individuals as authoritative evidence of status.[69]

65. Justice Thompson for the majority in Inglis v. Trustees of Sailor's Snug Harbor, 3 Pet. 99, 126 (U.S., 1830); but see Story's dissent at 164. The issue of infant election was discussed (but ultimately evaded) in Hollingsworth v. Duane, 12 F. Cas. 356 (U.S.C.C., 1801).

66. Martin v. Commonwealth, 1 Mass. 347, 391, 392 (Mass., 1805).

67. [New Jersey v. Marsh] (1778), entries of Jan. 10, 14, 1778, in *Minutes of Council of Safety of N.J.*, 186, 189.

68. Kelly v. Harrison, 2 Johns. Cas. 29, 35 (N.Y., 1800). And see the similar case, Sistare v. Sistare, 2 Root 468 (Conn., 1796).

69. See Camp v. Lockwood, 1 Dall. 393 (Pa., 1788), discussed in detail below, chap. 8, at n. 27, and Cooper v. Telfair, 4 Dall. 14 (U.S., 1800).

In the long run, the states' policy of claiming loyalty from the hostile or the uncommitted was not necessarily disadvantageous to such persons or to their descendants. The peace treaty provision barring "future loss or damage" on account of wartime activities reduced or removed the threat of further punishments for disloyalty, leaving the convicted or attainted loyalist the right to claim the advantages of citizenship. Persons whose sympathies lay with the British and who in fact (if not in law) had chosen to remain subjects of the king might use a wartime attainder to their own advantage after the war, citing it as evidence that the law had deemed them citizens rather than aliens and demanding the rights of the previously rejected status.

The case of *McIlvaine* v. *Coxe*, argued before the United States Supreme Court in 1805, illustrated the possibilities inherent in the situation for those who had been judged disloyal citizens during the Revolution. Daniel Coxe—a native of New Jersey, a onetime member of the colony's council, and a colonel in the provincial militia— had clearly chosen to side with the British during the war. In 1777 he had fled to British-occupied Philadelphia, where he held office under the king's authority. He followed the British troops to New York in 1779 and eventually left for England when the royal army evacuated the city. Coxe never swore allegiance to any American state, nor did he ever abjure George III. Indeed, he repeatedly represented himself as a British subject, traded in that capacity, and received a royal pension in compensation for his losses as a loyalist.[70]

Rebecca Coxe McIlvaine's counsel argued against Coxe's claim to the rights of citizenship, contending that Coxe's actions during the war showed his choice of British subjectship. The lawyers cited the Chapman precedent of 1781 to prove the right of election in revolutionary situations.[71] Even if Coxe had owed allegiance to New Jersey by continuing to reside there after the establishment of the new constitution (July 2, 1776) and the state's treason statute (October 4, 1776), his withdrawal, emigration to England, and self-identification as a British subject proved his expatriation. The right to choose a new allegiance was inherent in the Revolution, and its validity had been shown by the whole course of American development. "Of all people," argued counsel, "the Americans are the last

70. McIlvaine v. Coxe, 2 Cranch 280, 281–283 (U.S., 1805).
71. William Tilghman (for McIlvaine), *ibid*., 284. See also Jared Ingersoll's argument at 322.

who ought to call in question the right of *expatriation*. They have
derived infinite advantage from its exercise by *others* who have left
Europe and settled here."[72]

The old notion of perpetual allegiance founded on *Calvin's Case*
had been formulated "when the ideas of the royal prerogative were
extravagant and absurd."[73] The New Jersey constitution was based
on theories of contract and consent that rejected the immutability of
allegiance, and the ideology of the Revolution implied and included
both the right of election and that of expatriation. The new states,
rightly established, operated by the rule of the majority, of course;
but to institute that rule "*individual assent* is necessary, or it deserves
the name of usurpation, and ought to be execrated as tyranny."[74]
Coxe never gave his consent to the new government. If he had
owed temporary allegiance between the time of the state's treason
act and his withdrawal, his obligation ceased when he departed. If
he had become a citizen by coercion, he had the right to shake off
that compulsory allegiance which he never recognized.[75] In any
event, he must now be considered an alien, not qualified for the
rights of citizenship: "If expatriation be a right when legally exercised, it must induce alienage, and the revolution is a case in point to
show that a man is not obliged to continue the subject of that prince
under whose dominion he was born; otherwise . . . we must admit
that America was not independent until the King of Great Britain
acknowledged her independence; and that it was the consequence
of, and not antecedent to, the treaty of peace."[76]

Coxe's lawyers denied his alienage either during or after the
Revolution. The New Jersey constitution of July 2, 1776, had
considered every inhabitant a member of the new society, and the
decision for independence was an act of the majority binding the
minority. Coxe was an inhabitant, thus he became a citizen. Even
allowing a period of election did not change the case. Coxe had
continued in the state after the act of October 4, 1776, by which
New Jersey explicitly and unequivocally declared that all persons
abiding in its territory and deriving protection from its laws were
members owing allegiance. Coxe's attainder in 1778 and the confis-

72. Tilghman, Ingersoll, *ibid.*, 284, 325.
73. Tilghman, *ibid.*, 289.
74. Ingersoll, *ibid.*, 322.
75. Tilghman, *ibid.*, 285, 292.
76. Ingersoll, *ibid.*, 329.

cation that followed punished his disaffection, but did not alter his citizenship.[77]

Coxe's circumstance was not like that of Samuel Chapman of Pennsylvania, for he had remained in the state after legitimate government and effective protection had begun. Coxe rightly suffered the penalties "resulting from his civil relation to the commonwealth," and he should now be "entitled by natural and equal justice to the benefits of that relation."[78] The doctrine of perpetual allegiance could not decide this case, of course, for the revolutionary situation tore apart the community established under a common sovereign and enabled men to form new contracts of society and government. The place and circumstances of birth did not determine Coxe's allegiance, thus other criteria had to be applied: "Now, the natural, the only practicable substitute, is this, *that those residing at the time of the revolution in the territory separating itself from the parent country, are subject to the new government, and become members of the new community, on the ground either of tacit consent evidenced by their abiding in such territory; or on the principle that every individual is bound by the act of the majority."*[79]

By continuing to reside in New Jersey, Coxe had accepted the contractual relation of allegiance and protection that made him a citizen. He could not thereafter change his citizenship unilaterally. Even if the common law and the constitution of the state admitted the right of expatriation, there was no proof that Coxe had correctly exercised that right, for the contract could only be broken—in the absence of default by the government—by mutual consent.[80] "This public consent," insisted Coxe's counsel, "can be expressed only in one way, *by law*; hence it follows that if the right, strictly speaking, exists, it must be dormant until put in motion by law." The state of New Jersey had never officially recognized or regulated the right; certainly it had always treated Coxe as a citizen, albeit a disloyal one. But Coxe had been punished for his disloyalty, and the treaties of 1783 and 1794 prevented any further retribution. He remained a citizen, not an alien. The law must now enforce his rights.[81]

77. William Rawle (for Coxe), *ibid.*, 292–299.
78. Rawle, *ibid.*, 300.
79. Richard Stockton (for Coxe), *ibid.*, 312.
80. Stockton, *ibid.*, 318.
81. Stockton, *ibid.*, 320.

Justice William Cushing handed down the Court's opinion in the case on February 13, 1808.[82] The difficult problems of determining whether the right of expatriation existed in the absence of statutory recognition and of deciding when Coxe lost the right of election were evaded, for there was "no doubt that after the 4th of October 1776, he became a member of the new society, entitled to the protection of its government, and bound to that government by the ties of allegiance." The statute of that date was "conclusive upon the point, . . . [for] the legislature of that state by the most unequivocal declarations, asserted its right to the allegiance of such of its citizens as had not left the state, and had not attempted to return to their former allegiance." The peace treaty did nothing to change Coxe's citizenship; that agreement merely recognized the separate categories of British subject and American citizen without defining their membership. The decision "was left necessarily to depend upon the laws of the respective states, who, in their sovereign capacities, had acted authoritatively upon the subject." New Jersey had declared Coxe a citizen, and he must now be treated as such.[83]

The arguments in *McIlvaine* v. *Coxe* illustrate the impact of the Revolution on American concepts of allegiance and citizenship. The notion that a person was perpetually bound to the sovereign under whose protection he was born could not survive the actual dismemberment of the old empire.[84] The legitimacy of the new governments emerging from the wreckage of the old community of British allegiance was to derive from individual consent. Although lawyers debated the evidence for this consent and the precise time after which it could be presumed to have been given, and though they disagreed on the issue of unilateral expatriation, they agreed that citizenship began with an act of individual will. The opposing lawyers and the Court both sustained the right to elect citizenship as an inherent and necessary consequence of the Revolution.

Into the nineteenth century, courts generally pursued a conservative policy concerning the timing of election. As in *McIlvaine* v. *Coxe*, they insisted that a choice of loyalty had to be made within a

82. *Ibid.*, 4 Cranch 209 (U.S., 1808). Chancellor James Kent considered the principles enunciated in this opinion authoritative as late as 1827. James Kent, *Commentaries on American Law*, II (New York, 1827), 33–35.
83. McIlvaine v. Coxe, 4 Cranch 209, 212, 215.
84. For a more detailed discussion of British views on the issue, see Kettner, "Subjects or Citizens? A Note on British Views," *Va. Law Rev.*, LXII (1976), esp. 952–967.

short time after the Declaration of Independence, allowing no subsequent election of British allegiance *flagrante bello*.[85] The reasons for this conservatism can be inferred from the arguments and opinions in many of the reported cases. It took time to dissipate the bitterness felt toward natives or longtime residents who took up arms against their neighbors or who otherwise aided the enemy, despite the willingness of many to forgive and forget past hostilities. As the experience of the mixed commission set up by Jay's Treaty had shown, the legitimacy and the finality of punishments meted out to the disloyal on the grounds that they had implicitly chosen citizenship would have been called into question had the courts rejected the states' wartime restrictions on the time limits of election. Moreover, to defer the question of national status until the war's end and to legitimate multiple shifts of loyalty before 1783 seemed to belie the real independence of the states after 1776 and to sanction the British contention that they had remained rebellious colonies until the king and Parliament chose to acknowledge their freedom.

Eventually the initial insistence on the necessity of an early election would fade. If, during the war, the needs of security demanded that the states be able to identify those over whom they could exercise sovereign power, the concern for individual freedom later helped temper harsh policy. From a postwar vantage point, it often seemed reasonable to accept as decisive a person's choice of allegiance as it appeared at the time of the peace treaty. Even in Massachusetts, where the courts long assumed that all members of the society owed a debt of allegiance to the state at the moment of independence, judges could later conclude that

those who, from timidity, or doubt, or principles of duty and conscience, adhered to their former allegiance, were guilty of no crime for which a punishment could be justly inflicted; and if, from such opinions and impressions, they withdrew from the country, all the evils to which they could justly be subjected would be a complete dissolution of their connection with the country from which they voluntarily withdrew, and the national consequences thereof. They could not be punished for treason, for they had never been united with the new independent society. They had created no new allegiance, for it would be inconsistent with that to

85. The policy did not necessarily work both ways, for the courts proved willing to accept British deserters as citizens if they still adhered to the American cause in 1783. See above, n. 47, and Hebron v. Colchester, 5 Day 169 (Conn., 1811).

which they had a right to adhere. They had an election, and this was to be determined by their own opinions of interest and duty.[86]

It took time to bring about the spirit of conciliation that the framers of the peace treaty had hoped would characterize the relations between the now separate parts of what had once been a single community of allegiance. For at least a decade after 1783 many state courts and legislatures refused to concede even to acknowledged British subjects those rights expressly guaranteed by the treaty.[87] Not until the Supreme Court's determination of *Ware v. Hylton* (1796), for example, did the nation verify its pledge to enforce the prewar debts provision, regardless of state legislation designed to obstruct recovery.[88]

The task of determining the effect of the Revolution on other rights once held as a consequence of common subjectship continued well into the nineteenth century. American courts rejected the contention—based on Coke's dictum that a separation of crowns left the *antenati "ad fidem utriusque regis"* (in allegiance to both the old and the new sovereigns)—that all those born before independence remained, in some sense, fellow subjects.[89] Yet they hesitated to impose all the disabilities of alienage on those subjects who did not choose to become citizens. Theoretically, British-owned lands might have been claimed by the states on the grounds that the owners, as aliens, were not entitled to citizens' property rights; such non-penal actions would not necessarily have contravened the peace treaty's provision barring "future loss or damage" on account of

86. Judge Theodore Sedgwick, in Martin v. Commonwealth, 1 Mass. 347, 384–385 (Mass., 1805). See also Orser v. Hoag, 3 Hill 79 (N.Y., 1842).

87. E.g., Maryland's General Court initially (1790, 1793) upheld the right of British creditors to recover though the debtors had paid their debts into the state's treasury; but these decisions were reversed by the Court of Appeals: Dulany v. Wells, 3 Harris & McHenry 20 (Md., 1795); Court v. Vanbibber, *ibid.* 140 (Md., 1795). Ware v. Hylton, 3 Dall. 199 (U.S., 1796), in turn, reversed the appellate decision. For various legislative stratagems to prevent recovery, see Ritcheson, *Aftermath of Revolution*, 63–64.

88. Some states had already moved in this direction. See, e.g., Rutgers v. Waddington (N.Y., 1784), in Goebel, Jr., ed., *Law Practice of Alexander Hamilton*, I, 289–315; Hamiltons v. Eaton, 1 N.C. 641 (U.S.C.C., 1796); Page v. Pendleton, Wythe 211 (Va., 1793); and Georgia v. Brailsford, 2 Dall. 402, 3 Dall. 1 (U.S., 1792, 1794).

89. Above, chap. 1, at n. 22. It was recognized that Americans might use this principle in British courts to claim the rights of subjects. See esp. Read v. Read (above, n. 49); Lambert v. Paine, 3 Cranch 97 (U.S., 1805); Dawson v. Godfrey, 4 *ibid.* 321 (U.S., 1808). Several cases dealt with the impact of British statutes that extended subjectship to persons born abroad (above, chap. 1, n. 10) and the act of 1699 (Prologue, n. 8) that allowed subjects to inherit from distant ancestors though the parents were alien. See, e.g., Contee v. Godfrey, 6 F. Cas. 361 (U.S.C.C., 1808); Barzizas v. Hopkins, 2 Randolph 278 (Va., 1824); and Palmer v. Downer, 2 Mass. 179n (Mass., 1801).

wartime activities. But courts did not retain complete freedom to approve such actions, for Jay's Treaty explicitly guaranteed all lands still held as of 1794: neither British subjects, "their Heirs or assigns shall, so far as may respect the said Lands, and the legal remedies incident thereto, be regarded as Aliens."[90]

A long series of judicial decisions clarified the implications of the treaty guarantees and the rights of persons made aliens by the Revolution. The Supreme Court held that a dissolution of the royal government did not automatically effect "a dissolution of civil rights, or an abolition of the common law under which the inheritances of every man in the state were held."[91] In order for the states to claim lands held by British subjects, then, they had to complete official escheat proceedings; that is, they had to prosecute individual cases and could not rely upon a general claim that the Revolution had divested all such persons of titles to land in America.[92] The two treaties protected titles that accrued to British subjects before or during the war, but did not protect descents cast or titles acquired after 1783.[93] Thus British claimants had to prove actual possession of some form of title at the date of the treaty whose guarantees they invoked.[94]

Judicial decisions concerning the property of British subjects drew a clear dividing line between rights acquired before the peace treaty and those that might have accrued thereafter. The treaty date thus provided a fixed demarcation line beyond which those who had continued in allegiance to the king became aliens in the eyes of the law. By 1830 the Supreme Court was willing to adopt the treaty as a reference point not only for the rights of "real British subjects" but for general questions concerning loyalists as well.

Associate Justice Joseph Story twice urged his colleagues on the Court to take 1783 as the cutoff date for the period of election.[95] He

90. Jay's Treaty, Art. IX. Samuel Flagg Bemis, *Jay's Treaty: A Study in Commerce and Diplomacy*, 2d ed. rev. (New Haven, Conn., 1962), 466.
91. Terrett v. Taylor, 9 Cranch 43 (U.S., 1815).
92. Fairfax v. Hunter, 7 Cranch 603 (U.S., 1813). See also Terrett v. Taylor, 9 *ibid.* 43 (U.S., 1815); Jackson v. Clarke, 3 Wheat. 1 (U.S., 1818); Craig v. Radford, *ibid.* 594 (U.S., 1818); Orr v. Hodgson, 4 *ibid.* 453 (U.S., 1819); and Society for the Propagation of the Gospel v. New Haven, 8 *ibid.* 464 (U.S., 1823).
93. See Craig v. Radford, Orr v. Hodgson, and Dawson v. Godfrey (cited above, nn. 92, 89), and Blight v. Rochester, 7 Wheat. 535 (U.S., 1822).
94. Harden v. Fisher, 1 Wheat. 300 (U.S., 1816); Hughes v. Edwards, 9 *ibid.* 489, 501 (U.S., 1824).
95. Inglis v. Trustees of Sailor's Snug Harbor, 3 Pet. 99 (U.S., 1830); Shanks v. Dupont, *ibid.* 242 (U.S., 1830). In the first case, Story wrote a dissenting opinion on the major point,

had no doubt that the circumstances of the Revolution made it mandatory to allow individuals time to choose their allegiance. Certainly the common law could justify an immediate transfer of allegiance from one sovereign to another in cases involving a cession or a conquest of territory or a prince's abdication of government. But the case of a community divided by civil war was more intricate: "Where the old government, notwithstanding the division, remains in operation, there is more difficulty in saying, upon the doctrine of the common law, that their native allegiance to such government is gone, by the mere fact, that they adhere to the separated territory of their birth, unless there be some act of the old government, virtually admitting the rightful existence of the new."[96]

When two rival claimants demanded an individual's loyalty, neither could legitimately "make him responsible, criminally, to its jurisdiction. It may give him the privileges of a subject, but it does not follow, that it can compulsorily oblige him to renounce his former allegiance." The Declaration of Independence was the act of one party only: "It did not bind the British government, which was still at liberty to insist, and did insist, upon the absolute nullity of the act, and claimed the allegiance of all the colonists, as perpetual and obligatory." States had no right to force individuals caught up in the conflict to become members of the new communities by fiat: "In order, therefore, to make such persons members of the state, there must be some *overt* act or consent on their part, to assume such a character; and then, and then only, could they be deemed, in respect to such colony, to determine their right of election."[97]

The principle that the Americans generally adopted, Story rightly observed, was to consider each person free to choose his allegiance within a reasonable period of time, "and the fact of abiding within the state, after it assumed independence, or after some other specific period, was declared to be an election to become a citizen." However, such an implicit election "could be binding only between him and the state, and could have no legal effect upon the rights of the British crown. The king might still claim to hold him to his former allegiance, and until an actual renunciation on his part, according to the common law, he remained a subject. He was, or might be held

---

which involved the technicalities of a will. He spoke for the majority in the second case.
96. Inglis v. Trustees of Sailor's Snug Harbor, 3 Pet. 99, 157.
97. *Ibid.*, 157, 159.

to be, bound *ad utriusque fidem regis.*" Such a person would be deemed a citizen by the American courts, a subject by the British courts, and either by neutral courts, depending upon the circumstances.[98]

Historically it was true that some persons changed sides during the conflict, and their position remained ambiguous as long as both sides claimed their loyalty. But the peace treaty ended the anomaly. It "acted, by necessary implication, upon the existing state of things, and fixed the final allegiance of the parties on each side, as it was then *de facto.*" After 1783 American courts had no more right to "deem *all* persons citizens who at *any* time before the treaty were citizens" than Great Britain had "to claim as subjects all who previously were subjects." Rather the treaty "ought to be so construed, as that each government should be finally deemed entitled to the allegiance of those who were at that time adhering to it."[99]

Story found this principle simple, rational, and just. It allowed the courts to escape the inconvenience of concluding that the Revolution left many in the position of owing a double allegiance.[100] It had the advantage of giving due weight to the opinions of both the governments and the individuals concerned. Moreover, it could solve difficult questions concerning the evidence for and the timing of election in cases in which the individual's choice or capacity to choose was in some doubt.

The utility of this principle was illustrated in *Shanks* v. *Dupont* (1830), in which the Supreme Court considered the status of a woman who had been born in South Carolina and resided there during the war, but who had married a British officer and departed with him for Great Britain in 1782. The case might have involved a whole complex of considerations, including the relative weights of place of birth, duration of residence after independence, marriage to an alien enemy, and capacity of a woman *"sub potestate viri"* to choose her own allegiance. Instead, the case became a simple matter of determining de facto adherence at the time of the treaty, in which the opinions of both the governments and the individual could be duly considered: "The governments, and not herself, finally settled her national character. They did not treat her as capable by herself of changing or absolving her allegiance; but they virtually allowed her

---

98. *Ibid.*, 160, 161.
99. *Ibid.*, 162, 163, 164.
100. Shanks v. Dupont, 3 Pet. 242, 247 (U.S., 1830).

the benefit of her choice, by fixing her allegiance finally on the side of that party to whom she then adhered."[101]

After 1783, concluded Justice Story, Americans had no interest in discriminating against those who had become loyalists or in treating them other than as British subjects. Article VI of the peace treaty, he recalled, had barred future confiscations and further impairment of rights: "This part of the stipulation, then, being for the benefit of British subjects who became aliens by the events of the war; there is no reason why all persons should not be embraced in it, who sustained the character of British subjects, although one might also have treated them as American citizens." By international principles, the Americans and the British had equal rights to claim the allegiance of those who had confronted the Revolution. They could recognize or deny the other's claim. There was only one reasonable and just conclusion—the treaty of 1783 involved a mutual recognition by the governments of the individual choices made at the war's end.[102]

The status of "American citizen" was the creation of the Revolution. The imperial crisis of the prewar years and the formal separation from the mother country in 1776 stimulated the articulation of at least some of the major principles that were to shape and define the new status. Despite some initial confusion, Americans came to see that citizenship must begin with an act of individual choice. Every man had to have the right to decide whether to be a citizen or an alien. His power to make this choice was clearly acknowledged to be a matter of right, not of grace, for the American republics were to be legitimate governments firmly grounded on consent, not authoritarian states that ruled by force and fiat over involuntary and unwilling subjects.

Although the right to choose one's loyalty could be regulated, it could not be denied. Individual liberty and the security of the community as a whole could both be served—must both be served—by republican citizenship. Americans acknowledged the right of the state to dictate the timing of election, to establish the rules governing its exercise, and to determine its consequences. But the individual alone would be responsible for making the choice between subjectship and citizenship.

101. *Ibid.*, 248.
102. *Ibid.*, 249–250.

It was not yet clear how far this right of election could be extended. The notion that allegiance in an established political community could only be broken by default or by mutual consent still characterized most discussions of the relationship between a person who had explicitly or implicitly made his choice and the community that accepted him as a member. Some Americans pursued the logic of volitional allegiance to its limits, arguing that the right to join a community logically implied the right to leave it as well. Others hesitated, contending that in the absence of default both parties—the citizen and the community—must consent to expatriation. Although they acknowledged that allegiance began with an act of individual volition, they doubted that the right to terminate this obligation could safely be entrusted to an autonomous individual. The balance between the volitional and the contractual aspects of citizenship thus remained open to question even after the immediate effects of the Revolution on the status of its participants had been determined.

Even more perplexing was the question whether the Revolution had created one community of allegiance or many. The issue remained at the periphery of the problems of loyalty that Americans dealt with directly in these years; the particular questions discussed here—the validity of treason prosecutions and of wartime confiscations, and the postwar rights of British subjects in the new states—rarely required a close examination of the possible distinctions between a general American citizenship and a membership in a particular state. It was enough to decide that one was a subject or a citizen; to consider whether the latter meant membership in a state or in a nation of states seemed unnecessary.

The question would become a critical one in the years after the Revolution. It would appear in many different contexts and in many different guises: in the development of policies concerning naturalization and expatriation, in debates over the jurisdiction of courts and the status of inhabitants of the American territories, in conflicts between nationalists and advocates of states' rights, and ultimately in the soul-searing crisis of slavery.

By the beginning of the nineteenth century, then, Americans had only begun to discover the complexity of the question "Who are 'the People'?" They were committed to certain principles about the acquisition of citizenship, but they had yet to develop fully the meaning of that status.

PART IV

Principles, Politics, and Prejudice

CHAPTER 8

American Naturalization after Independence: Qualifications for Citizenship

The dissolution of the imperial bonds in 1776 gave the authority to admit members to the community to the individual state governments. Americans charged that the long list of grievances committed by George III amounted to a withdrawal of his protection over them, and they declared themselves absolved of their former allegiance as British subjects. In the king's place there now stood thirteen independent states, each claiming the fidelity of the inhabitants remaining within its bounds. The new states not only sought the loyalty of their present inhabitants and former fellow subjects; they also extended a broad welcome to the foreign-born.

The states developed the notion of volitional allegiance when assigning citizen or alien status to persons who had once shared British subjectship. It seemed unnecessary to inquire deeply into the individual qualifications of such persons or to provide elaborate procedures to guarantee their fitness for membership. The mere choice of the Revolutionary cause proved the former subject's qualification for republican citizenship. His willingness to risk life, fortune, and sacred honor in the struggle with Great Britain attested to his sincerity in embracing republican ideals; his familiarity with the forms of free government—no matter how degenerated in the mother country—presumably prepared him for full membership in polities that were widely thought to have essentially distilled, purified, and extended traditional British forms and principles.

The case of the foreign-born immigrant was not so easily decided. Americans continued to assume that the natural bounty of the New World would attract alien settlers; indeed, the promise of personal liberty and individual dignity under free and enlightened republican governments could only increase the flow of immigration from a Europe still sunk in vice, luxury, and oppression. But were these strangers, unaccustomed to responsible self-government, ready for membership in the new states? Could it be said of them, too, that a mere election of citizenship was proof of their capacity for republican life?

Explicitly or implicitly—by constitutional provision, legislative enactment, or mere exercise of power—the new republican governments assumed sovereign control over the naturalization of newcomers and established procedures for admitting aliens to citizenship. Pennsylvania, Vermont, North Carolina, and New York set the requirements and procedures in their first constitutions. Pennsylvania allowed every foreign settler "of good character" who took "an oath or affirmation of allegiance" to the state to acquire "land or other real estate." After one-year's residence he was to be deemed a "free denizen," entitled to "all the rights of a natural born subject of this state, except that he shall not be capable of being elected a representative until after two years residence."[1]

Drafters of Vermont's constitution copied Pennsylvania's clause.[2] North Carolina granted property rights to "every Foreigner" who settled in the state as soon as he swore allegiance, and after one-year's residence he was to be "deemed a free citizen."[3] New Yorkers lodged the power to naturalize in their legislature, providing only that the representatives at least require the candidate to settle in the state and "to abjure and renounce all allegiance and subjection to all and every foreign king, prince, potentate and state, in all matters ecclesiastical as well as civil."[4]

1. Pennsylvania constitution (Sept. 28, 1776), sec. 42, Thorpe, ed. and comp., *Constitutions, Charters, and Laws*, V, 3091.
2. Vermont constitution (July 8, 1776), Art. XLIII, *ibid.*, VI, 3748.
3. North Carolina constitution (Dec. 18, 1776), Art. XL, *N.C. Col. Recs.*, X, 1012.
4. New York constitution (Apr. 20, 1777), Art. XLII, Thorpe, ed. and comp., *Constitutions, Charters, and Laws*, V, 2637–2638.

Maryland, Virginia, South Carolina, and Georgia all established naturalization procedures by legislative enactment. Maryland's act of July 1779 required a declaration of "belief in the christian religion" and an oath of allegiance to be taken and subscribed before the governor and council, the General Court, or any general or county court, whereupon the foreigner would be reputed a "natural born subject of this state." A further residence of seven years was required before the person so naturalized could become eligible for any state office or for Congress.[5]

Virginia passed an act in 1779 declaring all white persons born within the territory and all who had resided there for the two years preceding citizens of the state. Subsequent immigrants would gain this status by proving their intent to reside in the state (by public oath or affirmation) and by giving "assurances of fidelity."[6] This act was modified in part by another in October 1783 that somewhat narrowed the rights granted. Naturalization was still accomplished by the procedure outlined in 1779, but the new citizen was not to be qualified for office until after he had resided in the state for two years and had "evinced a permanent attachment to the state, by having intermarried with a citizen of the commonwealth, or a citizen of any other of the United States, or purchased lands to the value of one hundred pounds therein."[7]

The citizenship laws of South Carolina and Georgia followed Virginia's pattern of progressive admission to rights, though both states included some idiosyncratic statutory provisions. South Carolina regarded as citizens all "free white persons" who resided in the state one year and swore allegiance. After two years such a "citizen" could gain the vote for the legislature or the city corporation of Charleston, but he would not be eligible for high office until admitted to that privilege by a special act of "naturalization."[8] Thus South Carolina preserved the idea—common in English law—that

---

5. Maxcy, ed., *Laws of Md.*, I, 362–364, amended and supplemented by an act of Nov. 1789, *ibid.*, II, 93–95.

6. Hening, ed., *Statutes of Va.*, X, 129–130.

7. *Ibid.*, XI, 322–324. An amending statute of 1786 extended the residence requirement to five years. *Ibid.*, XII, 261–265. Note that the word "white" in the 1779 act was changed to "free" in the acts of 1783 and 1786. The Virginia constitution as finally approved contained nothing about naturalization, though drafts written by Jefferson included an admission procedure. See Boyd *et al.*, eds., *Jefferson Papers*, I, 344, 353, 363.

8. Act of Mar. 26, 1784, *S.C. Statutes*, IV, 600–601. The term "naturalization" was applied to this special act by the statute of Mar. 26, 1786. *Ibid.*, 746–747.

"citizenship" could comprehend separate legal categories of membership. The "second-class citizen" could acquire full rights—or at least become legally eligible for those rights—only by obtaining a special act of the legislature and not merely by meeting a set of general, impersonal qualifications.

Georgia's citizenship laws reflected a cautious and suspicious attitude toward the political and personal character of foreigners in general and of Scotsmen in particular. One wartime measure required emigrants from other states to produce a certificate from a circuit or county court judge where they last resided verifying "his, or their Attachment to the liberties or Independence of the United States of America, And also of his or their honesty, Probity and Industry." If this certificate received the approval of the governor and council, the immigrants were thereupon "declared free Citizens of this State." The act further established that "WHEREAS the People of Scotland have in General Manifested a decided inimicallity to the Civil Liberties of America," they would not be allowed to benefit from the act. Scotsmen who arrived in the state were to be deported, except those "who have exerted themselves in behalf of the freedom and Independence of the United States."[9]

After the war Georgia reorganized its naturalization procedures. All "free white persons" seeking citizenship were to enroll their names in the superior court records of the county where they proposed to reside, thereby gaining the right of "acquiring possessing or holding and Selling devising or otherwise disposing of Personal property and renting houses or lands from Year to Year" and "the right of suing for all such debts, demands or damages other than for real estate." After a twelve-month residence an alien could gain the rights of a "free Citizen" by exhibiting a certificate from the county grand jury "purporting that he hath demeaned himself as an honest man and friend to the Government of the State" and by taking and subscribing an oath of allegiance. The new citizen could not vote for the legislature or hold any office of trust or profit until completing a seven-year residence and obtaining a special act of the legislature in his behalf. He was also to remain subject to aliens' duties for a period not specified by the general statute.[10]

The remaining states naturalized foreigners without explicitly

9. Act of Aug. 5, 1782, *Col. Recs. Ga.*, XIX, pt. ii, 162–166.
10. Act of Feb. 7, 1785, *ibid.*, 375–378.

claiming this right in their constitutions or without passing new enabling acts establishing requirements and procedures. Massachusetts—which had admitted few aliens before the Revolution—adopted a number of persons by special legislative acts after 1778. The only general regulation governing the passage of such acts was embodied in a resolve of October 19, 1787, that declared that every petition for admission received in the future needed to be "accompanied by sufficient Recommendations and a certifycate seting forth the length of time which such petitioner or petitioners, May have resided within this Commonwealth."[11] New Hampshire passed similar special acts of naturalization in 1785 and 1788, and Connecticut apparently followed the same procedure.[12] Rhode Island admitted two men in 1789, both Englishmen. Although the state still retained its colonial charter and never formally repealed the clauses that implied that all British subjects were subjects within Rhode Island, the state obviously assumed that the Revolution had made Englishmen aliens.[13]

Delaware—and, perhaps, New Jersey—followed Rhode Island's lead in simply continuing colonial practices. In 1788 Delaware passed an act supplementing the general naturalization act that had been in force in the colony since 1700. The revised law now required an oath or affirmation before the president of the state or the superior court of any county, whereupon the alien was to be "deemed, adjudged and taken to be a natural-born subject of the state." The new citizen was not eligible for civil or high political office until he had resided in the state five years and met the other qualifications of age and property established by law.[14]

11. *Acts and Laws of the Commonwealth of Massachusetts* (Boston, 1890–1898 [orig. publ. Boston, 1781–1805]), *1786–1787*, 744. The first act I have found is that for Peter Landais, Oct. 15, 1778, *Acts and Resolves, Mass. Bay*, VI, 225.

12. Batchellor, comp., *Laws of N.H.*, V, 44, 307. For Connecticut, see the comments of Representative Benjamin Huntington during debates on the first federal naturalization law, Feb. 14, 1790, [*Annals of the Congress of the United States.*] *The Debates and Proceedings in the Congress of the United States, 1789–1824* . . . (Washington, D.C., 1834–1856), 1st Cong., 2d sess., 1120, hereafter cited as *Annals of Congress*. A Connecticut act of May 1784 established special modes of naturalization for foreigners settling in the free ports of New London and New Haven. Charles J. Hoadly *et al.*, eds., *The Public Records of the State of Connecticut* . . . (Hartford, Conn., 1894–), V, 325–326.

13. Rider, *Denization and Naturalization in R.I.*, 12, 13; *R.I. Col. Recs.*, X, 317–318. The assembly also passèd special acts readmitting persons suspected of disloyalty to the privileges of citizenship. See, e.g., the petition and readmission of Stephen Deblois, *ibid.*, IX, 728–729, X, 46.

14. Supplementary act of June 11, 1788, *Laws of Del.*, II, 921–923.

218 Principles, Politics, and Prejudice

The procedures followed in New Jersey are obscure, and possibly the state felt no need to develop a specific naturalization policy. Certainly it liberally granted political rights to new settlers. The suffrage law passed on July 2, 1776, provided that "all Inhabitants of this Colony of full age who are worth fifty pounds, Proclamation money, clear Estate in the same, and have resided within the county in which they claim a vote for 12 months immediately preceding the election, shall be entitled to vote for representatives in council and assembly, and also for all other public officers that shall be elected by the people of the county at large."[15] Naturalization may still have been required for securing land titles—at least until the act of 1794 authorizing aliens to purchase and hold real estate on the same terms as natural-born citizens—but the published state records do not contain an established procedure for admitting aliens to citizenship.[16]

Although the naturalization policies of the individual states varied in detail, they reflected certain shared assumptions. Applicants for citizenship were expected to swear or affirm publicly their allegiance to the new states. Occasionally they were required to disavow explicitly all foreign attachments.[17] States passing general enabling laws sometimes required certificates, references, or other proof of good character, while most at least stated it as a general qualification. Where legislatures admitted aliens by special act, the character of an individual applicant was a customary subject of inquiry.[18] Virtually all the states required a specific period of residence either for the initial admission or for the full enjoyment of political rights.

The assumption underlying residence requirements was that the exercise of political rights required a clear and conscious attachment to and familiarity with republican principles. This idea was perhaps most clearly apparent in a provision of the Georgia act of February 7, 1785:

If any Person or persons under the age of sixteen Years shall after the passing of this Act be sent abroad without the limits of the United States and reside there three Years for the purpose of receiving an education

15. Act of July 2, 1776, quoted in N.J. Hist. Records Survey Program, *Guide to Naturalization Records*, 3.
16. Act of Feb. 1794, quoted *ibid.*, 39.
17. See, e.g., the naturalization of Anthony Smith *et al.*, Mar. 20, 1783, *Laws of the State of New York passed at the Sessions of the Legislature* (Albany, N.Y., 1886–1887), I, 557.
18. See, e.g., preamble to act naturalizing Michael Cunningham and John Prescott, June 27, 1782, *Mass. Acts and Laws, 1782–1783*, 9.

under a foreign power, such person or persons after their return to this State shall for three Years be considered and treated as Aliens in so far as not to be eligible to a Seat in the Legislature or Executive authority or to hold any office civil or Military in the State for that term and so in proportion for any greater number of Years as he or they shall be absent as aforesaid, but shall not be injured or disqualified in any other respect.[19]

Although the specific details of this provision were unique, it reflected a common assumption in states' naturalization policies: time alone could insure that those imbued with "foreign principles" had the opportunity to assimilate the habits, values, and modes of thought necessary for responsible participation in a virtuous, self-governing republican community.

The states' preoccupation with the qualifications for citizenship obscured the ill-defined nature of the status itself. Individual states naturalized foreigners—they would continue to do so into the 1790s—but naturalized citizens seemed to become members of a community that transcended state boundaries. There was no return to the chaotic and disorganized system that prevailed before 1740 in which persons adopted by one colony remained aliens in the others. The state governments were engaged in war against a common foe; they joined in a confederation that in practice, if not in theory, attenuated the sense of their individual sovereignty; and they clearly perceived a community of interests and ideals binding them together while separating them from truly "foreign" nations.

During the war various actions of Congress revealed the assumption that "national" goals and purposes ought to influence citizenship policies of the individual states. Congressional resolutions of June 24, 1776, defined treason and citizenship, providing authority for subsequent state legislation.[20] And although Congress itself did not naturalize foreigners, it adopted resolutions obliging the states to do so. For example, a committee was appointed August 9, 1776, "to devise a plan for encouraging the Hessians, and other foreigners, employed by the King of Great Britain, and sent to America for the purpose of subjugating these states, to quit that iniquitous service." On August 14 Congress approved the committee's report. Assuming "that such foreigners, if apprised of the practice of these states, would chuse to accept of lands, liberty, safety and a com-

19. Act of Feb. 7, 1785, *Col. Recs. Ga.*, XIX, pt. ii, 378.
20. See above, chap. 7, at n. 13.

munion of good laws, and mild government, in a country where many of their friends and relations are already happily settled," the body resolved

that these states will receive all such foreigners who shall leave the armies of his Britannic majesty in America, and shall chuse to become members of any of these states; that they shall be protected in the exercise of their respective religions, and be invested with the rights, privileges and immunities of natives, as established by the laws of these states; and, moreover, that this Congress will provide, for every such person, 50 Acres of unappropriated lands in some of these states, to be held by him and his heirs in absolute property.[21]

It was left to the individual states to carry out Congress's promises, and some evidently did so.[22]

The effects of such congressional directives depended on the voluntary compliance of the state governments. Not until March 1, 1781, were the Articles of Confederation ratified, and even then the central government was given no explicit power over citizenship. A new and portentous element of confusion, however, was introduced by the document's "comity clause." As finally ratified, Article IV read:

The better to secure and perpetuate mutual friendship and intercourse among the people of the different states in this union, the free inhabitants of each of these states (paupers, vagabonds, and fugitives from justice excepted) shall be entitled to all privileges and immunities of free citizens in the several states; and the people of each state shall have free ingress and regress to and from any other state, and shall enjoy therein all the privileges of trade and commerce, subject to the same duties, impositions, and restrictions, as the inhabitants thereof respectively; provided, that such restrictions shall not extend so far as to prevent the removal of property imported into any state, to any other state of which the owner is an inhabitant; provided also, that no imposition, duties, or restrictions, shall be laid by any state on the property of the United States, or either of them.[23]

21. *Jours. Cont. Cong.*, V, 640, 653–655. See also the resolutions of Aug. 27, 1776, and Apr. 29, 1778, increasing the inducements to such prospective citizens: respectively, *ibid.*, 707–708; *Secret Journals of the Acts and Proceedings of Congress . . .* , I (Boston, 1820), 67–72.
22. See the proclamation by Gov. Jefferson, Feb. 2, 1781, Palmer *et al.*, eds., *Cal. of Va. State Papers*, I, 482–483. On the other hand, North Carolina refused to admit four prisoners of war. See House Journal entry, Oct. 22, 1779, Walter Clark, ed., *The State Records of North Carolina, 1777–1790*, XIII (Winston and Goldsboro, N.C., 1896), 935.
23. *Secret Jours. Cong.*, I, 334–335. For a discussion of the drafting of this clause and an expansive reading of its import, see Chester James Antieau, "Paul's Perverted Privileges or the True Meaning of the Privileges and Immunities Clause of Article Four," *William and Mary Law Review*, IX (1967–1968), 2–5.

James Madison found this clause so vague and imprecise that it approached incoherence. The "confusion of language" he thought "remarkable," for it made it possible to argue that

those who come under the denomination of *free inhabitants* of a State, although not citizens of such State, are entitled, in every other State, to all the privileges of *free citizens* of the latter; that is, to greater privileges than they may be entitled to in their own State: so that it may be in the power of a particular State, or rather every State is laid under a necessity, not only to confer the rights of citizenship in other States upon any whom it may admit to such rights within itself, but upon any whom it may allow to become inhabitants within its jurisdiction.

The clause gave a "very improper power" to each state in effect to naturalize aliens in every other state.[24] An alien who was naturalized in Pennsylvania might remove to South Carolina, for example, and thereby evade the stiffer requirements established by the latter state. By virtue of the Articles of Confederation, citizenship conferred by a single state seemed to acquire a necessary national dimension.

The comity clause undercut state sovereignty by assuming that authorities outside the state could at least in part determine who could claim the rights of citizenship within it. The language of the provision was mandatory, not permissive: individual states were obliged to confer the privileges and immunities of free citizens on the free inhabitants of the other states of the Confederation. Comity implied one community in the United States, not many. Moreover, the concept of a "United States citizenship" implicit in the assumption of a national community seemed in certain contexts definable without reference to state membership. In 1783 commissioners appointed by Congress to meet with Indian leaders in the northwest territories were instructed to discover information regarding the French inhabitants of Illinois, Detroit, "and other villages within the territories of the United States." They were to "give assurances in the name of the United States to those inhabitants who shall profess their allegiance to the United States, that they shall be

24. [Alexander Hamilton, John Jay, and James Madison], *The Federalist; A Commentary on the Constitution of the United States . . .* , with an introduction by Edward Meade Earle (New York, 1937), No. 42, 276–277, hereafter cited as *The Federalist*. In 1823 the Kentucky Court of Appeals took "free inhabitants" here to mean "free citizens." "And however absurd it may appear that any state could naturalize and admit by law, and that law be so operative as to confer rights *extra territorium*, yet this phenomenon was presented under the articles of confederation." Elmondorff v. Carmichael, 14 Am. Dec. 86, 90 (Ky., 1823).

protected in the full enjoyment of their liberty and their just and lawful property."[25] Such persons would thus owe allegiance to and receive protection from the United States, not an individual state. Certainly this procedure closely resembled an admission into a national citizenship.

Occasionally state court judges implied that the concept of citizenship had a national dimension influencing decisions within the framework of local law. Judge Samuel Ashe of North Carolina argued in *Bayard* v. *Singleton* that the plaintiffs, "being citizens of one of the United States," were "citizens of this State, by the confederation of all the States; which is to be taken as part of the law of the land, unrepealable by any act of the General Assembly."[26] Citizens of other states who found themselves in North Carolina could not be denied the rights of citizens—as defined by North Carolina—or the equal application of its laws, for the comity clause of the Articles barred such discrimination.

The sense of a common citizenship and the implication of a national political community inevitably conflicted with the idea of full sovereignty of the individual states. Yet state courts were willing to affirm—as a matter of obligation and not of courtesy—that rights and duties, rewards and punishments, stemming from membership in a single state were to be enforced throughout the Confederation. The conflict was clearly illustrated in the case of *Camp* v. *Lockwood*, in which the Philadelphia County Court of Common Pleas considered the question whether Pennsylvania was obliged to recognize a confiscation meted out by Connecticut as punishment for the disloyalty of one of its own citizens.

The facts of the case were not contested. James Lockwood had become indebted to Abiathar Camp before the Revolution when both were residents of Connecticut. Camp joined the British during the war, and as a consequence, Connecticut instituted proceedings against him for disloyalty under its general confiscation act of May 1778. In September 1779 the state declared Camp's estate (including debts owed him) forfeited and actually seized part, though without acting specifically on the debt in question. After the war Camp fled to Halifax and Lockwood removed to Pennsylvania. In 1788 Camp brought suit in the Pennsylvania court for the recovery

25. Entry of Oct. 15, 1783, *Secret Jours. Cong.*, I, 244.
26. Judge Ashe, on motion to dismiss, in Bayard v. Singleton, 1 N.C. 5, 6 (N.C., 1787).

of the old debt. Lockwood contested the action, denying Camp's claim on the grounds that the debt had vested in the state of Connecticut as a result of the confiscation.[27]

Camp's counsel insisted that Pennsylvania and Connecticut were independent, sovereign states, whose relations were analogous to those between individuals in a state of nature. Camp's "offences as a Subject, though committed against a nation, confederated and allied with ours, do not allow us to join in the infliction of punishment." To accept the act of confiscation as in any way relevant to Camp's legal rights in Pennsylvania would contradict the fundamental axiom that one government could not intermeddle with the government of another state. Connecticut's act to void the debt thus barred recovery in the jurisdiction of that state alone; it did not affect Camp's rights in Pennsylvania courts.[28]

Responding to this argument, Lockwood's counsel cautioned that although it was "true, that these States are said to be sovereign and independent; . . . they are evidently bound by a link which must be taken into view, or we shall argue wrong in the abstract." The Articles declared that the citizen of one state was the citizen of all, thus "the United States, though individually sovereign and independent, must admit . . . a peculiar law resulting from their relative situation." Authorized public officials had proceeded against Camp for dereliction of his duties as a citizen. Since Pennsylvania recognized the general nature of that citizenship, it should similarly respect the rights and enforce the duties it entailed.[29]

President Edward Shippen, delivering the court's opinion, upheld the binding force of the Connecticut confiscation. The War of Independence began in common resistance to common grievances and was carried on as a common cause under the direction of the central Congress. Camp's status as a citizen of Connecticut entitled him to rights and privileges of citizenship in the other states; therefore his disloyalty was as extensive as his obligations and rights:

The offence, which incurred the forfeiture, was not an offence against the State of Connecticut alone, but against all the States in the Union: And the act, which directed the forfeiture, was made in consequence of the recommendations of Congress, composed of the Representatives of all the States, and was a case within the general powers vested in them as

27. Camp v. Lockwood, 1 Dall. 393 (Pa., 1788).
28. William Rawle (for Camp), *ibid.*, 395, 397.
29. Jared Ingersoll (for Lockwood), *ibid.*, 398, 399.

conductors of a war, in which all were equally principals. Our Courts, therefore, necessarily take notice of the confiscations made in a sister State on these grounds.[30]

Connecticut's law, authorized by Congress, punished persons for offenses against the United States, and the punishment meted out under the law was to be enforced throughout the nation. Shippen, like Ashe of North Carolina, thus insisted that in matters relating to citizenship, state courts should give legal reality to the idea of a national citizenship.

Although the primary locus of allegiance throughout the Confederation period was still in the individual sovereign state, the idea that citizens belonged to a larger national community surfaced frequently, never fully articulated or theoretically explored, but persuasive—almost instinctive—in certain contexts. The sense that citizenship was, at least in some respects, national eroded belief in full sovereignty of the individual states and played into a growing conviction that the Confederation was an inadequate expression of the community of interests and ideals existing among the states. The Confederation's ineffectiveness, amounting in some cases to virtual impotence, in implementing common goals moved many to search for new forms of political organization more consonant with the idea of a national community. In 1787 dissatisfaction with the Articles culminated in the Philadelphia Convention and the creation of a new federal constitutional order.

The framers of the Constitution failed to grapple with the relationship of state and national citizenship, but they did concern themselves with problems involving citizen status that had become apparent since independence. For example, the delegates generally acknowledged the desirability of ending the confusion inherent in a multiplicity of naturalization laws and procedures. Among the defects of the Articles of Confederation, according to James Madison, was the lack of "a uniformity" among the states "in cases requiring it, as laws of naturalization, bankruptcy, a Coercive authority operating on individuals, and a guaranty of the internal tranquility of the States."[31] The sixth resolution of Edmund Ran-

30. Shippen (for the Court), *ibid.*, 403.
31. James Madison, *Notes of Debates in the Federal Convention of 1787* (Athens, Ohio, 1966), preface, 15. Madison wrote the preface between 1830 and 1836, but he had discussed

dolph's "Virginia Plan," introduced May 29, would have given the national legislature the power to legislate "in all cases to which the separate States are incompetent, or in which the harmony of the United States may be interrupted by the exercise of individual Legislation." Randolph's intention to include naturalization in this grant of powers is indicated by his argument on June 16 that a "provision for harmony among the States, as in trade, naturalization, etc. . . . must be made."[32] William Paterson's "New Jersey Plan" also included the resolution that "the rule for naturalization ought to be the same in every State."[33]

The proposals of Randolph and Paterson differed subtly on whether the states were "incompetent" to naturalize or whether the role of the central government was merely to guarantee some uniformity among state practices. Indeed, the general attitude of the delegates on this question remained ambiguous. The Committee of Detail report of August 6 empowered the national legislature "to establish an uniform rule of naturalization throughout the United States," and the provision remained virtually unchanged in the final document.[34] The Convention did not explore the implications of the clause, nor did the delegates indicate whether the actual power to naturalize was to be exclusive or concurrent. These questions would remain open to debate into the nineteenth century.[35]

Although the delegates concurred on the desirability of uniform naturalization rules, they disagreed concerning the privileges that admission to citizenship ought to confer. In particular, the question whether naturalized citizens should acquire political rights equal to those of the native-born occasioned some debate. The issue emerged during the Convention in the attempt to define the qualifications for high political office.

The report of the Committee of Detail proposed that no person be qualified for election as a representative until he had been a citizen three years. A stipulation of four years of citizenship was

the problem in virtually the same terms in an exchange of letters with Edmund Randolph in Aug. 1782. *Ibid.*, 2n; Burnett, *Letters of Members of the Cont. Cong.*, VI, 455.

32. Madison, *Debates*, 31, 128.

33. Eighth resolution, introduced June 15, 1787, *ibid.*, 121.

34. Art. VII, sec. 1, in the committee report. *Ibid.*, 389. Art. I, sec. 8, now reads: "The Congress shall have the power . . . to establish a uniform rule of naturalization, and uniform laws on the subject of bankruptcies throughout the United States."

35. See below, chap. 9.

suggested for eligibility to the Senate.[36] On August 8 George Mason moved that the requirement for members of the House be increased to seven years. He "was for opening a wide door for emigrants; but did not chuse to let foreigners and adventurers make laws for and govern us. Citizenship for three years was not enough for ensuring that local knowledge which ought to be possessed by the Representative." Mason feared that "a rich foreign Nation, for example Great Britain, might send over her tools who might bribe their way into the Legislature for insidious purposes." Gouverneur Morris seconded the motion, and the amendment was passed with Connecticut alone opposing.[37]

The qualifications for senatorship were debated at length the next day. Gouverneur Morris opened discussion with the proposal to increase the four years recommended by the Committee of Detail to fourteen. Charles Pinckney seconded the motion, for because the Senate was to be given extensive powers over treaties and foreign affairs, there was "a peculiar danger and impropriety in opening its doors" to those who had "foreign attachments." George Mason thought the argument a valid one, asserting that "were it not that many not natives of this Country had acquired great merit during the revolution, he should be for restraining the eligibility into the Senate, to natives." Morris rose again to conclude the defense of his motion:

What is the language of Reason on this subject? That we should not be polite at the expence of prudence. . . . It is said that some tribes of Indians, carried their hospitality so far as to offer to strangers their wives and daughters. Was this a proper model for us? He would admit them to his house, he would invite them to his table, would provide for them comfortable lodgings; but would not carry that complaisance so far as, to bed them with his wife. He would let them worship at the same altar, but did not choose to make priests of them. . . . Admit a Frenchman into your Senate, and he will study to increase the commerce of France: an Englishman, he will feel an equal biass in favor of that of England.[38]

Other delegates objected to the proposed amendment. Oliver Ellsworth thought it would discourage "meritorious aliens from emigrating to this Country." Scottish-born James Wilson knew

---

36. Art. IV, sec. 2, and Art. V, sec. 3, of the committee's report, respectively. Madison, *Debates*, 386, 387.
37. *Ibid.*, 406.
38. *Ibid.*, 418–422.

from experience "the discouragement and mortification they [the foreign-born] must feel from the degrading discrimination, now proposed." Franklin opposed illiberality and argued that when foreigners searching for a "country in which they can obtain more happiness, give a preference to ours it is a proof of attachment which ought to excite our confidence and affection."[39] Madison strongly opposed extending the residence requirement because such a change would be both unnecessary and improper:

Unnecessary; because the National Legislature is to have the right of regulating naturalization, and can by virtue thereof fix different periods of residence as conditions of enjoying different privileges of Citizenship: Improper; because it will give a tincture of illiberality to the Constitution: because it will put out of the power of the National Legislature even by special acts of naturalization to confer the full rank of Citizen on meritorious strangers and because it will discourage the most desirable class of people from emigrating to the U.S. Should the proposed Constitution have the intended effect of giving stability and reputation to our Governments great numbers of respectable Europeans: men who love liberty and wish to partake its blessings, will be ready to transfer their fortunes hither. All such would feel the mortification of being marked with suspicious incapacitations though they should not covet the public honors.[40]

Edmund Randolph thought some temporary incapacitation appropriate—seven years was the maximum he would tolerate—but he would never agree to a fourteen-year bar on eligibility to the Senate. His position was grounded in both his sense of national honor and his awareness of contemporary political currents: "He reminded the Convention of the language held by our patriots during the Revolution, and the principles laid down in all our American Constitutions. Many foreigners have fixed their fortunes among us under the faith of these invitations. All persons under this description, with all others who would be affected by such a regulation, would enlist themselves under the banners of hostility to the proposed System."[41]

At the close of the long debate, Morris's motion for a fourteen-year citizenship requirement was defeated. So were subsequent motions for thirteen- and ten-year terms proposed by Morris and Pinckney. John Rutledge insisted that the Convention require a

39. *Ibid.*
40. *Ibid.*, 419.
41. *Ibid.*, 420.

longer term for the Senate than for the House, since the former had more power; as Hugh Williamson noted, "Bribery and cabal" could be more easily practiced in that body, for it was elected by fewer people. Randolph finally agreed to a proposed requirement of nine years with a guarantee of its reduction to seven if the citizenship requirement for the House were subsequently lowered. On that basis the Convention set the qualification for senatorship at nine years.[42]

The matter of the seven-year requirement for eligibility to the House came up for reconsideration on August 13. James Wilson proposed that the original term of four years be restored, Hugh Williamson favored the substitution of nine years, and Alexander Hamilton suggested that "citizenship and inhabitancy" alone be required, repeating Madison's earlier argument that Congress would have discretionary power over the political rights and capacities of immigrants under the naturalization power.[43]

The debate showed a continued division of opinion on the propriety of granting political rights to the foreign-born. Elbridge Gerry, fearful of persons "having foreign attachments" and conscious of the "vast sums laid out in Europe for secret services," voiced his hope "that in future the eligibility might be confined to Natives." Pierce Butler, too, was "strenuous against admitting foreigners into our public Councils." On the other hand, Hamilton advocated attracting Europeans "of moderate fortunes" who would "be on a level with the first Citizens." Madison wanted to maintain the "character of liberality" of the American governments and "to invite foreigners of merit and republican principles among us." He recognized the possible danger of men with "foreign predilections" gaining appointments, but trusted that the good judgment of the general electorate would prevent real abuses. James Wilson agreed, pointing to the experience of Pennsylvania—most of whose line officers during the late war had been foreigners—and noting his own and other delegates' foreign birth in order to deprecate the fear of subversion from within.[44]

The sense of the Convention was that a seven-year citizenship

---

42. *Ibid.*, 422. Art I, sec. 3, now reads: "No person shall be a senator who shall not have attained to the age of thirty years, and been nine years a citizen of the United States, and who shall not, when elected, be an inhabitant of that State for which he shall be chosen."
43. Madison, *Debates*, 437–439.
44. *Ibid.*

requirement struck the best balance between the desire to attract foreign settlers of merit and the dread of exposing the nation to foreign-spawned conspiracies. All three proposed amendments were defeated, and the citizenship requirement for the House of Representatives remained at seven years.[45]

Having done his best to dramatize the potential danger in liberally granting political rights to future immigrants, Gouverneur Morris now confidently proposed that the seven-year limitation "should not affect the rights of any person now a citizen." John Mercer seconded the proposal, which was necessary "to prevent the disfranchisement of persons who had become Citizens under and on the faith and according to the laws and Constitutions from being on a level in all respects with natives." But Roger Sherman impatiently rejected the claim that the Convention was obligated to meet the expectations of foreigners already admitted by the states: "The U. States have not invited foreigners nor pledged their faith that they should enjoy equal privileges with native Citizens. The Individual States alone have done this. The former therefore are at liberty to make any discriminations they may judge requisite." Noting that the Convention was engaged in "a sort of recurrence to first principles," Charles Pinckney agreed with Sherman: the new government should not be bound by troublesome obligations assumed by its predecessors.[46]

Such arguments disturbed other delegates. Nathaniel Gorman thought that when "foreigners are naturalized it would seem as if they stand on an equal footing with natives. He doubted the propriety of giving a retrospective force to the restriction." Madison, too, "animadverted on the peculiarity of the doctrine" advanced by Sherman and Pinckney: "It was a subtilty by which every national engagement might be evaded." Not only was it dishonorable to slough off obligations assumed under the Articles but the political ramifications could easily be disastrous: "It would expose us to the reproaches of all those who should be affected by it, reproaches which would soon be echoed from the other side of the Atlantic; and would necessarily enlist among the Adversaries of the reform a

45. *Ibid.* Art. I, sec. 2, now reads: "No person shall be a representative who shall not have attained to the age of twenty-five years, and been seven years a citizen of the United States, and who shall not, when elected, be an inhabitant of the State in which he shall be chosen."

46. Madison, *Debates*, 439, 440, 441.

very considerable body of Citizens: We should moreover reduce every State to the dilemma of rejecting it or of violating the faith pledged to a part of its Citizens." Wilson and Mercer agreed that the federal government should not begin its existence with a breach of faith.[47] Despite such arguments, the proposed amendment failed.[48]

Although the defeat of the Morris proposal meant that aliens already naturalized by the states might be temporarily barred from election to the House or Senate, the Convention did confirm their potential ability to qualify for the nation's highest offices, including the presidency. The initial Committee of Detail report had not established any personal qualifications for the chief executive. A report of August 22, however, proposed that "he shall be of the age of thirty five years, and a citizen of the United States, and shall have been an inhabitant thereof for twenty one years." This in turn was amended by the Committee of Eleven on September 4 to require that the president be a "natural born citizen or a Citizen of the U.S. at the time of the adoption of the Constitution." Persons naturalized before ratification, then, were eligible for the office on basically the same terms as native Americans; persons adopted thereafter were permanently barred from the presidency—the only explicit constitutional limitation on their potential rights.[49]

The debates over the citizenship qualifications for office reflected a clear concern about the "incidents" of the status—that is, the rights it conveyed—but they reveal a surprising insensitivity to the ramifications of its federal character. The delegates assumed that citizenship was a prerequisite for high political office and closely contested the length of time that one had to be a citizen in order to become eligible for a position in the government, but at no time did they discuss the relationship between state and national citizenship. The Constitution's comity clause—"The Citizens of each State shall be entitled to all Privileges and Immunities of Citizens in the several States"—occasioned little debate. The same is true of the

---

47. *Ibid.*, 440, 441.
48. *Ibid.*, 442.
49. Art. X of the Committee of Detail report referred to the powers but not the qualifications of the president, *ibid.*, 392–393. For the subsequent amendments—none of which occasioned any debate—see *ibid.*, 509, 575. Art. II, sec. 1, cl. 4, now reads: "No person except a natural born citizen, or a citizen of the United States, at the time of the adoption of this Constitution, shall be eligible to the office of President; neither shall any person be eligible to that office who shall not have attained to the age of thirty-five years, and been fourteen years a resident within the United States."

provisions giving the federal judiciary jurisdiction in disputes "between a State and Citizens of another State;—between Citizens of different States;—between Citizens of the same State claiming Lands under Grants of different States, and between a State, or the Citizens thereof, and foreign States, Citizens, or Subjects."[50]

The Constitution in its final form left critical questions relating to citizenship unanswered. Congress was empowered to establish a "uniform rule of naturalization"—but was this merely an administrative reform designed to standardize admission into state membership, or did it imply a recognition that citizenship fundamentally and primarily meant membership in a national community? There was an implicit assumption that birth within the United States conferred citizenship—the president was to be a "natural born citizen" resident in the United States—but did this encompass all persons born within the states and territories of the new nation, or could the states or federal government distinguish among natives, accepting some as birthright citizens while rejecting others? The comity clause placed a constitutional obligation on the states to confer "all privileges and immunities of citizens" upon the "citizens of each State"—but who was to determine what those privileges and immunities were? Citizens "of the United States" were eligible for federal offices by virtue of the Constitution, but their right to vote depended upon state laws. Many of their rights were protected against federal power; some were protected against the states; but in most cases state bills of rights were relied upon to guard against local encroachments on the "rights of citizens."[51]

The delegates at Philadelphia had tried to confront problems stemming from the diversity of naturalization policies under the Articles of Confederation, and in debating the qualifications for

50. Respectively, Art. IV, sec. 2, cl. 1, and Art. III, sec. 2, cl. 1. I have examined all references listed in the "Index by Clauses of the Constitution," in Max Farrand, ed., *The Records of the Federal Convention of 1787*, 2d ed. rev. (New Haven, Conn., 1966 [orig. publ. 1937]), IV, 107–123. The judiciary clause was debated, but at no point did the delegates question that national jurisdiction should extend over state citizens in some form. The privileges and immunities clause was barely discussed. See also Antieau, "Paul's Perverted Privileges," *W. and M. Law Rev.*, IX (1967–1968), 5–10.

51. Art. I, sec. 2 (House) and sec. 3 (Senate), and Art. II, sec. 1 (president) in effect allowed the states to define the electorate, and they could even confer this privilege on aliens. See Leon E. Aylsworth, "The Passing of Alien Suffrage," *Am. Pol. Sci. Rev.*, XXV (1931), 114–116. Art. I, secs. 9–10, placed certain restraints on the powers of Congress and the states; Art. III, sec. 2, guaranteed the right of trial by jury. The Bill of Rights, ratified Dec. 15, 1791, specified some rights, but this was held to limit the federal government only, in Barron v. Baltimore, 7 Pet. 243 (U.S., 1833).

office, they touched on the relationship between naturalized and native citizen status; however, the exact relations among the states and between the states and the nation as a whole would remain problematical until the ultimate question of the nature of individual citizenship was confronted directly. The framers dealt with the question tangentially, and, in consequence, the constitutional provisions involving citizenship contained profound ambiguities that would become apparent only long after the new government went into operation. The emergence of new problems of practical policy and political principle in the decades after 1789 would force later generations to deal with questions about the meaning of American citizenship—questions unseen or unattended to during the Philadelphia Convention—that lay at the heart of the federal system.

During the 1790s the subtler issues of federal relations hidden in the concept of citizenship were overshadowed by the continuing debate on the standards of admission and on the qualifications for membership. Growing partisan divisions within Congress and the country at large concentrated attention on the political activities of the foreign-born and brought a new, practical urgency to hopes and fears already raised in a theoretical way by the delegates to the Convention of 1787. Only gradually did conflicts within Congress or the courts begin to reveal the extent of the problems unsolved by the founders of the new constitutional order.

Both the persistence of old concerns and the outlines of new problems were evident in the political controversy following the election of Albert Gallatin to the Senate in 1793.[52] On December 2, 1793, a petition from Conrad Lamb and eighteen other residents of York, Pennsylvania, challenging the eligibility of the newly elected delegate was read before the Senate. The petition alleged that the Swiss-born Gallatin had not fulfilled the constitutional requirement of nine years of citizenship and asked that he not be seated. The petition was referred to committee on December 11, and a report was submitted December 31. Repeated postponements delayed substantive discussion until late February 1794.[53]

52. William Maclay's seat was vacated in Mar. 1791, but a dispute between the Pennsylvania House and Senate delayed the choice of Maclay's successor for two years. Raymond Walters, Jr., *Albert Gallatin: Jeffersonian Financier and Diplomat* (New York, 1957), 50.

53. This account is based on *ibid.*, 59–63, and on the Senate debates as reported in *Annals of Congress*, 3d Cong., 1st sess., *passim*, esp. 47–55.

On February 20 Gallatin rose to speak in his own behalf. He claimed that he had been an inhabitant of the United States since 1780, that he had taken oaths of allegiance and purchased lands in Massachusetts and Virginia between 1783 and 1785, and that he had fought for the American cause during the War of Independence. "He conceived himself a citizen in common with the other citizens of the United States, from the time of his first qualifying after his arrival and attachment to the country."[54]

William Lewis, counsel for the petitioners, insisted on proof of Gallatin's citizenship. According to the challengers, available evidence showed that Gallatin had never fully complied with the naturalization laws of any of the states. Virginia's law of 1783 required two separate oaths, yet the evidence indicated Gallatin had taken only one, and that before a magistrate rather than, as required, before a court. Furthermore, aliens admitted under Virginia's law were not considered eligible even for state political office until after a two-year residence in the state, and Gallatin had lived there only two months. None of the states had ever contemplated admitting "foreigners or persons from other States to citizenship, immediately on their entrance within their limits"; if Gallatin's brief residence could not qualify him for local office, it certainly ought not suffice to qualify him elsewhere. The comity clause of the Articles was, in Lewis's opinion, restricted to the "mass of citizens at the accomplishment of Independence" and did not extend to later immigrants. The notion that Gallatin was "entitled to be a citizen of the Union, or of any individual State of it, because he had qualified himself to be a citizen of one of them," was, according to Lewis, "a mere bubble." The Senate should therefore invalidate Gallatin's election, a most just and generous policy: "One of the ancient Republics made it death for an alien to intermeddle in their policies."[55]

Gallatin returned to his own defense the next day. Rather than directly confronting the question of his naturalization under state law, he emphasized theoretical points about the meaning of citizenship. The Revolution had totally changed the grounds of allegiance: "This country, before the Revolution, owed allegiance to the King, but that was destroyed by the Declaration of Independence, and

54. Senate debate, Feb. 20, 1794, *Annals of Congress*, 3d Cong., 1st sess., 48–49.
55. *Ibid.*, 49–50.

234 Principles, Politics, and Prejudice

then the inhabitants of the States became mutually citizens of every State reciprocally; and they continued so until such time as the States made laws of their own afterwards respecting naturalization." The new allegiance was "real"—being owed "to the Government and to society"—whereas the old allegiance had been "fictitious"—"being only to one man." Nor was citizenship confined to those resident when independence was declared. "Every man who took an active part in the American Revolution, was a citizen according to the great laws of reason and nature, and when afterwards positive laws were made, they were retrospective in regard to persons under this predicament, nor did those posterior laws invalidate the rights which they enjoy under the Confederation." Lewis had admitted that a person who had been "one of the mass of the people" at independence was a citizen. "On the same principle," Gallatin contended, "until a law passes to disprove that a man who was active in the Revolution previous to the Treaty of Peace, was a citizen, he must be one *ipso facto*." The Constitution established valid qualifications for members of Congress, but it did not take away the rights of those who were citizens before ratification. Gallatin was "one of the people" before the United States existed; he should not be deprived of that status now.[56]

Gallatin's arguments respecting his eligibility were unavailing. A motion to seat him was defeated, and his election was declared void by a vote of fourteen to twelve.[57] However, it would be dangerous to draw conclusions from this decision. The Senate was not required to justify its vote, and it is unclear which arguments the majority found convincing. Most likely, personal political opposition to Gallatin and a continued fear of "foreign influence" in the national government were more important than any single theoretical claim forwarded by Lewis. Certainly neither Congress nor other public bodies consistently adopted the counsel's idea that men naturalized by the states during the Confederation were excluded from national citizenship or federal office.[58] Nor did they insist on

56. Feb. 21, 1794, *ibid.*, 51–54.
57. Feb. 28, 1794, *ibid.*, 58. Walters, *Albert Gallatin*, 63, suggests that the vote ran "along strict party lines."
58. Gallatin himself served as a congressman after 1795. He was not then challenged either as an alien—assuming he had never been naturalized—or as a too-recent citizen— assuming that some might have thought his citizenship began with the Federal Union. Walters notes that the Federalists were outnumbered by the "Antis" in the House at this time, and it is possible that Gallatin's opponents realized the futility of challenging his eligibility. *Ibid.*, 87.

proof of explicit compliance with naturalization laws from all who immigrated during the Revolution and supported the American cause at the time of the peace treaty.[59]

The Gallatin affair did, however, reveal certain unresolved ambiguities about the constitutional concept of citizenship. The senators clearly had no consistent view of the relationship between state and national citizenship. Although the Senate qualification clause necessarily envisioned a continuity of membership in the Confederation and the Federal Union in terms of the "mass of citizens" (no one foresaw a delay of nine years before a senate of new "national" citizens could be formed), there was general agreement that not all persons adopted by the states could enter the Union fully qualified as national citizens. On the other hand, Gallatin was not formally declared to be incapable on the grounds of alienage; quite possibly some of those who voted against his being seated (assuming that some did vote on other than purely partisan grounds) did so because the date of his alleged naturalization was unclear.

Although the antagonism toward Gallatin illustrated, in part, a widespread doubt about the propriety of allowing the foreign-born to enjoy high office and political power, the form of the opposition was significant. Lewis concentrated his efforts on denying Gallatin's naturalization and on upholding the conscientious observation of all established membership requirements. On the other side, Gallatin took pains to argue that he had proven his suitability for membership by both word and deed; he had shown his attachment to government and society and thereby had substantiated his allegiance. The debate thus focused on the question whether Gallatin had become a citizen. Given that the Constitution itself defined the qualifications for high political office, no one suggested that political rights could be withheld, whether or not Gallatin was naturalized.

Suspicion of the foreign-born and a belief that citizenship conferred political rights combined to shape the development of a federal naturalization policy in the 1790s. The story of the successive acts of 1790, 1795, and 1798 is a familiar one.[60] The emergence

59. State courts certainly did not insist on a rigid compliance in the cases cited above, chap. 7, n. 85. Chief Justice Samuel Nelson held that a man who arrived before the Declaration of Independence must be deemed an "original citizen," in Young v. Peck, 21 Wendell 389, 391 (N.Y., 1839); upheld on appeal, Peck v. Young, 26 Wendell 613 (N.Y., 1841).

60. See generally Franklin, *Legislative History of Naturalization*; John P. Roche, *The Early Development of United States Citizenship* (Ithaca, N.Y., 1949); and *Naturalization Laws of the United States . . .* (Rochester, N.Y., 1855).

and intensification of partisan divisions, occasioned in large part by events in Europe following the French Revolution, heightened sensitivity to the political alignments of the foreign-born and led to an increasingly harsh and restrictionist naturalization policy under the Federalist administrations of Washington and Adams.

The first federal naturalization act of 1790 was fairly liberal. Any "free white person" who resided for two years within the United States and for at least one year in the state where he sought admission, proving his "good character" and taking an oath to "support the constitution of the United States," was to be "considered as a citizen of the United States." Children under twenty-one dwelling within the United States were to be included in the parent's naturalization, and foreign-born children of citizens were themselves to be deemed natural-born citizens, provided that "the right of citizenship shall not descend to persons whose fathers have never been resident in the United States."[61]

Congressional debates on the bill focused mainly on the residence requirement and on the extent to which immigrants could safely be entrusted with political rights. In the House, Thomas Tucker of South Carolina proposed a sliding scale that would permit aliens to acquire lands in less than one year, but would exclude them from office for at least three years. This, however, raised some problems—did the Constitution authorize a progressive admission to citizenship? "After a person has once become a citizen," argued Alexander White of Virginia, "the power of Congress ceases to operate on him." Property and political rights were to be governed in detail by the state laws. Congress was authorized to establish only a uniform rule of admission and could not legitimately attempt "a general definition of what constitutes the rights of citizenship in the several States." Joshua Seney of Maryland supported the argument that Congress's power was limited: "We can go no further than to prescribe the rule by which it can be

61. Act of Mar. 26, 1790. The provisions respecting children continued in later acts until 1802, when the language was altered in such a way as to render the status of children born of parents naturalized thereafter questionable. The issue was discussed in [Horace Binney], "The Alienigenae of the United States," *American Law Register*, II (1854), 193–210, and the problem was rectified by the act of Feb. 10, 1855 that declared children "heretofore" or "hereafter" born abroad of citizen fathers to be citizens. This act also declared that alien women qualified for admission would be deemed naturalized upon marriage to a U.S. citizen. Earlier practices are unclear, but a brief report of Ex parte Pic, 19 F. Cas. 580 (U.S.C.C., 1806), indicated that a *feme covert* (married woman) could be naturalized separately.

determined who are, and who are not citizens; but we cannot say they shall be entitled to privileges in the different States which native citizens are not entitled to, until they have performed the conditions annexed thereto." John Lawrence of New York also doubted the propriety of adding further requirements for office to those already established in the Constitution.[62]

Madison acknowledged the constitutional objections to step-by-step admission of aliens, but he saw no reason why Congress should not establish a uniform residence requirement for the bestowal of citizenship and allow the individual states to define in detail the rights of aliens and citizens.[63] Once a man became a citizen, he could immediately invoke the comity clause to demand the particular rights of citizenship as defined by the Constitution and state laws. If caution was necessary in conferring rights, Congress must exercise it in regulating admission to the status, not in distinguishing subsequent levels and grades of membership. Congress generally agreed that the Constitution barred attempts to establish gradations of rights among the mass of citizens, to fragment what appeared to be an indivisible status and to return to the British system of separate classes of membership.

Debate shifted to the proper residence requirement for naturalization. Thomas Hartley of Pennsylvania thought that the "terms of citizenship are made too cheap in some parts of the Union," and he wanted to delay admission long enough to insure the immigrant's "knowledge of the candidates" and "firm attachment to the Government." Michael Stone of Maryland also favored a term of residence long enough to guarantee "first, that he should have an opportunity of knowing the circumstances of our Government, and in consequence thereof, shall have admitted the truth of the principles we hold. Second, that he shall have acquired a taste for this kind of Government."[64]

Virginia's John Page advocated a liberal policy. "Bigotry and superstition, or a deep-rooted prejudice against the Government, laws, religion, or manners of neighboring nations," he argued, had a weight in Europe that should not influence policy here. Americans would "be inconsistent with ourselves, if, after boasting of

62. Tucker, *Annals of Congress*, 1st Cong., 2d sess., 1109; White, *ibid.*, 1113; Seney, *ibid.*, 1123; and Lawrence, *ibid.*, 1111.
63. *Ibid.*, 1111.
64. *Ibid.*, 1118.

having opened an asylum for the oppressed of all nations, and established a Government which is the admiration of the world, we make the terms of admission to the full enjoyment of that asylum so hard as is now proposed."[65] Page found a staunch ally in the Senate, William Maclay of Pennsylvania, who also thought the proposed two-year residence requirement "illiberal and void of philanthropy." Maclay saw in it a poorly disguised thrust by jealous and xenophobic New Englanders against the liberal and prosperity-producing admission policy of Pennsylvania:

We Pennsylvanians act as if we believed that God made of one blood all families of the earth; but the Eastern people seem to think that he made none but New England folks. It is strange that men born and educated under republican forms of government should be so contracted on the subject of general philanthropy. . . . They really have the worst characters of any people who offer themselves for citizens. Yet these are the men who affect the greatest fear of being contaminated with foreign manners, customs, or vices.[66]

In the end, Congress did include a two-year residence requirement in its first uniform rule of naturalization. Aliens seeking admission were thus obliged to spend at least that much time assimilating the habits and values of republican life before the federal government would confer upon them the status granting a constitutional right to the privileges and immunities of citizenship. This did not mean that aliens were in all cases without rights in the first two years of settlement, for the states were free to grant immigrants whatever privileges they wished within their own respective jurisdictions. The debates of 1790 specifically suggested that states could make their own regulations concerning the detailed rights of aliens and citizens, and many legislatures eased traditional alien disabilities by passing general or special acts permitting foreign immigrants to acquire and hold real property prior to their naturalization.[67]

What the discussions and act of 1790 did not clarify was whether

65. *Ibid.*, 1110.
66. Entry for Mar. 9, 1790, *The Journal of William Maclay, United States Senator from Pennsylvania, 1789–1791,* with an introduction by Charles Beard (New York, 1927), 205.
67. For examples of state laws conferring property rights on aliens, see Hoadly *et al.,* eds., *Conn. State Recs.,* VIII, 122 (Oct. 1793); *Pa. Statutes,* XIII, 179 (Feb. 11, 1789); *N.Y. State Laws,* III, 247–248 (Mar. 22, 1791); Hening, ed., *Statutes of Va.,* XIII, 122–124 (Dec. 24, 1790); *S.C. Statutes,* IV, 746–747 (Mar. 22, 1786); and Joseph Bloomfield, comp., *Laws of the State of New Jersey, from 1800 to 1811* . . . (Trenton, N.J., 1811), 172 (Nov. 7, 1806).

Congress's control over naturalization was now to be exclusive or whether it was merely to supplement state acts. The congressional statute did nothing to settle questions respecting the spheres of authority of the state and national governments, and many states continued to administer their own naturalization laws.[68] The vagueness of the Constitution's "uniform rule" provision allowed diverse interpretations concerning both the intent of the requirements for admission and the actual location of the power to naturalize. Alexander Hamilton had argued in *Federalist* Number 32 that the uniform rule provision necessarily conferred an exclusive power on Congress "because if each State had power to prescribe a DISTINCT RULE, there could not be a UNIFORM RULE."[69] Others argued that the apparent intent of the framers to eliminate inconvenience and to bar the free "introduction of obnoxious characters" also implied an exclusive congressional authority.[70] On the other hand, it was possible to claim that the intent of the naturalization clause was to prevent a too rigid policy toward immigrants. From this perspective, the individual states could still "enjoy a concurrent authority upon this subject," although they could not exercise their individual authority "so as to contravene the rule established by the authority of the Union." It was the considered opinion of the judges of the federal circuit court of Pennsylvania that the Constitution's clause was designed "to guard against too narrow, instead of too liberal, a mode of conferring the rights of citizenship." The individual states could not exclude those adopted by the United States, but they could adopt citizens on easier terms than those which Congress "may deem it expedient to impose."[71]

This interpretation posed a serious threat to the belief that existing naturalization requirements were already too liberal, an opinion widely shared in Congress by the mid-1790s. The European crisis touched off by the French Revolution flared into war after 1792, and refugees fled the scenes of military conflict and rebellion. The neutral United States attracted "disenchanted Englishmen, aristocratic Frenchmen, German Pietists fleeing forced military service,

68. See, e.g., *Mass. Acts and Laws, 1794–1795*, 39–40 (June 24, 1794); Maxcy, ed., *Laws of Md.*, II, 178–180, 199–200 (Nov. 1793, Nov. 1794). Vermont's constitution of 1793 retained a provision for state naturalization (chap. II, sec. 39) that was not amended until 1828. Thorpe, ed. and comp., *Constitutions, Charters, and Laws*, VI, 3770, 3772.

69. *The Federalist*, No. 32, 195.

70. See the arguments of counsel, Collett v. Collett, 2 Dall. 294, 295 (U.S.C.C., 1792).

71. *Ibid.*, 296 (Court opinion). See also the argument of Moses Levy, at 295.

French planters escaping from West Indian uprisings led by Toussaint l'Ouverture, and Irishmen in flight from British repression."[72] The massive influx of foreign immigrants might have increased fears of alien intermeddling in politics in any case; however, the large number of refugees with passionate political beliefs made all newcomers doubly suspect.

In light of these circumstances, both Federalists and Jeffersonian Republicans could agree on the desirability of tightening the government's naturalization policy. From the outset, Theodore Sedgwick of Massachusetts was dubious of the "rash theory, that the subjects of all Governments, Despotic, Monarchical, and Aristocratical, are, as soon as they set foot on American ground, qualified to participate in administering the sovereignty of our country." The current crisis in Europe, he thought, provided a particularly inauspicious time to admit aliens indiscriminately: "A war, the most cruel and dreadful which has been known for centuries, was now raging in all those countries from which emigrants were to be expected. The most fierce and unrelenting passions were engaged in a conflict, which shook to their foundations all the ancient political structures in Europe." Sedgwick could not conceive that "men, who, actuated by such passions, had fought on grounds so opposite, almost equally distant from the happy mean that we had chosen, would here mingle in social affections with each other, or with us." Therefore, he favored restrictions that would check the number of immigrants and improve their political character.[73]

Although many could agree with the general thrust of this argument, it was not easy to define the proper "political character" most conducive to domestic stability. Hidden behind the detailed proposals for revising the Naturalization Act of 1790 were sharply contrasting views concerning the proper control of the quality of immigration. In general, Federalists favored requirements designed to discourage "democratic 'disorganizers' "—or, as Sedgwick put it, "the discontented, the ambitious, and the avaricious"—while the Jeffersonians aimed at making citizenship difficult for merchants and aristocrats, whose "antirepublican principles" threatened to pervert the manners and ideals of the American community.[74]

72. James Morton Smith, *Freedom's Fetters: The Alien and Sedition Laws and American Civil Liberties* (Ithaca, N.Y., 1956), 23.
73. *Annals of Congress*, 3d Cong., 2d sess., 1006–1008.
74. Smith, *Freedom's Fetters*, 23; *Annals of Congress*, 3d Cong., 2d sess., 1006.

The various objectives of those who supported restricted naturalization raised charges and counter-charges of partisanship in heated congressional debates. Jonathan Dayton of New Jersey, for example, argued that a proposal requiring two witnesses of the applicant's moral character and attachment to republican government discriminated against "poor men" and "laboring people" who rarely "troubled their heads about forms of Government." But the objectionable clause "might suit extremely well with merchants and men of large capital." James Madison agreed. The requirement would discriminate against those who might shift their residence and those whose humble position might make it difficult to find "two reputable witnesses, who could swear to the purity of their principles for three years back." Whether they favored the policy or not, most saw a design behind the lengthy residence requirement and the cumbersome step-by-step procedure involving numerous oaths, declarations of intent, and character witnesses to guard the "Government against any disturbance from the people called Jacobins."[75]

These procedural revisions might appeal to political enemies of the "Jacobins," but they could also receive support from men in both parties who merely wished to improve the screening process and to lengthen the time in which aliens of every political persuasion could assimilate proper habits and values. More clearly discriminatory was the proposal—hotly debated, but eventually approved by roll call vote—that applicants for citizenship be required to renounce all titles of nobility. William B. Giles of Virginia, fearing an "inundation of titled fugitives," considered this measure necessary to minimize the danger that high-toned, aristocratic refugees would corrupt and subvert virtuous republicans. Opponents of Giles's amendment saw it as unnecessary and illiberal, a partisan ploy to label them as "friends of aristocracy."[76]

Although the debates on the bill reflected partisan hostilities, they also illustrated a shared assumption: the national government had a legitimate interest in controlling the character of potential citizens. There was fundamental agreement that the old term of residence

---

75. Dayton, *Annals of Congress*, 3d Cong., 2d sess., 1021; Madison, *ibid.*, 1022; Giles, *ibid.*, 1034.

76. Samuel Dexter (Mass.) proposed a counter-measure requiring all candidates for citizenship to renounce slavery and release all their slaves. Both amendments were pressed to a vote, Giles's passing, Dexter's failing. *Ibid.*, 1030–1032, 1034–1039, 1041–1058.

should be increased in order that the "prejudices which the aliens had imbibed under the Government from whence they came might be effaced, and that they might, by communication and observance of our laws and government, have just ideas of our Constitution and the excellence of its institutions before they were admitted to the rights of a citizen."[77]

Rarely did the debates extend to questions about the nature of citizenship—either the issue of volitional allegiance or the relationship between the states and the federal government. The propriety of expatriation was discussed briefly in connection with proposals respecting the readmission of persons who had renounced their membership (namely, the loyalist exiles); there was some reference to the notion of volitional allegiance as it was implied by naturalization and by the required oath of abjuration. But the speakers showed no real inclination to pursue this issue.[78] Similarly, the delegates avoided discussion of the federal character of citizenship and the relationship between membership in state and nation. A clause added to the draft bill in the Senate indicated that naturalization under state laws would no longer be tolerated, but this elimination of separate state procedures seemed to be simply another means of improving control of access to the rights of citizenship.[79]

The new naturalization act was approved January 29, 1795, increasing the period of residence from two to five years and requiring the applicant to declare publicly his intent to become a citizen three years before admission.[80] The potential citizen had to swear that he had completed the required residence, that he renounced and abjured his former allegiance, and that he would support the Constitution of the United States. Immigrants who had "borne any hereditary title, or been of the orders of nobility" were required to renounce that status, and all had to satisfy the court of admission that they had behaved as men of good moral character, were attached to the principles of the Constitution, and were "well disposed to the good order and happiness of the same." Aliens were to

77. Samuel Smith (Md.), *ibid.*, 1065.
78. Speech of William Vans Murray (Md.), Dec. 30, 1794, *ibid.*, 1028–1029.
79. *Ibid.*, 811, 812, 814.
80. Act of Jan. 29, 1795. Sec. 2 allowed aliens currently in the United States to be admitted under the old residence requirement; sec. 3 dealt with the children of naturalized parents, and it also required the consent of the state legislature for the readmission of any person proscribed by the state during the late war. This latter clause had been part of the 1790 act.

be naturalized on these conditions "and not otherwise"—a provision effectively ending admission under separate state laws.

The Naturalization Act of 1795 received widespread, if sometimes half-hearted, support from members of both major political factions. The barriers erected to improve the screening of applicants for citizenship were still low enough to be hurdled by those truly committed to becoming members of the American community, whatever their personal politics. The best hope of shaping the character of those who sought citizenship lay not in any prior selection by political tests applied during the process of admission, but in the extension of the period of "apprenticeship" to allow the individual immigrant to become firmly attached to the well-being of the Republic. Fisher Ames made the point clearly:

Now, said he, do we think of refusing this privilege [of citizenship] to all heretics in respect to political doctrine? Even that strictness would not hasten the millenium. For our own citizens freely propagate a great variety of opinions hostile to each other, and, therefore, many of them deviate widely from the intended standards of right thinking; good and bad, fools and wise men, the philosophers and the dupes of prejudice, we could live very peaceably together, because there was a sufficient coincidence of common interest. If we depend on this strong tie, if we oblige foreigners to wait . . . till they have formed it, till their habits as well as interests become assimilated with our own, we may leave them to cherish or renounce their imported prejudices and follies as they may choose.[81]

The argument seemed reasonable enough, but many Federalists were increasingly convinced that five years was much too short a time for the process to work. New citizens showed a disconcerting tendency to support the opposition. For every industrious, peaceable, and politically sound (that is, Federalist) immigrant, wrote Noah Webster, "we receive three or four discontented, factious men"—"the convicts, fugitives of justice, hirelings of France, and disaffected offscourings of other nations."[82] The sentiment was shared by the Connecticut Federalist Uriah Tracy, who found "many, very many Irishmen" in Pennsylvania, "and with a very few exceptions, they are United Irishmen, Free Masons, and the most God-provoking Democrats on this side of Hell."[83] A Federal-

81. Speech of Jan. 21, 1795, *Annals of Congress*, 3d Cong., 2d sess., 1048.
82. Quoted by John C. Miller, *Crisis in Freedom: The Alien and Sedition Acts* (Boston, 1951), 42.
83. Quoted in Smith, *Freedom's Fetters*, 24.

ist attempt to break the alliance between "the Democracy" and the new immigrants by levying a twenty-dollar tax on naturalization certificates failed to pass during a special session in 1797.[84] But the great wave of public anger raised by the exposé of the XYZ correspondence gave a Federalist-dominated Congress its opportunity to strike a devastating blow at the "alien menace."

The naturalization law and the Alien and Sedition acts passed by the Fifth Congress were clearly Federalist measures, designed both to increase national security at a time when war with France seemed imminent and to strike at an alleged source of Jeffersonian Republican strength.[85] "No acts ever passed by Congress had ever been so clearly the work of one party; no laws had ever been so unanimously opposed by the other party."[86] The law of 1795 was amended to require a residence of fourteen years before the applicant could be admitted and a declaration of intent to become a citizen five years before admission. On the motion of Albert Gallatin (and not without considerable reluctance on the part of some extremists) a one-year grace period was allowed for aliens already resident in the country to qualify under the terms of the old law of 1795. Special provisions were made for the central recording of all declarations and naturalizations, for the registration of all alien immigrants, and for the punishment of all persons who failed to comply with the registry provisions. Enemy aliens were barred from naturalization while their native country was at war with the United States.[87]

Drastic as these new provisions were, they were not as restrictive as some ideas propounded in the course of the House debates. Robert G. Harper of South Carolina thought "the time was now come when it would be proper to declare, that nothing but birth should entitle a man to citizenship in this country." Harrison Gray Otis of Massachusetts proposed an amendment to the residence requirement and a separate resolution to the effect that "no alien born, who is not at present a citizen of the United States, shall hereafter be capable of holding any office of honor, trust, or profit, under the United States."[88] In essence, Otis wished to return to a

84. *Ibid.*, 23.
85. For a thorough discussion of these measures, see *ibid.*, chaps. 2–8, App., 435–452 (texts of acts).
86. Noble E. Cunningham, Jr., *The Jeffersonian Republicans: The Formation of Party Organization, 1789–1801* (Chapel Hill, N.C., 1957), 126. The partisan character of the acts is evident in the debates. See *Annals of Congress*, 5th Cong., 2d sess., 1566–1582, 1777–1784.
87. Act of June 18, 1798.
88. *Annals of Congress*, 5th Cong., 2d sess., 1567, 1570.

concept of ranked and graded membership like that embedded in the English distinction between denizen, naturalized subject, and natural-born subject; he preferred legal discrimination between those born into the community and those subsequently adopted to uniform citizenship.

The Otis amendment/resolution was quickly and successfully opposed. Virginia's Abraham Venable insisted that any desire to exclude naturalized citizens from the rights enjoyed by natives could only be fulfilled by amending the Constitution: "After foreigners were admitted as citizens, Congress had not the power of declaring what should be their rights; the Constitution has done this. Foreigners must, therefore, be refused the privilege of becoming citizens altogether, or admitted to the rights of citizens." Otis disagreed: if Congress had the absolute power to exclude aliens from citizenship by extending the residence requirement to "the life of man," then surely it had the constitutional power to exclude them from some privileges while granting them others. The argument was ineffective. Too many members agreed with Nathaniel Macon of North Carolina that "after a man is a citizen, he must be entitled to the rights of a citizen."[89] The Otis amendment was withdrawn.

In any case, an amendment to the statute specifically limiting offices to native citizens was unnecessary. As Samuel Sitgreaves of Pennsylvania observed, Otis's aim could be achieved and "Constitutional embarrassment" avoided merely by extending the residence requirement for citizenship to prevent aliens from ever gaining that status. Although some extremists were willing to consider such a policy, Macon's apprehension that "gentlemen in their zeal to get at particular persons, will go too far in this business" was well taken and widely shared. Fourteen years seemed long enough to exclude all but the most persistent and committed aliens from the privileges of citizenship.[90]

Jefferson's election in 1800 was quickly followed by a repeal of the obnoxious Naturalization Act of 1798. A new law approved April 14, 1802, reinstated the general requirements established in

89. Venable, *ibid.*, 1570; Otis, *ibid.*, 1571, 1570; Macon, *ibid.*, 1571. A constitutional amendment excluding naturalized citizens from office was submitted to the House in July, but was tabled. Herman V. Ames, "The Proposed Amendments to the Constitution of the United States during the First Century of Its History," A.H.A., *Annual Report . . . for the Year 1896*, II (1897), 30, 74.

90. Sitgreaves, *Annals of Congress*, 5th Cong., 2d sess., 1572; Macon, *ibid.*, 1780.

1795: residence of five years with a declaration of intent three years before admission; oaths or declarations abjuring titles and foreign allegiance and swearing attachment to the principles of the Constitution; and satisfactory proof of good character and behavior. The act included provisions for the registration of all immigrants, and alien enemies were still barred from naturalization.[91]

The Naturalization Act of 1802 was the last major piece of legislation on this subject during the nineteenth century. A number of minor revisions were introduced before the Civil War, but these merely altered or clarified details of evidence, certification, and the like without changing the basic nature of the admission procedure.[92] At the heart of the naturalization process remained the idea that a prolonged term of residence was the surest way of guaranteeing an alien's attachment to the country and adoption of its ways. The declaration of intent gave notice to the public at large that the alien was committed to becoming a fellow citizen, and it served to focus closer attention on his behavior; but above all, continued residence "gave the knowledge and feeling, and gave the opportunity, for the intercourse that amalgamated the aliens with us, and gave them a common interest. It was the surest standard by which to test the desire for citizenship; it was action, and not declaration; it was fact and not theory."[93]

By the beginning of the nineteenth century Americans had begun to address some of the problems involved in the creation of a new concept of citizenship. Old bonds of personal allegiance that had

91. Act of Apr. 14, 1802.

92. An act of Mar. 26, 1804, exempted aliens resident between the acts of 1798 and 1802 from the declaration-of-intent requirement and also provided that widows and children of aliens dying before the completion of their admission be deemed naturalized. An act of Mar. 3, 1813, declared that aliens must reside five years continuously without at any time being out of the United States; but the clause was repealed June 26, 1848. A statute of July 30, 1813, allowed alien enemies who had already begun admission procedures before the outbreak of war to complete the process. Acts of Mar. 22, 1816, May 26, 1824, and May 24, 1828, regulated the evidence required in naturalization procedures. The act of Feb. 10, 1855, concerning the status of women and children has been mentioned above (n. 61). A wartime act of July 17, 1862, allowed aliens who had served in the regular or voluntary forces and who could prove their honorable discharge to be naturalized without the declaration of intent and with only two years' residence. After the 1840s, and particularly in the 1850s, nativism acquired considerable political strength. However, the nativists did not succeed in efforts to make the naturalization laws more restrictive, thus I have not dealt with this important movement in depth. For a brief assessment, see Eric Foner, *Free Soil, Free Labor, Free Men* (New York, 1970), 250–260.

93. Michael Leib (Pa.), *Annals of Congress*, 7th Cong., 2d sess., 576.

once united men in a common subjectship under the British king had been replaced by new contractual terms by which civil and political rights in the community were to be exchanged for support for republican principles, adherence to the Constitution, and responsible and virtuous behavior under enlightened forms of self-government.

The idea that citizenship must be complete in itself—that it was an undifferentiated status—was challenged by some who retained the traditional view that membership was appropriately divided by ranks and orders. But the majority resisted the notion that only those born under the principles of self-government could become citizens. Fears for the nation's security in the face of both external and internal threats produced a sometimes harsh and ultimately cautious naturalization policy, but they were not strong enough to override the sense that citizenship should ultimately depend not on some magical result of birth alone, but on belief, will, consent, and choice. Thus the legislators were most concerned with insuring a candidate's sincere commitment to the basic values and principles of the Republic. Once this commitment was shown, the naturalized alien had the right to claim virtually all the privileges of full membership.

CHAPTER 9

Citizenship and the Problem of Federal Relations

The debates of the 1790s established the terms upon which immigrants could become American citizens, but they failed to explore the political complexities of the status itself. It was readily apparent that American citizenship encompassed membership, rights, and obligations in both a local and a national community; yet the implications and ramifications of this dual status were never rigorously analyzed. The preliminary assumption seems to have been that the individual citizen, native or adopted, could bear his double membership in state and nation without inconsistency or conflict.

Tolerance of this conceptual ambiguity waned as new questions arose during the early years of the Republic. Problems in both foreign and domestic policy focused attention on the subtler aspects of the status of citizens and the meaning of citizenship in a federal system. Increasingly, politicians and jurists alike consciously attempted to delineate the boundaries of state and national authority. Theoretical coherence and logical consistency were not the primary goals here, especially for legislatures and executive officers. Rather, in dealing with problems involving citizenship—problems of naturalization, expatriation, and court jurisdiction—the chief aim was to maintain an acceptable pattern of federal relations.

The American courts played a central role in defining legislative principles. Conscious of the traditional responsibility of the judiciary to align positive legislation with the rules of "higher" law—natural, moral, or constitutional—lawyers and judges sought to go beyond the specific political or pragmatic factors that influenced legislators and to "discover" the ideals and principles that shaped or ought to shape republican citizenship. Aware of the uniqueness of the American experiment and the need for new law, yet cognizant, too, of the necessity of regular, coherent, and systematic law for stable governmental and societal order, the courts sought to enunciate a legal concept of citizenship that effectively preserved both liberty and security, individual rights and community safety.

The task was not easy, nor was it accomplished with complete success by the courts. Judges hesitated to carry the logic of their views to extreme conclusions, for to do so might threaten practical arrangements and understandings necessary for the stability of the young Republic. They unhesitatingly affirmed the equality of native and naturalized citizens, but were loath to conclude that the authority which admitted foreigners could also decide who qualified as birthright citizens. They drew a practical line of demarcation between the state and national aspects of citizenship, but refused to determine the delicate issue of the locus of the citizen's primary allegiance. And though they frequently (if cautiously) acknowledged that every citizen ought to be free to relinquish his allegiance, they were reluctant to suggest the means by which this could be done.

No one seriously questioned that American citizenship involved a double allegiance to state and nation. As long as the two operated together, or as long as particular issues could be determined within a discrete state or national context, the courts could take firm, decisive steps toward creating a systematic doctrine of citizenship. But when national and state interests diverged, when the two aspects of citizenship became inconsistent and contradictory, judges, lawyers, and legislators alike halted. Until Americans could reach some conclusive agreement on the proper character of federal relations, the meaning of citizenship would remain ambiguous and incomplete.

The centralization of the naturalizing authority in the national government began with the law of 1795, which established that aliens could be admitted by its provisions "and not otherwise." Although several states apparently still continued to naturalize aliens under their own separate laws for a time, few opposed the argument that standards of admission ought to be set exclusively by Congress rather than concurrently by the state and national governments.[1] A federal circuit court held in 1797 that Pennsylvania had no right under its own constitution to adopt foreigners, and though Justice Iredell avoided any direct discussion of federal relations in deciding the case, he noted his inclination to see naturalization as Congress's exclusive prerogative.[2]

The United States Supreme Court had no occasion to deal with this issue explicitly until 1817, by which time the matter seemed closed in practice. In *Chirac* v. *Chirac*, Chief Justice John Marshall observed that Congress's claim to sole power here "does not seem to be, and certainly ought not to be controverted."[3] Thereafter both state and federal courts affirmed the rule. The circuit court for the District of Columbia ruled that the federal naturalization laws "superseded and annulled" state procedures.[4] North Carolina's Supreme Court declared that the Constitution of 1789 had voided the portion of the state's constitution establishing rules for conferring citizenship on aliens, and according to state courts in South Carolina, New York, and Wisconsin, the "power of passing laws on the subject of naturalization exclusively appertains to the general government."[5]

Throughout there was little discussion of the grounds for locating the admitting power in the central government. Certainly none of these cases justified the rule in terms of theoretical doctrines stressing the national character of citizenship. Rather lawyers and judges merely inferred exclusivity from the "uniform rule" provision of the Constitution, occasionally noting that "the greatest confusion would be produced" by having a "variety of rules," for under the comity clause a "naturalized citizen of one state would be entitled to all the privileges of a citizen in every other state."[6]

States were, of course, involved in the actual procedure of admis-

1. Before the statute of 1795, several courts upheld the right of states to naturalize under their own laws: see Collet v. Collet, 2 Dall. 294 (U.S.C.C., 1792), and Portier v. LeRoy, 1 Yeates 371 (Pa., 1794). See also the remarks of Gallatin (Pa.) and William Craik (Md.) in Congress, *Annals of Congress*, 5th Cong., 2d sess., 1777, 1779.
   2. United States v. Villato, 2 Dall. 370, 372 (U.S.C.C., 1797).
   3. Chirac v. Chirac, 2 Wheat. 259, 269 (U.S., 1817).
   4. Matthew v. Rae, 16 F. Cas. 1112, 1113 (U.S.C.C., 1829).
   5. Quotation from Davis v. Hall, 1 Nott & McCord 292, 293 (S.C., 1818). See also Rouche v. Williamson, 3 Iredell 141 (N.C., 1842); Lynch v. Clarke, 1 Sandford Ch. 583 (N.Y., 1844); In re Wehlitz, 16 Wisc. 468 (Wisc., 1863).
   6. Argument of counsel, Houston v. Moore, 5 Wheat. 1, 10 (U.S., 1820).

sion because the federal laws established the administration of that procedure in both federal and state courts. For a time it was uncertain how conclusive state court action was in this area.[7] The Supreme Court implied in opinions of 1810 and 1813 that certificates of naturalization from state courts were sufficient evidence that all requirements had been met, but several decisions from South Carolina held that such certificates could be challenged later.[8] Although the nation's highest tribunal did not clearly deny that naturalizations could be directly contested, it decided in *Spratt* v. *Spratt* (1830) that the admitting court's decision was final in cases where the validity of a naturalization was involved indirectly—for example, in disputes where contested property titles depended on the alien or citizen status of one of the parties.[9] The rule was consistently maintained by the judiciary thereafter.[10] In effect, both federal and state courts acknowledged the authority of the others' decisions respecting the qualifications of alien applicants for citizenship.

If the courts interpreted the "uniform rule" clause in such a way as to bar states from adopting foreigners on their own authority, they were not ready to restrict Congress to this one method of naturalization. The scope of the national government's power was first questioned following the acquisition of Louisiana. At issue was Congress's right to accept territorial inhabitants as citizens by means other than individual naturalization under the uniform rule.[11] The Constitution (Article IV, section 3) authorized the admission of new states into the Union and clearly implied that the nation might acquire new territories, but the status of territorial inhabitants was open to judicial interpretation.

The question was first tested in the Superior Court of Louisiana

7. See generally John P. Roche, "Pre-Statutory Denaturalization," *Cornell Law Quarterly*, XXXV (1949–1950), 123–125.

8. Campbell v. Gordon, 6 Cranch 176, 182 (U.S., 1810); Stark v. Chesapeake Ins. Co., 7 Cranch 420, 423 (U.S., 1813). Justice John S. Richardson of South Carolina held that naturalizations irregularly obtained could be set aside: Richards v. M'Daniel, 2 Nott & McCord 351 (S.C., 1820), discussed and affirmed in Vaux v. Nesbit, 1 McCord Ch. 352, 371 (S.C., 1826).

9. Spratt v. Spratt, 4 Pet. 393, 408 (U.S., 1830). See also Roche, "Pre-Statutory Denaturalization," *Cornell Law Qtly.*, XXXV (1949–1950), 123–125.

10. See, e.g., Commonwealth v. Towles, 5 Leigh 743 (Va., 1835); State v. Penney, 10 Ark. 621 (Ark., 1850); and White v. White, 2 Metcalf 185 (Ky., 1859).

11. See generally Everett Somerville Brown, *The Constitutional History of the Louisiana Purchase, 1803–1812* (Berkeley, Cal., 1920), 18–19, 26, 46–47, 52, and *passim*. Relevant documents relating to the purchase and admission to statehood are in Thorpe, ed. and comp., *Constitutions, Charters, and Laws*, III, 1359–1392.

when Jean Baptiste Desbois, an immigrant who had settled in the territory after the cession but before statehood, applied for a license to practice in the courts. The law restricted this privilege to citizens, and Desbois could only claim citizenship by virtue of his inhabitancy when Louisiana became a state, for he had no claim to that status by birthright or naturalization. Judge François X. Martin ruled that Desbois was indeed a citizen. Under unrepealed Spanish laws and in light of an American policy of fostering immigration that went back to earliest colonial times, all immigrants to Louisiana acquired by the very act of migration "an inchoate right of naturalization or territorial citizenship." Martin observed that Congress had conferred political privileges on "inhabitants" in its laws regulating the territory; therefore all bona fide inhabitants of the territory gained all the rights and privileges of United States citizenship when Louisiana became a state.[12]

Martin's decision was corroborated by the federal circuit court in *United States* v. *Laverty* (1813). A number of Louisianians had been arrested for failure to register as alien enemies, and the United States district attorney contended that these persons would remain aliens until admitted to citizenship under the federal naturalization laws. But the court disagreed: "The government has a right, by treaty, or by the admission of a new state to naturalize, and such naturalization is equal to the other." Every bona fide inhabitant— that is, every person "whose domicil is here and [who] settled here with an intention to become a citizen of the country"—became a citizen when Louisiana gained statehood.[13]

Both the *Desbois* and *Laverty* cases affirmed the power of Congress to naturalize groups collectively by admitting territories to statehood. Subsequent decisions went beyond this to hold that territorial inhabitants gained citizenship when the government acquired the territory. In *American Insurance Company* v. *Canter* (1828), Chief Justice Marshall contended that when the United States assumed control of a territory, the relationships among the inhabitants did not change, but the tie to their former sovereign was dissolved. "The same act which transfers their country transfers the allegiance of those who remain in it." If the inhabitants did not

---

12. Desbois's Case, 2 Martin 185, 196, 201 (La., 1812).
13. United States v. Laverty, 3 Martin 733, 738, 739, and 26 F. Cas. 875, 877 (U.S.D.C., 1813).

automatically acquire political rights analogous to those enjoyed by state citizens, they clearly did become American citizens.[14]

In light of these decisions, the government's power to confer citizenship by treaty or cession could not be questioned. The "uniform rule" still established admission procedures for single persons—for example, special private acts like those frequently passed during the colonial period were not revived. But special groups could be admitted in consequence of the federal government's power to make treaties and acquire territory.[15] On the basis of this power, citizens of Texas were deemed to have become United States citizens when annexation resulted in their "collective naturalization."[16] Similarly, treaties with Indian tribes occasionally established procedures for the admission of tribal members to citizenship, though Indians were barred from naturalization under the general statutes.[17] Thus while the national government alone had the authority to naturalize, it was not restricted to a single method of conferring citizenship.

Whatever method of naturalization the government chose to use, its special authority ended once the alien was a citizen. Court decisions clearly reaffirmed the principle stated in the debates of the 1790s that once a person was naturalized, he could claim all the

14. American Ins. Co. v. Canter, 1 Pet. 511, 542 (U.S., 1828). Compare Attorney General William Wirt's opinion of Sept. 3, 1819, that a British subject who had settled in the Michigan Territory in 1787 and resided there since was not a citizen until he met the requirements of the naturalization laws. Henry D. Gilpin, ed., *Opinions of the Attorneys General of the United States, from the beginning of the Government to March 1st, 1841* . . . , I (Washington, D.C., 1841), 218–219.

15. According to the Treaty of Guadaloupe-Hidalgo (1848), Mexican citizens in ceded territories would automatically become U.S. citizens unless they publicly elected to remain Mexican citizens within one year. Mexicans in California and Indians in California and New Mexico—Mexican citizens since the 1820s—thus could claim citizenship under this treaty. See People v. Naglee, 52 Am. Dec. 312, 326–328 (Cal., 1850); United States v. Ritchie, 17 How. 525, 539 (U.S., 1854); United States v. Lucero, 1 N. Mex. 422, 434 (N. Mex. Terr., 1869). On the other hand, a decision of 1856 declared that an Englishman naturalized in Mexico reverted to his original subject status and did not become a U.S. citizen. Circuit Judge Matthew H. McAllister held that Mexico had no right to transfer, nor the U.S. to receive, "the voluntary or statutory allegiance of a naturalized citizen." Tobin v. Walkinshaw, 23 F. Cas. 1346, 1348 (U.S.C.C., 1856).

16. Opinion of Attorney General Amos Akerman (1871), quoted in John Bassett Moore, ed., *A Digest of International Law*, III (Washington, D.C., 1906), 314.

17. Indian citizenship issues are discussed below, chap. 10. For a list of treaties containing citizenship provisions, see Felix S. Cohen, *Handbook of Federal Indian Law* (Washington, D.C., 1942), 153. These are discussed in some detail in Arnold J. Lien, *The Acquisition of Citizenship by the Native American Indians*, Washington University Studies, Humanistic Series No. 1 (Concord, N.H., 1925), 164–176.

rights of a native citizen with the sole exception of eligibility for the presidency. The New York Supreme Court held in 1815 that a naturalized person could not be tried as an enemy spy by court-martial, though he "might be amenable to the civil authority for treason."[18] A number of decisions guaranteed full property rights to naturalized citizens and restated the old English principle that naturalization operated retrospectively to validate titles acquired before admission.[19] On the other hand, the United States Supreme Court declared that admission to citizenship could not destroy special rights and privileges that a man had enjoyed prior to natu-ralization under laws granting special benefits to alien settlers.[20]

Chief Justice Marshall summed up the situation clearly in 1824:

> A naturalized citizen is indeed made a citizen under an act of Congress, but the act does not proceed to give, to regulate, or to prescribe his capacities. He becomes a member of the society, possessing all the rights of a native citizen, and standing, in the view of the constitution, on the footing of a native. The constitution does not authorize Congress to enlarge or abridge those rights. The simple power of the national Legislature, is to prescribe a uniform rule of naturalization, and the exercise of this power exhausts it, so far as respects the individual. The constitution then takes him up, and, among other rights, extends to him the capacity of suing in the Courts of the United States, precisely under the same circumstances under which a native might sue. He is distinguishable in nothing from a native citizen, except so far as the constitution makes the distinction.[21]

Questions concerning the naturalization power seemed simple and rather easily solved in comparison with the intricate issues of federal relations raised by other constitutional provisions involving citizenship. In particular, interpretation of the clauses respecting the privileges and immunities of citizenship (Article IV, section 2) and the jurisdiction of the federal courts (Article III, section 2) forced the courts to consider the state and national dimensions of the status. As Justice Bushrod Washington noted, "Every citizen of a state owes a double allegiance: he enjoys the protection and participates in the

18. Smith v. Shaw, 12 Johns. Rep. 257, 265 (N.Y., 1815).
19. Jackson v. Beach, 1 Johns. Cas. 399 (N.Y., 1800), held that naturalization retroac-tively confirmed property titles, acting as "a waiver of all liability to forfeiture." The principle was affirmed in Governeur v. Robertson, 11 Wheat. 332, 350 (U.S., 1826), and Jackson v. Green, 7 Wendell 333 (N.Y., 1831).
20. Spratt v. Spratt, 1 Pet. 343 (U.S., 1828).
21. Osborn v. Bank of United States, 9 Wheat. 738, 827 (U.S., 1824).

government of both the State and the United States."[22] Yet in what sense and in what contexts was American citizenship to be considered a national status conferring national rights as opposed to a state status more circumscribed in operation and effect?

Article IV, section 2, clause 1, established that "the citizens of each State shall be entitled to all privileges and immunities of citizens in the several States." Antebellum jurists generally agreed that the intent of the clause was to give legal-constitutional force to the notion of a national community by assuring that no state would impose the disabilities of alienage on citizens of other states. Judge William H. Cabell of Virginia, for example, contended in 1811 that "the citizens of the other states, although contradistinguished from citizens of this state, [are] not . . . *aliens* with respect to this state, inasmuch as both the articles of confederation, and the constitution of the United States, entitle them to the privileges and immunities of citizens of this state."[23] Ten years later Justice Washington affirmed this idea in federal circuit court: "With respect to the immunities which the rights of citizenship can confer, the citizen of one state is to be considered as a citizen of each, and every other state in the union."[24] Alabama's Judge William P. Chilton sounded the same note in 1848 when explaining the clause: "By it, the citizens of the different states are, as it respects the privileges and immunities they enjoy in their respective states, brought into a general citizenship with each other."[25]

If the privileges and immunities clause had been intended to recognize a "general citizenship" as Judge Chilton and others believed, the precise wording of the clause made it possible to argue that some American citizens could not claim the benefit of the provision. In 1787 no one seems to have considered the possible distinction to be drawn here between state citizens and citizens of the United States. It did not take long for the courts to realize, however, that when strictly construed, the language of the clause ("The citizens of each State") excluded some persons who were national, but not state, citizens. Chief Justice Marshall held in 1805

22. Houston v. Moore, 5 Wheat. 1, 33 (U.S., 1820).
23. Murray v. M'Carty, 2 Munford 393, 399 (Va., 1811). See generally Antieau, "Paul's Perverted Privileges," *W. and M. Law Rev.*, IX (1967–1968), 1–38, and Arnold J. Lien, *Concurring Opinion: The Privileges or Immunities Clause of the Fourteenth Amendment* (St. Louis, Mo., 1957), esp. chaps. 1–2.
24. Butler v. Farnsworth, 4 F. Cas. 902, 903 (U.S.C.C., 1821).
25. Wiley v. Parmer, 14 Ala. 627, 629 (Ala., 1848).

that citizens of the District of Columbia were not state citizens, and the same reasoning was applicable to American citizens resident abroad or in the territories.[26] Such persons could only qualify under the clause by removing to a state, for, in the words of another of Marshall's opinions in 1832, "a citizen of the United States, residing in any state of the Union, is a citizen of that state."[27]

Clearly some United States citizens might not be citizens of a state, but it was never contemplated that some state citizens might be excluded from the privileges of "general citizenship" that this clause was designed to protect. Although Roger B. Taney would later attempt to justify just such an exclusion of free black state citizens in the Dred Scott case, he had no doubts about the correlation of state and national citizenship when he wrote his dissenting opinion in the *Passenger Cases* (1849), insisting that "every citizen of a State is also a citizen of the United States."

Living as we do under a common government, charged with the great concerns of the whole Union, every citizen of the United States, from the most remote States or Territories, is entitled to free access, not only to the principal departments at Washington, but also to its judicial tribunals and public offices in every State and Territory of the Union. And the various provisions in the Constitution of the United States—such, for example, as the right to sue in a federal court sitting in another State, the right to pursue and reclaim one who has escaped from service, the equal privileges and immunities secured to citizens of other States, and the provision that vessels bound to or from one State to another shall not be obliged to enter and clear or pay duties—all prove that it intended to secure the freest intercourse between the citizens of the different States. For all great purposes for which the Federal government was formed, we are one people, with one common country. We are all citizens of the United States; and, as members of the same community, must have the right to pass and repass through every part of it without interruption, as freely as in our own States.[28]

All American citizens residing in a state seemed to be protected by the privileges and immunities clause, but it was unclear which of their specific rights were thus guaranteed. Were the "privileges and immunities of citizens" to be deduced from the nature of free republican governments? Were they rights specifically defined or

26. Hepburn v. Ellzey, 2 Cranch 445, 452–453 (U.S., 1805).
27. Gassies v. Ballon, 6 Pet. 761, 762 (U.S., 1832).
28. Passenger Cases, 7 How. 283, 482, 492 (U.S., 1849). The Dred Scott case is discussed in detail below, chap. 10.

implied by federal statutes, treaties, and the Constitution? Were they the rights enjoyed under the constitutions and laws of the separate states? Or were the privileges and immunities of citizenship—the incidents of the status, in technical terms—to be defined by some combination of these ideas? The answer to these questions was crucial, for the rights comprehended in the phrase "privileges and immunities of citizens" were under a constitutional guarantee, presumably enforceable by the national government against the states and thus directly pertinent to the problem of federal relations.[29]

A leading case decided in the aftermath of the Civil War held that Article IV, section 2, was designed only to secure an equality of rights between out-of-state citizens and state citizens, thus recognizing a national citizenship status while allowing the individual states to define separately the incidents of that status. In *Paul* v. *Virginia* (1869), Justice Stephen J. Field held that "the privileges and immunities secured to citizens of each State in the several States, by the provision in question, are those privileges and immunities which are common to the citizens in the latter States under their Constitution and laws by virtue of their being citizens."[30] Several antebellum cases had apparently pursued the same logic. In the opinion of Chancellor James Kent of New York in *Livingston* v. *Van Ingen* (1812), the clause "means only that citizens of other states shall have equal rights with our own citizens."[31] Alabama's Chief Justice Henry W. Collier agreed with his colleague Justice Chilton in 1848 that the "general citizenship" conferred by Article IV, section 2, was meant "to communicate all the privileges and immunities, which the citizens of the same State would be entitled to, under the like circumstances."[32] Chancellor Nicholas Ridgely of Delaware also argued that the clause was designed to confer all rights enjoyed by state citizens upon citizens of other states: "To

29. The Constitution did not specifically authorize congressional enforcement of this clause, an apparent "defect" that would not be repeated in drafting the Fourteenth Amendment. Still, even without specific authorization, courts upheld federal legislation to enforce clause two (extradition of fugitives from justice) and clause three (rendition of fugitive slaves) of Art. IV, sec. 2. See Antieau, "Paul's Perverted Privileges," *W. and M. Law Rev.*, IX (1967–1968), 26–27, and his discussion of Prigg v. Pennsylvania, 16 Pet. 539 (U.S., 1842), and Kentucky v. Dennison, 24 How. 66 (U.S., 1860).
30. Paul v. Virginia, 8 Wall. 168, 180 (U.S., 1869).
31. Livingston v. Van Ingen, 9 Johns. Rep. 507, 577 (N.Y., 1812).
32. Wiley v. Parmer, 14 Ala. 627, 631 (Ala., 1848).

what purpose are all privileges and immunities reserved to the citizens of each State, if a State can discriminate between its own citizens and the citizens of another State in the privileges of a citizen, and unless the same method to protect their property is allowed to them. If we may cut and carve and limit and restrain other citizens in the exercise of our privileges as citizens, it is evident that they are not entitled to all privileges and immunities of citizens in this State."[33]

Most judicial interpretations of the privileges and immunities clause in the antebellum years led in a different direction. Instead of conceiving the clause as a guarantee of the separate "packages of rights" associated with state citizenship, most judges seemed to assume that the privileges and immunities secured by the clause were rights valid nationally, either by virtue of their fundamental nature or by their inclusion in federal law or federal purposes. As early as 1795 the Supreme Court affirmed that "the right of acquiring and possessing property, and having it protected, is one of the natural, inherent and inalienable rights of man," and a number of state and federal judicial decisions acknowledged this right to be among the privileges and immunities of citizenship.[34] The right of access to federal tribunals was also beyond state interference, though this was an example of a right attached to national citizenship by the federal compact rather than by its inherent character.[35] Chief Justice Isaac Parker of Massachusetts argued that the Constitution made "the people of the United States subjects of one government *quoad* every thing within the national power and jurisdiction," and Justice Washington, speaking for the Supreme Court, agreed: "For all national purposes, embraced by the federal constitution, the states and the citizens thereof are one, united under the same sovereign authority, and governed by the same laws."[36] Such

33. Douglass v. Stephens, 1 Del. Ch. 465, 472–473 (Del., 1821).
34. Vanhorne v. Dorrance, 2 Dall. 304, 310 (U.S.C.C., 1795). See also Campbell v. Morris, 3 Harris & McHenry 535, 554 (Md., 1797, 1800); Terrett v. Taylor, 9 Cranch 43, 50 (U.S., 1815); Douglass v. Stephens, 1 Del. Ch. 465, 477; and Delassus v. United States, 9 Pet. 117, 133 (U.S., 1835). See also Justice Story's claim in Wilkinson v. Leland, 2 Pet. 627, 657 (U.S., 1829), that the "fundamental maxims of free government seem to require, that the rights of personal liberty and private property should be held sacred."
35. Catlett v. Pacific Ins. Co., 5 F. Cas. 291, 296 (U.S.C.C., 1826); Suydam v. Broadnax, 14 Pet. 67, 74 (U.S., 1840); Marshall v. Baltimore & Ohio R.R. Co., 16 How. 314, 326 (U.S., 1853); Union Bank of Tennessee v. Jolly's Adm'rs, 18 How. 503, 507 (U.S., 1855).
36. Abbot v. Bayley, 6 Pickering 89, 91 (Mass., 1828); Buckner v. Finley, 2 Pet. 586, 590 (U.S., 1829).

statements clearly presumed that certain rights not dependent on the laws of the separate states were associated with national citizenship.

The clearest and most detailed attempt to elucidate the meaning of the privileges and immunities clause before the Civil War was made by Justice Bushrod Washington in 1823 in the circuit court case of *Corfield* v. *Coryell*. Washington felt "no hesitation" in restricting the meaning of the clause to those privileges "which are, in their nature, *fundamental*; which belong, of right, to the citizens of all free governments; and which have, at all times, been enjoyed by the citizens of the several states which compose this union, from the time of their becoming free, independent and sovereign." His enumeration of these fundamental rights comprehended

protection by the government; the enjoyment of life and liberty, with the right to acquire and possess property of every kind, and to pursue and obtain happiness and safety; subject nevertheless to such restraints as the government may justly prescribe for the good of the whole. The right of a citizen of one state to pass through, or to reside in any other state, for the purposes of trade, agriculture, professional pursuits, or otherwise; to claim the benefit of the writ of habeas corpus; to institute and maintain actions of any kind in the courts of the state; to take, hold and dispose of property, either real or personal; and an exemption from higher taxes or impositions than are paid by the other citizens of the state; may be mentioned as some of the particular privileges and immunities of citizens, which are clearly embraced by the general description of privileges deemed to be fundamental: to which may be added the elective franchise, as regulated and established by the laws or constitution of the state in which it is to be exercised.[37]

"Judge Washington's words, as reported, far over-leaped his thought," one modern constitutional historian has contended, insisting that it would have been "preposterous" for any judge to argue that the clause "forced each State to accord citizens from sister States whatever the Supreme Court might hold to be 'fundamental' in 'free governments,' regardless of whether the State made

---

37. Corfield v. Coryell, 4 Wash. C.C. 371, 380–381 (U.S.C.C., 1823). The opinion was followed in Bennett v. Boggs, 3 F. Cas. 221 (U.S.C.C., 1830), and Chief Justice Lemuel Shaw described it as "plausible, if not satisfactory," in Dunham v. Lamphere, 3 Gray 268, 276 (Mass., 1855). For similar attempts to list rights included in the guarantee, see Taney's dissent in the Passenger Cases (quoted above, text at n. 28); Crandall v. Nevada, 6 Wall. 35, 43–44 (U.S., 1867); Ward v. Maryland, 12 Wall. 418, 430 (U.S., 1870).

any such provisions for its own citizens."[38] Justice Washington and those judges who held that the clause referred only to rights enjoyed under state laws were not thinking in such terms, however. Whether the privileges and immunities of citizenship were to be defined by the states or with reference to "national purposes," no one doubted that certain fundamental rights were included; neither state nor federal judges believed that the law granted them the arbitrary, "instrumentalist" power to make the clause mean "whatever they wished."

The idea that a core of fundamental rights lay at the heart of the privileges and immunities of citizenship pervaded the judicial interpretation of the clause. Whether the courts determined that the constitutional provision guaranteed out-of-state citizens an equality of rights enjoyed by citizens of the state or that it protected a configuration of privileges attached specifically to national citizenship, they never questioned that certain broadly defined rights were included in its scope. The conflicting opinions in the Delaware case of *Douglass* v. *Stephens* (1821) illustrate this assumption clearly. In his dissenting opinion, Chancellor Ridgely thought that Article IV, section 2, required the state to confer the privileges of state citizenship on citizens of other states, but that fundamental rights defined those privileges: "The rights of enjoying and defending life and liberty, of acquiring and protecting reputation and property,—and, in general, of attaining objects suitable to their condition, without injury to another, are the rights of a citizen; *and all men by nature have them.*" Chief Justice Kensey Johns, on the other hand, voiced the majority contention that "the privileges and immunities to be secured to all citizens of the United States are such only as belong to the citizens of the several States; which includes the whole United States, and must be understood to mean, such privileges as *should be* common, or the same in every State." Johns concluded: "The privileges and immunities, etc., are not enumerated or described; but they *are* all privileges common in the Union,—which certainly excludes those privileges which belong only to citizens of one or more States, and not to those in every other State."[39] The majority

38. Charles Fairman, *Reconstruction and Reunion, 1864–88, Part One*, in Paul A. Freund, ed., *The Oliver Wendell Holmes Devise History of the Supreme Court of the United States*, VI (New York, 1971), 1123.
39. Ridgely, Douglass v. Stephens, 1 Del. Ch. 465, 470 (Del., 1821); Johns, *ibid.*, 476–477, my emphasis.

here held that not all rights were fundamental, that not all rights "were" or "should be" common in fact throughout the nation. Hence, not all differentiations between privileges enjoyed by state citizens and citizens from out-of-state were unconstitutional.[40] But some rights were fundamental, and these constituted the privileges and immunities of national citizenship.

If judicial interpretations of the privileges and immunities clause focused primarily on the problem of what rights persons could claim as a consequence of their "general citizenship," those of Article III, section 2, directly addressed the question of who qualified as state citizens. Of particular importance in this article was the clause investing the federal judiciary with jurisdiction in cases "between citizens of different States." In determining whether the federal courts could hear specific cases under this provision, judges were forced to consider how state citizens were to be identified.[41]

As Justice Washington pointed out in federal circuit court in 1821, the "only rational construction of the constitution, in relation to federal jurisdiction, is to limit it to cases where the suit is between the resident citizens of different states, or where an alien is a party." To be sure, "the citizen of one state is to be considered as a citizen of each, and every other state in the union" in questions involving privileges and immunities; but diversity jurisdiction could not logically depend upon the national dimension of citizenship.[42] If the courts allowed a citizen of Pennsylvania to bring fellow Pennsylvanians into federal tribunals by claiming that they were equally citizens of other states, state courts would in effect be rendered

40. A number of the cases cited above justified different regulations for the exercise of property rights, e.g., by in-state and out-of-state citizens. Disputes often centered on whether a particular regulation constituted an infringement or denial of the fundamental right. In Conner v. Elliott, 18 How. 591, 593, 594 (U.S., 1856), Justice Benjamin Curtis argued that the meaning of privileges and immunities should be determined on just such a case-by-case basis, noting that not all rights were incidents of citizen status. Along the same lines, see Smith v. Maryland, 18 How. 71 (U.S., 1855).

41. See above, chap. 8, at n. 50. The specific jurisdiction of the federal courts was, of course, regulated in detail by statute, beginning with the Judiciary Act of 1789. For discussions of such statutes, see Max Farrand, "The Judiciary Act of 1801," *AHR*, V (1899–1900), 682–686; Kathryn Turner, "Federalist Policy and the Judiciary Act of 1801," *WMQ*, 3d Ser., XXII (1965), 3–32; Dwight F. Henderson, *Courts for a New Nation* (Washington, D.C., 1971); and Felix Frankfurter and James M. Landis, *The Business of the Supreme Court: A Study in the Federal Judicial System* (New York, 1928), esp. 4–55. About 140 statutes dealing with jurisdiction before 1875 are listed, *ibid.*, 331–335. I have examined these, but have found no additional light on citizenship issues.

42. Butler v. Farnsworth, 4 F. Cas. 902, 903 (U.S.C.C., 1821).

superfluous. By the same token, if the courts looked to a person's "general citizenship" rather than his particular state membership—for example, allowing a Pennsylvanian to claim that all New Yorkers were equally citizens of Pennsylvania—then federal diversity of citizenship jurisdiction would be meaningless.

Early Supreme Court decisions ruled that when a case was submitted to the federal courts under diversity jurisdiction the citizenship of the parties had to be stated explicitly. One of the counsel in *Bingham* v. *Cabot* (1798) argued that "a citizen of one state may reside for a term of years in another state, of which he is not a citizen; for citizenship is clearly not co-extensive with inhabitancy." The Court agreed with the proposition, and since the record in the case did not explicitly set forth the status of the parties, jurisdiction was denied.[43] The rule was steadfastly followed by the federal courts; an analogous rule was adopted by the state tribunals when establishing their own jurisdiction.[44]

The courts gradually worked out the standards by which they would judge the validity of claims to citizenship in a particular state. In 1802 the circuit court for the district of Pennsylvania suggested that a person was to be considered a citizen of the state in which he was permanently domiciled.[45] Justice Washington later confirmed the rule when he declared that for purposes of determining jurisdiction, citizenship "means nothing more than residence. . . . If a citizen of one state should think it proper to change his domicil, and to remove himself and family, if he have one, into another state, with a bona fide intention of abandoning his former place of residence, and to become an inhabitant or resident of the state to which he removes; he becomes, immediately upon such removal, accompanied with such intention, a resident citizen of that state."[46] Justice Thompson elaborated this principle when he stated that "the party so removing" from one state to another need not acquire all the

---

43. Bingham v. Cabot, 3 Dall. 382, 383–384 (U.S., 1798).
44. See, e.g., Abercrombie v. Dupuis, 1 Cranch 343 (U.S., 1803); Wood v. Wagnon, 2 Cranch 9 (U.S., 1804); Capron v. Van Noorden, 2 Cranch 126 (U.S., 1804); Brown v. Keene, 8 Pet. 112, 115 (U.S., 1834). In 1841 the New Hampshire Superior Court held that it was not sufficient to state a party's alien birth in order to claim that he was an alien, since naturalization or the parent's citizenship might mean that he was in fact a citizen. In this instance, it was alien status that had to be pleaded specifically. Campbell v. Wallace, 37 Am. Dec. 219 (N.H., 1841).
45. Knox v. Greenleaf, 4 Dall. 360 (U.S.C.C., 1802).
46. Cooper v. Galbraith, 6 F. Cas. 472, 476 (U.S.C.C., 1819).

privileges of state citizenship "before he can come into the circuit court of the United States."[47]

Still, residence alone was not in itself sufficient evidence for sustaining a claim to citizenship. As Justice Story noted in 1828, temporary or fraudulent residence without a bona fide *"animo manendi"* or an intent to remain would not cause the court to hear cases in which one party had removed solely for the purpose of gaining access to federal tribunals.[48] Justice John McLean agreed that in such instances "citizenship may depend upon the intention of the individual." This intent was most clearly shown by acts, not by declarations: "An exercise of the right of suffrage is conclusive on the subject; but acquiring a right of suffrage, accompanied by acts which show a permanent location, unexplained, may be sufficient."[49]

For the purposes of diversity jurisdiction, the federal courts demanded that the parties be citizens of different states. Although judges recognized the inequity of the situation, they construed the Constitution to exclude persons who were United States citizens but not state citizens from the purview of this clause. Citizens of the District of Columbia were not "State citizens" within the meaning of the Constitution, argued Chief Justice Marshall in 1805, though the seat of the government could be considered a "state" in a "general theoretical sense." The anomaly could only be rectified by legislative, not judicial, action.[50] The same exclusion applied to territorial citizens.[51] Justice Samuel Nelson acknowledged in 1851 that a "person may be a citizen of the United States, and not a citizen

47. Catlett v. Pacific Ins. Co., 5 F. Cas. 291, 296 (U.S.C.C., 1826).
48. Case v. Clarke, 5 F. Cas. 254 (U.S.C.C., 1828). In Burnham v. Rangeley, 4 F. Cas. 773 (U.S.C.C., 1845), the court denied jurisdiction, although the party's removal from the state had been bona fide and not merely a ploy to evade jurisdiction. Here, the defendant's removal took him out of this circuit.
49. Shelton v. Tiffin, 6 How. 163, 185 (U.S., 1848). Conversely, the court held in Evans v. Davenport, 8 F. Cas. 845 (U.S.C.C., 1849), that when a person did not exercise the rights of a citizen in the new state, it could not be presumed that he lost his original citizenship. The state courts generally agreed that residence and citizenship were not coextensive. See, e.g., Curd v. Letcher, 3 J. J. Marshall 443 (Ky., 1830); Harris v. John, 6 J. J. Marshall 257 (Ky., 1831); Gilman v. Thompson, 34 Am. Dec. 714 (Vt., 1839). On the other hand, "citizen" as used in various statutes was sometimes interpreted to mean "inhabitant" or "permanent resident," as in Risewick v. Davis, 19 Md. 82 (Md., 1862). In this sense, a resident alien could be considered, for commercial purposes, a citizen: Field v. Adreon, 7 Md. 209 (Md., 1854).
50. Hepburn v. Ellzey, 2 Cranch 445, 452–453 (U.S., 1805); also Reily v. Lamar, 2 Cranch 344 (U.S., 1805).
51. Corp. of New Orleans v. Winter, 1 Wheat. 91 (U.S., 1816).

of any particular state," but it was the latter status, not the former, that sustained the federal courts' authority to hear disputes "between citizens of different States."[52]

Judicial rulings on the meaning of the privileges and immunities and of the diversity jurisdiction clauses helped clarify the peculiarly dualistic character of American citizenship. However, they by no means fully determined the political questions that might arise from the definition of that status. Interpretations of Article IV, section 2, focused primarily on the rights attached to the status of citizen rather than on how to determine who was qualified to claim citizenship. Similarly, the contested issues in the diversity jurisdiction decisions for the most part raised discussion of practical matters of operational policy rather than consciously devised statements or principles of political philosophy. In none of the instances cited above was there any implication that the individual states were bound to accept the federal judges' rulings on a party's citizenship other than in the particular case in question. Judicial pronouncements on the relevance of intent, residence, and so forth aimed at providing a working definition of state citizenship for the purpose of establishing diversity jurisdiction; they did not purport to create general criteria that the states were obliged to use in identifying their own members. That is, one could argue, consistently with these decisions, that a man whom the federal courts described as a New York citizen for purposes of sustaining jurisdiction did not have to be considered a state citizen by New York itself.

Considerable ambiguity thus remained at the heart of this notion of dual citizenship. Perhaps the most crucial unresolved question was whether the individual citizen owed his primary loyalty to his state or to the United States as a whole, and this determination involved the issue of whether state citizenship flowed from national

52. Prentiss v. Brennan, 19 F. Cas. 1278, 1280 (U.S.C.C., 1851). Special problems were involved when an "artificial person" (corporation) was a party. In Bank of United States v. Deveaux, 5 Cranch 61 (U.S., 1809), and Hope Ins. Co. v. Boardman, *ibid.* 57, the Supreme Court held that a corporation could only litigate in federal courts in consequence of the citizenship of its members, which must appear on the record. If all members were from one state, the corporation could sue as a citizen of that state. Bank of Augusta v. Earle, 13 Pet. 519 (U.S., 1839), denied, however, that corporations could claim citizenship rights under the privileges and immunities clause. Louisville, Cincinnati, & Charleston R.R. v. Letson, 2 How. 497 (U.S., 1844), created a presumption or legal fiction that all members of a corporation were citizens of the state of incorporation, thus vitiating the Deveaux rule. For a complete discussion of this issue, see Edwin Merrick Dodd, *American Business Corporations until 1860, with Special Reference to Massachusetts* (Cambridge, Mass., 1954), 150–155.

citizenship or vice versa. The courts dealt directly with this problem only in reference to naturalized citizens. There, membership in the nation, conferred under the authority of the central government, clearly preceded and drew forth membership in the state.[53] With respect to the primary loyalty and status of native citizens, however, the courts maintained a judicious silence.

This silence was broken in one hotly contested case arising from the nullification crisis in South Carolina. The convention that met in March 1833 to respond to President Jackson's Force Bill included among its acts an authorization for the state legislature to bypass the ordinary constitutional amendment procedure and to establish immediately a new oath of allegiance for state officers.[54] Deep divisions between nullifiers and unionists prevented the convention from specifying the exact wording of this oath, but the nullifiers did manage to add an amendment, hoping to control its future interpretation: "The allegiance of the citizens . . . is due to the . . . State, and . . . obedience only, and not allegiance, is due . . . to any other power or authority, to whom a controul over them has been or may be delegated by the state."[55]

Under the authority of the convention's instructions, the legislature passed an act requiring all militia officers to swear that they would "be faithful and true allegiance bear to the State of South Carolina." The constitutionality of the act was quickly challenged. In two separate cases, persons elected as militia officers refused to take the oath and sued for their commissions. Judge Elihu H. Bay denied the suit of Edward McReady, upholding the oath and denying the commission; Judge John S. Richardson upheld James McDonald's claim to his commission and declared the state militia oath unconstitutional. The two cases were taken together to the South Carolina Court of Appeals.[56]

Justices John B. O'Neall, David Johnson, and William Harper divided over the issue, with unionists O'Neall and Johnson successfully holding the oath unconstitutional against the protestations of

53. See Marshall's statement in Gassies v. Ballon, above at n. 27, made with reference to a naturalized citizen.
54. For an excellent analysis of the Nullification Crisis in general and of this episode in particular, see William W. Freehling, *Prelude to Civil War: The Nullification Controversy in South Carolina, 1816–1836* (New York, 1966), esp. 309–321.
55. Quoted *ibid.*, 312.
56. *Ibid.*, 314, 316–317.

the nullifier Harper.[57] O'Neall was the only one to claim specifically that the oath, as explained in advance by the convention, violated the Federal Constitution and the allegiance owed by every citizen of the United States.[58] He contended that in this country sovereign authority had been delegated to two levels of government acting together. "They must together be sovereign," he declared, "for together they constitute the entire will of the people, by which the government is to be administered in the State and in the United States." Allegiance was owed to both governments, which, operating correctly within their respective spheres, constituted a single sovereign in a "legal point of view."[59] As Judge Johnson stated, "The Government of the State is a compound of the State and Federal Government, and to demand the allegiance of the citizen to one only and exclusively, is to require of him only half his duty."[60]

O'Neall denied Harper's nullificationist contention that the United States was essentially a confederation in which each member state retained complete sovereignty and in which the people —associated and organized into local communities of allegiance— merely submitted to the central government for specified limited purposes.[61] He disdained Harper's argument that the Union was a government from which the states could withdraw voluntarily and unilaterally:

It seems to me to be perfectly clear, that the government created by the Federal Constitution, is strictly speaking and in every sense, a government of the people; not of the whole people in the United States, as among themselves, but in this point of view, of the people of each State. As between it and foreign states, or nations it is a government of all the people of the United States, in one aggregate community. It is a government: for within its prescribed constitutional limits, it acts upon the people, and enforces against them its laws, through its own judiciary, or that of each State.[62]

---

57. For the opinions, see State v. Hunt, 2 Hill 1, 209–282 (S.C., 1834).

58. Johnson stressed that the oath act violated the state constitution's amendment procedure, though the oath itself was innocuous, being open to judicial interpretation that could require allegiance to state and nation. *Ibid.*, 243–244.

59. O'Neall, *ibid.*, 215.

60. Johnson, *ibid.*, 247.

61. Harper, *ibid.*, 256–258.

62. O'Neall, *ibid.*, 219.

Since the militia oath, as explained by the convention, demanded that state officers swear exclusive allegiance to South Carolina, it violated the principles of government embedded in the Federal Constitution and must be held void.

William Harper, the dissenter, was actually the only judge to consider the issue of double allegiance in the hypothetical case of fundamental conflict between state and nation. If a state chose to withdraw from the Union, he asked, would all its citizens be bound in law to withdraw, or could they refuse out of obedience to a higher power? In other words, did the national dimension of citizenship—the allegiance purportedly owed to the United States—override and control an individual's obligation to his state? Harper clearly thought not. Since he viewed citizenship as membership in and allegiance to the state, he denied that any other authority could command the individual citizen's ultimate obedience.[63]

O'Neall and Johnson did not provide a clear answer to Harper's hypothetical dilemma; both were content to focus their attention on the case at hand and to aver simply that every citizen owed a double allegiance. A conflict between one's duties to the state and to the nation was unthinkable as long as the federal system operated correctly. The law in question could be declared void without deciding which allegiance was primary, and the national harmony was better preserved by evading, rather than by directly confronting, the deeply disturbing problem raised by Judge Harper.

The question of where the citizen's primary loyalty lay arose not only in the South Carolina controversy over allegiance but also in the more general, long-term debate over the idea of expatriation.[64] The peculiar facts surrounding the birth of the Republic made it difficult, if not impossible, for Americans to deny the general right of expatriation, and there were few who thought to do so, at least in theory. The Revolution and the practice of naturalization proved that men could abjure their old allegiance and embrace new loyal-

---

63. Harper, *ibid.*, 257, 270.
64. See generally Tsiang, *Question of Expatriation*; Rising Lake Morrow, "The Early American Attitude toward the Doctrine of Expatriation," *American Journal of International Law*, XXVI (1932), 552–564, and his more detailed study, "Citizenship in Anglo-American Diplomacy from 1790 to 1870" (Ph.D. diss., Harvard University, 1931); Duane Douglas Smith, "The Evolution of the Legal Concept of Citizenship in the United States" (Ph.D. diss., Ohio State University, 1936), chap. 6.

ties. Yet unanticipated difficulties awaited legislators and jurists who sought to translate this abstract right into concrete procedures for renouncing the peculiarly dualistic allegiance characteristic of federal citizenship. Officers of the executive branch felt little hesitation in defending expatriation in clashes with foreign governments; but Congress and the courts proved far more cautious, for to institutionalize the right in the domestic sphere necessitated a direct confrontation with complex and potentially divisive problems of federal relations.

The claim that every man had the right to slough off his allegiance and to discard his citizenship was a direct extrapolation and generalization of the right of election affirmed during the Revolution.[65] Indeed, it was Virginia's wartime citizenship statute of 1779 that most unequivocally affirmed the right. In order to "preserve to the citizens of this commonwealth that natural right which all men have of relinquishing the country in which birth or other accident may have thrown them, and seeking subsistence and happiness wheresoever they may be able, or may hope to find them," the act provided a simple public procedure by which a man could renounce his citizen status and exercise "his natural right of expatriating himself."[66]

Virginia was virtually alone in establishing such a statutory provision, but many Americans recognized expatriation as an inherent and fundamental right.[67] When Congress discussed the terms of the naturalization bill of 1795, William Vans Murray insisted that the government's policy of adopting aliens necessarily implied the acceptance of expatriation: "The very proviso to naturalize an alien, without inquiry as to the consent of his own country having been previously obtained, seems to be predicated on the principle for which he contended—that a man has the right to expatriate himself without leave obtained; if he has not, all our laws of this sort, by which we convert an alien into a citizen completely, must be ac-

65. See above, chap. 7.
66. Law of May 1779, Hening, ed., *Statutes of Va.*, X, 129. The person had to declare, orally or in writing, in any county or general court, that he wished to renounce his citizenship, then actually remove from the state.
67. Morrow, "Citizenship in Anglo-American Diplomacy," 82, notes that Kentucky passed a similar statute "years later." St. George Tucker observed that the constitutions of Pennsylvania and Vermont explicitly guaranteed the right of emigration, "or, as I rather chuse to call it, expatriation," Tucker, ed., *Blackstone's Commentaries*, I:2, Note K, "The Right of Expatriation Considered," 96.

knowledged to be a violation of the rights of nations."[68] The United States upheld the power of aliens to renounce their native allegiance; it thus could not consistently deny that right to its own citizens.

Executive officers for the most part agreed that expatriation was valid, though they qualified this acceptance with certain restrictions and limitations. Secretary of State Thomas Jefferson stated his opinion in 1793:

Our citizens are entirely free to divest themselves of that character by emigration, and other acts manifesting their intention, and may then become the subjects of another power, and free to do whatever the subjects of that power may do. But the laws do not admit that the bare commission of a crime amounts of itself to a divestment of the character of citizen, and withdraws the criminal from their coercion. They could never prescribe an illegal act among the legal modes by which a citizen must disfranchise himself; nor render treason, for instance, innocent, by giving it the force of a dissolution of the obligation of the criminal to his country.[69]

Similar principles were repeatedly affirmed by the secretaries of state—by James Madison in 1803, John Quincy Adams in 1823, John Forsyth in 1839, Daniel Webster in 1842, John C. Calhoun in 1844, and Edward Everett and William L. Marcy in 1853 and 1855.[70]

There were special reasons why diplomatic officers preferred to acknowledge the right of expatriation. Disputes over the allegiance of individuals born in one country and naturalized in another could build into serious international crises. The impressment controversy with Great Britain—a long-festering sore even before 1776— was exacerbated after independence by the conflicting claims of the two nations; the United States insisted that naturalized subjects had lost their native allegiance and had become citizens, while Great Britain denied the right of expatriation and maintained the doctrine of perpetual allegiance.[71] The right to adopt new citizens was

68. *Annals of Congress*, 3d Cong., 2d sess., 1028.

69. Jefferson to Gouverneur Morris, Aug. 16, 1793, Francis Wharton, ed., *State Trials of the United States during the Administrations of Washington and Adams* (Philadelphia, 1849), 89n.

70. See Madison to Murray, June 16, 1803, Moore, ed., *Digest of Int. Law*, III, 735; J. Q. Adams to Anderson, May 27, 1823, *ibid.*, 563–564; Forsyth to Emerson, Jan. 23, 1839, *ibid.*, 718–719; Webster to Thompson, July 8, 1842, *ibid.*, 564–565; Calhoun to Pageot, Nov. 30, 1844, *ibid.*, 565; Everett to Marsh, Feb. 5, 1853, *ibid.*, 759; and Marcy to Kinney, Feb. 4, 1855, *ibid.*, 759.

71. See generally Kettner, "Subjects or Citizens? A Note on British Views," *Va. Law. Rev.*, LXII (1976), *passim*.

stoutly defended by Secretary of State James Monroe, who insisted
to the British minister on the eve of the War of 1812, "It is impossible for the United States to discriminate between their native and
naturalized citizens, nor ought your Government to expect it, as it
makes no such discrimination itself."[72]

This rigorous policy was capable of leading to deadlocks that
could only be settled by force or by the threat of force. When Great
Britain refused to release six seamen captured on the U.S.S. *Nau-
tilus*, claiming that they were British subjects, the American government immediately declared that a double number of British
prisoners would be held as hostages and meet the same fate as the
Americans. Britain seized six more seamen, then twenty-three,
then forty-six; the United States retaliated, number for number.
Cooler minds ultimately prevailed, and Britain eventually agreed
to exchange her captives without trying them for treason.[73] But the
lesson seemed clear enough. It was more conducive to international
harmony to affirm the right of one's citizens or subjects to expatriate themselves than to insist upon their continued and immutable
allegiance.

In practice, American diplomatic officials often acknowledged
that their policies should be flexible in cases of contested national
status. Secretary of State Marshall tempered his claim that "no nation has a right to question the validity" of an American naturalization by admitting a possible exception in the case of any nation
"which may have a conflicting title to the person adopted."[74] Following the war with Great Britain the government often compromised its generally affirmed principle that naturalized and native
citizens deserved equal protection abroad. Secretary of State Marcy
illustrated this when he wrote to the minister to Sardinia, "This
government cannot rightfully interpose to relieve a naturalized

72. Monroe to Foster, May 30, 1812, Moore, ed., *Digest of Int. Law*, III, 563. The right of
naturalized citizens to diplomatic protection even against their native country was also
affirmed by Secretaries of State James Buchanan and Lewis Cass, *ibid.*, 566, 576, 574.
Attorney General Jeremiah S. Black advised President Buchanan, July 4, 1859, that "naturalization does ipso facto place the native and the adopted citizen in precisely the same
relations with the government under which they live, except in so far as the express and
positive law of the country has made a distinction in favor of one or the other." Benjamin F.
Hall, comp., *Official Opinions of the Attorneys-General of the United States . . .* (Washington,
D.C., 1852–1858), IX, 356.
73. Morrow, "Early American Attitude toward Expatriation," *Am. Jour. Int. Law*,
XXVI (1932), 559–561. See also Tsiang, *Question of Expatriation*, 45–49.
74. Marshall to Humphreys, Sept. 23, 1800, Moore, ed., *Digest of Int. Law*, III, 563.

citizen from the duties or penalties which the laws of his native country may impose upon him on his voluntary return within its limits."[75] By mid-century the government's working policy seemed to be to extend diplomatic protection to naturalized citizens except in cases when the native government, within its own jurisdiction, sought to enforce obligations owed by the expatriate antecedent to his original departure.[76]

Although the executive branch vigorously affirmed the right of expatriation, either to defend American naturalization policies or to forestall potentially explosive international conflicts, the judiciary proved to be extremely circumspect in dealing with the issue. Whenever cases involving the question of expatriation arose, judges frequently avoided making categorical statements of right, preferring instead to find other less controversial grounds for their decisions. As a result, state and federal courts followed no clear and coherent doctrine in this area. Some judges showed a great reluctance to diverge too widely from the old English notion of perpetual allegiance, though the traditional version of this doctrine was never applied in full force. Rather, even the most conservative American jurists accepted the possibility of expatriation by consent, relying on the concept of contractual allegiance articulated in the years immediately preceding the Revolution.[77]

The conservatives' theory of expatriation was simply stated. Citizenship implied a contract between the individual and the society of which he was a member. The contract could be broken when one of the parties defaulted on his obligations, but it could not be dissolved unilaterally. The right of expatriation thus was not fully analogous to the right of election in cases involving the dissolution of an old government or society. Rather it was a conditional, limited right that could be exercised only in specific circumstances and with the government's consent.

This doctrine was fully acknowledged in the opinion delivered by Chief Justice Oliver Ellsworth in the case of *United States* v. *Williams* (1799).[78] Isaac Williams, a citizen from Connecticut, had accepted a privateering commission from French authorities in

75. Marcy to Daniel, Nov. 10, 1855, *ibid.*, 569. See also Forsyth to Strobecker, Apr. 15, 1835, and Henry Wheaton to Knoche, July 24, 1840, *ibid.*, 564.
76. Cass to Schleiden, Apr. 9, 1859, and Cass to Hofer, June 14, 1859, *ibid.*, 571–573.
77. See generally chap. 6 above.
78. United States v. Williams, Wharton's *State Trials* 652 (U.S.C.C., 1799).

alleged violation of the treaty of amity between the United States and Great Britain. Williams's defense argued that he had gone to France in 1792, had explicitly renounced his American citizenship, and had been duly naturalized. He had served in the French military forces even before the treaty in question had been ratified, and he had lived in French territories for over three years. According to his counsel, these facts sufficiently proved that Williams had forsaken his American character and could not be charged with violating laws requiring a neutral conduct of citizens.[79]

Ellsworth refused to agree that the stated facts absolved Williams of his responsibilities as a citizen. The two "great principles" deciding this case were first, "that all members of a civil community are bound to each other by compact" and, second, "that one of the parties to this contract cannot dissolve it by his own act." There was no default here, nor was there any explicit governmental consent to Williams's expatriation. The nation was sparsely settled with "no inhabitants to spare." It was publicly committed to neutrality, and thus its policy was to restrain its citizens from acts supporting any belligerent power that might result in international hostilities. The government's naturalization policies did not contradict this position, but implied merely a willingness to allow individuals to acquire a dual allegiance; there was no affirmation of an absolute right of expatriation. Since neither explicit nor implicit consent could be shown, Williams remained a citizen, subject to the penalties established for those who violated the neutrality regulations.[80]

When read carefully Ellsworth's opinion neither denied the possibility of expatriation nor upheld the rule that allegiance was inherently natural and perpetual, but its qualifications were not apparent to less conservative spirits. Ellsworth's decision was criticized immediately and bitterly by the Jeffersonian-Republican press, which saw the decision as part of a broad Federalist attempt to impose the old tyrannical principles of English law on the new Republic. "T. C. of Northumberland" wrote to the Philadelphia *Aurora* that the decision was "manifestly unjust," charging that the "birth-duty of allegiance is a fraud upon infancy. It is the adult only who can decide what country best suits his interest, but the chains of slavery are fastened upon him while he is incapable of resisting,

79. *Ibid.*, 652–653.
80. *Ibid.*, 653, 654. See also the Trial of Gideon Henfield, Wharton's *State Trials* 49, esp. 78, 85 (U.S.C.C., 1792).

and ignorant of the evil."[81] Another outraged Virginian quoted in the New London (Connecticut) *Bee* agreed:

The natural right previously secured to the citizens of this State [Virginia] by law to expatriate themselves is abrogated; by what? Not by the Constitution of the United States, not by laws made under it, but by the judgment of a Federal Court. An obsolete principle, applicable only to the personal right of the former feudal sovereigns of England, is enforced by a free republic founded on a total denial of such rights. . . . By the Chief Justice's opinion, we are still the subjects of Great Britain.[82]

The reaction to the *Williams* decision may have helped persuade the courts that categorical denials of the validity of unilateral expatriation were unwise. At any rate, subsequent decisions were much more tentative in suggesting the necessity of explicit governmental consent for the renunciation of allegiance. Judge Gabriel H. Ford of the New Jersey Supreme Court denied that the law permitted a "man to lay aside his allegiance as he puts off a garment," but he did not clearly disavow the right in all cases.[83] Although Justice Washington was not prepared in 1815 to "admit, that a citizen of the United States can throw off his allegiance to his country, without some law authorizing him to do so," his mind was still open on the subject.[84]

In essence, the contention of these opinions was that, for all practical purposes, no right of expatriation existed until competent legal authorities prescribed a mode for its exercise. Both state and national courts challenged this claim, maintaining that every individual had the right to expatriate himself under general principles of natural, common, or international law. When positive statutes did not provide specific guidelines, such courts cited universal theoretical principles in determining cases concerning the validity of an individual's renunciation of citizenship.

As might be expected, the Virginia judiciary stoutly affirmed the right of every American citizen to "become an alien by expatriation."[85] In the case *Murray* v. *M'Carty* (1811), Judge Cabell specifi-

81. Quoted in Tsiang, *Question of Expatriation*, 35.
82. *Ibid.*
83. Coxe v. Gulick, 5 Halstead 328, 331 (N.J., 1829).
84. United States v. Gillies, 25 F. Cas. 1321, 1322 (U.S.C.C., 1815). For an able discussion of the issue, see [John Lowell], *Review of a Treatise on Expatriation by George Hay, Esq. . . . By a Massachusetts Lawyer* (Boston, 1814).
85. Justice Roane, Read v. Read, 5 Call 160, 191 (Va., 1804).

274 Principles, Politics, and Prejudice

cally declared that this right was not dependent upon positive law: "Nature has given to all men the right of relinquishing the society in which birth or accident may have thrown them; and of seeking subsistence and happiness elsewhere; and it is believed that this right of emigration, or expatriation, is one of those 'inherent rights, of which, when they enter into a state of society, they cannot, by any compact, deprive, or devest their posterity.' " Positive laws (like the Virginia statute of 1779) could regulate the manner and prescribe the evidence necessary to prove the exercise of the right; but "in the absence of regulations *juris positivi*, the right must be exercised according to the principles of general law."[86]

Kentucky judges followed Virginia's lead. Several decisions of the court of appeals acknowledged that persons emigrating from Kentucky to the independent Republic of Texas could be deemed to have expatriated themselves, given proof of their intent. Justice George Robertson disclosed the theoretical grounds for this policy, declaring in *Alsberry* v. *Hawkins* (1839): "Allegiance, in these United States, whether local or national, is, in our judgment, altogether *conventional*, and may be repudiated by the native as well as adopted citizen, with the *presumed* concurrence of the government, without its formal or express sanction. Expatriation may be considered a practical and fundamental doctrine of America."[87] The court looked to the specific circumstances of individual cases to determine whether the intent of the parties had been to remove temporarily without renouncing their citizenship or to reject consciously their old allegiance in favor of a new one.[88]

---

86. Murray v. M'Carty, 2 Munford 393, 396–397 (Va., 1811). Roane observed apropos of the expatriation statute that "the exercise of that right, under the act, is as free as air, and depends on volition only." *Ibid.*, 405.

87. Alsberry v. Hawkins, 9 Dana 177, 178 (Ky., 1839), my emphasis. The same court had evaded the question earlier in Brooks v. Clay, 3 A. K. Marshall 545, 549 (Ky., 1821).

88. Alsberry v. Hawkins held that the woman had expatriated herself by remaining in Texas long after her husband's death, and she was therefore incapable of taking a dower in lands purchased before removal. A similar conclusion was reached in Trimbles v. Harrison, 1 B. Monroe 140 (Ky., 1840). In Moore v. Tisdale, 5 B. Monroe 352, 354 (Ky., 1845), Justice Thomas A. Marshall observed that in cases like these—all of which involved the status of married women—the principle was the same as in cases respecting infant election during the Revolution. "[I]nfants and others under disability, tho' bound for the time, by the elections of those having authority over them, have still the right, within a reasonable time after the disability is removed, to determine for themselves, and that a disaffirmation of the election which had been made for them, relating back, defeats, so far as they are concerned, the election itself, and fixes their character from the beginning according to their own choice, made when they had a right to decide for themselves."

It was not enough merely to affirm that the doctrine of perpetual allegiance was "not compatible with" republican constitutions or to conclude that the idea of expatriation followed "necessarily from our naturalization laws."[89] If the courts were to follow any consistent policy in distinguishing between real and pretended acts of expatriation, they must articulate broad principles regulating the right. It was almost self-evident that not "every act inconsistent with the duty is inconsistent with the state of a citizen."[90] The nation could not allow an individual to cast off his allegiance at whim or under all circumstances, "otherwise he might appear in arms against his country without being guilty of treason."[91] "The cause of removal must be lawful," declared Supreme Court Justice Paterson; "otherwise the emigrant acts contrary to his duty, and is justly charged with a crime."[92] Expatriation was a "reasonable and moral right which every man ought to be allowed to exercise," agreed Justice Iredell, but it was subject to such limitations "as the public safety or interest requires, to which all private rights ought and must forever give way." Surely no citizen should be allowed to renounce his allegiance until he had fulfilled the obligations he owed as a member of society.[93]

The courts frequently contended that no citizen could discard his status in the midst of war. However, the New York Supreme Court and Court of Errors disagreed with the arguments of Alexander Hamilton that this prohibition was absolute and universal; they sustained the validity of a Frenchman's expatriation and his subsequent naturalization in the United States, although he had left his homeland while it was engaged in mortal war against Great Britain.[94] On the other hand, New York judges recognized the relevance of national security interests when they denied that a person

89. Jackson v. Burns, 3 Binney 75, 85 (Pa., 1810); Beavers v. Smith, 11 Ala. 20, 29 (Ala., 1847).

90. Justice James Wilson, Trial of Gideon Henfield, Wharton's *State Trials* 49, 85 (U.S.C.C., 1792).

91. Judge Gabriel H. Ford, Coxe v. Gulick, 5 Halstead 328, 331 (N.J., 1829).

92. Talbot v. Janson, 3 Dall. 133, 153 (U.S., 1795). In the lower court, Judge Thomas Bee implied that expatriation could never be complete, for the expatriate could never "injure the country of his first and native allegiance, by open violation of her treaties with foreign powers." Jansen v. Vrow Christina Magdalena, 13 F. Cas. 356, 360–361 (U.S.D.C., 1794).

93. Talbot v. Janson, 3 Dall. 133, 163, 162 (U.S., 1795).

94. Duguet v. Rhinelander (N.Y., 1800, 1802), in Goebel, Jr., ed., *Law Practice of Alexander Hamilton*, II, 649–650, discussed and sustained in Coulon v. Bowne (N.Y., 1803), *ibid.*, 552–554.

could divest himself of his American citizenship without leaving the country. To rule otherwise would be to admit that American armies could be transformed into enemy hosts by wholesale expatriations on the battlefield.[95]

The courts insisted that a citizen who wished to expatriate himself must do so in a regular manner and in full knowledge of the consequences of his act. Justice Joseph Story, like many others, was dubious about the right of a citizen to renounce his allegiance in the absence of specific legislative permission. "Assuming, for the purposes of argument" that such a renunciation was possible, however, Story insisted that it be performed in a proper manner and spirit: "[I]t is perfectly clear, that this cannot be done without a *bona fide* change of domicil under circumstances of good faith. It can never be asserted as a cover for fraud, or as a justification for the commission of a crime against the country, or a violation of its laws, when this appears to be the intention of the act."[96] In a rare instance when a federal court acknowledged a man's successful removal from the country and assumption of a foreign allegiance in good faith, the former citizen paid a high personal cost: "He has lost his character as a citizen of the United States; he has abandoned his rights as such; he cannot now claim them, and cannot be called upon to perform any of the duties incident to that character."[97] As Chief Justice Marshall warned, the successful expatriate "loses the rights which are connected with those obligations. He becomes an alien."[98]

Not surprisingly, both state and federal courts frequently preferred to evade adjudicating the question of expatriation instead of confronting it squarely; alternative legal doctrines were available that often allowed the courts to sidestep citizenship questions. Perhaps most useful was the tenet that residence or domicil could establish a person's "national character" for certain purposes, for it permitted the courts to determine many specific controversies without ruling on more sensitive and difficult problems of expatriation.

A complex maritime prize case of 1804 illustrated the utility of

95. Fish v. Stoughton, 2 Johns. Cas. 407, 408 (N.Y., 1801).
96. The Santissima Trinidad, 7 Wheat. 283, 348 (U.S., 1822).
97. Juando v. Taylor, 13 F. Cas. 1179, 1182 (U.S.D.C., 1818). Although this is the only early federal court affirmation of the right I have found, Justice William P. Van Ness claimed that the right "is constantly recognized, and has never in any way been restrained." *Ibid.*, 1181.
98. Chacon v. Eighty-Nine Bales of Cochineal, 5 F. Cas. 390, 393 (U.S.C.C., 1821).

the doctrine of domicil. The controversy arose when a United States naval vessel commanded by Captain Alexander Murray seized the schooner *Charming Betsy* for alleged violations of the Non-Intercourse Act prohibiting trade with France.[99] Jared Shattuck, owner of the captured vessel and of most of its cargo, had been born in Connecticut, but had resided for many years in the Danish island of St. Thomas. There he received the privileges of a Danish *burgher* and swore allegiance to the king of Denmark. The question raised now was whether Murray had acted legitimately in seizing the *Charming Betsy*, or whether the captured schooner should be considered the property of a Danish subject immune to the restrictions imposed on American citizens.[100]

The central issue was the validity of Shattuck's expatriation. Shattuck's lawyers argued the right of every citizen to choose a new allegiance if he did so with "a *bona fide and honest intention, at a proper time, and in a public manner*." Shattuck had left the United States when the world was at peace, he had resided, married, and acquired land abroad, and he had taken an oath of allegiance to the Danish monarch. Although the United States lacked a prescribed means of expatriation, Shattuck had done all he could to make his intention public and notorious.[101] On the other hand, opposing counsel denied that Shattuck's actions met the three general requirements for expatriation: fitness in time, fairness of intent, and publicity of the act. He had not definitely settled abroad until the mid-1790s, when war raged in Europe; he had not shown a foreign naturalization, but a "burgher's brief," a "mere license to trade"; and he had never formally disclaimed his right to the protection of the American government.[102]

Chief Justice John Marshall finally delivered the opinion of the Supreme Court in February 1804. He reasoned that it was not necessary to decide whether a person "can divest himself absolutely of that character [of citizenship] otherwise than in such a manner as may be prescribed by law." Rather the issue could be settled by the notion that domicil or permanent residence established national

---

99. For a general discussion of the trade restrictions, see Alexander DeConde, *The Quasi-War: The Politics and Diplomacy of the Undeclared War with France, 1797–1801* (New York, 1966), 266.
100. Murray v. The Charming Betsy, 2 Cranch 64, 65–66 (U.S., 1804).
101. *Ibid.*, 71, 92–94.
102. *Ibid.*, 75–87.

character for commercial purposes. Whether Shattuck was in fact a Danish subject or an American citizen—whether he had truly expatriated himself—was irrelevant. He had settled on St. Thomas and had traded in the character of a Danish subject. Thus the Court could hold that he was not affected by the law banning Americans from trade with the French.[103]

The doctrine that residence or domicil could define "national commercial character" was eminently useful. The federal courts quickly adopted it to settle a number of prize cases resulting from the War of 1812 and the international hostilities that accompanied the revolutionary convulsions in Latin America. Although some details respecting evidence for domicil remained to be worked out, the courts generally found little difficulty in pursuing a consistent policy. Americans who resided abroad in the jurisdiction of an enemy nation during wartime were to be considered subjects of that foreign power for the purposes of commercial retaliation, marine insurance, and the like. Citizens could not change their domicil *flagrante bello* in order to acquire the trading advantages of neutrals or to achieve other fraudulent aims. But they could live abroad, acquire foreign privileges, and trade as foreign subjects without fearing punishment from United States tribunals as lawbreakers or traitors.[104]

The doctrine of domicil allowed the courts to dispose of the particular cases brought before them; it did nothing to resolve the ambiguity of the government's policy toward expatriation. Clearly the majority opinion in the country acknowledged the existence of the right itself. The differences focused primarily on determining how the right could be exercised without jeopardizing the safety and security of the community as a whole. Expatriation was distinguished from the right of election in revolutionary situations: the former ended a relationship of rights and obligations; the latter

103. *Ibid.*, 120.
104. For examples of the use of this doctrine, see The Venus, 8 Cranch 253 (U.S., 1814); The Frances, 8 Cranch 335 (U.S., 1814); The Mary & Susan, 1 Wheat. 46 (U.S., 1816); The Dos Hermanos, 2 Wheat. 76 (U.S., 1817); and The Pizarro, 2 Wheat. 227 (1817). Similar ideas were applied in state cases dealing with the effect of domicil in Texas: Wooldridge v. Wilkins, 3 Howard (Miss.) 360 (Miss., 1839); Wynn v. Morris, 16 Ark. 414 (Ark., 1855). And the executive branch denied that foreign residence was the same as expatriation for political purposes when it insisted that a New Yorker who had fled to Canada could not be tried by court-martial as a spy, though he might be liable to charges of treason. Elijah Clark Case (1812), discussed at length, with documents, in Hugh Henry Brackenridge, *Law Miscellanies* . . . (Philadelphia, 1814), 409–419.

created such a bond. The acts were related, but not identical. Each individual stood alone and made a unilateral decision when he accepted the rights and obligations of citizenship; but it was not quite so clear that he could lay down those obligations without considering the interests of others. Although no relationship based on volition and consent could be deemed perpetual without becoming a travesty, its severance or dissolution ought to conform to broad principles of justice and equity.

Significantly, those who sought precise guidelines institutionalizing expatriation thought more in terms of a "uniform rule"—a standardized, impersonal procedure—than in terms of special private acts of legislation releasing named individuals from their allegiance. The fundamental assumption seems to have been, in the words of Justice Robertson of Kentucky, that American allegiance was "altogether conventional."[105] Rules regulating time, place, manner, and intent would help protect the community's interests and expectations by giving order and predictability to the general process of expatriation; but the individual's choice to remain or to leave must be preserved. Positive laws were to regulate the exercise, not to create the right.

Given the broad theoretical consensus on the legitimacy of the right of expatriation, what made the courts so cautious in affirming the right in practice? The major obstacle to vigorous action was revealed as early as 1795 in the case of *Talbot* v. *Janson*.[106] The controversy, ultimately brought to the Supreme Court, originated when Edward Ballard, operating in obvious collusion with William Talbot, captured a Dutch brigantine commanded by Joost Janson. Although Ballard and Talbot were both from Virginia, they claimed to have had expatriated themselves. Ballard specifically averred that he had conformed to the provisions of Virginia's statute of 1779. The weight of the evidence indicated that both men had obtained their French naturalizations purely for the purpose of undertaking privateering expeditions illegal for American citizens, and no convincing proof existed that either man had removed or intended to remove permanently from the United States. However, Virginia authorities had formally declared that Ballard, at least, was no longer a citizen.[107]

105. Alsberry v. Hawkins, 9 Dana 177, 178 (Ky., 1839).
106. Above, n. 92.
107. Talbot v. Janson, 3 Dall. 133, 133–137 (U.S., 1795).

The case clearly raised the significant issue of "dual citizenship." Talbot's counsel insisted on the general legitimacy of expatriation and doubted the propriety and safety of any regulation of the right. They also disputed the authority of the Supreme Court to prescribe the proper form of expatriation, especially in Ballard's case. Since Ballard had already conformed to the provisions of the Virginia law of 1779, no further action was necessary or possible: "Not being a citizen of *Virginia*, he cannot be deemed a citizen of the *United States*."[108]

Janson's lawyers disagreed. In the first place, fraud and duplicity discredited the bona fide intent of the expatriations. More important, even if Ballard's Virginia expatriation were valid, it did not necessarily end his status as a citizen of the United States. Emigration and expatriation were matters incidental to the regulation of naturalization, and their control ought to be vested exclusively in Congress. A Virginia expatriation might therefore have some local impact, but it could "have no effect on the political rights of the Union."[109]

The justices delivered their opinions seriatim, and William Paterson alone confronted this issue directly:

The act of the legislature of Virginia, does not apply. Ballard was a citizen of Virginia, and also of the United States. If the legislature of Virginia pass an act specifying the causes of expatriation, and prescribing the manner in which it is to be effected by the citizens of the state, what can be its operation on the citizens of the United States? If the act of Virginia affects Ballard's citizenship, so far as it respects that state, can it touch his citizenship so far as it regards the United States? Allegiance to a particular state, is one thing; allegiance to the United States is another. Will it be said, that the renunciation of allegiance to the former implies or draws after it a renunciation of allegiance to the latter? The sovereignties are different; the allegiance is different; the right, too, may be different.[110]

The other justices stressed rampant fraud and illegality without mention of the central nation/state issue. Their response symbolized the cautious attitude that both jurists and legislators would adopt almost invariably in the future.[111]

108. *Ibid.*, 145.
109. *Ibid.*, 151.
110. *Ibid.*, 153–154.
111. James Iredell affirmed the general right of expatriation, but doubted that it had been properly exercised here. James Wilson had heard the case below, and gave no opinion here. William Cushing stated *obiter* that expatriation must be bona fide and manifested at least by

Justice Paterson pointedly noted in his opinion in *Talbot* v. *Janson* that "a statute of the United States relative to expatriation is much wanted."[112] Indeed, Congress considered the possibility of such a statute several times. One section of a bill of 1797 that would have banned American citizens from serving in foreign military forces proposed a mode of renunciation similar to that established in Virginia. W.C.C. Claiborne urged the House to accept the bill, for it was "no more binding for citizens born in the United States to continue citizens of the United States, than it was for a Roman Catholic or Protestant to continue of that opinion, when he arrived at years of maturity, and could judge for himself." William Smith added his support, observing that the "idea of a man being compelled to live in this country, contrary to his will, seemed to be repugnant to our ideas of liberty."[113] Again in 1808 the right of expatriation was virtually admitted in a bill proposing "that if any citizen shall expatriate himself, he shall, *ipso facto*, be deemed an alien, and ever after, be incapable of becoming a citizen."[114] In these instances, discussion of the issue was brief and opposition to legislation general, but unfocused. Some members hesitated to provide for expatriation at a time when international tension was high and the security of the nation itself was threatened. Others found the thought of regularizing the process by which a citizen renounced his country distasteful and wished to avoid any appearance of sanctioning the act. A few speakers voiced doubts about Congress's constitutional authority to legislate on this matter.[115]

The legitimacy of a national expatriation act was finally discussed in full during the winter of 1817–1818. Representative Thomas B. Robertson of Louisiana submitted a bill modeled on the Virginia statute of 1779 providing an easy, convenient procedure by which American citizens could exercise the right to renounce their citizenship. Robertson had already introduced a proposal to this effect in 1814, but the bill had been shelved on the grounds that it might

---

emigration. John Rutledge denied the necessity of deciding this issue, noting only that a French naturalization did not absolutely prove an intent to relinquish American allegiance. *Ibid.*, 159–170.

112. *Ibid.*, 154.

113. *Annals of Congress*, 5th Cong., 1st sess., 350.

114. *Ibid.*, 10th Cong., 1st sess., 1871.

115. Detailed summaries of the proposals and debates can be found in Morrow, "Early American Attitude toward Expatriation," *Am. Jour. Int. Law*, XXVI (1932), 555–556; and Tsiang, *Question of Expatriation*, 37–40, 56–57.

complicate current negotiations with England. He now sought decisive action in order to clarify the government's policy with respect to this vital and fundamental right.[116]

The fate of the earlier bill had deeply disturbed the Louisiana congressman: "It was considered, as most principles are that are not borrowed from the common law—that beautiful system which, next to special pleading, receives the most rapturous encomiums from a certain quarter in this House—as fraught with great mischief; it was said to interfere with pending negotiations; to encourage desertion, piracy, and I do believe every sin in the decalogue." To his mind, the right of expatriation—"an acknowledged, a natural right"—needed no defense: "Let the enemies of human rights—at all times the real innovators—support their claim." Ancient practice and the best republican theory agreed that all men should enjoy the unimpeded "right to pursue their own happiness." The ambiguous decisions of the American courts could not be allowed to stand. It was the duty of the legislature to act with honesty, vigor, and high principle, affirming the right of expatriation on the basis of "its own abstract truth."[117]

The ensuing debate on Robertson's bill reveals that politicians were fully aware of the delicate nation/state issues involved in expatriation. Kentucky Representative Richard C. Anderson, Jr., set the tone for much of the discussion when he affirmed the right, but denied Congress's constitutional power to regulate it. No clause of the fundamental law justified this exercise of authority. "If the power [to regulate the mode of expatriation] exists in any legislative body," Anderson argued, "it is in the State Legislatures." If they did not have this power, then the individual citizen retained the absolute and untrammeled exercise of the right. Although Anderson was inclined to think that the latter alternative was the most appropriate, he had no doubt that the present bill was "unnecessary and unconstitutional."[118]

James Pindall of Virginia agreed with Anderson that Congress lacked constitutional authority here, not only because no clause delegated power in this area but also because the whole idea of a national expatriation statute violated the principles of the American system: "Allegiance is fitted to sovereignty, and, whenever we

116. *Annals of Congress*, 15th Cong., 1st sess., 448, 495.
117. *Ibid.*, 1029, 1030, 1035.
118. *Ibid.*, 1039, 1040, 1042; speech of William Lowndes (S.C.), *ibid.*, 1050–1052.

discover sovereignty, we affirm that a correspondent allegiance must exist elsewhere. The States of this Union are sovereign, and . . . every citizen sustains a two-fold political capacity first, with respect to the State; secondly, with respect to the United States." Congress had no authority to release a citizen from the allegiance he owed his state, and unless a national expatriation statute could have this effect, it was virtually meaningless.[119] Louis McLane of Delaware explained: "The relation to the State government was the basis of the relation to the General Government, and therefore, as long as a man continues a citizen of a State, he must be considered a citizen of the United States. I affirm that the Government of the United States cannot withhold its protection from, or dispense with its duties to any man, while he remains a citizen of any individual State, and that any act of the General Government, absolving him from such duties, would be inoperative."[120] A person remaining a state citizen could always invoke the privileges and immunities clause to claim the rights of a United States citizen, rendering a "national expatriation" meaningless and absurd.[121]

Speeches in support of the bill failed to come to terms with this argument. Richard M. Johnson of Kentucky pointed out that judicial decisions against attempted expatriations imperiled the right itself and made some practical provision for its exercise "not only expedient, but indispensable." Thomas W. Cobb of Georgia denied that the proposed measure would in any way affect state sovereignty, but he gave no convincing arguments in support of this view. Neither man could refute the arguments directed against the bill.[122] Even those who, like James Johnson of Virginia, were "humiliated" to hear the right called into question preferred the measure's defeat, holding that any regulation might threaten the right.[123] In the end, the bill was rejected.[124]

Why did Congress refuse to act? Theoretical objections to expatriation constituted no effective barrier to legislation, tainted as they were by an apparent kinship with "the old feudal doctrine of

119. *Ibid.*, 1045, 1047–1050.
120. *Ibid.*, 1057.
121. *Ibid.*, 1079.
122. Johnson, *ibid.*, 1044; Cobb, *ibid.*, 1069.
123. *Ibid.*, 1063–1064; and see the speeches of William Lowndes (S.C.) and Joel Abbott (Ga.), *ibid.*, 1050–1052, 1086–1087.
124. For the initial vote on the bill and the final vote on subsequent alternative amendments, see *ibid.*, 1070, 1107.

perpetual allegiance."[125] Nor is the answer to be found in practical difficulties and general policy considerations. Some congressmen may have been swayed by fears that legislation would permit and even promote defections in wartime, complicate diplomatic relations with foreign powers, or encourage emigration and depopulation. However, such issues were superficial and easily provided for by carefully constructed laws. Rather the opposition in Congress reflected the same fears that lay behind the conservative policies of the courts: to act on expatriation meant confronting, determining, and perhaps overturning the delicate balance between the respective authority of nation and state.

By the end of the second decade of the nineteenth century the close connection between the concept of citizenship and the issue of federal relations was clear. Because jurists and legislators were aware that their actions concerning the law of citizenship had significant implications for the political structure of the Republic, they often hesitated to extend the full logic of their ideas. The courts quickly held that the national government alone could regulate the admission of aliens to citizenship, but they refused to specify that all citizens, native or naturalized, derived their character as citizens in the first instance from the central government. Judges drew the lines dividing the state and national aspects of citizenship in order to define jurisdiction and the rights that were actionable in federal tribunals, but they did not claim to decide who had the authority to establish conclusively who were citizens of each state. Jurists and politicians acknowledged that citizens had the right to renounce their allegiance, but they declined to say who could regulate the right and thus in essence determine who did and who did not owe obedience to government.

The remaining ambiguity about the nature of citizenship reflected a fundamental uncertainty about the structure of the nation created by the Revolution. In the conflict with Great Britain Americans had argued that they owed their primary loyalty to George III in his capacity as the head of the individual colonial governments. They denied any primal obligation to Parliament or to the imperial community in which they were not represented. Rather their allegiance, their membership, was defined with reference to the local

125. Johnson (Va.), *ibid.*, 1063.

community and the parochial government authorized by their direct consent. When the colonists withdrew from the British empire, they did so as separate, organized, and self-governing communities.

The shared experience of the Revolution blurred the sense of the individuality of the separate colonial societies and made the idea of a common nationality more convincing. The idea acquired legal force under the comity clause of the Articles, though most Americans still considered the states to be the primary object of political allegiance. The central government during the 1780s, much to the despair of a growing body of nationalists, was still very much the creature of the states, clearly subordinate to the sovereign local communities. Yet the idea that citizens of the several states were fellow citizens had a persuasiveness, sustained by the evidence of obvious common interests, that contributed to the creation of a strong and truly national central government.

The creation of the federal system at the Convention of 1787 would not have been possible without this sense of a national community. But the older concept that gave primacy to the local group, the smaller and more immediate community, did not simply fade. It took time for Americans to adjust their political thinking to recognize that every citizen could be a member of two societies, delegating authority to two levels of governmental institutions, receiving protection from and owing obedience to two embodiments of the sovereign people.

The Revolutionary generation had fought against the pretensions of Parliament in defense of the belief that the people were truly sovereign, that all legitimate government rested on the consent of the people. They now justified the hitherto unthinkable notion of two governments in the same state by contending that political institutions were simply agents of the people and not in themselves sovereign. Yet this contention did not destroy *"imperium in imperio"* as a political solecism; the concept was simply transformed to a new kind of problem. Governments gained legitimacy by representing the sovereign people, by operating within the limits imposed by the people. But at the very core of the American experiment remained the question "Who are 'the People'?"

Although the question was perhaps not immediately obvious, it gradually became apparent in the specific problems involving citizenship and federal relations. The individual citizen was the basic irreducible unit. The crucial issue that almost invariably arose in the contexts discussed here was whether those individual units combined to form one sovereign people or many. If national citizenship was primary, then the will of the people was to be determined by the majority of the national community, regardless of state groupings. If state citizenship was fundamental, then government by consent meant a mandatory recognition of the majority will in each and every state.

American leaders preferred not to choose between these two alternatives. As long as state and national interest could be balanced by compromise and mutual good will, there was no need to confront the matter. But there was no guarantee that this evasion could be sustained indefinitely. Indeed, the nullifying South Carolina judge William Harper had already posed the issue in sharp form. Could the citizen of any state disobey the claims of his fellow state citizens in the name of a higher authority? Did the allegiance each citizen owed to the national community override and control the obligations he owed to his state? Were the people sovereign in their national character, or was the Union truly formed of multiple sovereign communities?

The problems of naturalization, expatriation, and court jurisdiction were all intertwined with these questions, yet they could be partially answered without a definitive theory of federal relations. It was the different and vastly more difficult problem of slavery that moved Americans to confront the matter. Increasingly, the subtle, slow-working dynamic of Revolutionary ideals highlighted the moral, ideological, and legal anomalies inherent in the status of the black man. The position of the Negro—and, to a lesser extent, of the Indian—contradicted the Republic's fundamental principles of equality and consent. And Americans could not resolve these contradictions without either destroying central components of the concept of citizenship or facing the potentially explosive question of whether nation or state was supreme.

CHAPTER 10

Birthright Citizenship and the Status of Indians, Slaves, and Free Negroes

By about 1820 certain central assumptions regularly appeared in discussions of American citizenship. The status was based on individual consent. It entitled the citizen to fundamental privileges and immunities and in return bound him to assume duties and obligations toward the community as a whole. Citizenship constituted membership in a federal community requiring allegiance to nation and state. Aliens who proved capable of meeting impersonal requirements, who conformed to standard measures of fitness for membership, could be admitted into the ranks of the sovereign people by naturalization. With the single exception of eligibility for the presidency, they thereby acquired the same status and rights as native citizens.

But who counted as native citizens? No one appeared to reexamine and justify Coke's idea of the "natural-born citizen." Americans merely continued to assume that "birth within the allegiance" conferred the status and its accompanying rights. Natives were presumably educated from infancy in the values and habits necessary for self-government, and there was no need to worry about their qualifications for membership. To be sure, it might trouble some that the volitional, consensual character of birthright citizenship was in fact more theoretical than real owing to the lack of concrete legislation regulating the abstract right of expatriation; but this concern led only to agitation for laws that would allow citizens to withdraw from membership. It did not shake the presumption that membership was acquired automatically by all those born under the Republic.

Because these assumptions about the origins, character, and effects of citizenship were so pervasive, the clash of principle and prejudice marking the period between 1820 and the Civil War was intensified and rendered virtually insolvable. The confrontation began, in effect, with the debates over Missouri; some Americans found themselves facing glaring inconsistencies between their professed principles of citizenship and their deep-seated desire to exclude certain groups permanently from the privileges of membership. For two of these pariah groups—Indians and slaves—the exclusion could be rationalized within the stated framework of broad principles. But for free blacks, no compromise seemed possible without surrendering either principle or prejudice. Here the problem of citizenship focused; here the lines were drawn.

The Indians were perhaps the most easily isolated group excluded from the privileges and immunities of citizenship. Throughout the colonial period Americans had distinguished Indians according to their individual circumstances.[1] Government officials dealt with independent and unconquered tribes on the fringes of the white settlements as sovereign political communities, negotiating with them as with foreign nations.[2] Tributary tribes who remained within the effective jurisdiction of the local governments and who, like the Narragansetts of Rhode Island, did "confesse, and most willingly and submissively acknowledge" themselves "to be the humble, loving and obedient servants and subjects of his Majestie" formally enjoyed the protection of the monarch; but they

1. See generally W. Stitt Robinson, Jr., "The Legal Status of the Indian in Colonial Virginia," *VMHB*, LXI (1953), 247–259; Yasu Kawashima, "Jurisdiction of the Colonial Courts over the Indians in Massachusetts, 1689–1763," *NEQ*, XLII (1969), 532–550; Yasu Kawashima, "Legal Origins of the Indian Reservation in Colonial Massachusetts," *American Journal of Legal History*, XIII (1969), 42–56; and James P. Ronda, "Red and White at the Bench: Indians and the Law in Plymouth Colony, 1620–1691," Essex Inst., *Hist. Colls.*, CX (1974), 200–215.
2. William S. Johnson contended that whites dealt with the Indians not as independent states, but "as with savages, whom they were to quiet and manage as well as they could, sometimes by flattery, but oftener by force." Quoted in Smith, *Appeals to the Privy Council*, 434n.

customarily retained a subordinate jurisdiction and a separate legal existence under the crown.[3] Individual Indians who had lost or relinquished their tribal connection apparently merged into the white population.[4]

The status of the tribes that were gradually encompassed by the white settlements posed the most perplexing problems. For example, between 1704 and 1773 a series of three royal commissions, each of whose judgments was appealed to the Privy Council, wrestled with the adjudication of conflicting claims over lands in Connecticut put forward by the Mohegan Indians, the government, and certain private landholders.[5] Connecticut argued that the dispute was one between parties equally subject to the laws and courts of the colony and alleged that the Indians' claims had been extinguished in the seventeenth century—with the exception of a few reserved tracts that the tribe held from and under the guardianship and protection of the colonial government. The Mohegans, on the other hand, insisted that their claims rested on their original possession of all the lands, only part of which had ever been surrendered. Moreover, they contended, the matter should be determined by the commission and the Privy Council rather than by Connecticut's courts and laws, for the Mohegans were not subjects of the colony, but either subjects of the king or independent.[6]

The royal commission of 1743 upheld its own jurisdiction over

3. Act of Apr. 19, 1664, *R.I. Col. Recs.*, I, 134. See also Labaree, ed., *Royal Instructions*, II, 463–481, esp. secs. 663, 666, 679, 683, 688, 690, and Kawashima, "Jurisdiction of the Colonial Courts," *NEQ*, XLII (1969), 538–540.
4. *Ibid.*, 546–547. But Ronda, "Red and White at the Bench," Essex Inst., *Hist. Colls.*, CX (1974), 200–215, finds an increasingly "separate and unequal" treatment of Plymouth's Indians.
5. For accounts of the case, see Smith, *Appeals to the Privy Council*, 422–442, and E. Edwards Beardsley, "The Mohegan Land Controversy," New Haven Colony Historical Society, *Papers*, III (New Haven, Conn., 1882), 205–225. Richard S. Dunn, *Puritans and Yankees: The Winthrop Dynasty of New England, 1630–1717* (Princeton, N.J., 1962), 339–343, discusses the role of local white political factionalism in the first (Dudley) commission; P. Richard Metcalf, "Who Should Rule at Home? Native American Politics and Indian-White Relations," *Journal of American History*, LXI (1974), 654–657, deals suggestively with factionalism within the Mohegan tribe.
6. See the plea to the jurisdiction of the 1743 commission, *Governor and Company of Connecticut and Moheagan Indians, by their Guardians. Certified Copy of Book of Proceedings before Commissioners of Review, MDCCXLIII* (London, 1769), 122–125, hereafter cited as *Procs. Conn. v. Moheagans*. See also Richard Jackson to William Pitkin, Feb. 6, 1767, in [Albert C. Bates, ed.], *The Pitkin Papers: Correspondence and Documents during William Pitkin's Governorship of the Colony of Connecticut, 1766–1769* . . . (Connecticut Historical Society, *Collections*, XIX [Hartford, Conn., 1921]), 68–69.

the controversy.[7] Daniel Horsmanden, one of the commissioners, argued that the "Indians, though living amongst the king's subjects in these countries, are a *seperate* [sic] *and distinct people from them*," and as a consequence he concluded "that a matter of property in lands in dispute between the Indians *a distinct people* (for no act has been shown whereby they became *subjects*) and the English subjects, cannot be determined by the laws of our land, but by a law *equal to both parties*, which is the law of *nature* and *nations*; and upon *this foundation*, as I take it, these commissions have most properly issued."[8] The commission's president, Cadwallader Colden, dissented:

I can in no manner consider the Moheagan Indians as a *separate* or *sovereign state* . . . ; such a position in this country, where the state and condition of Indians are known to everybody, would be exposing majesty and sovereignty to ridicule, it might be of dangerous consequence, and not to be suffered in any of his majesty's courts, could I imagine it could have any influence on the minds of the people who heard it advanced; . . . every one of the Moheagan nation, are born under *allegiance* to the crown of Great Britain; and if any or all of them should make war upon the subjects of Great Britain, and afterwards be brought to justice, they must be adjudged *traitors*, and would be as justly hanged, drawn, and quartered, as any *other* the *king's subjects* could be in the like case.[9]

Although the majority sustained the commission's authority, overruling the plea to its jurisdiction, it is not certain that others shared Horsmanden's opinion on the independence of the tribe.[10] He seemed more favorable to the Indians than the other members, and when the commission finally ruled on the merits—against the Mohegans, and in favor of the colony—he entered a dissent.[11] In 1773 when the Privy Council finally ended the case by ruling in favor of the colony, no formal opinion was given on the tribal sovereignty issue.[12] As a result, the long proceedings left the status of

7. *Procs. Conn. v. Moheagans*, 126.
8. Opinion of Commissioner Horsmanden, *ibid.*, 126–127.
9. Opinion of President Colden, *ibid.*, 127.
10. No reasons were given by the majority for overruling the plea. Jurisdiction might have been sustained for the reasons given by Horsmanden, but it might equally well have been upheld on the grounds that the Mohegans were royal, but not local, subjects.
11. *The Moheagan Indians against the Governor and Company of Connecticut, and others. The Case of the Respondents the Governor and Company of the Colony of Connecticut . . .* ([n. p., 1770]), 34. My thanks to Professor J. Youngblood Henderson for allowing me to consult his copies of these documents, which he obtained from Houghton Library, Harvard University.
12. *Acts of Privy Council, Col.*, V, 218.

"remnant tribes" undetermined. Their condition seemed independent enough to sustain the extraordinary jurisdiction of a royal
commission, but their rights to ancient tribal lands were not protected against the encroachments of the surrounding white community.

With the completion of independence the central government
assumed primary authority over Indian affairs—or at least over
tribes outside the boundaries of existing states.[13] In 1775 the Continental Congress established northern, middle, and southern departments with boards of commissioners authorized to conclude treaties
with organized tribes, and the next year Congress established a permanent standing committee on Indian affairs. Under the Articles of
Confederation the central government retained the "exclusive right
and power of . . . managing all affairs with the Indians, not members of any of the states," and after 1789 Congress held the power to
"regulate commerce with foreign nations, and among the several
States, and with the Indian tribes."[14] From 1789 to 1848 organized
tribes were dealt with through treaties executed by the Department
of War under Congress's statutory guidelines, after which military control was replaced by civilian superintendence under the
Department of the Interior.[15]

Although the federal naturalization laws restricted admission
under the "uniform rule" to free white aliens—thus excluding
Indians—a number of treaties and statutes contemplated the possi-

13. The following summary is based principally on Lien, *Acquisition of Citizenship*,
134–150; Michael T. Smith, "The History of Indian Citizenship," *Great Plains Journal*, X
(1970), 25–35; and Francis Paul Prucha, *American Indian Policy in the Formative Years: The
Indian Trade and Intercourse Acts, 1790–1834* (Cambridge, Mass., 1962), chaps. 2–3.

14. Articles of Confederation, Art. X; U.S., *Constitution*, Art. I, sec. 8. The scope and
exclusiveness of Congress's power has been disputed from the beginning. Questions of
whether the power extended to all tribes (and tribal "remnants") or only to those not
already under one of the states in 1789, and whether this power lapsed when tribal organization "disintegrated," have been particularly difficult to resolve. For the confusion of
policies on such issues, see J. Youngblood Henderson and Russel L. Barsh, "Oyate kiN
hoye keyuga u pe (The Tribe Sends a Voice as They Come)," *Harvard Law School Bulletin*
(Apr. 1974), 10–15, (June 1974), 10–15, (Fall 1974), 17–20; Robert Ericson and D. Rebecca
Snow, "The Indian Battle for Self-Determination," *California Law Review*, LVIII (1970),
445–490; Gerald Gunther, "Governmental Power and New York Indian Lands—A Re-
assessment of a Persistent Problem of Federal-State Relations," *Buffalo Law Review*, VIII
(1958–1959), 1–26; and Francis J. O'Toole and Thomas N. Tureen, "State Power and the
Passamaquoddy Tribe: 'A Gross National Hypocrisy?'" *Maine Law Review*, XXIII (1971),
1–39. See also the cases cited below, n. 24.

15. Lien, *Acquisition of Citizenship*, 147.

bility of Indian citizenship under certain conditions.[16] The treaty with the Delawares in 1778 envisioned the admission of a separate Indian state into the Confederation; later treaties with the Cherokees in 1785 and 1835 and with the Choctaws in 1830 raised the possibility of congressional representation for these tribes.[17] None of these provisions was put into operation, but they did suggest that tribes within the nation's borders ought to be incorporated into the body politic in a more systematic way.

Other treaties and statutes indicated that an Indian who left his tribe and received a land allotment in fee simple from the government could or would thereby become a citizen. The Cherokee treaties of 1817 and 1819 provided for land grants to heads of families "who may wish to become citizens of the United States," and a treaty of 1830 explicitly established that "each Choctaw head of a family being desirous to remain and become a citizen of the States, shall be permitted to do so, by signifying his intention to the agent within six months from the ratification of this treaty."[18] In such cases, the individual Indians had to choose between tribal

16. Chief Justice Taney considered that Indians were aliens incapable of qualifying for naturalization because of the law's color restrictions, in Scott v. Sandford, 19 How. 393, 404, 420 (U.S., 1857). See also Parent v. Walmsly, 20 Ind. 82 (Ind., 1863). Jeffries v. Ankeny, 11 Ohio 372 (Ohio, 1842), allowed a person of mixed white-Indian ancestry to vote on the grounds that he was "nearer white than black"; but Judge Matthew P. Deady denied that such a person could be naturalized even after the naturalization law had been amended to allow the admission of persons of African nativity or descent—an alteration Deady considered "merely a harmless piece of legislative buncombe." In re Camille, 6 F. Rep. 256, 258 (U.S.C.C., 1880).

17. Lien, *Acquisition of Citizenship*, 135, 163–164; Annie H. Abel, "Proposals for an Indian State, 1778–1878," A.H.A., *Annual Report . . . for the Year 1907*, I (1908), 89–104.

18. Quoted in Lien, *Acquisition of Citizenship*, 164, 165. These and similar treaties often required a period of residence "with the intention of becoming citizens" before the titles became valid. See, e.g., the opinions of Attorneys General Roger B. Taney (Sept. 9, 1831) and Henry D. Gilpin (Aug. 3, 1840), in Hall, comp., *Opinions of Attorneys-General*, II, 462, III, 585–586. The Cherokee treaties of 1817 and 1819 generated a number of cases concerning requirements or proofs for citizenship. For North Carolina, see, e.g., Eu-che-lah v. Welsh, 3 Hawks 155 (N.C., 1824), and Yo-na-gus-kee v. Coleman, *ibid.* 174; and for Tennessee, Blair v. Pathkiller, 2 Yerger 407 (Tenn., 1830), Riley v. Elliston, *ibid.* 431, M'Connell v. Mousepaine, *ibid.* 438, West v. Donoho, 3 Yerger 445 (Tenn., 1832), Jones v. Evans, 5 Yerger 323 (Tenn., 1833), and State v. Ross, 7 Yerger 74 (Tenn., 1834). The Choctaw treaty of 1830 required five years' residence, and courts held that flight to avoid felony prosecution before completing this forfeited the rights to land and citizenship, though removal motivated by force, fear, or fraud did not: respectively, Newman v. Doe, 4 Howard (Miss.) 522 (Miss., 1840); and McIntosh v. Cleveland, 7 Yerger 46 (Tenn., 1834). Alabama's Supreme Court held that Indians did not become citizens under the Choctaw treaty, since they could not, "consistently with the constitution and laws, be invested with all the rights, and bound to all the duties, of citizens." Wall v. Williams, 11 Ala. 826, 837 (Ala., 1847).

membership and removal, on the one hand, and land and citizenship, on the other.[19]

The offer of citizenship to a whole tribe generally entailed the destruction of the tribal organization and government. Successive agreements with the Stockbridge Indians of Wisconsin in 1843, 1846, 1848, 1856, and 1864 vacillated between dissolving the tribe and admitting all members or retaining the separate organization and allowing individuals to choose either citizenship or tribal membership. Treaties of 1855 and 1862 with the Wyandots and Ottawas required the Indians to relinquish their tribal organization in return for the privileges of full citizenship and individual land ownership. A series of treaties in the 1860s gave the president and the courts the power to determine when adult male allottees had become sufficiently "intelligent and prudent" to warrant admission.[20] The number of Indians who gained citizenship before 1870 in such a fashion is unknown, but the commissioner of Indian affairs reported in 1891 that before 1887 only 3,072 persons had been admitted by virtue of such treaties and congressional acts.[21]

Although most Indians were barred from citizenship, their exclusion was not initially justified in theoretical terms. Several early decisions merely suggested that the "peculiar" status of individual Indians or tribes legitimized the denial of equal treatment and the special restrictions on their rights.[22] Others sustained discriminatory legislation by stressing that Indians had to be protected against the superior intelligence—and "sometimes" the "cupidity"—of whites; they should not be deemed citizens, but rather considered the "unfortunate children of the public," creatures "incapacitated, from their mental debasement" of dealing on equal terms with their white neighbors.[23] Tribal organization, however, became the primary fact justifying the denial of privileges within the accepted principles of citizenship law. Indians who could not prove admis-

19. Cohen, *Handbook of Federal Indian Law*, 153.
20. Lien, *Acquisition of Citizenship*, 164–170.
21. [U.S. Dept. of Interior], *Sixtieth Annual Report of the Commissioner of Indian Affairs to the Secretary of the Interior, 1891*, Pt. i (Washington, D.C., 1891), 21.
22. See, e.g., Peters' Case, 2 Johns. Cas. 344 (N.Y., 1801), and Jackson v. Wood, 7 Johns. Rep. 290, 295 (N.Y., 1810), where James Kent argued that Indians were not aliens in every sense, but not subjects or citizens either.
23. Quotations from Chandler v. Edson, 9 Johns. Rep. 362, 364 (N.Y., 1812); Andover v. Canton, 13 Mass. 547, 554 (Mass., 1816); and Jackson v. Reynolds, 14 Johns. Rep. 335, 337 (N.Y., 1817). See also St. Regis Indians v. Drum, 19 Johns. Rep. 127 (N.Y., 1821); Thaxter v. Grinnell, 43 Mass. 13 (Mass., 1840).

sion to citizen status under the laws or treaties above (thus presumably retaining tribal membership) could be considered aliens, for the tribes themselves—though within the jurisdiction and "protection" of the government and dependent upon it to a large degree—could be considered quasi-sovereign nations, enforcing their own laws and customs and requiring the immediate allegiance of their members.[24]

Both state and federal tribunals effectively applied the argument that individual Indians did not qualify as citizens because of their birth "within the allegiance of the tribe." Chancellor James Kent was the first to formulate the argument explicitly when he spoke for the New York Court of Errors in overturning a lower court's decision that an Oneida Indian could inherit property as a citizen. Kent observed: "Though born within our territorial limits, the *Indians* are considered as born under the jurisdiction of their tribes. They are not our subjects, born within the purview of the law, because they are not born in obedience to us. They belong, by birth, to their own tribes, and these tribes are placed under our protection and dependent upon us; but we still recognize them as national communities."[25] The party here could claim no naturalization, nor could he prove his birth under the immediate personal protection of the government; thus he was an alien. Judge Charles J. Colcock of the South Carolina Court of Appeals evinced a similar attitude in upholding the rejection of the vote proferred by John Marsh, a

24. Some states—especially those already in existence before 1789—contended that members of "remnant tribes" were under the ordinary jurisdiction of the local government and had no special national status. New York courts took this position, e.g., in Peters' Case (above, n. 22), and they argued that with respect to non-tribal lands, individual Indians came under the ordinary property laws of the state, in Jackson v. Sharp, 14 Johns. Rep. 472 (N.Y., 1817), and Jackson v. Brown, 15 Johns. Rep. 264 (N.Y., 1818). Jackson v. Goodell, 20 Johns. Rep. 188, 193 (N.Y., 1822), even held that the Oneida Indians were citizens, though this ruling was later reversed. Maine and Massachusetts denied any special national jurisdiction over tribes within their borders: Murch v. Tomer, 21 Me. 535, 537 (Me., 1842); Moor v. Veazie, 32 Me. 343, 366, 368 (Me., 1850); Danzell v. Webquish, 108 Mass. 133, 134 (Mass., 1871). New York accepted those Indians who remained in the state after 1843 as "remnants" qualified for citizenship in Strong v. Waterman, 11 Paige 607, 612 (N.Y., 1845); this was later affirmed by the federal court in United States v. Elm, 25 F. Cas. 1006 (U.S.D.C., 1877). California's Supreme Court held that Indians living apart from their tribe came under the ordinary laws of the state, and North Carolina agreed that Cherokees remaining after the removal of the main tribe were the same as other citizens: respectively, People v. Antonio, 27 Cal. 404, 405 (Cal., 1865); State v. Ta-cha-na-tah, 64 N.C. 614, 615–616 (N.C., 1870).

25. Goodell v. Jackson, 20 Johns. Rep. 693, 712 (N.Y., 1823). See also Lee v. Glover, 8 Cowen 189, 190 (N.Y., 1828); Cornet v. Winton, 2 Yerger 143, 146, 150 (Tenn., 1826); and Murray v. Wooden, 17 Wendell 531, 536, 538 (N.Y., 1837).

Pamunkey Indian who had served in the Continental army, taken an oath of allegiance, and received a federal pension. Although Marsh was a man of "unexceptionable character," the judge "regretfully" held that he was not a citizen, belonging to that "race of people, who have always been considered as a separate and distinct class, never having been incorporated into the body politic."[26]

The federal courts and executive officers concurred in excluding the Indian tribes and tribal members from citizenship. The counsel in *Johnson v. McIntosh* (1823) argued that Indians were "of that class who are said by jurists not to be citizens, but perpetual inhabitants, with diminutive rights." They were considered an "inferior race of people, without the privileges of citizens, and under the perpetual protection and pupilage of the government."[27] The Supreme Court did not comment on the citizenship issue here, merely holding that the Indian tribes did not enjoy full sovereign power over the lands they occupied; however, a clear statement was forthcoming in *Cherokee Nation v. Georgia* (1831). In this case the Cherokees sought to enjoin the state of Georgia from enforcing state laws within the territory reserved for the tribe, for the Cherokee Nation was "a foreign State, not owing allegiance to the United States, nor to any state of this Union, nor to any prince, potentate or State, other than their own." The Supreme Court could and must hear the case under the constitutional clauses giving it jurisdiction "between a State, or the citizens thereof, and foreign States, citizens or subjects" and original jurisdiction over cases "in which a State shall be a party."[28]

Although several members of the Court found this argument reasonable, the majority rejected the claim that the Cherokees constituted a "*foreign* state in the sense of the constitution." According to Chief Justice Marshall, the Indian tribes within the United States

26. State ex rel. Marsh v. Managers of Elections for District of York, 1 Bailey 215, 216 (S.C., 1829). Although race discrimination undoubtedly bolstered legal punctiliousness here, the status of Indians was not the same as that of blacks, who also were generally excluded. See, e.g., Davis v. Hall, 1 Nott & McCord 292 (S.C., 1818), where the child of a white father and an Indian mother was recognized as a citizen.

27. Johnson v. McIntosh, 8 Wheat. 543, 569 (U.S., 1823). This case was primarily important for defining the Indians' right to the land as a right of occupancy only, with the ultimate fee title residing in the government. See also Mitchel v. United States, 9 Pet. 711 (U.S., 1835); Clark v. Smith, 13 Pet. 195, 201 (U.S., 1839).

28. Cherokee Nation v. Georgia, 5 Pet. 1, 3, 16 (U.S., 1831); U.S., *Constitution*, Art. III, sec. 2, cl. 1–2. For an excellent discussion of the controversy, see Joseph C. Burke, "The Cherokee Cases: A Study in Law, Politics, and Morality," *Stanford Law Review*, XXI (1968–1969), 500–531.

were "domestic dependent nations," occupying a "state of pupilage" with respect to the United States that resembled the relation
"of a ward to his guardian." Justice William Johnson felt that the
tribes' lack of sovereign control over their territory and the unequal
conqueror-to-conquered language of the treaties were insuperable
obstacles to the recognition of Indian sovereignty. Justice Henry
Baldwin agreed that "Indian sovereignty cannot be roused from its
long slumber, and awakened to action by our *fiat*." Thompson and
Story disagreed: the tribes were foreign states and individual tribal
members were aliens.[29]

Indeed, although the disagreement on the "foreign" or "domestic dependent" character of the tribes was crucial to the jurisdictional question posed, the matter was irrelevant to the question of
individual Indian status, for the Court unanimously held that the
tribes were, in some sense, nations. In *Worcester* v. *Georgia* (1832),
these implications were clarified.[30] Marshall explained that the
relation of the Cherokees to the federal government "was that of a
nation claiming and receiving the protection of one more powerful:
not that of individuals abandoning their national character, and
submitting as subjects to the laws of a master." Justice McLean
observed that "no one has ever supposed that the Indians could
commit treason against the United States," though they could be
punished as a nation for treaty violations.[31] The tribes, in short,
were sovereign enough to give protection to and demand allegiance
from their members. All Indians who retained this relationship—
regardless of their ultimate dependency on the United States—
were aliens.

The logic was eminently serviceable, but certainly not impec-
cable. To the extent that the tribes were separate nations, their
individual members could not successfully claim to be American
citizens by birthright.[32] They were barred from ordinary natural-

29. Marshall, Cherokee Nation v. Georgia, 5 Pet. 1, 16, 17 (U.S., 1831); Johnson, *ibid.*,
22–23; Baldwin, *ibid.*, 47; Thompson, with Story concurring, in dissent, *ibid.*, 66. Indians at
peace with the U.S. could not be considered "alien enemies": Attorney General Hugh S.
Legaré to Sec. of War, Aug. 13, 1842, Hall, comp., *Opinions of Attorneys-General*, IV, 82.
And crimes committed by members of a tribe in amity with the U.S. could not be deemed
acts of war by an independent nation: United States v. Cha-to-kah-na-pe-sha, Hempst. 27
(Ark. Terr., 1824).
30. Worcester v. Georgia, 6 Pet. 515 (U.S., 1832).
31. Marshall, *ibid.*, 555; McLean, *ibid.*, 583.
32. The federal courts continued to rule against birthright citizenship for Indians even
after the ratification of the Fourteenth Amendment (discussed below, Epilogue). See McKay

ization as long as that procedure was restricted to "free white aliens," and they could gain admission only under the special statutory or treaty provisions.[33] Individuals might have the right to "expatriate" themselves from their tribe and to merge with the white population; however, this alone could not make them citizens without a positive act of the government.[34] On the other hand, if they remained members of the tribes—"nations" that were neither fully sovereign nor fully foreign—they could not demand access to the federal courts under the constitutional clause establishing federal jurisdiction over suits "between a State, or the citizens thereof, and foreign States, citizens, or subjects."[35]

The quasi-sovereign character of the tribes raised some perplexing theoretical questions concerning the extension of white jurisdiction over their members or territories. A few state courts assumed that they ought to apply tribal rather than state law where tribal members were concerned.[36] Yet states sometimes seized the initiative in extending their laws to tribes within their borders, particularly in the period when the federal executive turned wholeheartedly to a policy of removal.[37] State judicial decisions justifying such extensions tended to reject claims of exclusive or paramount federal power over the tribes, stating either that the Indians concerned

---

v. Campbell, 2 Sawyer 118 (U.S.D.C., 1871); United States v. Osborne, 6 Sawyer 406 (U.S.D.C., 1880); and the majority opinion in Elk v. Wilkins, 112 U.S. 94, 98–109 (U.S., 1884).

33. See above, n. 16.

34. The Indian's right to expatriate himself from his tribe was explicitly affirmed in United States ex rel. Standing Bear v. Crook, 25 F. Cas. 695, 699 (U.S.C.C., 1879). This did not mean that he was automatically naturalized; see above, n. 32. Ex parte Kenyon, 14 F. Cas. 353 (U.S.C.C., 1878), sometimes cited in support of the contrary opinion, actually involved a native-born white citizen who first joined, then left, the Cherokee tribe.

35. Art. III, sec. 2, cl. 1. See, e.g., Karrahoo v. Adams, 1 Dillon 344 (U.S.C.C., 1870).

36. Holland v. Pack, Peck (Tenn.) 151, 153 (Tenn., 1823), held that a Cherokee entering the white-settled part of the state should be treated the same as a sojourning Frenchman; thus the courts should apply tribal laws for offenses committed within tribal territory. Wall v. Williamson, 8 Ala. 48 (Ala., 1845), and Wall v. Williams, 11 Ala. 826 (Ala., 1847), confirmed the validity of a marriage contracted and dissolved according to Choctaw usages. Jones v. Laney, 2 Tex. 342 (Tex., 1847), sustained the validity of a slave's manumission under Chickasaw law, though the act would not have been valid under the laws of Georgia, Mississippi, or Texas. In 1855 the Supreme Court reaffirmed that the Cherokees governed themselves by their own laws, considering the tribe's situation similar to that of a territory in the second stage of development under the Ordinance of 1787: Mackey v. Coxe, 18 How. 100, 103 (U.S., 1855).

37. See particularly Glasgow v. Smith, 1 Overton (Tenn.) 144, 167 (Tenn., 1805?); State v. Tassels, Dudley (Ga.) 229 (Ga., 1830); Caldwell v. State, 1 Stewart & Porter 327 (Ala., 1832); and State v. Foreman, 8 Yerger 256 (Tenn., 1835).

were wards of the state rather than of the nation, that both state and national authorities had power in this area, or that tribal degeneration had vitiated the Indians' quasi-sovereign powers and thus the demand for a special relationship with the central government.[38] Although the federal courts generally challenged such arguments with claims of exclusive national power in this sphere and of exclusive federal authority to determine when a tribe ceased to exist in a constitutional sense, even federal decisions showed some inconsistencies and occasional retreats.[39]

The concept of tribal sovereignty had serious inherent weaknesses, but it did allow courts and executive officers considerable flexibility in determining issues of citizenship concerning white-Indian relations. For example, a number of instances occurred in which white citizens sought to gain special privileges or to evade punishment for certain offenses by contending that they had "expatriated themselves" through adoptions into Indian tribes.[40] In 1830

38. See, e.g., Hicks v. Ewhartonah, 21 Ark. 106 (Ark., 1860); McCracken v. Todd, 1 Kans. 148 (Kans., 1862); and the cases cited above, nn. 24, 37. United States v. Cisna, 1 McLean C.C. 254, 258 (U.S.C.C., 1835), suggested that concurrent state-federal jurisdiction over tribes within state borders was appropriate and that both parties ought to decide when federal responsibilities were to be terminated.

39. Worcester v. Georgia (above, n. 30) made a broad claim to exclusive national power, and this line was followed in Fellows v. Blacksmith, 19 How. 366 (U.S., 1856); United States v. Holliday, 3 Wall. 407 (U.S., 1865); The Kansas Indians, 5 Wall. 737 (U.S., 1866); and The New York Indians, *ibid.* 761. The Court generally gave Congress wide latitude in Indian affairs, affirming its right to supersede a treaty exemption by subsequent statute, though an analogous state act had earlier been deemed an unconstitutional violation of contract: see respectively The Cherokee Tobacco, 11 Wall. 616 (U.S., 1870); New Jersey v. Wilson, 7 Cranch 164 (U.S., 1812). Congress's extension of criminal jurisdiction to offenses committed by Indians within Indian territory was also upheld, though treaty exemptions for such crimes had earlier been sustained: United States v. Kagama, 118 U.S. 375 (U.S., 1886); Ex parte Crow Dog, 109 U.S. 556 (U.S., 1883). State jurisdiction over offenses committed by whites within Indian country and state laws protecting Indians against white trespassers, e.g., were upheld in United States v. Bailey, 1 McLean C.C. 234 (U.S.C.C., 1834), and New York ex rel. Cutler v. Dibble, 21 How. 366 (U.S., 1858). The absence of specific treaty exemptions or the fact that the Indian offense had been committed off the reservation could lead the courts to sustain state jurisdiction: United States v. Ward, 1 Woolw. 17 (U.S.C.C., 1863); United States v. Yellow Sun alias Sa-coo-da-cot, 1 Dillon 271 (U.S.C.C., 1870). Indeed, the deference shown by the courts to Congress and the difficulty in enforcing decisions against the states (as in the Cherokee cases) might well have led one to challenge Judge Samuel A. Kingman's assertion in Wiley v. Keokuk, 6 Kans. 94, 110 (Kans., 1870), that "it is not in the power of any tribunal to say, 'You are an Indian, and your rights rest in the arbitrary decrees of executive officers, and not in the law.'"

40. The peculiar wording of the Cherokee treaties of 1817 and 1819 allowed some whites to qualify for land allotments as "heads of Indian families," without having to claim expatriation. See Grubbs v. M'Clatchy, 2 Yerger 432 (Tenn., 1830); Morgan v. Fowler, *ibid.* 450; and Tuten v. Martin, 3 Yerger 452 (Tenn., 1832).

Attorney General John M. Berrien dismissed one such argument on the grounds that the adopted man remained within federal jurisdiction (though in Indian territory): "A citizen of the United States cannot divest himself of his allegiance to this government, so long as he remains within the limits of its sovereignty."[41] Attorney General Benjamin F. Butler contended four years later that even slaves whose masters resided with and were adopted by the Choctaws were not under the jurisdiction of Indian laws. The political condition of such slaves depended upon that of their masters, and the latter could never divest themselves of their allegiance and evade the jurisdiction of federal laws by becoming Indians.[42]

The Supreme Court formally affirmed this position in *United States* v. *Rogers* (1846). The lower circuit court had divided on a number of questions relating to expatriation and the status of adopted members of Indian tribes. Chief Justice Taney simply held that the tribes within the jurisdiction of the government remained subject to its ultimate authority: "Congress may by law punish any offense committed there [in Indian territory], no matter whether the offender be a white man or an Indian." Whatever special obligations the man in question "may have taken upon himself by becoming a Cherokee by adoption, his responsibility to the laws of the United States remained unchanged and undiminished."[43] Whites might gain additional privileges by becoming adopted Indians—although Richard Newland, a white man adopted by the Cherokees, hardly benefited from this policy when his Cherokee murderer, Thomas Ragsdale, evaded punishment by virtue of a treaty provision pardoning crimes committed by one Indian against another.[44] However, a white man's tribal adoption ultimately could not alter the obligations he owed as a consequence of his primary citizenship.

The peculiar "domestic dependent nation" status of the tribes thus ultimately served the purposes of those who wished to maintain control over Indians without fully incorporating them into the community of citizens. Because the tribes were "domestic" and "dependent," white laws could be extended over them. Yet such extension did not constitute the kind of protection that elicited

41. Opinion of Dec. 21, 1830, Hall, comp., *Opinions of Attorneys-General*, II, 405.
42. Opinion of Dec. 26, 1834, *ibid.*, 693–696.
43. United States v. Rogers, 4 How. 567, 572, 573 (U.S., 1846).
44. United States v. Ragsdale, 27 F. Cas. 684 (U.S.C.C., 1847). See also Jackson v. Porter, 13 F. Cas. 235 (U.S.C.C., 1825).

allegiance and sustained citizenship as long as political and judicial authorities considered the tribes, in some sense, "nations" whose members were aliens. The logic of combining dependency and wardship with the idea of a separate allegiance and nationality was perhaps inconsistent; but it sufficed to exclude the Native Americans from the status and the privileges of American citizenship.[45]

If the fact of tribal organization allowed Americans to exclude Indians from citizenship within the framework of accepted legal principles, the exclusion of the Negro was much more difficult to justify. Here there was no intermediate organization that, like the tribe, could be considered "alien" and with respect to which individual members could be deemed to owe a foreign allegiance. Slavery constituted a complex institution both in formal law and social practice, of course, but in no sense could slaves be considered to form a nation with a quasi-sovereign status. And free blacks even more clearly lacked an institutional or corporate embodiment that might justify their characterization as aliens.

Negro slavery and the system of racial subordination that accompanied it created profound moral, philosophical, and legal dilemmas in a society committed to the idea that the end of all law, government, and social organization ought to be the maintenance and expansion of liberty.[46] It was not surprising that principles of citizenship became entangled with these dilemmas. Jurists and legislators might have preferred to avoid the task of defending the exclusion of blacks from citizenship, but evasion ultimately proved impossible. When the problem arose in connection with Negro slaves, the law did allow some room for maneuvering, and the question of citizenship could be begged with relative ease. When free blacks were involved, however, the question had to be confronted.

A combination of economic needs, cultural prejudices, and psy-

45. Indians who broke their tribal relations and accepted grants of land in severalty were admitted to citizenship under the General Allotment or Dawes Act of Feb. 8, 1887. Indian women marrying citizens became citizens under the act of Aug. 9, 1888, and Indian men who enlisted to fight in World War I could become citizens under the act of Nov. 6, 1919. The Citizenship Act of June 2, 1924, admitted all Indians born within the territorial limits of the United States to citizenship, approximately two-thirds having already been admitted under the acts and treaties above. Cohen, *Handbook of Federal Indian Law*, 153–154.

46. The literature on slavery is enormous. Two of the most stimulating recent works among those used here are David Brion Davis, *The Problem of Slavery in the Age of Revolution, 1770–1823* (Ithaca, N.Y., 1975), and Robert M. Cover, *Justice Accused: Antislavery and the Judicial Process* (New Haven, Conn., and London, 1975).

chological pressures led to the crystallization of the colonial system of chattel slavery in the late seventeenth century.[47] As the system gradually took shape, most blacks were reduced to the general status of commodities—of things, of property. This process was never complete, for judges and lawmakers could never fully ignore the slave's obvious humanity. English courts found it difficult to deal with this anomaly within the traditions of the common law, and a persistent, though not altogether consistent, line of judicial opinions reflected the English judges' uneasy view of the emergence of chattel slavery in the colonies.[48] The colonial courts, too, obviously had to deal with slaves as persons for such purposes as criminal jurisdiction, and the northern colonies especially extended some privileges and legal benefits to them in this capacity.[49] Yet as long as slaves could be viewed in some sense as property, judges could avoid fitting them into established categories of membership or non-membership. As chattels, slaves were neither aliens nor citizens: "Persons in the status of slavery are, in contemplation of law, slaves."[50]

The Revolution greatly stimulated antislavery sentiment, for the

---

47. Among the more useful works, see Oscar and Mary F. Handlin, "Origins of the Southern Labor System," *WMQ*, 3d Ser., VII (1950), 199–222; Winthrop D. Jordan, *White over Black: American Attitudes toward the Negro, 1550–1812* (Chapel Hill, N.C., 1968), esp. 3–98; and Edmund S. Morgan, *American Slavery—American Freedom: The Ordeal of Colonial Virginia* (New York, 1975).

48. For an excellent discussion of the early English cases, see William M. Wiecek, "*Somerset*: Lord Mansfield and the Legitimacy of Slavery in the Anglo-American World," *University of Chicago Law Review*, XLII (1974–1975), esp. 88–95. The major opinions before the famous case of Somerset v. Stewart, Lofft 1 (1772)—which was widely read as forbidding slavery within England itself—were unclear and inconsistent. One line of opinions seemed to affirm that Englishmen could have property rights in slaves: see Butts v. Penny, 2 Lev. 201, 3 Keb. 785 (1677); Chambers v. Warkhouse, 3 Lev. 336 (1693/1694); Gelly v. Cleve, 1 Ld. Raym. 147 (1694); Pearne v. Lisle, Amb. 75 (1749); and the joint opinion by Attorney General Philip Yorke and Solicitor General Charles Talbot, 1729, quoted in Knight v. Wedderburn, 17 Mor. Dict. of Dec. 14545, 14547 (1778). Contemporaneously, another series of cases seemed to deny property rights in men, even while sometimes upholding property rights in a man's service or labor: see Chamberlain v. Harvey, Carthew 396, 5 Mod. 182, and 1 Ld. Raym. 146 (1695/1696); Smith v. Brown & Cooper, 2 Salk. 666, Holt K.B. 495 (1702?); Smith v. Gould, 2 Salk. 666, 2 Ld. Raym. 1274 (1705/1706); and Shanley v. Harvey, 2 Eden 126 (1762).

49. For brief surveys, see Arthur Zilversmit, *The First Emancipation: The Abolition of Slavery in the North* (Chicago, 1967), chap. 1, and Ira Berlin, *Slaves without Masters: The Free Negro in the Antebellum South* (New York, 1974), 3–12.

50. Peter v. Hargrave, 5 Grattan 12, 17 (Va., 1848). See also Jarman v. Patterson, 7 T. B. Monroe 644, 645 (Ky., 1828). Helen Tunnicliff Catterall, ed., *Judicial Cases concerning American Slavery and the Negro*, Carnegie Institution of Washington, Publication No. 374 (Washington, D.C., 1926–1937) serves as an excellent guide to slavery cases. Where I have quoted opinions or arguments, I have examined the original reports.

disparity between the deeply felt ideals of individual liberty and the widespread system of bondage was too blatant to be overlooked.[51] In the North, bold legal decisions or more cautious gradual emancipation statutes signaled slavery's slow disappearance as a legally sanctioned institution.[52] In the South, too, public disparagement of the institution increased, and though the majority of blacks in the southern states remained slaves, manumissions created a sizable free black caste.[53] "Necessity" in the shape of huge economic investments and fears of social control prevented Southerners from forcefully moving toward outright abolition; however, the legislatures and courts of the South in the immediate post-Revolutionary period did generally liberalize manumission laws and interpret their technical provisions and procedures "*in favorem libertatis.*"[54]

While the first decades of the nineteenth century witnessed the decline of slavery in the North and the formal outlawing of the slave trade by the federal government, the rapid extension of cotton cultivation and the continued fear of an ever-expanding black population led to a reversal of early antislavery tendencies in the South. There the states moved once more to tighten white control, passing laws increasing the difficulty of private manumission, elaborating the black codes, and improving the machinery of enforcement.[55] The

51. See especially William W. Freehling, "The Founding Fathers and Slavery," *AHR*, LXXVII (1971–1972), 81–93. Duncan J. MacLeod, *Slavery, Race, and the American Revolution* (Cambridge, 1974), 12–13, and *passim*, contends that the Revolutionary ideology in the long run stimulated the articulation of a more openly racial justification of slavery.

52. Zilversmit, *The First Emancipation*, chaps. 5–8; Leon F. Litwack, *North of Slavery: The Negro in the Free States, 1790–1860* (Chicago, 1961), 3–15; Benjamin Quarles, *The Negro in the American Revolution* (Chapel Hill, N.C., 1961), chaps. 3, 10. For reports of Walker v. Jennison and Jennison v. Caldwell (Mass., 1781)—cases generally considered to have abolished slavery in that state—see "A Note by Chief Justice Gray," Mass. Hist. Soc., *Procs.*, XIII (1873–1875), 296.

53. For an example of southern criticism of slavery, see Tucker, ed., *Blackstone's Commentaries*, I:2, Note H: "On the State of Slavery in Virginia," 31–85. See also MacLeod, *Slavery, Race, and the American Revolution*, chap. 2; Berlin, *Slaves without Masters*, chap. 1.

54. Berlin, *Slaves without Masters*, 28–34; Cover, *Justice Accused*, chap. 4. MacLeod, *Slavery, Race, and the American Revolution*, 117–118, sees a hardening of policy here after 1813.

55. For a convenient summary, see Lawrence M. Friedman, *A History of American Law* (New York, 1973), 192–201. Slave states still upheld the freedom of those lawfully manumitted or those whose masters had violated local laws against the importation of slaves. See, e.g., Stewart v. Oakes, 5 Harris & Johnson 107n (Md., 1813); Spencer v. Negro Dennis, 8 Gill 314 (Md., 1849); Vansant v. Roberts, 3 Md. 119 (Md., 1852); Hunter v. Fulcher, 1 Leigh 172 (Va., 1829); Wilson v. Isbell, 5 Call 425 (Va., 1805); Commonwealth v. Pleasant, 10 Leigh 697 (Va., 1840); Foster v. Fosters, 10 Grattan 485 (Va., 1853); Jacob v. Sharp, Meigs 114 (Tenn., 1838). See also Donald J. Senese, "The Free Negro and the South Carolina Courts, 1790–1860," *South Carolina Historical Magazine*, LXVIII (1967), 140–153.

result of this divergent sectional development was the creation of a complicated "conflict-of-laws" situation within the Federal Union: in the South, slaves remained property; in the North, abolition gave them legal recognition as free men.[56]

At first, the federal and state courts reacted to this situation by acknowledging the need for moderation and compromise. Building upon a persistent natural law tradition hostile to slavery and buttressed by an expansive reading of Lord Mansfield's opinion in the leading British case of *Somerset* v. *Stewart* (1772), American jurists generally adopted the position that slavery could only exist with the support of positive state laws.[57] In the absence of complicating factors, courts could determine cases involving slavery or the status of alleged slaves within a framework of legal theory that stressed the primacy of local law, but permitted judges to give some effect to the laws of other states through comity.[58] In other words, courts would begin with a presumption of freedom or slavery, depending upon whether the constitution and laws of the "forum state" opposed or sanctioned the "peculiar institution." When the "vital interests" of the forum state did not seem to be involved, however, and when judges were not specifically bound by statute, the courts were free to accommodate the interests of sister states by giving some judicial recognition to their laws and institutions.[59] This meant in practice that free states might, for some purposes, recog-

56. For recent analyses, see Wiecek, "*Somerset*," *U. of Chicago Law Rev.*, XLII (1974–1975), esp. 128–146; Davis, *Slavery in the Age of Revolution*, chap. 10; "American Slavery and the Conflict of Laws," *Columbia Law Review*, LXXI (1971), 74–99; Harold W. Horowitz, "Choice-of-Law Decisions Involving Slavery: 'Interest Analysis' in the Early Nineteenth Century," *UCLA Law Review*, XVII (1969–1970), 587–601; Kempes Schnell, "Anti-Slavery Influence on the Status of Slaves in a Free State," *Journal of Negro History*, L (1965), 257–273; and Thomas D. Morris, *Free Men All: The Personal Liberty Laws of the North, 1780–1861* (Baltimore, 1974), 1–23, and *passim*.
57. Cover, *Justice Accused*, 8–116.
58. Joseph Story, *Commentaries on the Conflict of Laws, Foreign and Domestic . . .* (Boston, 1834), esp. secs. 27, 38, 96–97, 101–106. In Polydore v. Prince, 19 F. Cas. 950 (U.S.D.C., 1837), Judge Asher Ware attempted to distinguish between "natural" statuses and "artificial" statuses founded in the "*lex domicilii*" (law of the place of domicil). Slavery was of the latter type, and Ware contended that where the laws of the forum state (*lex fori*) did not recognize slavery, the incidents of slave status could not be enforced. For a useful introduction to some of the theoretical problems of the law of slave status, see Ronald Harry Graveson, *Status in the Common Law* (London, 1953), esp. 25–29.
59. States increasingly prescribed the policy judges should take in conflicts cases, as when Louisiana instructed judges not to sustain claims to freedom grounded on residence in a free state in 1846, or when northern legislatures set guidelines in their personal liberty laws. See respectively Cover, *Justice Accused*, 96–97, and Morris, *Free Men All*, App., 219–222.

nize slave status, while slave states might acknowledge freedom acquired by the operation of free state laws.

Questions concerning the extent to which the laws and institutions of one state or section would acquire, through comity, an extraterritorial acceptance in another section of the Union arose when slaves removed to free states or territories. The case of runaways was somewhat special, for the fugitive clause of the Constitution and the Fugitive Slave Act passed by Congress in 1793 imposed obligations on free states that were not the subject of comity.[60] Fugitive slaves were still slaves—still property—liable to recaption and return if found anywhere within the nation.[61] On the other hand, when masters and their slaves immigrated to free areas, made a temporary sojourn in non-slave jurisdictions, or merely passed through free states or territories in transit to another slave state, questions of comity and conflicting legal systems did arise.

Initially, even the slave states recognized that slaves might gain freedom by immigrating to free states or territories with the consent of their masters. The Maryland Court of Appeals held in 1799 that a slave hired out to labor in Pennsylvania was freed by the operation of that state's abolition laws.[62] According to a Mississippi Supreme Court ruling in 1818, slaves resident in the Northwest Territory when the Ordinance of 1787 abolished slavery there were released from their "absolute subjection" and could defend their subsequent status as free men in the Mississippi courts. Illustrating the continued ambivalence of southern views respecting the morality of the institution, the court declared: "Slavery is condemned by reason and the laws of nature. It . . . can only exist, through municipal regulations, and in matters of doubt, . . . courts must lean *'in favorem vitae et libertatis.' "*[63]

---

60. Art. IV, sec. 2, cl. 3, established that persons "held to service or labor in one State under the laws thereof, escaping into another, shall . . . be delivered up on claim of the party to whom such service or labor may be due." For the origins of the clause and the federal enforcement laws of 1793 and 1850, see Morris, *Free Men All,* 15–22, 130–147, and Stanley W. Campbell, *The Slave Catchers: Enforcement of the Fugitive Slave Law, 1850–1860* (Chapel Hill, N.C., 1970), 7–8, and *passim.*

61. According to Blackstone, "recaption" was an "extra-judicial or eccentrical kind of remedy" involving the customary right of an individual to recapture and restrain runaways and strays without judicial formality if the public peace was not violated. Slaveholders tried to make this a major right and to ignore the traditional limitations. Morris, *Free Men All,* 3–4.

62. Negro David v. Porter, 4 Harris & McHenry 418 (Md., 1799).

63. Harry v. Decker, Walker (Miss.) 36, 42 (Miss., 1818).

Virginia also recognized the laws of free states, holding in 1820 and 1833 that slaves carried to Ohio and Massachusetts were free and could not again be reduced to slavery.[64] Judge François X. Martin of Louisiana noted that the "right of a State to pass laws dissolving the relation of master and servant, is recognized in the constitution of the United States, by a very forcible implication," thus the Ohio constitution "emancipates, *ipso facto*, such slaves whose owners remove them into that state, with the intention of residing there."[65] Slaves who were carried to France were also judged free, even after they returned to Louisiana.[66] The courts of Kentucky, Tennessee, Missouri, and South Carolina agreed that slaves taken with their master's consent to free states or to foreign countries where slavery did not exist were consequently emancipated.[67] Courts in the free states, of course, sustained the doctrine that slavery could not exist without the support of positive laws, and slaves voluntarily brought within their jurisdiction were adjudged entitled to their freedom.[68]

Freedom suits hinging on the slave's presence in free states did not always yield results favorable to the slave, however. Both northern and southern courts were ready to give judgment for the master when residence in the free area was only temporary or when it was the result of a fraudulent attempt to evade state regulations respecting emancipation. Judge Robert Wash of the Missouri Supreme Court admitted that even the most temporary residence in

64. Griffith v. Fanny, Gilmer 143 (Va., 1820); Betty v. Horton, 5 Leigh 615 (Va., 1833).

65. Lunsford v. Coquillon, 2 Martin N.S. 401, 403, 408 (La., 1824). See also Frank v. Powell, 11 La. 499 (La., 1838); Thomas v. Generis, 16 La. 483 (La., 1840); Josephine v. Poultney, 1 La. An. 329 (La., 1846). The statute of 1846 (above, n. 59) was prospective only and did not apply to slaves whose claim rested on free-state residence before the act. Cover, *Justice Accused*, 96.

66. Marie Louise v. Marot, 8 La. 475, 9 La. 473 (La., 1835, 1836); Smith v. Smith, 13 La. 441 (La., 1839); Eugenie v. Préval, 2 La. An. 180 (La., 1847); Arsène v. Pignéguy, 2 La. An. 620 (La., 1847).

67. For Kentucky: Stanley v. Earl, 5 Littell 281 (Ky., 1824); Bush v. White, 3 T. B. Monroe 100 (Ky., 1825); Davis v. Tingle, 8 B. Monroe 539 (Ky., 1848); Mercer v. Gilman, 11 B. Monroe 210 (Ky., 1851); Ferry v. Street, 14 B. Monroe 355 (Ky., 1854). For Tennessee: Blackmore v. Negro Phill, 7 Yerger 452 (Tenn., 1835); Laura Jane v. Hagen, 10 Humphreys 332 (Tenn., 1849). For Missouri: Winny v. Whitesides, 1 Mo. 472 (Mo., 1824); Milly v. Smith, 2 Mo. 36 (Mo., 1828); Vincent v. Duncan, 2 Mo. 214 (Mo., 1830); Ralph v. Duncan, 3 Mo. 194 (Mo., 1833); Julia v. McKinney, 3 Mo. 270 (Mo., 1833); Rachael v. Walker, 4 Mo. 350 (Mo., 1836); Wilson v. Melvin, 4 Mo. 592 (Mo., 1837). For South Carolina: Guillemette v. Harper, 4 Richardson 186 (S.C., 1850); Willis v. Jolliffe, 11 Richardson Eq. 447 (S.C., 1860).

68. See, e.g., Commonwealth v. Robinson, Thacher Crim. Cas. 488 (Mass., 1837); Hone v. Ammons, 14 Ill. 29 (Ill., 1852); Anderson v. Poindexter, 6 Ohio St. 622 (Ohio, 1856).

Illinois "contrived or permitted by the legal owner, upon the faith of secret trusts or contracts, in order to defeat or evade the ordinance [of 1787], and thereby introduce slavery *de facto*, would doubtless entitle a slave to freedom, and should be punished by a forfeiture of title to the property." But transient presence without such an intent did not emancipate the slave: "The ordinance was intended as a fundamental law, for those who may choose to live under it, rather than as a penal statute to be construed by the letter against those who may choose to pass their slaves through the country."[69]

Although the courts of Kentucky and Louisiana earlier had held that residence in free states with the master's consent effected an emancipation ipso facto, they increasingly stressed that the master's consent must embrace a permanent residence. Decisions in Kentucky in 1849 and 1852 denied freedom to slaves who had been sent to Ohio or who had sojourned in Pennsylvania by consent, but for temporary purposes.[70] Similarly, Chief Justice George Eustis of the Louisiana Supreme Court reinterpreted the meaning of earlier decisions when he held in 1852 that the status of a slave was not affected "by a transit [to France] for a temporary purpose."[71] Furthermore, southern courts did not feel bound to recognize emancipations accomplished outside the state when the intention was to circumvent local rules regulating manumission.[72]

The extent to which the principles of comity would be observed in slave status cases largely depended on the discretion of the courts concerned, and this in turn reflected broader currents of public opinion.[73] As already noted, the southern states began to shift to

69. LaGrange v. Chouteau, 2 Mo. 20, 22 (Mo., 1828). On appeal, Marshall held that no congressional act had been misconstrued: LaGrange v. Chouteau, 4 Pet. 287 (U.S., 1830). The policy was later affirmed by Missouri in Nat v. Ruddle, 3 Mo. 400 (Mo., 1834), and by Illinois in Willard v. People, 4 Scammon 461 (Ill., 1843).

70. Collins v. America, 9 B. Monroe 565 (Ky., 1849); Maria v. Kirby, 12 B. Monroe 542 (Ky., 1852).

71. Liza v. Puissant, 7 La. An. 80, 83 (La., 1852). Compare with the earlier statement of Judge George Mathews that, "being free for one moment in France, it was not in the power of her former master to reduce her again to slavery." Marie Louise v. Marot, 9 La. 473, 476 (La., 1836).

72. Lewis v. Fullerton, 1 Randolph 15 (Va., 1821); Hinds v. Brazealle, 2 Howard (Miss.) 837 (Miss., 1838); Green v. Lane, 8 Iredell Eq. 70 (N.C., 1851); Henriette alias Mary v. Heirs of Barnes, 11 La. An. 453 (La., 1856).

73. Individual judges could play a large role. When John B. Gibson succeeded William Tilghman as Pennsylvania's chief justice in 1827, the state's supreme court became less sensitive to claims of slaveholders. Cover, *Justice Accused*, 64–65. Similarly, John B. O'Neall

more restrictive policies on manumission and the control of both slaves and free blacks early in the nineteenth century.[74] By the 1830s southern courts—responding to the emergence of an aggressive northern abolition movement, the nullification crisis, Nat Turner's rebellion, and the increasing vehemence of proslavery apologists— more and more stressed the primacy of their own local preference in conflict-of-laws cases concerning questions of slave or free status.[75] Chief Justice William L. Sharkey of the Mississippi Supreme Court reflected the progressively bitter tone of the debate when he coldly refused to acknowledge the validity of a deed of emancipation executed in Ohio that would have freed the black mistress and mulatto son of one of the state's white citizens. "No state is bound to recognize . . . a contract made elsewhere, which would . . . exhibit to the citizens an example pernicious and detestable," especially when the contract originated in "an offense against morality."[76] Judge Thomas A. Marshall of Kentucky argued in *Graham v. Strader* (1844) that residence in a free state destroyed the master's ability to enforce his dominion over his human property, but did not touch his right and title; once the slave returned from Ohio to Kentucky, he could not successfully sue for his freedom, for the Kentucky courts were not bound by any rule of comity or by past policies of courtesy to acknowledge the force of a sister state's obnoxious laws.[77]

This hardened attitude was evident throughout the southern states. In one of the preliminary stages of the Dred Scott case, Judge William Scott of the Missouri Supreme Court rejected the state's earlier policy of conciliation and bluntly announced that "no State is bound to carry into effect enactments conceived in a spirit hostile to that which pervades her own laws. . . . Times are not now as they were when the former decisions on this subject were made. Since then not only individuals but States have been possessed with a dark

---

fought stubbornly for liberal decisions in South Carolina. Senese, "The Free Negro and South Carolina Courts," *S.C. Hist. Mag.*, LXVIII (1967), 143–150.

74. Above, at nn. 54–55.

75. Schnell, "Anti-Slavery Influence," *Jour. Negro Hist.*, L (1965), 265–266, attributes the breakdown of the initial compromise to the rise of militant northern abolitionism; but the recent studies by MacLeod, Berlin, Cover, and Morris cited above have illustrated a more complex interaction of slavery and the law that produced a steady escalation of tension from at least the turn of the century.

76. Hinds v. Brazealle, 2 Howard (Miss.) 837, 843 (Miss., 1838).

77. Graham v. Strader, 5 B. Monroe 173, 179–182 (Ky., 1844).

and fell spirit in relation to slavery, whose gratification is sought in the pursuit of measures, whose inevitable consequence must be the overthrow and destruction of our government. Under such circumstances it does not behoove the State of Missouri to show the least countenance to any measure which might gratify this spirit."[78]

As the sectional conflict over slavery broadened and deepened, both sides closed ranks. Northern courts forsook the policy of accommodation as antislavery forces increased their agitation against the expansion of slavery into the territories, the rendition of fugitive slaves, and the political and legal compromises that subordinated the principles of liberty to the imperious demands of slaveholders.[79] And the spirit of moderation that had once enjoined the southern courts to acquiesce in the manumission of slaves by northern laws was replaced by a stubborn and defiant defense of the "peculiar institution."

While state courts moved from a policy of conciliation toward a policy of resistance and confrontation, the nation's highest tribunal did its best to avoid involvement in the growing controversy.[80] The goal was inevitably unattainable, for not only did cases directly involving slave status arise within the Supreme Court's jurisdiction, but major constitutional decisions on other points of law could be extended to imply controversial policies toward slavery. Marshall's expansive interpretation of Congress's power over commerce, for example, could be cited to justify national regulation of the interstate slave trade, and the Court's expansion or limitation of the state's "police power" could have an immediate effect on local governmental authority to control the internal movements of both free blacks and slaves.[81]

The Supreme Court tried to pursue a cautious policy on explicit

78. Scott v. Emerson, 15 Mo. 576, 583, 586 (Mo., 1852). Followed in Calvert v. Steamboat Timoleon, *ibid.* 595, and Sylvia v. Kirby, 17 Mo. 434 (Mo., 1853).

79. Although to some degree superseded by the works of Morris and Cover, Jacobus tenBroek, *The Antislavery Origins of the Fourteenth Amendment* (Berkeley and Los Angeles, Cal., 1951), is still informative on legal theories and tactics advocated by the various abolitionist factions.

80. An excellent brief summary of the Supreme Court's involvement with the slavery issue is Leo Pfeffer, *This Honorable Court: A History of the United States Supreme Court* (Boston, 1965), 137–163. See also Donald M. Roper, "In Quest of Judicial Objectivity: The Marshall Court and the Legitimation of Slavery," *Stanford Law Review*, XXI (1968–1969), 532–539, and Kent Newmyer, "On Assessing the Court in History: Some Comments on the Roper and Burke Articles," *ibid.*, 540–547.

81. See, e.g., the discussion of McCulloch v. Maryland, 4 Wheat. 316 (U.S., 1819), and New York v. Miln, 11 Pet. 102 (U.S., 1837), in Pfeffer, *This Honorable Court*, 138–139.

slavery issues—and thus antagonized both the proponents and the enemies of the institution. In several prize cases involving captured slave-trading vessels, the Court had to confront the status question directly. In 1825 Marshall held that the Court could not declare illegal that which was sanctioned by another nation's laws. In this instance, slaves hijacked from Spanish and Portuguese ships off the African coast (and subsequently recaptured by an American revenue cutter) were returned as the property of their original foreign owners. On the other hand, the slaves who mutinied and seized the Spanish-owned *Amistad* were released as free men in 1841, for Spain had since outlawed the trade, and the mutineers could no longer be considered as property.[82] As one modern historian has recently pointed out, such cases disturbed both antislavery and proslavery forces: "For the slaveholder it [the *Amistad* decision] was a Supreme Court declaration that in the natural order of things—even though not in the legal order—his slave had a right to kill him. For antislavery forces, the *Amistad* and *Creole* together were a confession in open court of the depths of the difference between the order of right and the order of law."[83]

With respect to the internal slave trade and disputes between free and slave states over questions of status, the Court refused to develop a consistent, independent policy, following instead the principle that state decisions were conclusive. In *Groves* v. *Slaughter* (1841), the Court upheld the right of Mississippi to ban the importation of slaves as merchandise, and several of the justices suggested in separate opinions that the states had exclusive power in this area. Justice Baldwin supposed that Congress was barred from any interference with the master's control of his "property" by the Fifth Amendment's guarantee of "due process"; Chief Justice Taney insisted that the national government had no power to prohibit the internal commerce in slaves; and Justice McLean contended that

---

82. The Antelope, 10 Wheat. 66 (U.S., 1825); United States v. The Schooner Amistad, 15 Pet. 518 (U.S., 1841). Justice Story had earlier asserted a broad federal judicial power to enforce natural law principles against the international slave trade in United States v. La Jeune Eugenie, 26 F. Cas. 832 (U.S.C.C., 1822), but later cases shifted from natural law arguments toward doctrines of comity and choice-of-law rules in conflicts situations. For excellent discussions, see Wiecek, "*Somerset*," *U. of Chicago Law Rev.*, XLII (1974–1975), 129–132; Cover, *Justice Accused*, 100–116; and "American Slavery and the Conflict of Laws," *Col. Law Rev.*, LXXI (1971), 88–89.

83. Cover, *Justice Accused*, 116. The Creole case occurred two years after the Amistad and involved a mutiny on an American-owned slaver. *Ibid.*, 109–116.

Congress could do nothing to sustain that "evil" trade.[84] Similarly, the Court ruled in *Strader* v. *Graham* (1851) that the status of persons who had resided in both slave and free states depended upon the law of the state in which the persons were finally settled.[85] Since such cases usually originated as freedom suits by slaves who had resided in a free territory and had later been returned to bondage in a slave state, the Court in effect upheld the growing tendency of the southern courts to ignore the antislavery statutes and constitutional provisions of the free states.

The Supreme Court did seem firmly committed to the primacy of federal power in disputes over fugitive slaves. Yet even here, the crucial opinion satisfied neither the advocates nor the opponents of the "peculiar institution." In *Prigg* v. *Pennsylvania* (1842), the justices unanimously declared Pennsylvania's "personal liberty law" of 1826 unconstitutional on the grounds that it operated to obstruct and delay the rendition of fugitive slaves.[86] Justice Story's opinion for the majority upheld the right of the master to recover his slave as a national right "which no state law or regulation can in any way qualify, regulate, control or restrain." Indeed, he asserted that federal power to implement the fugitive slave clause was exclusive.[87] Although historians have debated ever since whether a majority of the Court supported Story on this point, the antislavery forces in the northern states quickly seized upon this part of an otherwise obnoxious decision to justify new state laws barring state officials from aiding in the enforcement of the federal act.[88] The new fugitive slave law passed in 1850 multiplied the number of federal officials obliged to assist slaveholders in recovering runaways, but

84. Groves v. Slaughter, 15 Pet. 449 (U.S., 1841). Compare Boyce v. Anderson, 2 Pet. 150 (U.S., 1829), where Marshall held that several slaves who drowned in a boating accident "resembled" passengers—persons, i.e., and not property—for purposes of recovery from the boat's owner. At common law, carriers were liable for damages to merchandise, but not to passengers, unless negligence was involved. See Pfeffer, *This Honorable Court*, 141–143, and Charles Warren, *The Supreme Court in United States History*, rev. ed., II (Boston, 1926), 67–73.

85. Strader v. Graham, 10 How. 82 (U.S., 1851). Earlier decisions often had the effect of sustaining judgments in favor of freedom. See, e.g., LaGrange v. Chouteau, 4 Pet. 287 (U.S., 1830); Menard v. Aspasia, 5 Pet. 505 (U.S., 1831); Rhodes v. Bell, 2 How. 397 (U.S., 1844).

86. Prigg v. Pennsylvania, 16 Pet. 539 (U.S., 1842). For discussions of this leading case, see Campbell, *The Slave Catchers*, 10–12, and Morris, *Free Men All*, 94–106.

87. Prigg v. Pennsylvania, 16 Pet. 539, 611, 622 (U.S., 1842).

88. Joseph C. Burke, "What Did the Prigg Decision Really Decide?" *PMHB*, XCIII (1969), 73–85; Morris, *Free Men All*, 94–106.

northern antikidnapping and personal liberty laws continued to place the responsibility for the rendition of fugitives squarely on federal courts and agents. Slaveholders' demands for effective enforcement of the new law met intransigent resistance in the North, and federal courts were increasingly drawn into the political maelstrom surrounding the conflict of slavery and freedom.[89]

Slavery remained an established legal fact throughout the entire antebellum period, an institution sanctioned by positive laws in the southern states and by a persistent policy of compromise and withdrawal on the part of the federal government. An inherent and essential part of the compromise was the continued readiness of the nation's political and judicial leaders to accept the master's definition of the slave as property. Although it was impossible to avoid confronting problems of slave status—problems involving complex legal questions as well as stark moral and ideological dilemmas —the debates could be argued in terms that did not raise the issue of citizenship explicitly. At least in the first instance, the decisive question was not whether the Negro was a citizen, but whether he was a slave or a free man, property or person. Property had no national character. It was neither alien nor citizen. Thus, like the Indian, the slave could "logically" be excluded from the privileges of membership in the society of which he was so obviously a part.

Of course, not all blacks were slaves. Negroes born in free states or of free parents and those manumitted by their masters could not be considered as property. Neither slavery nor tribal character could provide a convenient justification for excluding these persons from membership. Indeed, when free Negroes were considered within the context of the general assumptions governing the concept of citizenship, there seemed to be no theoretically consistent way to deny them the rights and privileges of citizens.[90]

Although the federal statutes excluded blacks from ordinary naturalization, traditional principles of the law, unquestioned since the seventeenth century, could logically lead to the conclusion that they were entitled to claim citizenship by birthright. Yet to admit

89. Morris, *Free Men All*, 130–201; Campbell, *The Slave Catchers*, esp. chaps. 6–7. And see especially Jones v. Van Zandt, 15 How. 215 (U.S., 1847), and Ableman v. Booth, 21 How. 506 (U.S., 1859).

90. For excellent general histories of the free blacks in the North and South, respectively, see Litwack, *North of Slavery*, and Berlin, *Slaves without Masters*.

this implied a number of consequences that were absolutely unacceptable to many Americans. First, citizenship was generally assumed to confer a right to demand the protection of a broad range of rights and privileges whites were often unwilling to extend to blacks. Second, the peculiarly dualistic character of citizenship meant that both the national and the state governments were obliged to foster and protect these rights. And third, acknowledging free blacks' citizenship raised complex questions about manumission that could easily challenge the idea that black slaves were property, thus threatening the pattern of compromise that enabled the nation to tolerate the existence of slavery.

In such circumstances, the question of black citizenship took on tremendous political and ideological significance. A resolution of the problem acceptable to both North and South was impossible within the framework of ideas comprising the concept of citizenship. There seemed to be only two alternatives: either to extend the concept to free blacks and thus confront directly the ensuing implications or to insist upon a continued exclusion of Negroes and thus reinterpret the concept of citizenship.

The outlines of the problem were fully apparent from the moment it appeared in congressional debates over Missouri's admission to statehood. By late 1820 the major issue of the extension of slavery at least had been temporarily settled. The compromise agreement—permitting the institution to expand into Missouri and below its southern border (the 36°30′ line), but prohibiting it in the remainder of the Louisiana Purchase territory—appeared to clear the way for the state's admission into the Union. But in December 1820 a second dispute arose over a provision in the proposed Missouri constitution barring free Negroes and mulattoes from entering the state. A number of senators and representatives objected to the clause on the grounds that many free blacks were citizens and that the proposed prohibition violated the Constitution's guarantee of equal privileges and immunities. When southern spokesmen defended the controverted clause and denied that free Negroes were citizens, the crucial issue was joined.[91]

Opponents of the clause argued that since free blacks were "not aliens or slaves, . . . [they] were of consequence free citizens."[92]

---

91. The debates on this issue are extensively discussed in Smith, "Evolution of the Legal Concept of Citizenship," chap. 4.

92. Sen. Harrison Gray Otis (Mass.), *Annals of Congress*, 16th Cong., 2d sess., 93. For

Most states' discrimination against this caste—as well as against
women, paupers, minors, and non-freeholders—could not effect
"a total extinguishment of citizenship." Disabilities imposed on
free blacks could not obscure other important precedents: such
persons had not been considered foreigners when the state constitutions were formed; they had since enjoyed the right to acquire
property by inheritance, the right of religious freedom and personal
protection, and the broad guarantees of the Bill of Rights; and they
had been obliged to pay taxes and defend their country in arms.
More important, free blacks clearly belonged to that category of
persons denominated "natives." As one spokesman pointed out, "If
being a native, and free born, and of parents belonging to no other
nation or tribe, does not constitute a citizen of this country, I am at a
loss to know in what manner citizenship is acquired by birth."[93] If
Missouri were allowed to make an arbitrary distinction between
citizens on the basis of color alone, then every state could claim a
similar authority to grant or withhold rights, despite the Constitution's guarantees. In such a case, "your national existence is lost; the
Union is destroyed; the objects of confederation annihilated, and
your political fabric is demolished."[94]

Southern spokesmen were aghast at the radical and innovative
arguments advanced against the Missouri constitution: "These freed
negroes and mulattoes are now for the first time, called citizens of
the United States, entitled to all the privileges and immunities of the
citizens of the several States."[95] In their view, "not every person
who is born in a State, and born free" could become "a member of
the political community."[96] No one could be considered to have
that status unless he "possessed all at least of the civil rights, if not of
the political, of every other person in the community, under like
circumstances, of which he is not deprived for some cause personal
to himself."[97] Although free blacks were obviously free, they could
not be citizens and must be considered aliens or denizens.[98]

similar arguments, see Sen. James Burrill (R.I.), *ibid.*, 47–48; Rep. Rollin C. Mallary (Vt.),
ibid., 629–633; and Rep. William Eustis (Mass.), *ibid.*, 637.
  93. Rep. Joseph Hemphill (Pa.), *ibid.*, 596, 598, 599.
  94. Sen. David L. Morril (N.H.), *ibid.*, iii. Morril argued that "citizens" in the privileges
and immunities clause comprehended all inhabitants who were neither aliens nor slaves.
Ibid., 105.
  95. Sen. William Smith (S.C.), *ibid.*, 57.
  96. Rep. Alexander Smith (Va.), *ibid.*, 556.
  97. Rep. Philip Barbour (Va.), *ibid.*, 545.
  98. Rep. A. Smith (Va.), *ibid.*, 557.

If even the most cursory survey showed that free Negroes "were everywhere excluded from an equality with even the lowest rank of citizens," a more technical objection to black citizenship could be derived from Congress's exclusive power to naturalize.[99] Slaves, of course, were property, and though emancipation might make them "persons," it could not serve to naturalize them: "The most of them [free Negroes] were born slaves, and the act of manumission by the masters could not constitute them citizens. If the master can make a citizen, it must be by some other process than his sign manual on paper."[100] Emancipation was "merely the relinquishment of [the master's] claim to the services of the negro; it gives freedom to the slave, but it is not competent for the owner, a single individual, by any act of his, to constitute him a citizen."[101]

In the end, Congress did not resolve the citizenship issue. After interminable debates that occupied both houses through the winter months, a compromise solution was finally reached. Congress agreed to the admission of Missouri on the "fundamental condition" that the controverted clause would never be construed to authorize the exclusion of "any citizen of either of the States in this Union . . . from the enjoyment of any of the privileges and immunities to which such citizen is entitled under the Constitution of the United States."[102] In view of the continued disagreement over whether blacks and mulattoes were or could be citizens, the declaration was a hollow one. The question thus remained open and would continue to trouble the other branches of government until the Civil War.

The Missouri debates outlined the major positions on the issue of black citizenship taken by Americans in the following decades. On the one hand, many northern and at first some southern courts defended the idea that free native-born blacks were citizens entitled to the general benefits of membership. Although such courts often sustained harsh discriminatory laws against this group, they consistently held that special regulations and limitations did not deny citizenship and the basic rights incidental to that status. On the other hand, the courts of the slave states increasingly closed ranks and rejected the contention that Negroes could be citizens. In the

99. Rep. William S. Archer (Va.), *ibid.*, 585.
100. Sen. W. Smith (S.C.), *ibid.*, 58.
101. Rep. Louis McLane (Del.), *ibid.*, 616.
102. Glover Moore, *The Missouri Controversy, 1819–1821* (Lexington, Ky., 1953), 155, and chap. 5 generally.

process, they challenged some of the fundamental assumptions about the source, character, and effects of citizenship that hitherto had remained unquestioned.

The Supreme Judicial Court of Massachusetts was perhaps the first state tribunal to uphold formally the right of Negroes to be considered citizens. Even before the creation of the Union, the state's highest court held in *Commonwealth v. Jennison* (1783) that slavery was repugnant to republican liberty and that Negroes were free members of the community:

Whatever sentiments have formerly prevailed in this particular or slid in upon us by the example of others, a different idea has taken place with the people of America, more favorable to the natural rights of mankind, and to that natural, innate desire of Liberty, with which Heaven (without regard to color, complexion, or shape of noses, features) has inspired all the human race. And upon this ground, our Constitution . . . sets out with declaring that all men are born free and equal—and that every subject [that is, citizen] is entitled to liberty, . . . as well as life and property—and in short is totally repugnant to the idea of being born slaves.[103]

Fifty-three years later Chief Justice Lemuel Shaw affirmed that all persons, black and white, who came into the state's limits (with the exception of fugitives) became "subject to all its municipal laws; . . . and entitled to the privileges which those laws confer."[104] Although the state's courts tolerated a "separate but equal" treatment of black citizens—conceding in 1849 that prejudice "not created by law . . . probably cannot be changed by law"—they never retreated from the position that Negroes could be and were citizens of the state.[105]

To be sure, northern courts trod carefully in this area, upholding both black citizenship and discriminatory laws that in practice vitiated the status. Chief Justice David Daggett of the Connecticut bench delivered one widely known opinion denying blacks' claim to the benefits of the privileges and immunities clause when he upheld a state law designed to prevent Prudence Crandall from operating her school for out-of-state Negro children: "To my mind, it would be a perversion of terms, and the well known rules of construction, to say, that slaves, free blacks, and Indians, were

103. Commonwealth v. Jennison (Mass., 1783), quoted in Mass. Hist. Soc., *Procs.,* XIII (1873–1875), 293.
104. Commonwealth v. Aves, 18 Pickering 193, 209 (Mass., 1836).
105. Roberts v. City of Boston, 5 Cushing 198, 209 (Mass., 1849).

citizens, within the meaning of that term, as used in the constitution. God forbid that I should add to the degradation of this race of men; but I am bound, by my duty, to say, they are not citizens."[106] Daggett's opinion was reversed on appeal (the higher court remained silent on this particular point), and some evidence suggests that his colleagues did not share his views.[107] At any rate, five years later the Connecticut Supreme Court of Errors held that an emancipated slave "became *sui generis*, and entitled to all the rights and privileges of *other* free citizens of the state."[108]

Like Connecticut, Pennsylvania maintained an ambivalent policy toward her free black population. In *Hobbs* v. *Fogg* (1837), the state's supreme court observed that these people, "tho' free as the winds, might be unsafe depositories of public power"; Chief Justice John B. Gibson specifically pointed to the privileges and immunities clause as "an obstacle to the political freedom of the negro, which seems . . . insuperable."[109] In 1843 this precedent was interpreted as a bar only to high political rights, not as an implication that free blacks were "destitute of the rights of citizenship."[110] Ten years later, however, the Pennsylvania Supreme Court again held that neither "the black population of Africa, [nor] the red aborigines of America" had as yet been admitted "into political partnership." Blacks might be citizens, but they could not yet aspire to "the exercise of the elective franchise, or to the right to become our legislators, judges and governors."[111]

For a time this logic appealed to several of the southern states as well, producing opinions surprisingly libertarian in tone. Judge Henry Crabb of Tennessee spoke for a unanimous court in 1827 when he argued that freedom "transfers its possessor, even if he be black, or mulatto, or copper-colored, from the kitchen and the cotton-field, to the court house, and the election ground."[112] Chief Justice John Catron admitted in 1834 that manumission, assented to by the state, meant "adopting into the body politic a new member," and he stressed the vast importance of the process in Tennessee,

106. Crandall v. State, 10 Conn. 339, 347 (Conn., 1834).
107. See comments in Catterall, ed., *Judicial Cases*, IV, 415.
108. Colchester v. Lyme, 13 Conn. 274 (Conn., 1839), my emphasis.
109. Hobbs v. Fogg, 6 Watts 553, 557, 560 (Pa., 1837).
110. Blenon's Estate, Brightly 338, 345 (Pa., 1843).
111. Foremans v. Tamm, Grant 23 (Pa., 1853).
112. Vaughan v. Phebe, Martin & Yerger 5, 22–23 (Tenn., 1827). See also Ford v. Ford, 7 Humphreys 92, 95–96 (Tenn., 1846).

where the vote of the free Negro was "of as high value as that of any man."[113]

The North Carolina Supreme Court analyzed the problem with particular care in *State* v. *Manuel* (1838). Here Judge William Gaston acknowledged that the principles of the law irresistibly led to the conclusion that free blacks were citizens. Under Great Britain's imperial rule, all free persons, regardless of color, were subjects if born within the allegiance; all others were aliens. "Slaves were not in legal parlance persons, but property." Yet as soon as they were released from the "disqualification of slavery," they became persons —and hence either subjects or aliens, according to the circumstances of their birth. During the Revolution slaves remained slaves, but all British subjects who remained in North Carolina became freemen: "Slaves manumitted here became freemen—and therefore if born within North Carolina are citizens of North Carolina—and all free persons born within the State are born citizens of the State."[114]

Gaston noted that since the state's first constitution extended the suffrage to freemen, it was a "matter of universal notoriety" that free men of color had exercised the franchise until the constitution's revision in 1835. But this reduction of free blacks' rights did nothing to change the fact of their citizenship:

Surely the possession of political power is not essential to constitute a citizen. If it be, then women, minors, and persons who have not paid public taxes are not citizens. . . . The term "citizen" as understood in our law, is precisely analogous to the term *subject* in common law, and the change of phrase has entirely resulted from the change of government. The sovereignty has been transferred from one man to the collective body of the people—and he who before was a "subject of the king" is now "a citizen of the state."[115]

The principles of the law were clear: "all human beings" within the state who were not slaves were either citizens or aliens. There was no intermediate status; therefore free native blacks were citizens.[116] The idea that the place and circumstances of birth determined citizenship or alienage had never before been seriously challenged.

113. Fisher's Negroes v. Dabbs, 6 Yerger 119, 126 (Tenn., 1834).
114. State v. Manuel, 4 Devereaux & Battle 20, 24, 25 (N.C., 1838).
115. *Ibid.*, 25–26.
116. *Ibid.*, 24. The court had taken a similar position earlier in State v. Edmund, 4 Devereaux 340 (N.C., 1833), holding that a free black was a citizen within the meaning of a state law protecting the citizen's right to hold property in slaves.

The Constitution itself assumed the continued relevance of the concept of the "natural-born citizen" in establishing qualifications for the presidency, and discussions and controversies over naturalization invariably measured the status of adopted aliens against that enjoyed by natives as their birthright. When the question was formally adjudicated with respect to the status of a white child born in the United States of temporarily resident alien parents, the familiar principle was unhesitatingly affirmed: "Upon principle . . . I can entertain no doubt, but that by the law of the United States, every person born within the dominions and allegiance of the United States, whatever were the situation of the parents, is a natural-born citizen."[117]

If the circumstances of birth determined the natural alien or citizen status of whites, they were equally relevant evidence for determining whether black men were property or persons. The courts of Kentucky, Virginia, Louisiana, and Alabama affirmed the free status of Negro children born of parents who were in the process of gaining their freedom.[118] The Louisiana Supreme Court ruled that a Negro plaintiff must be presumed free by reason of his long residence in free territory and the absence of evidence that he had been born in the dominions of slavery.[119] Missouri, Louisiana, and Illinois courts agreed that blacks born in Illinois after the abolition of slavery by the Northwest Ordinance were born free, and the same principle determined the condition of the descendants of a Negro born in Canada.[120]

Any examination of the laws showed that free birth placed the black man above the slave in a position to enjoy many rights. Judge Alexander M. Buchanan observed in 1856 that "in the eyes of the Louisiana law, there is, (with the exception of political rights, of certain social privileges, and of the obligations of jury and militia service), all the difference between a free man of color and a slave,

117. Lynch v. Clarke, 1 Sandford Ch. 583, 663 (N.Y., 1844).
118. Violet v. Stephens, Littell's Sel. Cas. 147 (Ky., 1812); Barringtons v. Logan, 2 Dana 432 (Ky., 1834); Gentry v. McMinnis, 3 Dana 382 (Ky., 1835); Spotts v. Gillaspie, 6 Randolph 566 (Va., 1828); Phillis v. Gentin, 9 La. 208 (La., 1836); Union Bank of Tennessee v. Benham, 23 Ala. 143 (Ala., 1853).
119. Forsyth v. Nash, 4 Martin 385 (La., 1816).
120. Merry v. Tiffin, 1 Mo. 725 (Mo., 1827); Merry v. Chexnaider, 8 Martin N.S. 699 (La., 1830); Jarrot v. Jarrot, 2 Gilman 1 (Ill., 1845). A whole series of cases and appeals on the status of descendants of a Canadian Negro woman was begun by Chouteau v. Pierre, 9 Mo. 3 (Mo., 1845). The final case—Charlotte v. Chouteau, 33 Mo. 194 (Mo., 1862)—was in favor of the Negro party. For a list and summary of the cases, see Catterall, ed., *Judicial Cases*, V, 113n.

that there is between a white man and a slave."[121] Judge Henry St.
George Tucker of Virginia acknowledged the right of free Negroes
to the benefit of habeas corpus, without which "their personal
liberty would be an insubstantial shadow."[122] Chief Justice John C.
LeGrand of the Maryland Court of Appeals contended that the state
should insure these persons' property rights and their access to the
courts, for such rights could not be taken away unless their exercise
threatened the good of the whole community.[123] The Mississippi
Supreme Court affirmed the same principle in 1858: "Free negroes
are only debarred, by our laws, of the rights secured to them . . .
so far as the exercise of those rights may be positively prohibited,
or may be directly dangerous to the condition of our slaves, by
exposing them to improper interference, or to . . . mischievous
example."[124]

Yet the rights and privileges that freedom brought to the black
man were invariably less than those enjoyed by white citizens. Free
Negroes appeared to occupy a middle ground in terms of the rights
they were allowed to claim in practice, a status that could not be
described in the traditional language of slave, alien, or citizen.
Slaves they might once have been, but now they were free. Aliens
they were not, for they owed no foreign (or tribal) allegiance. Yet
acknowledging their citizenship implied the illegitimacy of many
of the discriminatory laws levied against them—unjust and unconstitutional infringements of the privileges and immunities inherent
in the status.

It was difficult to define this intermediate status within the traditional vocabulary of the law, however. Judge Colcock of South
Carolina admitted that free Negroes were "not aliens," but he
insisted that they had "not, like the freed men of Rome, or Athens,
become incorporated into the body politic." But they were under
the control of the government and the laws of the state: "If not
citizens," they were "subjects."[125] Judge Benjamin Mills of Kentucky contended that the limited rights and the obligations of free
blacks identified the group as "quasi citizens, or at least denizens," a

121. State v. Harrison, 11 La. An. 722, 724 (La., 1856).
122. De Lacy v. Antoine, 7 Leigh 438, 444 (Va., 1836). Compare Hudgins v. Wright, 1
Hening & Munford 134, 144 (Va., 1806), and Aldridge v. Commonwealth, 2 Va. Cas. 447
(Va., 1824).
123. Hughes v. Jackson, 12 Md. 450, 463 (Md., 1858).
124. Shaw v. Brown, 35 Miss. 246, 320 (Miss., 1858).
125. Estate of Hardcastle, Harper (2d ed.) 495, 463 (S.C., 1826).

suggestion that found favor with Judge Edward Cross of Arkansas and with United States Attorney General Hugh S. Legaré.[126] Judge Hiram Warner of the Georgia Supreme Court considered this class to be "our wards"; Judges William L. Harris and Cotesworth P. Smith of Mississippi's highest court thought the African race *"alien strangers"*; and Judge Buchanan of Louisiana considered all Negroes "strangers to our Constitution."[127] Other tribunals merely defined such persons as a "degraded race" or as a "third class."[128]

Most of these denotations violated the general understanding of familiar legal terms. Free blacks who had been born within the "dominion and jurisdiction" of the United States could in no legal sense be deemed aliens. Nor did the revived concept of the denizen fit their situation, for as Representative James Strong of New York observed in the Missouri debates: "No one can be a denizen who has not been an alien. Denizenship is the modification of alienage. But Congress can pass laws of naturalization only, and not of denization. It would seem to follow, therefore, that these persons cannot be denizens."[129] "Subject" was a term of English law, and as North Carolina's Judge Gaston pointed out, "subjects" and "citizens" equally signified full membership and rights.[130] None of the other alternatives provided a solution, however; "wards" and "degraded persons" could still be citizens.

Nevertheless, decisions favoring blacks' citizenship grew increasingly untenable in the South. Both Tennessee and North Carolina retreated from their initial stand, emphasizing more and more the actual discriminations against free blacks and mulattoes as indicators of their separate status as a "degraded race" or "third class."[131] Elaborating upon the arguments advanced by southern spokesmen in the Missouri debates, the courts of the South now inverted

126. Rankin v. Lydia, 2 A. K. Marshall 467, 476 (Ky., 1820); Pendleton v. State, 6 Ark. 509, 511 (Ark., 1846); Attorney General Legaré to Sec. of Treas., Mar. 15, 1843, Hall, comp., *Opinions of Attorneys-General*, IV, 147–148. Mills himself was unable to sustain this definition for long. See his dissent in Amy v. Smith, 1 Littell 326, 337–347 (Ky., 1822).

127. Cooper v. Mayor & Aldermen of Savannah, 4 Ga. 68, 75 (Ga., 1848); Heirn v. Bridault, 37 Miss. 209, 224 (Miss., 1859); African Methodist Episcopal Church v. New Orleans, 15 La. An. 441, 443 (La., 1860).

128. State v. Claiborne, Meigs 331, 339 (Tenn., 1838); Cox v. Williams, 4 Iredell Eq. 15, 17 (N.C., 1845); Bryan v. Walton, 14 Ga. 185, 198 (Ga., 1853).

129. *Annals of Congress*, 16th Cong., 2d sess., 571.

130. See above, n. 115.

131. See above, n. 128; State v. Newsom, 5 Iredell 250 (N.C., 1844); and State v. Jowers, 11 Iredell 555 (N.C., 1850).

traditional legal logic, reversing the assumption that citizenship conferred a legal claim to rights to contend that a lack of rights proved that free blacks were not citizens. Rather than examining the circumstances of birth that had long provided the definitive evidence of status, the courts focused their attention on the facts of prejudice and discrimination, which they attempted to use as the basis for a new classification.

The new argument won the approval of some executive officials as well as many southern judges. Attorney General William Wirt confessed in 1821 that "if nativity, residence, and allegiance combined, (without the rights and privileges of a white man,) are sufficient to make [a free Negro] a 'citizen of the United States' in the sense of the constitution, then free negroes and mulattoes are eligible to those high offices [in the national government], and may command the purse and sword of the nation." Since the very thought was abhorrent, Wirt concluded that the Constitution must be interpreted to embrace no person "in the description of citizen of the United States who has not the *full* rights of a citizen in the State of his residence."[132]

The Kentucky Court of Appeals also reached the conclusion that it was "not the place of a man's birth, but the rights and privileges he may be entitled to enjoy, which makes him a citizen." The actual exercise of those rights was not necessary, of course, for many acknowledged citizens could not meet that criterion. Women and infants, for example, "are generally dependent upon adult males, through whom they enjoy the benefits of those rights and privileges; and it is a rule of common law, as well as of common sense, that females and infants should, in this respect, partake of the quality of those adult males who belong to the same class and condition in society, and of course they will or will not be citizens, as the adult males of the same class are or are not so." But for a man "to be a citizen, *it is* necessary, that he should be *entitled* to the enjoyment of those privileges and immunities, upon the same terms upon which they are conferred upon other citizens; and unless he is so entitled, he cannot, in the proper sense of the term, be a citizen."[133]

132. Attorney General Wirt to Sec. of Treas., Nov. 7, 1821, Hall, comp., *Opinions of Attorneys-General*, I, 507.
133. *Amy v. Smith*, 1 Littell 326, 333 (Ky., 1822), one of the best examples of a very common argument.

Judge Mills dissented from his colleagues' opinion in this case and pointed to the clearly unacceptable conclusions implicit in their argument. By the logic of the majority, "widows and maids of mature age," as well as "the unprotected orphan," were not citizens —thus numerous statutes and judicial precedents to the contrary must be discountenanced. Similarly, one must overturn the established practice of the federal courts in examining birth and residence —not privileges virtually or actually held—for purposes of deciding jurisdiction in diversity of citizenship cases. A consistent view of law and practice must yield a different conclusion. Citizenship conferred a right to broadly defined rights that the courts were obliged to protect: "A citizen . . . is one who owes to the government, allegiance, service, and money by way of taxation, and to whom the government in turn, grants and guarantees liberty of person and of conscience, the right of acquiring and possessing property, or marriage and the social relations, of suit and defence, and security in person, estate and reputation."[134] All persons— including free blacks—who were neither slaves nor aliens were citizens. If an individual lacked essential rights, it was not his status but the discriminatory laws that should be called into question.

Two central aspects of the concept of citizenship brought the North and South to this confrontation over the status of free blacks. The first was the assumption that citizenship was a status without gradations of rank; that is, whatever the social practice, the law in principle would not envision a hierarchy of fundamental privileges separating citizenship into categories of "first class," "second class," and the like. The second was the presumption that citizenship normally involved a double membership in state and nation and that the national dimension of the status entailed certain "incidents" obligatory to the states. Both ideas had developed within American law before the status of the free black became a publicly debated issue. Neither seemed particularly controversial when attention was solely confined to the condition of white men.[135] But once

134. *Ibid.* (dissent), 339, 341, 342. Note also the attempt here to define in general terms the privileges and immunities that formed the incidents of citizen status.
135. See generally chap. 9 above. The frequent discussions of "dual allegiance," the clear assumption of a distinct national dimension of citizenship in debates on naturalization and expatriation, and the efforts to define in broad terms the "incidents" of national citizenship have convinced me that the assumptions mentioned in the text were not aberrational, despite later decisions questioning the substantive content of "privileges and immunities." For these later decisions (often read back into the antebellum period), see below, Epilogue.

Americans seriously began to consider the legal status of the black population, the working categories of slave, alien, and citizen operated as constraints, limiting the alternatives available to men who wished to exclude the Negro within the framework of law. The federal character of citizenship—its implication of rights enforceable in and against both state and nation—insured that the resolution of this status question would inevitably have a profound effect upon the principles and practices of both North and South.

The northern states for the most part yielded to the logic of past principles and admitted the citizenship of free Negroes, but they did so largely at the cost of reversing one conceptual development that had slowly been emerging in the courts—namely, that the fundamental privileges conferred by citizenship included the potential enjoyment of full political rights. In many northern states Negroes were excluded from the suffrage and from high office, and the determination to maintain this barrier strengthened during the antebellum years.[136] However, the right to the elective franchise had never seemed absolutely inherent in the status; it had always been subject to a wide range of limitations and qualifications even among the white citizenry. The exclusion of black citizens here seemed no more illegitimate than the unquestioned exclusion of women, children, and the mentally incompetent or morally unfit. A few northern states rejected the analogy as tainted with special pleading, concluding that adult male blacks ought to be allowed the vote; but for most, high political privileges were simply divorced from the fundamental incidents of citizen status.

On the other hand, certain fundamental privileges did clearly seem to follow from citizenship—the rights to property, liberty of person and conscience, and access to the courts—and the recognition of Negro citizenship committed the North to extend these rights to native free blacks. Moreover, the federal character of citizenship suggested that black citizens were entitled to demand the protection of these fundamental "privileges and immunities" within, and if necessary against the wishes of, individual states in the Union.[137] And this the southern states were not prepared to accept.

136. Williamson, *American Suffrage*, 278; Litwack, *North of Slavery*, 74–75.
137. Smith v. Moody, 26 Ind. 299, 301, 306–307 (Ind., 1866), held Indiana's statutes and constitutional provisions barring the immigration of free blacks unconstitutional violations of Art. IV, sec. 2. Chief Justice Robert Gregory cited the Civil Rights Act of Apr. 9, 1866, as "declaratory" in its definition of citizenship, concluding that blacks had been citizens even before that statute was passed.

Before the question of Negro citizenship was raised, it was assumed that the status involved a double membership in nation and state.[138] When the free states began to acknowledge blacks as citizens, however, the slave states had to challenge this assumption. Ohio might do as she wished and "confer citizenship on the chimpanzee or ourang-outang," observed Judge Harris of Mississippi sarcastically; but no rule of comity and no technicality of the law or the Constitution would force "states not thus demented, to forget their own policy . . . and lower their own citizens."[139] Whatever their condition in the northern states, Negroes could not be considered to enjoy the sort of national character that could impose obligations on the South. If membership in the Union meant that under the Constitution the southern states were not free to identify their own citizens and were subject to the dictates of other governments, then the Constitution must be broken and the Union must fall.

The conclusion was obvious and frightening, undoubtedly a major reason why the Supreme Court delayed so long in attempting to enunciate an authoritative doctrine of citizenship. Any effort to eliminate the inconsistencies and ambiguities in the law ultimately would have to address the problem of Negro citizenship, and any definitive statement here was bound to evoke organized hostile opposition. Thus the nation's highest court remained silent, rejecting, evading, or distinguishing away arguments and precedents that threatened to raise the controverted issue.

This policy of silence and evasion came to an end with the Dred Scott case.[140] In 1834 Scott had been carried by his owner, Dr. John Emerson, to the free state of Illinois and to the Wisconsin Territory. Emerson, a physician attached to the United States Army, had returned to Missouri with Scott in 1838. When the doctor died, Scott sued Emerson's widow for his freedom, arguing that residence with his master's consent in areas made free by the Missouri Compromise had effected his emancipation. Judging from the earlier case of *Rachael* v. *Walker* (1836)—which duplicated almost

138. The exception of persons in the territories or the District of Columbia in fact helped prove the rule. In their case, national status was clear, and state membership followed on the territory's admission to statehood or the individual's permanent removal to an existing state of the Union. See above, chap. 9, at nn. 43–52.

139. Mitchell v. Wells, 37 Miss. 235, 264 (Miss., 1859).

140. For a detailed narrative and analysis, see Vincent C. Hopkins, *Dred Scott's Case* (New York, 1951).

exactly the details of the Scott case—there was good reason to hope that the Missouri courts would affirm the right of the slave to be free.[141]

But times had changed. The Missouri Supreme Court held in 1852 that Scott's slave status—unenforceable in free areas—reattached as soon as he returned to the state, and his plea for freedom was rejected.[142] The case might have ended here had not Mrs. Emerson married Dr. Calvin C. Chaffee, an abolitionist congressman, who devised the scheme to use Scott's case to test the constitutionality of the Missouri Compromise and the power of Congress over slavery in the territories. Since Chaffee did not wish to appear as the slave-holding defendant in such a suit, Scott was sold to Mrs. (Emerson) Chaffee's brother-in-law, John F. A. Sanford of New York, and the suit was brought to the federal circuit court in Missouri under diversity of citizenship jurisdiction. Surprisingly, the lower court held that Scott could sue as a citizen, but finally ruled that he remained a slave under Missouri law.[143] When Scott subsequently appealed the decision to the Supreme Court, the questions involved included not only Scott's free or slave status and the power of Congress over slavery in the territories but also the perplexing and explosive issue of Negro citizenship.

Scott v. *Sandford* [*sic*] was argued in February 1856 and reargued the following December. Initially, the majority of the Court wished to evade comment upon congressional power and to dispose of the case by relying on the principle stated earlier in *Strader* v. *Graham* (1851), namely, that the status of persons in Scott's situation depended upon the laws of the state in which they finally resided.[144] Since the Missouri Supreme Court had declared Scott to be a slave, the justices could decide the citizenship question on the limited grounds that slaves, as property, had no status as citizens or aliens, avoiding a more expansive analysis. Yet when two of the justices— John McLean and Benjamin Curtis—made it known that they in-

141. In Rachael v. Walker, 4 Mo. 350 (Mo., 1836), an army officer had taken his slave to free territories, then returned to Missouri. The court agreed that the officer was bound to reside in free areas if so ordered by the army, "yet no authority of the law or the government compelled him to keep the plaintiff there as a slave." *Ibid.*, 354.

142. Scott v. Emerson, 15 Mo. 576 (Mo., 1852); Hopkins, *Dred Scott's Case*, chaps. 2–3.

143. In the circuit court, the defendant's lawyers did not plead Scott's slave status in abatement, only averring that he was "a negro of African descent, whose ancestors were of pure African blood, and who were brought into this country and sold as slaves." Hopkins, *Dred Scott's Case*, 24.

144. *Ibid.*, 41–42. For Strader v. Graham, see above, at n. 85.

326 Principles, Politics, and Prejudice

tended to write full and vigorous dissents, their colleagues could not afford to keep silent. Chief Justice Taney assumed the task of writing and delivering the majority opinion, covering all the controverted issues. Justices John Catron, John A. Campbell, Peter Daniel, James Wayne, and Robert Grier submitted concurring opinions, while Justice Samuel Nelson alone refused to do more than stand by the *Strader* precedent and maintain silence on the divisive issues.[145]

Taney's majority opinion denied that Scott or any other black man could be a citizen of the United States within the meaning of the Constitution.[146] According to the Chief Justice, the words "citizens" and "people of the United States" were synonymous: "They both describe the political body who, according to our republican institutions, form the sovereignty, and who hold the power and conduct the government through their representatives. They are what we familiarly call the 'sovereign people,' and every citizen is one of this people, and a constituent member of this sovereignty." State and United States citizenship were, however, separate terms relating to separate sovereignties. Both before and after 1789, argued Taney, states could confer local membership within their own boundaries upon whomever they chose. Every person and "every class and description of persons, who were at the time of the Constitution recognized as citizens in the several States," became national citizens with the creation of the Union; but those locally admitted after 1789 enjoyed no national status. The power to naturalize, to adopt persons into this new sovereignty, belonged exclusively to Congress:

It is very clear, therefore, that no State can, by any act or law of its own, passed since the adoption of the Constitution, introduce a new member into the political community created by the Constitution of the United States. It cannot make him a member of this community by making him a member of its own. And for the same reason it cannot introduce any person, or description of persons, who were not intended to be embraced in this new political family, which the Constitution brought into existence, but were intended to be excluded from it.[147]

145. Hopkins, *Dred Scott's Case*, chaps. 6–7.
146. Scott v. Sandford, 19 How. 393 (U.S., 1857). The opinions are given as follows: Taney, *ibid.*, 399–454; Wayne, *ibid.*, 454–456; Nelson, *ibid.*, 457–469; Grier, *ibid.*, 469; Daniel, *ibid.*, 469–493; Campbell, *ibid.*, 493–518; Catron, *ibid.*, 518–529; McLean, *ibid.*, 529–564; Curtis, *ibid.*, 564–633.
147. *Ibid.*, 404, 406.

For Taney, the key question here was an historical one. Were free blacks state citizens before the ratification of the Constitution and thus granted national status and guaranteed privileges and immunities by Article IV, section 2? To his mind, all the evidence suggested that members of the "African race" were not included in the meaning of this clause. Taney argued that the Constitution clearly showed the inferior position of the "negro race" in its clauses respecting the slave trade and the extradition of fugitives— though here he generalized from slaves and fugitives to all blacks. State legislation, too, discriminated against this class—though Taney would admit later that discrimination per se did not exclude women, minors, and other whites from citizenship. The explicit restriction of naturalization to white aliens, according to the terms of the federal statutes passed since 1790, barred blacks from this mode of admission and constituted still further evidence of their degradation —though again Taney overlooked the "collective naturalization" of all "inhabitants" in territories acquired by treaty or cession.[148]

This "uniform course of legislation . . . by the colonies, by the States, and by Congress, running through a period of time of more than a century," made it impossible for Taney to admit that Negroes could be citizens of the United States. Local citizenship they might enjoy, but unless they were members of both a state and the nation, they could not claim the protection of the privileges and immunities clause: "These rights are of a character and would lead to consequences which would make it absolutely certain that the African race were not included under the name of citizens of a State, and were not in the contemplation of the framers of the Constitution when these privileges and immunities were provided for the protection of the citizens in other States." As purely local citizens, blacks might have rights at the discretion of the individual state; but once they removed beyond that state's jurisdiction, their condition depended absolutely on their new place of residence. And if this reasoning held good against a free black, it certainly applied against Scott, who by the laws of Missouri was "still a slave, and certainly incapable of suing in the character of a citizen."[149]

Taney's conclusion that blacks could not enjoy the privileges and immunities of citizenship under the Constitution rested upon

148. *Ibid.*, 411, 412–417, 422, 419–420.
149. *Ibid.*, 421, 423, 427.

two premises. First, one had to accept the separation of state and national citizenship not only in theory but in fact. For Taney, the guarantees made to the "citizens of each State" in Article IV, section 2, protected only those members of the national community, and the clause must therefore be interpreted to read "the United States citizens of each State." Second, this national citizenship could not be held to derive automatically from birth "within the dominion and jurisdiction" of the national government. Rather those citizens who created the Union in 1789 formed a closed community in which membership was restricted to descendants of the founders and to aliens co-opted by the process of naturalization.

In seeking to derive consistent exclusionist principles from an ambivalent legal tradition, Taney could only succeed by distorting history and making "bad law." His conclusion that Negroes had never been citizens in any of the states before 1789 was reached in the face of clear historical evidence to the contrary, evidence that the dissenters quickly brought forward. Similarly, his insistence on a fundamental disjunction between state and national citizenship countered a long popular and judicial tradition of considering the two as inseparable dimensions of the same status. In making national citizenship exclusively the effect of naturalization or pedigree, he disregarded volumes of judicial precedents emphasizing place of birth without regard to ancestry. Taney's opinion rested instead on the social fact of prejudice and discrimination.

Despite this questionable reasoning, two of the associate justices concurred generally with Taney's opinion, and four others accepted the chief justice's overall decision without challenging his view of citizenship. Justices Nelson and Catron declined to comment specifically on the issue of membership status, holding that Scott remained a slave by Missouri law and the *Strader* v. *Graham* precedent.[150] Justices Grier and Campbell extended this logic: Scott could not sue because he was a slave, and slaves were not citizens.[151] Justices Wayne and Daniel alone fully agreed with Taney on black citizenship, the former stating his agreement without extensive argument and the latter elaborating his own reasons for barring all blacks from participation in the national sovereignty.[152] Justices John McLean and Benjamin Curtis dissented from the

150. Nelson, *ibid.*, 459, 469; Catron, *ibid.*, 518.
151. Grier, *ibid.*, 469.
152. Wayne, *ibid.*, 454; Daniel, *ibid.*, 475–481.

majority opinion in the Dred Scott case. McLean did not consider the citizenship question to be legitimately before the Court, and he devoted most of his attention to the other crucial issues—that is, to the constitutionality of the Missouri Compromise and to congressional power over slavery in the territories. However he did contend that Scott was a citizen to the extent that he could rightfully bring suit in a federal court, thus disagreeing with the majority's claim that the circuit court had erred in sustaining jurisdiction: "Being born under our Constitution and laws, no naturalization is required, as one of foreign birth, to make him a citizen. The most general and appropriate definition of the term citizen is 'a freeman.' Being a freeman, and having his domicil in a State different from that of the defendant, he is a citizen within the act of Congress, and the courts of the Union are open to him."[153]

McLean denied that African ancestry alone was enough to exclude Scott from citizenship, and since this had been the only fact alleged in the lower court as a bar to its jurisdiction, the circuit court had been correct in hearing the case. Although he admitted that no person of foreign birth could "legally be made a citizen of a State, and *consequently* a citizen of the United States," except by congressional naturalization, McLean rejected Taney's contention that blacks had never been so admitted.[154] Whether or not Negroes were "agreeable members of society" was for McLean more "a matter of taste than of law. . . . On the question of citizenship, it must be admitted that we have not been very fastidious. Under the late treaty with Mexico, we have made citizens of all grades, combinations, and colors. The same was done with the admission of Louisiana and Florida."[155] Because the laws in force suggested that black men could be citizens, and because no proof other than Scott's color and African ancestry had been adduced to deny his claim to citizenship, McLean was satisfied that the circuit court's decision to determine the case on its merits (as opposed to abating the case on the jurisdictional issue) was entirely valid.

Justice Curtis thought it appropriate to consider this question more deeply, analyzing not only the particular problem of jurisdiction but also the whole complex issue of federal citizenship. According to Curtis, if any person of Scott's description—that is, "a

153. *Ibid.*, 531.
154. *Ibid.*, 533, my emphasis.
155. *Ibid.*

negro of African descent, whose ancestors were of pure African blood, and who were brought into this country and sold as slaves" —could be a citizen, then Scott should be presumed one also, for no reason to the contrary other than this description had been given. Unless such a description constituted an absolute disproof of citizenship—unless it was clear that blacks had never been and could never be United States citizens—then the Court's presumption should be in favor of Scott.[156]

Curtis contended that the question of United States citizenship could only be answered by examining the state of affairs during the Confederation period. He agreed with Taney that citizens of the several states became constituent members of the national sovereignty at the moment the Union was created, but read the historical record differently—and more accurately. By the laws and constitutions of New Hampshire, Massachusetts, New York, New Jersey, and North Carolina, all free native-born inhabitants, regardless of color or ancestry, were citizens, and those who enjoyed this status and met other requirements possessed and exercised the elective franchise. Under the comity clause of the Articles, "free inhabitants" were guaranteed rights in all the states. Curtis pointedly reminded the Court that the Continental Congress had overwhelmingly rejected a proposal to qualify this guarantee by restricting it solely to white inhabitants. Nothing in the Constitution implied an intention to deprive citizens of their rights; and since some free blacks, at least, had been citizens and had even voted in the contests over ratification, then it was impossible to assume now that all blacks were excluded from citizenship, even by Taney's reasoning.[157]

However, descent from the founding generation was not the only criterion for determining citizenship. According to Curtis, "under the Constitution of the United States, every free person born on the soil of a State, who is a citizen of that State by the force of its Constitution or laws, is also a citizen of the United States." The Constitution's reference to "natural born citizen" in the presidential qualification assumed the acquisition of citizenship by birth. Logically, this could only be interpreted four ways: (1) the Constitution itself determined which native-born persons should be United States citizens; (2) it empowered Congress to make this

156. *Ibid.*, 569–571; and above, n. 143.
157. *Ibid.*, 572–576.

decision; (3) it assumed that all natives were citizens; (4) or it left this decision to the states, who by defining which of their native-born inhabitants were state citizens would also conclusively establish those who were national citizens.[158]

The first three possibilities could be dismissed. The Constitution contained no clause explicitly defining citizens, nor did it give Congress more than the power to naturalize aliens. The third possibility, that by virtue of the Constitution all natives became citizens, Curtis thought doubtful; the document specifically granted Congress power over naturalization only (not over citizenship generally), and other references to the status—in the privileges and immunities clause and in the sections establishing the jurisdiction of federal courts—referred specifically to state citizens as forming the national citizenry. The fourth possibility, then, appeared to be the correct one. In Curtis's opinion, the individual states had the right to define which of their native inhabitants were to be considered citizens, and from this local citizenship, national status followed inevitably.[159]

Curtis and Taney thus sharply differed on the relationship between state and national citizenship. The chief justice contended that national authority created national citizenship by naturalization and the adoption of all (white) persons who were state citizens in 1789. These persons and their descendants composed the national citizenry. State authority could create only local citizens after 1789, a class that had no national standing and no constitutional claim to privileges and immunities in other states. Curtis, on the other hand, argued that although Congress held the power of naturalization, the individual states retained the right to define who qualified as national citizens. He attempted to soften the impact of this assertion by acknowledging the right of state governments to define the incidents of citizenship—especially with respect to the sensitive rights of suffrage and officeholding—but he nevertheless concluded that if individual blacks were citizens in Ohio or Massachusetts, they remained citizens in Mississippi and South Carolina.[160]

The conflicts between Taney and Curtis were clear, but their agreement on several important issues should not be overlooked.

158. *Ibid.*, 576–577.
159. *Ibid.*, 576–582.
160. *Ibid.*, 580–584, for Curtis's argument concerning privileges and immunities.

Both discountenanced the idea, prevalent in many earlier state decisions, that citizenship could be determined by examining the rights a person actually enjoyed. Although Taney emphasized discriminatory laws as evidence relevant to the question whether blacks had been intentionally included under the rubric "citizens," he did not argue that rights created citizens. Rather the two major opinions agreed: the status conferred the rights, and national citizenship, once established, imposed obligations upon the individual states.

Moreover, Taney and Curtis alike concluded that national citizenship—however defined and however inclusive—implied membership in a sovereign political community transcending state boundaries. The "people of the United States," and not "the people of the states united," formed the inner community of citizens, owing allegiance to the national government as well as to their states. The Dred Scott decisions thus upheld the dualistic nature of national citizenship, but left unresolved the question of what should happen if these two allegiances collided.

For the moment, the conflicts were more apparent than the consensus, both within the Court and the country at large.[161] The attempt to resolve the question of Negro citizenship and to eliminate the ambiguities in the law by judicial fiat failed. Indeed, the Dred Scott case mainly succeeded in underscoring the continued uncertainty and renewed ambiguity of the meaning of citizenship. The highest court in the nation had failed to agree on the respective authority of the state and national governments to determine who owed allegiance and who could demand protection under the Constitution. It had divided on the status of free black Americans and had simultaneously called into question, by the majority's challenge to birthright citizenship, the status of natives born of unnaturalized alien parents. By its silence it had left unresolved the question of the primacy of the allegiance to nation or to state. North and South continued to dispute the origins, character, and effects of citizenship. Logic and precedent, principle and law, failed to produce a clear understanding of the meaning of citizenship.

161. For the reaction to the decision, see generally Pfeffer, *This Honorable Court,* 156–158; Hopkins, *Dred Scott's Case,* chap. 11; Smith, "Evolution of the Legal Concept of Citizenship," chap. 8; and Stanley I. Kutler, ed., *The Dred Scott Decision: Law or Politics?* (Boston, 1967), pt. iii.

Perhaps the result was inevitable. The problem of citizenship involved interests and emotions that were unlikely to be affected by logical argument. Ultimately, the questions of community, power, and sovereignty so integrally bound up with the concept would be decided not by the rule of law, but by the verdict of armed force. Only after four long years of carnage would it be possible to affirm Negro citizenship, to confirm the principle of birthright membership, and to eliminate many of the ambiguities that had riddled the concept of American citizenship from the beginning.

Resolution?

The outbreak of war removed obstacles that had long prevented Americans from achieving a consistent concept of citizenship. The compromises tolerated for the sake of national unity ended with the crisis of secession, and after four years of carnage on the battlefield, the North emerged with the conqueror's right to impose its will on the devastated South. The war effectively determined the location of sovereign power in the United States, establishing the Union's primacy over the individual states. But the military decision could not stand alone. Statutes and constitutional amendments were needed to transfer the verdict of the sword into the body of the law. In the end, the national government and the victors of the North strove to extend their ideas of sovereignty and community over the South and to resolve authoritatively problems of citizenship that had plagued the Republic since its founding.

The ideals of the South had been expressed in secession and in the subsequent creation of the Confederacy.[1] In essence, the South insisted that the Union had been the analogue of the old British empire—that is, a political community formed of separate sovereign peoples that in itself lacked ultimate coercive power over its members. To southern leaders like Jefferson Davis and Alexander Stephens, fundamental sovereignty under the Constitution remained

---

1. See generally James G. Randall, *Constitutional Problems under Lincoln*, rev. ed. (Urbana, Ill., 1951), chap. 1; Charles P. Roland, *The Confederacy* (Chicago, 1960), chap. 2; and Charles Robert Lee, Jr., *The Confederate Constitutions* (Chapel Hill, N.C., 1963).

vested in the people of the several states, not in the aggregate community. The people of the individual states had submitted to the national government for limited and specified purposes, and they had voluntarily accepted the rights and obligations of national citizenship. As long as the central authority was exercised properly and with due regard for the powers reserved by the states, citizens owed obedience to the national government. But once the people— that is, a majority of citizens within the respective states—determined that national power had become tyrannical, they could appeal to the principles of 1776 and withdraw their allegiance.[2]

The dissolution of national allegiance did not cancel the obligations that southern citizens owed to their local communities. These duties predated the Union, persisted throughout its existence, and survived its destruction. Indeed, secession did nothing to impair the authority of the individual sovereign states, which was rooted in the sovereign will of the people. That authority was ultimate, commanding the southern citizen to relinquish his ties to the United States and to follow his fellow citizens into independence in accordance with the principles of his highest and truest allegiance. The seceding states remained whole and continued in full sovereignty, thus their individual members did not gain the right to choose sides or elect their allegiance. Citizens of the North became alien enemies.[3] And citizens of the South who sided with the Union were liable to the penalties of treason.[4]

The fundamental idea that sovereignty, community, and citizenship should be defined with reference to the individual states was

2. Randall, *Constitutional Problems*, 13–16.
3. Northern citizens resident in southern states who declared their intent to become Confederate citizens and acknowledged the authority of the Confederate government were not liable to apprehension, imprisonment, or removal under the alien enemies act of Aug. 8, 1861. Nor were citizens of Delaware, Maryland, Kentucky, Missouri, the District of Columbia, the territories of Arizona and New Mexico, or the Indian Territory south of Kansas. In 1862 Attorney General Thomas H. Watts held that C. H. Lovejoy, a native of New York who had resided in Virginia from before the war and whose actions since showed his attachment to the southern cause, was to be considered a Virginia citizen liable to conscription. T. H. Watts to Secretary of War G. W. Randolph, Aug. 13, 1862, Rembert W. Patrick, ed., *The Opinions of the Confederate Attorneys General, 1861–1865* (Buffalo, N.Y., 1950), 134–135.
4. Acting Attorney General Wade Keyes to Secretary of War G. W. Randolph, Richmond, Va., July 10, 1862, Patrick, ed., *Opinions of Confed. Attorneys General*, 114–115. For an extended opinion on this issue explicitly denying a right of election on the grounds that "the Citizens of the States were never, since the Declaration of Independence of the King of Great Britain, member-citizens of the same [national] political community," see T. H. Watts to President [Jefferson Davis], Richmond, Va., Mar. 4, 1863, *ibid.*, 231–242.

fixed in the Constitution of the Confederacy framed in the early months of 1861. The preamble left no doubt that state sovereignty was the basis for this new union: "We, the people of the Confederate States, each State acting in its sovereign and independent character, in order to establish justice, insure domestic tranquillity, and secure the blessings of liberty to ourselves and our posterity— invoking the favor and guidance of Almighty God—do ordain and establish this Constitution for the Confederate States of America."[5] All powers delegated to the central government remained dependent upon the continued assent of the people in their respective states.

Given this fundamental understanding that the states formed the primary locus of authority, the Confederate Constitution could safely repeat or paraphrase many of the familiar provisions involving citizenship that had previously caused national controversies. Representatives and senators had to be citizens of the Confederate States, and the president was required to be "a natural born citizen of the Confederate States, or a citizen thereof at the time of the adoption of this Constitution, or a citizen thereof born in the United States prior to the 20th of December, 1860."[6] The framers specified that "no person of foreign birth, not a citizen of the Confederate States, shall be allowed to vote for any officer, civil or political, State or Federal."[7] The central Congress was given power to "establish uniform laws of naturalization," a power exercised in August and December 1861 when all foreigners serving in the land and naval forces of the Confederacy were given the full protection of the government and allowed naturalization on easy terms. An alien admitted under these statutes was to take an oath to the specific state in which he wished to become a citizen as well as to the Confederate Constitution and laws.[8] The acts revealed the assump-

5. Permanent Constitution of the Confederate States of America, preamble. For the full text of the document, see Lee, Jr., *Confederate Constitutions*, App. C, 171–200.

6. C.S.A., *Constitution*, Art. I, sec. 2, cl. 2 (House); Art. I, sec. 3, cl. 3 (Senate); Art. II, sec. 1, cl. 7 (president).

7. *Ibid.*, Art. I, sec. 2, cl. 1.

8. *Ibid.*, Art. I, sec. 8, cl. 4. See the naturalization laws of Aug. 22, 1861, and Dec. 24, 1861. Except for these acts concerning foreigners in the army and navy, the Confederacy applied the naturalization laws of the old Union. An attempt to repeal these laws (thereby leaving naturalization to the states) was made in 1862 but vetoed by Davis. See E. Merton Coulter, *The Confederate States of America, 1861–1865* (Baton Rouge, La., 1950), 67–68, and William M. Robinson, Jr., *Justice in Grey: A History of the Judicial System of the Confederate States of America* (Cambridge, Mass., 1941), 57, 178–181.

tion that Confederate citizenship began with state citizenship; indeed, Congress's "uniform laws" did not prevent several of the states from enacting their own naturalization legislation.[9]

Perhaps surprisingly, the Confederate Constitution did not explicitly define citizenship, though several amendments to this effect were proposed during the debates on the draft instrument.[10] Christopher Memminger of South Carolina urged a clause specifying that "every free white citizen of any one of the Confederate States shall be deemed a citizen of the Confederate States." John Gregg of Texas proposed instead a more elaborate amendment: "Every free white person who is a citizen of any one of the Confederate States at the time of its ratification of this Constitution, and every person born of parents domiciled in any of the States or Territories of the Confederate States, shall be deemed a citizen of the Confederate States." Georgia's Thomas R. R. Cobb suggested a version of his own: "All free white citizens of the several States forming this Confederacy at the time of the adoption of this Constitution are hereby declared citizens of the Confederate States. And all persons hereafter declared to be citizens by any one of the States (except aliens or persons having one-eighth or more of African blood in their veins) shall be citizens of the Confederate States."[11] None of these amendments passed, and the exact relationship between state and Confederate citizenship remained undefined.

The framers of the Confederate Constitution did insure that southern state citizenship would confer rights throughout the new nation by repeating the privileges and immunities guarantee that had been the source of so much difficulty in years past, but they expanded the clause to include an explicit affirmation of slavery and the property status of slaves. Slaveholders in this union would not be subject to the challenges to their rights that had bedeviled them in the old. Confederate citizens were free to carry their human property from state to state as they had not been permitted to do in the

9. Coulter, *Confederate States of America*, 67–68. In 1861 Georgia declared all aliens resident in the state to be citizens unless they decided to the contrary within three months. In 1862 Florida perpetually banned all U.S. citizens from state citizenship.

10. The Congress resolved itself into convention and debated the draft instrument between Feb. 28 and Mar. 11, 1861. The journals of the proceedings are sketchy and lack details on the debates. See *Journal of the Congress of the Confederate States of America, 1861–1865*, I (Washington, D.C., 1904), 851–896.

11. Feb. 28, 1861, *ibid.*, 859–860. Similar attempts to explain the relation of state and Confederate status were made in debates on the naturalization clause. *Ibid.*, 866–867.

United States: "The citizens of each State shall be entitled to all the privileges and immunities of citizens in the several States, and shall have the right of transit and sojourn in any State of this Confederacy, with their slaves and other property; and the right of property in said slaves shall not be thereby impaired."[12] The central Congress and the governments of new territories admitted to the Confederacy were obliged to recognize and protect the institution that made slaves property and barred them from citizenship.[13]

The Confederate founding fathers felt no need to go beyond these clauses to formulate a detailed definition of citizenship. The South's position had already been made clear by years of debate: citizenship was properly defined with reference to the states and rightly confined to the white population. Slaves were unquestionably excluded from the privileges and immunities of membership by their status as property. Although the precise status of free blacks was not specified in the Confederate Constitution, the legal decisions of southern state courts in the years immediately preceding secession and the majority arguments in the Dred Scott case could be used to exclude free blacks from Confederate citizenship in the unlikely event that their status as non-citizens was questioned.[14]

The principles of secession and of the Confederate Constitution drew strength and persuasiveness from their apparent correspondence with the principles of the American Revolution and from theories about the nature of the United States Constitution that southern spokesmen had voiced frequently in the antebellum years. Secession was defended as the ultimate right of revolution inherent in the sovereign people under any form of government. The right to withdraw was also derived from the doctrine that the Union was the creation, the agent, or the trustee of the people of the states. From this perspective, secession was a lawful procedure implicitly legitimized by the nature of the federal government itself. Both arguments rested upon the basic premise that the citizens of each state comprised a separate sovereign power and retained the natural and the constitutional right to determine the fate of the Union.

12. C.S.A., *Constitution*, Art. IV, sec. 2, cl. 1. There was apparently no debate on this clause or the amendment. *Jours. Confed. Cong.*, I, 881.

13. C.S.A., *Constitution*, Art. IV, sec. 3, cl. 3.

14. For a prewar southern affirmation of the Dred Scott opinion see Clark v. Gautier, 8 Fla. 360, 362 (Fla., 1859). My assumption is that Taney's reasoning would have been sustained in the South throughout the period of the Confederacy, though I have not investigated this point in depth.

Unionists in the North rejected the southern argument. In their view, the Constitution was the creation of the sovereign people in their aggregate capacity and their national character. Even if it was conceded that the people of the individual states had been sovereign and independent before 1789—a point some considered debatable in itself, given that Congress declared the states independent in 1776—there was no doubt that they relinquished their separate sovereignty upon entering the Union. Thereafter, according to President Lincoln, the continued existence of the states depended upon the terms of the Constitution: "The States have their status in the Union, and they have no other legal status. If they break from this, they can do so only against law and by revolution." It was absurd to suppose that any fundamental law could legitimize its own destruction by affirming secession as a legal right. Such a principle was "one of disintegration, . . . upon which no government can possibly endure."[15]

In the opinion of John Lothrop Motley, the acknowledged right of revolution was not the same as the purported legal right of secession. Quoting Daniel Webster, Motley insisted that secession "as a practical right, existing under the Constitution," was "nothing but an absurdity, for it supposes resistance to Government under the authority of Government itself; it supposes dismemberment without violating the principles of the Union; it supposes opposition to law without crime; . . . it supposes the total overthrow of Government without revolution."[16] If the Union was to be dissolved peaceably, it could only be done at the behest and with the consent of the majority of the people. And the "majority of the people" could only be defined with reference to the whole community, to the aggregate citizenry that created the Union and subordinated the states.

If the pretended constitutional right of secession could not be sustained, neither could northerners accept the claim that the South was acting upon the principles of 1776. In the first place, the Revolution had been waged in defense of liberty, not of slavery, and to consider secession as an analogue of the Revolution was to pervert the past and dishonor the founders' libertarian principles. Moreover, the crucial distinction between legitimate revolution

15. Message to Congress, July 4, 1861, quoted in Randall, *Constitutional Problems*, 17.
16. "J.L.M.," in the London *Times*, May 23–24, 1861, *ibid.*, 19.

and unlawful insurrection lay in the former's dependence upon an authoritative judgment that government had become tyrannical and had violated its duties and responsibilities.

In 1776 the American people had been driven to exercise their ultimate right of revolution, for they lacked a systematic means of controlling the king's tyrannical actions. The situation now was different, however, for southerners were not discrete and sovereign peoples, unrepresented at the center of power and independent of the wider political community. The Constitution had institutionalized methods of expressing and redressing grievances; Congress was no local parliament, representing only part of an empire, but was the legitimate embodiment of the whole people. The people of the southern states were not in the same situation as the people of the individual colonies, who had formed separate communities under a common king. Under the Constitution southerners were citizens of the United States, receiving protection from the national government, owing allegiance to the supreme law of the land, and legally obliged to submit to the will of the majority. In 1776 the majority of the several sovereign peoples that formed the American colonies had determined the issue of legitimacy and revolution; now, a minority of the sovereign people sought to impose its will upon the whole. Secession was rebellion, and secessionists were not expatriates, but rebels and traitors.[17]

From this point of view, the Civil War was a struggle over the nature of the community created in 1789—a bloody contest over allegiance. The lines now were sharply drawn between those who stressed the primacy of the state communities of allegiance and those who insisted that the Union had created one nation and one people. Years of evasion and compromise in Congress and the courts had delayed the confrontation between these two points of view. But now the time of decision was at hand, and open conflict would determine which side would prevail.

In the moment of its triumph the North sought to impose its own ideas of citizenship and community upon the nation. A succession of laws and constitutional amendments was passed over the objec-

17. Many Northerners thought that persons who supported the Confederacy were legally traitors, but in practice the South and its defenders were accorded the status of belligerents. For a full discussion of the issue of treason and of northern views of the South's legal status, see *ibid.*, chaps. 3–4.

tions of the recalcitrant President Johnson and forced upon the southern states as a condition of their readmission to the privileges forfeited by their disloyalty. These laws constituted a major effort to resolve problems of allegiance that had long plagued the nation, to bring consistency of principle at last to the concept of American citizenship.[18]

Congressional action—not the action of the states—was responsible for the first clear statutory definition of citizenship. The Thirteenth Amendment abolishing slavery and involuntary servitude throughout the nation had already been passed and ratified in 1865, and many believed that Congress had the national responsibility to guarantee the status and rights of freedmen.[19] In March 1866 Congress passed and sent to the president the Civil Rights Act, based explicitly upon the principle that citizenship derived from birth within the allegiance and entitled persons enjoying the status to basic rights throughout the nation. The statute declared that

all persons born in the United States and not subject to any foreign power, excluding Indians not taxed, are hereby declared to be citizens of the United States; and such citizens, of every race and color, . . . shall have the same right, in every State and Territory in the United States, to make and enforce contracts, to sue, be parties, and give evidence, to inherit, purchase, lease, sell, hold and convey real and personal property, and to full

---

18. Heated controversies have taken place concerning the intent of the post-Civil War statutes and constitutional amendments. My interpretation of these acts requires that they be seen first as the culmination of the developments described in this work, rather than as the starting point for problems still very much alive today. Of course they are both; but to approach the question of the "true intent" or "original understanding" of the framers with an eye to contemporary problems is perhaps more appropriate for the lawyer than the historian. For examples of recent—and fundamentally divergent—interpretations of these acts, see Alexander M. Bickel, "The Original Understanding and the Segregation Decision," *Harv. Law Rev.*, LXIX (1955–1956), 1–65; Alexander M. Bickel, "Citizenship in the American Constitution," *Arizona Law Review*, XV (1973), 369–387; Fairman, *Reconstruction and Reunion, 1864–88*, esp. chaps. 19–20; tenBroek, *Antislavery Origins of the Fourteenth Amendment*; Howard Jay Graham, "The 'Conspiracy Theory' of the Fourteenth Amendment," *Yale Law Journal*, XLVII (1937–1938), 371–403, and XLVIII (1938–1939), 171–194; and Robert J. Kaczorowski, "Searching for the Intent of the Framers of Fourteenth Amendment," *Connecticut Law Review*, V (1972–1973), 368–398. My summary below rests on these works and the following: Benj. B. Kendrick, *The Journal of the Joint Committee of Fifteen on Reconstruction* (New York, 1914); U.S., Congress, Senate, *Congressional Globe*, 39th Cong., 1st sess., 1865–1866; Joseph B. James, *The Framing of the Fourteenth Amendment*, Illinois Studies in the Social Sciences, XXXVII (Urbana, Ill., 1956); W. R. Brock, *An American Crisis: Congress and Reconstruction, 1865–1867* (New York, 1963); and James M. McPherson, *The Struggle for Equality: Abolitionists and the Negro in the Civil War and Reconstruction* (Princeton, N.J., 1964).

19. See generally Brock, *An American Crisis*, chap. 4.

and equal benefit of all laws and proceedings for the security of persons and property, as is enjoyed by white citizens, and shall be subject to like punishments, pains, and penalties, and to none other, any law, statute, ordinance, regulation, or custom, to the contrary notwithstanding.[20]

Johnson vetoed the act. He objected to Congress's attempt to legislate Negro citizenship while the southern states were still unrepresented and he pointed out that the proposed rights to be guaranteed by the national government had traditionally fallen within the jurisdiction of the separate states—a claim that many supporters of the bill would have denied and one that ran counter to one major antebellum interpretation of the privileges and immunities clause.[21] Johnson found the federal enforcement machinery established by the bill an unconstitutional encroachment upon local authority; therefore he refused to approve a measure violating what he deemed fixed principles of federal relations.[22] But Congress was in no mood for arguments tinged with the stain of antebellum states' rights doctrine. The Senate and House overrode the president's veto, and on April 9, 1866, the Civil Rights Act became law.

What one Congress enacted another could repeal, and the surest guarantee that the view of citizenship embodied in the Civil Rights Act would survive lay not in statutes but in constitutional amendment. The Joint Committee of Fifteen on Reconstruction had been considering proposed revisions since January, and on April 30 the draft of the Fourteenth Amendment was introduced in the House and Senate.[23] By June 13 Congress had approved the amendment, affirming the primacy of national over state citizenship, acknowledging the principle of birthright membership, and guaranteeing the privileges and immunities of citizens against state power: "All persons born or naturalized in the United States, and subject to the jurisdiction thereof, are citizens of the United States and of the State wherein they reside. No State shall make or enforce any law which shall abridge the privileges or immunities of citizens of the United States; nor shall any State deprive any person of life, liberty, or

20. Act of Apr. 9, 1866.
21. See, e.g., the speech of Sen. Lyman Trumbull (Ill.), Jan. 29, 1866, U.S., Congress, Senate, *Congressional Globe*, 39th Cong., 1st sess., 1865–1866, pt. 1, 474–476; or that of Rep. William Lawrence (Ohio), Apr. 7, 1866, *ibid.*, pt. 2, 1832–1837. See also the discussion of Art. IV, sec. 2, above, chap. 9.
22. Brock, *An American Crisis*, 113; McPherson, *Struggle for Equality*, 341–350.
23. See generally Kendrick, *Jour. of Joint Committee*, and James, *Framing the Fourteenth Amendment*.

property, without due process of law; nor deny to any person within its jurisdiction the equal protection of the laws."[24]

By March 1867 twelve states had refused to ratify the amendment, but Congress made clear its determination to write the principle of national citizenship into the fundamental law. In the Reconstruction Act of March 2, 1867, Congress formally provided that no state could be restored until it had ratified and until the amendment had become part of the Constitution. Legislatures in the South now had no choice.[25] Thus the triumph of the Fourteenth Amendment in July 1868 secured the ideas that citizenship flowed from birth as well as from naturalization and that the status insured the protection of fundamental rights, ending the challenges of the antebellum years. All persons born within the dominion and allegiance of the United States were citizens and constituents of the sovereign community. Their status with respect to the states depended upon this national status and upon their own choice of residence, and it could not be impeached or violated by state action.

The Fourteenth Amendment seemed to settle questions about the relationship between state and national citizenship; therefore Congress was finally free to take a firm position on the long-debated issue of expatriation. The North had waged four bitter years of war to combat the idea that individual states could withdraw from the Union against the will of the majority, and in some respects this seemed to leave little recourse but bloody rebellion to citizens who considered their government tyrannical or merely unconducive to the successful pursuit of happiness. The collective expatriation of whole communities from the United States in the form of secession was clearly not tolerable, certainly not within the physical confines of the nation. Yet if the possibility of secession was denied, and if citizenship and allegiance depended upon circumstances of birth beyond the individual's control, what options remained? How real was an individual's consent to be governed if he could not choose to repudiate his citizenship?

Expatriation had long been recognized as the solution to this problem, but the doctrinal conflict of state and national sovereignty during the antebellum years had made it impossible for Americans

24. U.S., *Constitution*, Amend. 14, sec. 1.
25. See generally James G. Randall and David Donald, *The Civil War and Reconstruction*, 2d ed. (Boston, 1961), 584–585, 633–634, and Brock, *An American Crisis*, chap. 5.

to make a formal affirmation of this right. Now that the war had cut that Gordian knot by determining the ultimate sovereignty of the national community, Congress could act decisively. Declaring that "the right of expatriation is a natural and inherent right of all people, indispensable to the enjoyment of the rights of life, liberty, and the pursuit of happiness," Congress fully recognized its legitimacy on July 27, 1868: "Any declaration, instruction, opinion, order or decision of any officers of this government which denies, restricts, impairs, or questions the right of expatriation, is hereby declared inconsistent with the fundamental principles of this government."[26] With the affirmation of this principle, citizenship was squarely placed on a foundation of consent and individual choice: aliens could choose to become citizens by meeting the standardized, impersonal requirements for naturalization, and native citizens could choose to relinquish their birthright allegiance by expatriating themselves and electing citizenship elsewhere.

In one important respect, the Civil War settlement failed to extend to their fullest the more nationalistic and democratic ideas involved in post-Revolutionary discussions of citizenship. The crucial right of eligibility for the suffrage remained "in a fringe area," frequently linked with citizenship, but not yet "nationalized" and guaranteed by the government as an automatic corollary of the status.[27] To be sure, section two of the Fourteenth Amendment reduced the congressional representation of states "when the right to vote at any [state or federal] election" was "denied to any of the male inhabitants of such State, being twenty-one years of age, and citizens of the United States, or in any way abridged, except for participation in rebellion, or other crime." And the Fifteenth Amendment, ratified February 3, 1870, even more pointedly stated: "The right of citizens of the United States to vote shall not be denied or abridged by the United States or by any State on account of race, color or previous condition of servitude."[28] But in both clauses, the language was indirect and negative, open to interpretations that left states with wide powers to curtail access to the suffrage.

---

26. Act of July 27, 1868.
27. Bickel, "The Original Understanding," *Harv. Law Rev.*, LXIX (1955–1956), 7, 46. In this connection, see also [Edward Bates], *Opinion of Attorney General Bates on Citizenship* [Nov. 29, 1862] (Washington, D.C., 1862). Bates affirmed at this point that blacks were citizens, but he denied that eligibility for suffrage was an inherent incident of the status.
28. U.S., *Constitution*, Amend. 14, sec. 2, Amend. 15, sec. 1.

Neither the Fourteenth nor the Fifteenth Amendment stated affirmatively that all adult citizens—or even all adult male citizens—were entitled to the vote. The states remained free to establish qualifications—of age, sex, literacy, education, or property—that "impartially" identified those citizens entitled to the vote (and consequently to federal protection of their right).[29] This crucial "political right" thus remained outside the core privileges and immunities guaranteed by the Constitution as an attribute of citizenship. It is by no means clear that this outcome was universally intended by the framers of these amendments.[30] But unquestionably this was the interpretation imposed on the clause by several generations of political and judicial leaders after 1870. The ambiguous linkage between citizenship and suffrage inherent in the Constitution would later support a more expansive interpretation. Yet well into the twentieth century, suffrage was commonly restricted to white adult male citizens under state laws that claimed legitimacy from a strict construction of the post-Civil War amendments.

By 1870 statutes and constitutional amendments seemed to have resolved the problems of citizenship that had troubled many Americans since independence. The Fourteenth Amendment defined citizen status as the product of birth within the allegiance or of naturalization; along with the Civil Rights Act of 1866 and the Fifteenth Amendment, it seemed to assure national protection of privileges and immunities that perhaps included the vote and certainly included fundamental rights of life, liberty, and property. The congressional resolution of 1868 affirming expatriation placed birthright citizenship as well as the status of the naturalized alien on a volitional basis, and legislation of 1870 finally amended the naturalization laws to permit the adoption of black immigrants.[31]

The consistency of principle brought to the concept of citizen-

29. Brock, *An American Crisis*, 288. See also Richard Claude, "Constitutional Voting Rights and Early U. S. Supreme Court Doctrine," *Jour. Negro Hist.*, LI (1966), 114–124, and, for a denial that Amend. 14 gave women citizens the right to vote, Minor v. Happersett, 21 Wall. 162 (U.S., 1875).
30. See generally LaWanda Cox and John H. Cox, *Politics, Principle, and Prejudice, 1865–1866: Dilemma of Reconstruction America* (New York, 1963), 207, 228, and LaWanda and John H. Cox, "Negro Suffrage and Republican Politics: The Problem of Motivation in Reconstruction Historiography," *Journal of Southern History*, XXXIII (1967), 303–330.
31. Act of July 14, 1870. Sec. 7 declared that "the naturalization laws are hereby extended to aliens of African nativity and to persons of African descent." For the continued exclusion of Indians under the revised naturalization laws, see above, chap. 10, n. 16.

ship by the Reconstruction Congresses was in some respects transitory, for the Supreme Court decision in *The Slaughter-House Cases* (1873) reopened questions that seemed settled in 1870. At issue in the cases was the meaning of the Fourteenth Amendment; the particular question to be determined was whether an 1869 grant of a monopoly in the slaughtering of livestock to a New Orleans corporation by the Louisiana legislature infringed the privileges and immunities of citizenship of other New Orleans butchers. By a narrow five to four majority, the Court held that the grant was not unconstitutional on these grounds. And the majority opinion of Justice Samuel F. Miller significantly altered the way problems of national citizenship would be approached in the future.[32]

In constructing his opinion, Miller insisted that section one, clause two, of the amendment—"No State shall make or enforce any law which shall abridge the privileges or immunities of citizens of the United States"—had to be interpreted in light of the section's first clause, which distinguished between United States and state citizenship. He argued that the amendment and its enforcement provisions were restricted to the rights of national citizenship only —rights he defined not in terms of their fundamentality or as the rights the several states gave their own citizens, but as those rights only that were specified in the Constitution or the laws and treaties of the United States.[33] In his view, the Fourteenth Amendment had "nothing to do" with the bulk of rights traditionally regulated by the states. Article IV, section 2, left such rights under state jurisdiction: "Its sole purpose was to declare to the several states, that whatever those rights, as you grant or establish them to your own citizens, or as you limit or qualify, or impose restrictions on their exercise, the same, neither more nor less, shall be the measure of the rights of citizens of other states within your jurisdiction." Miller denied that the new amendment authorized national intervention when a state "limited" or "qualified" the non-federal rights of citizens:

Was it the purpose of the 14th Amendment, by the simple declaration that no State should make or enforce any law which shall abridge the privileges and [*sic*] immunities of citizens of the United States, to transfer the security

32. The Slaughter-House Cases, 16 Wall. 36 (U.S., 1873).
33. *Ibid.*, 74. For earlier understandings of privileges and immunities, see above, chap. 9, at nn. 23–40.

and protection of all the civil rights which we have mentioned, from the States to the Federal Government? And where it is declared that Congress shall have the power to enforce that article, was it intended to bring within the power of Congress the entire domain of civil rights heretofore belonging exclusively to the States?[34]

Miller concluded that this had not been Congress's intent, and thus drastically limited the national government's power to the protection only of the "federal" rights of citizens.

Miller might have reached a different conclusion had he examined the actions and debates of Congress more closely. Supporters of the Fourteenth Amendment and the bills that preceded it—the Freedmen's Bureau Bill, the Civil Rights Bill, and the abortive Bingham Amendment especially—frequently indicated that their aim was to provide explicitly for the enforcement of Article IV, section 2, and the "fundamental" rights of citizenship that clause envisioned.[35] Miller's attempt to separate state citizenship rights in Article IV, section 2, and national citizenship rights in the Fourteenth Amendment by using the amendment's first clause (defining citizenship) to control the interpretation of the second clause (privileges or immunities) was dubious; the first had been added much later, after a secret Senate caucus had agreed on the body of the text.[36] Although the debates were not marked by precision of

34. Slaughter-House Cases, 16 Wall. 36, 77 (U.S., 1873). For a much broader interpretation arguing that Amend. 14 incorporated the Bill of Rights and gave the federal government power to protect fundamental rights against the states, see United States v. Hall, 26 F. Cas. 79 (U.S.C.C., 1871). Antieau, "Paul's Perverted Privileges," *W. and M. Law Rev.*, IX (1967–1968), esp. 22–25, has indicted Justice Stephen J. Field for developing the view of Art. IV, sec. 2, used by Miller. But Field's position in Paul v. Virginia, 8 Wall. 168 (U.S., 1869), though arguing that the states defined the privileges and immunities referred to in that clause, seems to have assumed that the states would include and protect "fundamentals." Field's dissent in the Slaughter-House Cases, 16 Wall. 36, 83–111 (U.S., 1873), certainly argued in these terms.

35. My reading of the debates conforms more closely to Robert Kaczorowski's than to Charles Fairman's on this issue. Both provide useful summaries of the debates while disagreeing on how they should be interpreted (see above, n. 18). The Bingham Amendment read: "The Congress shall have power to make all laws which shall be necessary and proper to secure to the citizens of each state all privileges and immunities of citizens in the several states (Art. 4, Sec. 2); and to all persons in the several States equal protection in the rights of life, liberty and property (5th Amendment)." Kendrick, *Jour. of Joint Committee*, 61. The amendment was reported out of committee on Feb. 10, debated in the House on Feb. 26–28, then postponed to Apr. 10, when it was not revived. For a brief discussion, see Brock, *An American Crisis*, 131–132.

36. Fairman, *Reconstruction and Reunion, 1864–88*, 1296; James, *Framing the Fourteenth Amendment*, chap. 10.

thought, clearly both supporters and opponents of the Fourteenth Amendment conceived of it as protecting an indefinite—but not an unlimited or undefinable—set of fundamental privileges attached of right to citizenship. These fundamental rights—not merely a limited set of rights defined by a test of "federal relation"—were now to be enforceable by federal authority against every state on behalf of every citizen.

Given that the Thirty-Ninth Congress was concerned about the plight of freedmen and white unionists in the southern states, certainly the amendment envisioned the use of federal power to protect the fundamental rights of citizens even against their own states. This need had not been foreseen in 1787 when the old Article IV, section 2, was adopted, simply because it was assumed that every state in fact already provided for this protection in their own laws and constitutions. The language of that provision made the federal government's jurisdiction here questionable, for it referred to the "citizens of each state" in the several states; by shifting to the "privileges or immunities of citizens of the United States," the new amendment should have eliminated this difficulty. The class of rights protected by the amendment remained the same as that envisioned by Article IV, section 2, and broadly defined as early as 1823 by Justice Washington's opinion in *Corfield* v. *Coryell*.[37] The amendment was designed to insure that all United States citizens— not merely state citizens or the even narrower class of "United States citizens of each state" envisioned by Taney in 1857—could now claim these rights under national authority and protection.[38]

Miller rejected the test of "fundamentality" implicit in earlier conceptions and adopted instead a test of "federal relations" in defining the meaning of the Fourteenth Amendment's privileges or immunities clause. In so doing he frustrated the intent and narrowed the scope of the amendment and set the development of

37. Above, chap. 9, at n. 37. Washington's definition of the rights of citizenship was cited with approval a number of times during the Reconstruction debates. See, e.g., Sen. Lyman Trumbull (Ill.), Jan. 29, 1866, U.S., Congress, Senate, *Congressional Globe*, 39th Cong., 1st sess., 1865–1866, pt. 1, 475; Rep. Henry Wilson (Iowa), Mar. 1, 1866, *ibid.*, pt. 2, 1117–1118; Rep. William Lawrence (Ohio), Apr. 7, 1866, *ibid.*, pt. 2, 1835–1836; Sen. Jacob M. Howard (Mich.), May 23, 1866, *ibid.*, pt. 3, 2765. See also Antieau, "Paul's Perverted Privileges," *W. and M. Law Rev.*, IX (1967–1968), esp. 32–36.

38. For Taney's attempt to narrow the class of persons covered by Art. IV, sec. 2, see above, chap. 10, nn. 146–149.

American citizenship on a tortuous new path whose end has not yet been reached.

Although new and crucial questions about the incidents of status emerged in 1873 to throw the concept of citizenship once more into confusion, Americans in 1870 could feel that the inconsistencies in the law had been resolved as a consequence of the Union's victory. Force had finally settled issues that could not be determined by logical argument and reasoned discourse. American citizenship had been firmly placed on a consensual, volitional basis, originating in birth or naturalization, but continuing only as long as the individual citizen chose to adhere to his allegiance. The status remained uniquely dualistic, involving membership and rights in the nation and state, but there was no longer any doubt that national citizenship was primary. "We the people of the United States" symbolized and defined the location of the ultimate and undivided sovereign power in the American Republic.

The resolution of the problems surrounding the concept of American citizenship came only as the result of war, but the form and content of that resolution were shaped by intellectual and ideological forces rooted deeply in the American past. The theoretical formulations of seventeenth-century English jurists were still dimly perceptible in American law—in the vocabulary of "natural-born citizen" and "naturalization," in the concept of birthright citizenship, and in the assumption that membership status conferred rights distinguishing citizens from aliens. These terms and ideas had defined a broad conceptual framework within which Americans worked out their own notion of citizenship, and if that notion ultimately acquired a distinctive character of its own, it also reflected the marks of its origin.

The Americanization of English ideas had begun almost immediately. The circumstances of life in a strange and frightening, yet immensely rich and promising, wilderness had gradually led the colonists to simplify and eliminate complex legal distinctions among members of society. Emergent forms and habits of self-government legitimized theories that all obligation rested upon individual volition and consent and attenuated the sense, still firmly embedded in English laws, that political obligation and status depended upon natural relations of superiority and dependency. Instead, all who chose to contribute to the survival and prosperity of the community at large seemed equally entitled to the rights and privileges offered by law and government.

The crisis of the Revolution and the achievement of independence provided both the occasion and the impetus for articulating American theories of allegiance, political obligation, and sovereignty. The dissolution of the imperial connection and the creation of new republican states impelled political and judicial leaders to express the principles upon which membership in free communities ought to rest. For Americans, these principles of liberty led inevitably to the conclusion that all legitimate power over men depended upon their own consent to be governed. All citizenship—and not just that which was created by naturalization or revolutionary election—seemed definable in terms of a legal contract between the individual and the community at large.

The Revolution itself illustrated the principle that the contract of allegiance could be broken when one of the parties defaulted. By a logical extension of this idea, Americans would eventually acknowledge the individual's right to relinquish his allegiance—with due regard for the interests of the community—whenever such a relinquishment facilitated his pursuit of happiness. Allegiance and citizenship in a free republican society could only be considered conventional and conditional, not natural and perpetual.

Two distinctive features of American government and society delayed the full realization of ideas of citizenship expressed in general form during the Revolutionary era. The first was the residual uncertainty concerning the form of the community of allegiance and the location of ultimate sovereign power. The federal system created in 1789 both reflected the continued viability and authority of the individual states and gave legal force and substance to an already pervasive sense of a wider national community. The ideals of the Revolution embraced the concept that ultimate sovereignty was vested in "the people." What remained uncertain was whether "the people" formed one sovereign community or many. American citizenship implied membership in both state and nation, but the relationship between these two aspects of the status remained the topic of frequent and increasingly heated debate.

The second factor complicating the situation was the presence of the black man in American society. In practice, he was under the authority of the government; nevertheless, in half the nation he was fully excluded from membership in the sovereign community. The fixed determination of many white Americans to continue that exclusion, bolstered by a virtually universal attitude of color prejudice and by a long-standing policy of withdrawal and evasion, meant that questions about the extent, the shape, and the inclusiveness of the community of citizens would remain open.

Not logic, but force, finally answered these questions. The triumph of the Union in the Civil War and the passage of the postwar amendments brought a fundamental coherence to the law. New questions most certainly would emerge after 1870—vital questions involving the precise content of "privileges and immunities," the significance of female citizenship, the relationship between the status and the right to vote—but these would be addressed within the framework of a concept that at last was fundamentally outlined in the Constitution. And the answers would be determined by the authority of a sovereign people, a community of citizens, that formed a single and united nation.

A Note on Citation
Table of Cases
Table of Statutes
General Index

A Note on Citation

In this work I have used a combination of reference styles. Notes citing books, periodicals, articles, and the like are in the familiar "historical" form, but references to judicial cases follow the form used in legal works. In that system a full entry includes: (1) the name of the case; (2) the volume number and short reference to the work in which the case appears; (3) the page number on which the report of the case begins, followed by the page(s) actually cited; (4) the court of jurisdiction and date of decision. For example, Abbot v. Bayley, 6 Pickering 89, 90 (Mass., S.J.C., 1828), indicates a reference to page 90 of the case of Abbot v. Bayley, Pickering's *Reports*, VI, 89ff, decided in the Supreme Judicial Court of Massachusetts, 1828.

For most English cases I have referred in the footnotes only to the original nominative reporter, although the entry in the Table of Cases also includes a reference to the full reprint of such reports in the authoritative *The English Reports, Full Reprint* (Edinburgh and London, 1900–1932). Thus, Andrews v. Baily, Style 139; 82 E.R. 593 (K.B., 1648), indicates the case of Andrews v. Baily, originally reported in Style's *Reports*, 139ff, reprinted in *The English Reports*, LXXXII, 593ff, and decided in the Court of King's Bench, 1648. In the more recent cases the report itself indicates the court of jurisdiction. For example, A.C. indicates *Appeals Cases* heard in the House of Lords; Ch. D. indicates *Chancery Division*; Q.B.D. indicates *Queen's Bench Division*. A few cases lacked jurisdictional information.

A complete explanation of abbreviations commonly used in referring to reports can be found in Henry Campbell Black, *Black's Law Dictionary: Definitions of the Terms and Phrases of American and English Jurisprudence, Ancient and Modern*, 4th ed. rev. (St. Paul, Minn., 1968), 1797–1882. Below is a list of abbreviations I have used in presenting the jurisdictional information.

A.C.	Appeals Cases, House of Lords
Ch.	Chancery
Const. Ct.	Constitutional Court
C.P.	Common Pleas
Ct. App.	Court of Appeals
Ct. Err.	Court of Errors
Ct.-Martial	Court Martial
Eq.	Equity
Ex.	Exchequer
Ex.-Cham.	Exchequer-Chamber
Gen. Ct.	General Court
H.L.	House of Lords
K.B.	King's Bench
Mayor's Ct.	Mayor's Court
Mun. Ct.	Municipal Court
O. & T.	Court of Oyer and Terminer
Q.B.D.	Queen's Bench Division
S.C.	Supreme Court
Scot. Ct. Sess.	Scottish Court of Sessions
S.J.C.	Supreme Judicial Court
Star-Cham.	Star-Chamber
Super. Ct.	Superior Court
U.S.	United States Supreme Court
U.S.C.C.	United States Circuit Court
U.S.D.C.	United States District Court

Table of Cases

See A Note on Citation, p. 355, for an explanation of the form of these entries.

British Cases

Andrews v. *Baily*, Style 139; 82 E.R. 593 (K.B., 1648): 31n

[Anonymous], 2 Peere Williams 75; 24 E.R. 646 (Ch., 1722): 59, 135–136nn

Attorney General v. *Prince Ernest Augustus of Hanover*, Appeal Cases 436 (H.L., 1957): 7–8n

Attorney General v. *Stewart*, 2 Merivale 143; 35 E.R. 895 (Ch., 1816–1817): 57n

Bacon v. *Bacon*, Croke Car. 601; 79 E.R. 1117 (K.B., 1641): 14–15, 33n

Blankard v. *Galdy*, 4 Modern 222; 87 E.R. 359 (K.B., 1693). Also, 2 Salkeld 411 (91 E.R. 356): 56, 135n

Butts v. *Penny*, 2 Levinz 201; 83 E.R. 518 (K.B., 1677). Also, 3 Keble 785 (84 E.R. 1011): 301n

Calvin's Case, 7 Coke's Rep. 1a; 77 E.R. 377 (Ex.-Cham., 1608). Also, 2 Howell's *State Trials* 559. *See* General Index under *Calvin's Case*

Campbell v. *Hall*, 1 Cowper 204; 98 E.R. 1045 (K.B., 1774): 57, 57n

Chamberlain v. *Harvey*, 5 Modern 182; 87 E.R. 596 (K.B., 1695/1696). Also, Carthew 396 (90 E.R. 830); 1 Ld. Raymond 146 (91 E.R. 994): 301n

Chambers v. *Warkhouse*, 3 Levinz 336; 83 E.R. 717 (C.P., 1693/1694): 301n

Collett v. *Keith*, 2 East 260; 102 E.R. 368 (K.B., 1802): 57n

Collingwood v. *Pace*, 1 Levinz 59; 83 E.R. 296 (C.P. and Ex.-Cham., 1661–1664). Also, 1 Keble 65 and *passim* (83 E.R. 814); 1 Ventris 413 (86 E.R. 262); O. Bridgman 410 (124 E.R. 661). *See* General Index under *Ramsey* cases

Commendam Case, Hobart 140; 80 E.R. 290 (Ex.-Cham., 1612): 150n

Courteen's Case, Hobart 270; 80 E.R. 416 (Star-Cham., ca. 1618): 31

Cranburn's Case, 2 Salkeld 633; 91 E.R. 534 (K.B., 1696): 49n

Craw v. *Ramsey*, 2 Keble 601; 84 E.R. 378 (C.P. and Ex.-Cham., 1669/1670). Also, T. Jones 10 (84 E.R. 1122); 2 Ventris 1 (86 E.R. 273); Carter 185 (124 E.R. 905); Vaughan 274 (124 E.R. 1072). *See* General Index under *Ramsey* cases

De Geer v. *Stone*, 22 Chancery Division 243 (1882): 15n

Duchy of Lancaster Case, 1 Plowden's Commentaries 212; 75 E.R. 325 (Ex.-Cham. [?], 1561): 22, 22n, 27n

Dutton v. *Howell*, Shower's Parliamentary Cases 24; 1 E.R. 17 (H.L., 1693): 135n

East India Company v. *Sandys*, 10 Howell's *State Trials* 371 (1683–1685): 32

Fish v. *Klein*, 2 Merivale 431; 35 E.R. 1004 (Ch., 1817): 33–34n

Foster v. *Ramsey*, 2 Siderfin 23; 82 E.R. 1235 (K.B., 1656). *See* General Index under *Ramsey* cases

Table of Statutes

The following table includes only British, United States (federal), and Confederate statutes. Acts of the individual colonies and states regulating naturalization, suffrage, and the like may be found under topical headings in the General Index. The acts are listed chronologically; full entries include the technical citation, title of act, source, subject matter, and index reference(s). The short-title references are explained below in order of their appearance in the table.

Short Titles

Ruffhead
  Owen Ruffhead *et al.*, eds., *The Statutes at Large* ... (London, 1763–1800).
Jones, *British Nationality*
  J. Mervyn Jones, *British Nationality: Law and Practice* (Oxford, 1947).
Parry, *British Nationality Law*
  Clive Parry, *British Nationality Law and the History of Naturalisation* (Milan, 1954).
Shaw, ed., *Denization and Naturalization, 1603–1700*
  W. A. Shaw, ed., *Letters of Denization and Acts of Naturalization for Aliens in England and Ireland, 1603–1700* (Huguenot Society of London, *Publications*, XVIII [Lymington, 1911]).
U.S. Stats.
  Statutes at Large of the United States of America, 1789–1873, 17 vols. (Boston, 1850–1873); continued as *United States Statutes at Large* (Washington, D.C., 1874–).
C.S.A. Stats.
  James M. Matthews, ed., *The Statutes at Large of the Provisional Government of the Confederate States of America, from the Institution of the Government, February 8, 1861, to its Termination, February 18, 1862, Inclusive* ... (Richmond, Va., 1864).

British Statutes

17 Edw. II, stat. 1 (1324). *Praerogativa regis.* Ruffhead, I, 180 (escheat of French lands): 5

17 Edw. III, Parliament Roll (1343). Jones, *British Nationality*, 66 (birth abroad, royal succession): 13–14

25 Edw. III, stat. 2 (1350). *De natis ultra mare.* Ruffhead, I, 254 (birth abroad): 14–15, 84n

25 Edw. III, stat. 5, c. 2 (1350). Statute of Treasons. Ruffhead, I, 261 (treason): 49, 49n

42 Edw. III, c. 10 (1368). Ruffhead, I, 326 (birthright subjectship): 13, 13n

1 Hen. VII, c. 2 (1485). Ruffhead, II, 65 (denizens and aliens' duties): 34

14 & 15 Hen. VIII, c. 4 (1522/23). Ruffhead, II, 131 (aliens' duties): 50n

32 Hen. VIII, c. 16 (1540). Ruffhead, II, 283 (denizens and aliens' duties): 34

3 Jac. I, c. 4 (1605). Ruffhead, III, 39 (secs. 22–23 expand treason): 49n

7 Jac. I, c. 2 (1609). Ruffhead, III, 73 (naturalization and restoration to blood): 67

10 Car. I, c. 4 [Ireland] (1634). Parry, *British Nationality Law*, 47n; Shaw, ed., *Denization and Naturalization, 1603–1700*, xxii (Irish naturalization of Scots): 37, 39–42

United States Statutes

General Index

371

Barbados, 135n
Barbour, Philip (representative, Va.), 313
Bard, Peter, 123
Barrington, Lord. *See* Wildman, William
Bartheleme, Claudius, 88n
Bas, Joseph, 88n
Bates, Edward (attorney general, U.S.), 344n
Bay, Elihu H. (judge), 265
Beccaria, [Cesare], 188
Bedford, duke of. *See* Russell, John
Bee, Thomas (judge), 275n
Bellomont, Earl. *See* Coote, Richard
Berkeley, Lord John, 89
Bernard, Sir Francis (governor), 147, 158–159
Bernon, Gabriel, 69
Berrien, John M. (attorney general, U.S.), 299
Bingham Amendment, 347, 347n
Birth, circumstances of: and denization, 31–33, 33–34n; as indicator of citizenship, 184, 191–193, 215, 231, 287, 313, 317–318, 320–322, 341–345 (*see also* Citizenship, birthright); as indicator of free or slave status, 311, 317–321; as indicator of subjectship, 6, 8, 9, 13–28 *passim*, 13n, 28n, 29, 37, 39, 41–42, 47, 49n, 50–51, 54–55, 65, 80n (*see also* Allegiance, natural); and naturalization, 32–33, 32n, 33–34n, 40–43, 51, 60. *See also* Citizens, natural-born; Subjects, natural-born
Black, Jeremiah S. (attorney general, U.S.), 270n
Black codes, 302, 306–307
Blacks. *See* Freedmen; Free Negroes; Slaves
Blackstone, Sir William, 54–55, 57–59, 83n, 136, 139–141, 140n, 152, 167, 170n, 304n; quoted, 6, 30, 35, 136
Blake, Joseph (deputy governor), 113
Bland, Richard, 152
Blazo, William, 88n, 100–101n
Board of Trade, 96, 103, 104. *See also* Trade, Lords of
Bolzius, Rev. Martin, 101–102, 102n, 123n
Bomont, Giles de, 66
Boot, Nicholas, 84
Bouquet, Col. Henry, 104, 104n
Bridgman, Sir Orlando (Eng. judge), 33–34n, 38
Brooke, Christopher, 58n
Brunett, Henry, 94
Brunetti, Francis, 68n
Buchanan, Alexander M. (judge), 318–319, 320

Buchanan, James (secretary of state, president), 270n
Bueno, Joseph, 68, 68n
Bunker Hill, battle of, 168, 176
Burnaby, Rev. Andrew, 158
Burrill, James (senator, R.I.), 312–313n
Butler, Benjamin F. (attorney general, U.S.), 299
Butler, Pierce, 228
Byrd, William, II, 113

C
Cabell, William H. (judge), 255, 273–274
Calhoun, John C. (secretary of state), 269
California (state), 253n, 294n
Calvert, Cecelius, 81n
Calvert, George, 1st Lord Baltimore, 58, 58n, 80
Calvert family, 89
Calvin, Robert, 16–17, 19–20, 27, 28, 33n. See also *Calvin's Case*
Calvin's Case, 7–8, 15–28, 36–37, 37–38n, 45–47, 48, 52, 135; American use of, as precedent, 17, 28, 158–160, 159–160n, 192, 200; dominance of, in English law, 7–8n, 17n, 28, 45; and law of treason, 48–52; and Lockean theory, 45, 52–53, 55–56
Camden, Lord. *See* Pratt, Charles
Camp, Abiathar, 222–224
Campbell, John A. (justice), 326, 328
Campbell, Lord William (governor), 168
Canada, 278n, 318
Capacity, natural. *See* King, two capacities of
Capacity, political. *See* Crown; King, two capacities of
Cape of Good Hope, 57n
Carlisle, Abraham, 183n
Carstens, Johannes, 93n
Carteret, Sir George, 89
Carteret, John, earl of Grenville, 76
Cass, Lewis (secretary of state), 270n
Catholics: in colonies, 114, 114n, 119–121; and English naturalization, 67, 67n, 68n, 70, 70n, 71n, 75
Catron, John (justice), 316–317, 326, 328
Chaffee, Dr. Calvin C., 325
Chaffee, Mrs. Calvin C. (formerly Mrs. John Emerson), 324–325
Chamier, Daniel, 118
Champante, John, 123, 123n
Chapman, Samuel, 195–196, 199, 201
Character, proof of: assumed requirement for naturalization, 69, 85, 88–89, 99, 218;

explicit requirement for naturalization, 214–219 *passim*, 236, 241, 242, 246; for freemanship, 88

Charles I, king of England, 58n, 80, 80n, 170, 170n

Charles II, king of England, 15, 44, 45, 68–69

Charters, colonial, 66, 80–82, 134; as contracts, 128, 161, 166; and naturalization, 66, 78–80, 79n, 85, 101; and rights of Englishmen, 65, 82. *See also* names of individual colonies

Cherokees, 294n, 296, 297nn, 299; treaties with, 292, 292n, 298n, 299

Chickasaws, 297n

Child, Robert, 81

Children: born in colonies, 65, 80n, 84n, 91–93 *passim*, 91n, 191–192; citizenship and political rights of, 295n, 313, 317–318, 321–322, 323, 327; denization and naturalization of, 31–33, 33–34n, 35–36, 84n, 91–93 *passim*, 91n, 236, 236n, 242n, 246n; of denizens, 31–33, 32nn, 33nn, 36, 91n; and expatriation, 198, 274n; foreign-born, of citizen parents, 204n, 236, 236n, 246n; foreign-born, of subject parents, 13–15, 15nn, 204n; legal dependency of, 15, 33–34n, 198, 321–322; of naturalized aliens, 32–33, 32n, 33nn, 91n, 236, 236n, 242n; of resident aliens, 13n, 80n, 246n, 318; and right of election, 198, 274n

Chilton, William P. (judge), 255, 257

Choctaws, 297n, 299; treaties with, 292, 292n

Church, Benjamin, 177

Citizens, natural-born, 229–231, 236, 244–245. *See also* Citizens, naturalized; Citizenship, birthright

Citizens, naturalized: constitutional restriction on rights of, 229–231, 230n, 318; diplomatic protection of, 269–271, 270n; equality of, with native citizens, 229–231, 235, 244–245, 253–254; fear of foreign attachments of, 216–219, 226–229, 232, 235, 237–246; rights of, in state naturalization laws, 214–219. *See also* Naturalization, federal; Naturalization, state

Citizens, territorial, 251–253, 253n, 255–256, 263–264

Citizenship (general), 3, 7–10, 208–209, 349–351; attainders as proof of, 185n, 187, 199; of children born abroad, 204n, 236, 236n, 246n; of corporations, 264n; defined by congressional statute, 341–342; defined by constitutional amendment, 342–343;

defined by Continental Congress, 179, 187, 190, 219; defined by rights held, 313, 320–322, 332; as freemanship of city corporation, 88–89n; of free Negroes (*see* Free Negroes, citizen status of, controverted); gradations of, 236–237, 244–245, 247, 322, 322n; of Indians (*see* Indians, citizenship of); and loyalists, 172, 174, 179–208 *passim*, 217n, 222–224, 242, 242n; qualifications for, 213–247 (*see also* Naturalization, federal; Naturalization, state); renunciation of (*see* Expatriation); rights of, 197, 199–202, 204–205, 214–219, 225–231 (*see also* Articles of Confederation, Art. IV; Suffrage; United States Constitution, Art. IV, sec. 2, cl. 1, Amendments XIV–XV); volitional character of (*see* Allegiance, volitional; Election, right of); of women, 313, 317, 321–322, 323, 327, 345n. *See also* Citizenship, birthright; Citizenship, Confederate; Citizenship, federal; Citizenship, national; Citizenship, state; People, the; Sovereignty; Treason

Citizenship, birthright: challenges to, 317–322, 324–332; and expatriation, 272–273, 281, 287–288, 343–344; and free Negroes, 311, 313, 314, 317–322, 324–332 *passim*; recognition of, in state laws and constitutions, 214–215, 217–218; recognition of, in U.S. laws and Constitution, 230–231, 318, 340–343; and volitional allegiance, 287–288, 343–344. *See also* Allegiance, natural; Citizens, natural-born; Indians: citizenship of

Citizenship, Confederate, 335–338

Citizenship, federal (dual), 248–286; ambiguity of, pre-1789, 209, 224, 230–231, 235, 242, 255; and diversity jurisdiction, 261–264; and expatriation, 267–284; and naturalization, 249–254; and rights of citizenship, 254–261, 312, 322–324, 322n (*see also* Articles of Confederation, Art. IV; United States Constitution, Art. IV, sec. 2, cl. 1, Amendments XIV–XV). *See also* Allegiance, double; Citizenship (general); Citizenship, national; Citizenship, state; People, the; Sovereignty

Citizenship, national, 209, 224, 230–231, 235, 242; and American Revolution, 233–234, 284–285, 339–340; and Continental Congress, 219–220, 220n, 223–224; primacy of, controverted, 233, 264–267, 280–284, 286, 325–332, 334–340, 342–343; qualifications for (*see* Naturalization,

Orders-in-council, *continued*
appeals), 81n; (1699/1700, banning colonial denization), 95–96, 102; (1705/06,
repealing Pa. law), 97, 97n, 119n; (1773,
local naturalization and alien titles), 105,
105n, 121; (1773, Mohegan lands), 290–
291
Ordinance of 1787, 297n, 304–306 *passim*,
318
Otis, Harrison Gray (representative, Mass.),
244–245; (senator, Mass.), 312
Otis, James, 150–157 *passim*, 150n, 151n,
155–156n
Ottawas, treaty with, 293

P
Pace, Perses, 38n
Page, John (representative, Va.), 237–238
Pamunkeys, 295
Pardons, 47, 47n, 182
Parker, Isaac (judge), 258
Parliament, English/British: and Act of
Union of 1707, 48, 56, 59, 146, 160; acts of,
include consent of all, 32, 32n, 39, 55; and
colonial charters, 81, 161; and common
law, 22n, 134–140, 149–150, 154; and
discovered colonies, 59, 135–139, 135–
136n, 141, 155–157; eligibility for, 34–35,
35n, 77–78, 123, 125n, 126; as embodiment of the people, 56, 59, 144–146, 147n;
and Isle of Man, 145, 155; jurisdiction of,
over America, 57–59, 58n, 81–83, 132–
134, 136–171 *passim*; and kingdoms acquired by conquest, 23–26, 40–41, 56–57,
57nn, 135–137, 139–141, 146, 151–155;
and kingdoms acquired by descent, 24,
46–47, 56, 57–58, 135, 146, 158, 160–161;
and naturalization, 27n, 29–30, 30n,
35–36, 40–41, 69–70, 81–82, 132–133 (*see
also* Naturalization, English); and personal
union with Scotland, 16, 23–24, 46–47,
158; self-controlling character of, 144–
146, 155–156, 155n; and social contract,
59–60, 141–146, 155, 156, 171;
sovereignty of, 44–45, 48, 56, 58–59,
132–133, 136–171 *passim. See also* Allegiance, community of; Empire,
English/British; *Imperium in imperio*
Parliament, Irish. *See* Ireland, parliament of
Parliament, Scottish. *See* Scotland, parliament of
Parsons, Theophilus (judge), 191–192, 191n
Paterson, William (justice), 275, 280–281;
and New Jersey Plan, 225
Penal statutes, 46–47, 306

Penn, William, 73–74
Pennsylvania (colony): alien disabilities in,
112, 119, 122; Catholics in, 114; charter of,
65–66n, 80n; denization and naturalization in, 86, 97, 100, 104nn, 105, 105n, 109;
Germans in, 73, 108–110, 122; immigration to, 73, 108–111; oaths in, 114;
suffrage in, 122–123
Pennsylvania (state), 176n, 232–235 *passim*,
238, 243; Constitution of 1776, 195, 214;
Constitution of 1790, 250, 268n; judicial
decisions in, 181, 194–196, 222–224, 306n,
316; loyalists in, 181–183, 181nn, 183nn,
185n, 194–196; naturalization in, 214, 250;
right of election in, 194–196; status of
Negroes in, 304, 306, 310, 316; statutes of,
195–196, 238n, 304, 310; treason in,
181–183, 181n, 183nn, 185n, 194–196
People, the: as judge of government legitimacy, 144, 188–189, 191, 335, 338–340;
national vs. state character of, 209, 221,
233–234, 266–267, 284–286, 326, 332,
334–336, 338–340; Parliament as embodiment of, 56, 59, 144–146, 147n;
sovereignty of, 171–172, 191, 233–234,
266–267, 284–286, 326, 334–336, 338–340
Personal liberty laws, 303n, 310–311
Peterson, Jacob, 96, 96n
Philadelphia Aurora, 272
Philadelphia Convention: Committee of
Detail, 225–226, 230, 230n; Committee of
Eleven, 230; debates and proceedings,
224–232. *See also* New Jersey Plan; United
States Constitution; Virginia Plan
Philips, Josiah, 181n
Phipps, George, case of, 192n
Phocion (pseudonym), 165
Pinckney, Charles, 226, 227, 229
Pindall, James (representative, Va.), 282–283
Plockhoy, Cornelius, 86n
Plymouth (colony), 289n
Portugal, 309
Portuguese, naturalization of, 115n
Postnati: effects of conquest on rights of, 19;
Scots, status of, 16, 22–23, 22n, 27, 27n,
33, 33n, 41, 45–47, 65. See also *Antenati*
Postnati, Case of the. See Calvin's Case
Poynings's Law, 154
Pratt, Charles, Baron Camden, 150
Prescott, John, 218n
Prewar debts, 184–187, 185n, 204, 204n. *See
also* Jay's Treaty; Treaty of peace (1783)
Prisoners of war, 181, 181n, 195, 220n
Privy Council. *See* Orders-in-council
Protection: default of, 151n, 166–171, 176,

DATE DUE

GAYLORD			PRINTED IN U.S.A